Ronald Reagan,
the Movie

Ronald Reagan, the Movie

and Other Episodes in Political Demonology

Michael Paul Rogin

UNIVERSITY OF CALIFORNIA PRESS
Berkeley · *Los Angeles* · *London*

The photographs in this volume are reproduced courtesy of Paul Conrad and the *Los Angeles Times*; Movie Star News; Museum of Modern Art, New York; Pacific Film Archive, University Art Museum, University of California, Berkeley; Stanislav Rembski; Ben Weaver and Camera 5.

"The King's Two Bodies: Lincoln, Wilson, Nixon, and Presidential Self-Sacrifice," in J. David Greenstone, ed., *Public Values and Private Power in American Politics* (Chicago, 1982), © University of Chicago, reprinted by permission.

"Liberal Society and the Indian Question," *Politics and Society* 1 (May 1971), © Geron-X, Inc., reprinted by permission.

"Nature as Politics and Nature as Romance in America," *Political Theory* 5 (February 1977), © Sage Publications, reprinted by permission.

"Nonpartisanship and the Group Interest," in Philip Green and Sanford Levinson, eds., *Power and Community* (New York, 1970), © Pantheon Books, Random House, reprinted by permission.

Earlier versions of "*Ronald Reagan*: the Movie" appeared in *democracy* 1 (April and October 1981), © The Common Good Foundation; of "Political Repression in the United States," in Jack P. Greene, ed., *Encyclopedia of American Political History* (New York, 1984), © Charles Scribner's Sons; of "*Kiss Me Deadly*: Communism, Motherhood, and Cold War Movies" and "'The Sword Became a Flashing Vision': D. W. Griffith's *The Birth of a Nation*," in *Representations* 6 (Spring 1984) and 9 (Winter 1985), © The Regents of the University of California. All used with permission.

University of California Press
Berkeley and Los Angeles, California

University of California Press, Ltd.
London, England

© 1987 by
The Regents of the University of California
First Paperback Printing 1988
Library of Congress Cataloging-in-Publication Data

Rogin, Michael Paul.
  Ronald Reagan, the movie.

  Includes index.
    1. United States—Politics and government—
Miscellanea.   2. Conspiracies—United States—History—
Miscellanea.   I. Title.
E183.R64   1987   320.973   86-19229
ISBN 0-520-05937-9 (Cloth)
ISBN 0-520-06469-0 (Ppbk)

Printed in the United States of America

  2   3   4   5   6   7   8   9

for Isabelle and Madeleine

Contents

Illustrations

Preface

The aim of this book is to name and characterize a countersubversive tradition at the center of American politics. Although some of the chapters were originally written to stand on their own and others were conceived with the larger project in mind, all examine moments or strands in the history of political demonology. These terms, *countersubversive tradition* and *political demonology*, are not in common discourse. I use them to call attention to the creation of monsters as a continuing feature of American politics by the inflation, stigmatization, and dehumanization of political foes. These monsters—the Indian cannibal, the black rapist, the papal whore of Babylon, the monster-hydra United States Bank, the demon rum, the bomb-throwing anarchist, the many-tentacled Communist conspiracy, the agents of international terrorism—are familiar figures in the dream-life that so often dominates American politics. What do they signify?

American demonology has both a form and a content. The demonologist splits the world in two, attributing magical, pervasive power to a conspiratorial center of evil. Fearing chaos and secret penetration, the countersubversive interprets local initiatives as signs of alien power. Discrete individuals and groups become, in the countersubversive imagination, members of a single political body directed by its head. The countersubversive needs monsters to give shape to his anxieties and to permit him to indulge his forbidden desires. Demonization allows the countersubversive, in the name of battling the subversive, to imitate his enemy.

Demonology as a political form is not restricted to the United States, but this book is an inquiry into its specifically American variant. American countersubversion has taken its shape from the pervasiveness of propertied individualism in our political culture; the expansionist character of our history; and the definition of American identity against racial, ethnic, class, and gender aliens. My concern is with the symbiotic bond that joins the countersubversive to his foe and with the sources of that antagonistic connection in American history and in the countersubversive mind.

It is by now usual to worry about American political extremism. When Richard Hofstadter published his classic book on that subject in 1965, he even found "the paranoid style in American politics" in a major-party presidential candidate.[1] But that candidate, Barry Goldwater, was defeated and discredited, and he lacked significant defenders among scholars or intellectual opinion makers as a whole. If, however, the countersubversive tradition occupies not the political margins of America but its mainstream, then we are going to have to confront dominant figures not only in American history but in the political present as well. Let us begin with an example.

"Will we permit the Soviet Union to put a second Cuba, a second Libya, right on the doorsteps of the United States?" President Ronald Reagan asked a nationwide television audience on 16 March 1986. The president was justifying military aid for the Nicaraguan contras. "The Soviets . . . Fidel Castro . . . Arafat, Qadaffi, and the Ayatollah have made their decision to support the Communists," said Reagan, and America must sponsor the other side or face the danger of imminent invasion.

Nicaragua was a "Soviet ally on the American mainland"; it was also a "safe house, a command post for the international terror." "Gathered in Nicaragua," the president explained, "are . . . all the elements of international terror—from the P.L.O. to Italy's Red Brigades . . . [to] Colonel Qadaffi." Nicaragua threatened the entire western hemisphere. Pointing to a map of Latin America that showed Sandinista targets in color, Reagan illustrated Nicaraguan military support for subversives operating not only against Nicaragua's "democratic neighbors" in Central America but against "Colombia, Ecuador, Brazil, Chile, Argentina, Uruguay, and the Dominican Republic." Once established in Nicaragua, the president warned, the Soviet Union would threaten the Panama Canal and "ultimately move against Mexico. Should that happen, desperate Latin peoples by the millions would begin fleeing north into the cities of the southern United States."

The Sandinistas had chosen international subversion at a secret meeting two months after taking power. But they "followed the advice of Fidel Castro," said Reagan, and put on "a facade of democracy." Now the mask had fallen. The government had destroyed the only synagogue in Managua, Reagan charged, and forced "the entire Jewish community" to flee the country. In addition—and the president showed a photo of a "top aide" to prove his point—"top Nicaraguan Government officials are deeply involved in drug trafficking." Invoking the Truman doctrine and the spirit of John F. Kennedy, President Reagan called on Americans to support the "freedom fighters" who had opposed "the old Somoza dictatorship" and were now fighting against the revolution that had betrayed them. "I have only three years left to serve my country," he concluded. "Could there be any greater tragedy than for us to sit back and permit this cancer to spread?"[2]

By making Nicaragua a symbol that condensed all the forces threatening America, President Reagan brought together in a single speech the historic themes of American political demonology. Like earlier countersubversives, Reagan warned against the menace threatening America, and he identified the secret, conspiratorial meetings in which world conquest was planned. He named names, fascinated by the concrete particulars of Communist subversion. But these names had a misplaced concreteness, for they signified multiplying instances of a single disease rather than discrete people and places with lives of their own. The president attributed magical power to a single, central source by wiping out separate, local initiatives. He imagined a titanic struggle between the forces of good and an empire of evil.

President Reagan also sought to rouse the nation to the danger of alien contamination. Vulnerable American frontiers, in the countersubversive view, forced a choice between American expansion and foreign invasion. The warning that millions of Latins could flood the United States, moreover, paid homage to the racial phobias that were until recently an open part of American politics. In the demonological tradition, the president's speech confused Communism with terrorism and political opposition with crime, drugs, and disease. Even the bodily well-being of the leader was equated with the health of the body politic (for the cancer that had been cut out of the president's body must now, before he left office, be excised from "the American mainland" as well).

A small country in Central America had lost its autonomous existence and been transformed—whether by Communist design or presidential imagination—into a sign. All evil, as the president saw it, was concentrated in "the malignancy in Managua." In the name of describing a centralized, apocalyptic struggle, the president was trying to create one. He was replacing history by visionary myth.

Some commentators raised doubts about whether President Reagan's Nicaragua was real or imaginary, and isolated factual items appeared in several newspapers in the days surrounding the speech. Brazil denied it was a target of Sandinista subversion. Strong evidence of drug smuggling by contra forces was contrasted to the absence of such evidence about the Sandinistas. (In fact, the major "international drug trade" derives from the "democratic countries" Reagan had listed as Nicaraguan targets.) The Nicaraguan government had neither burned synagogues nor mounted an assault on Jews. With few exceptions, the contras were led by former Somocistas, not early supporters of the revolution. Sandinista violations of human rights paled before brutal contra terrorism. (Reagan had earlier blamed contra atrocities on Sandinistas dressed up as contras and insisted that a CIA manual did not advocate assassinating local Sandinista leaders when it proposed "neutralizing" them.)[3]

These correctives were themselves questioned by the president's supporters. But even if the empirical truth value of Reagan's speech was larger than zero, it was somehow beside the point, for the speech inhabited a wholly different realm from the one in which reporters tried to hold it to account. The fractured reality principle could coexist alongside the speech, for the two operated on different planes. Like earlier demonologists, President Reagan was soaring above the real. His maps, pictures, and visionary worldview, exhibited on the television screen, replaced the world they claimed to represent.

The most believable presence on the television screen was that of the president himself. Nicaragua—"only two hours' flying time from our own borders" in the speech—was actually far away, distant from the experience of the president and his audience. As Reagan's words and pictures brought his Nicaragua into American living rooms, the real Latin American country disappeared; it was in danger of symbolic and physical obliteration. The president himself, by contrast, inspired belief. A majority of Americans opposed military aid to the contras after Reagan's speech, and many of his other policies were unpopular as well.[4] But personal approval overwhelmed political disapproval. Reagan's return to himself at the end of his performance was thus no afterthought: it counterposed danger from alien forces to the reassuring (but mortal) presidential presence.

Unlike any other president since the end of World War II, Reagan has succeeded in making himself the benign center of America and placing malignancies outside our borders. Having raised anxiety about the permeability of American boundaries, President Reagan splits the good within the country from the bad without. Evil, he reassures us, is out there in visible spots that can be identified and removed. It is not (any longer) in us or in me. In personalizing the political, Reagan stands squarely within the countersubversive tradition. But whereas most earlier countersubversives, as we shall see, failed to separate themselves from the demons that plagued them, Reagan has escaped contamination. His self-presentation as a figure unimplicated in personal or political trouble invites us to investigate the making of his presidential character.

"*Ronald Reagan*, the Movie," like most of the chapters that follow it, examines the convergence in American political demonology between political discourse and personal symbols, between private and public history. It analyzes the formation of President Reagan through his Hollywood roles. Although each of the remaining chapters has a subject of its own, they can be read together as a genealogy for the Reagan administration. Chapter 2 offers an interpretive history of political repression in the United States. It addresses racial, class, and sexual conflict on the one hand and institutional power on the other. Chapter 2 connects the countersubversive mentality to political repression and institution building. Chapters 3 and 4 examine the efforts of political elites to substitute themselves for their constituencies. "The King's Two Bodies" shows how American presidents who aspired to greatness confused their own mortal bodies with the mystic body, America. "The King's Two Bodies" analyzes political religion, the vocabulary of the sacred in American political life. "Nonpartisanship and the Group Interest" argues that the mundane language of interest group liberalism also allows leaders to absorb the group members they claim to represent. Although the replacement of the constituency by the leader aggrandizes the leader, it may also separate leaders from their sources of power. That is what ultimately happened to Richard Nixon, by a process we shall examine, and it is now happening to interest group liberal leaders as well. Interest group liberalism—the labor, business, ethnic, and public interest coalition centered in the Democratic party—was the governing American political system from Roosevelt's New Deal to the election of Ronald Reagan. Reagan's ability to speak religiously for America corresponds to the atrophy of the interest group liberal mass base in trade unions and the Democratic party. "Nonpartisanship and the Group Interest" examines how an earlier labor movement and the liberal political scientists who defended it merged leaders with members in an effort to rationalize popular disenfranchisement and to turn weakness into strength.

The next two essays turn from political leaders in settled society to nature, the West, and American expansion. "Liberal Society and the Indian Question" looks at the theory and practice of Indian removal in the Age of Jackson. "Nature as Politics and Nature as Romance" traces the history of nature in American political discourse as a whole. As these essays show how nature and westward expansion gave America its sacred political identity, they interpret political demonology as the flight from historically based social and personal conflicts to a false or imposed unanimity. Like earlier chapters, those on the West point to the imperial presidency as the climax of American countersubversion; in them I analyze presidents who personified America by absorbing the members of the body politic into their own mystic bodies and leading the regenerated American nation against its alien, demonic foes.

The penultimate two essays concern movies. Taken together with the Reagan chapter, they examine the relationship between movies and politics from the origin of the motion picture in the political movie *The Birth of a Nation* to the origins of President Reagan in the motion picture. "The Sword Became a Flashing Vision" places in history the racial and sexual fantasies of *The Birth of a Nation*. "*Kiss Me Deadly*" links anti-Communism to sexual fantasies in cold war films. Traditional countersubversive demons are visible on the screen in these movies. My turn to movies also responds to a shift in American politics from appeals to history (however mythicized) to the more immediate power of the screen. *The Birth of a Nation* is the movie that founded modern American mass culture. The cold war movies return us to where we began, for they show us the worldview of the president who was produced along with them.

This collection of essays does not pretend to offer a comprehensive account of American political demonology. The essays make choices, both of method and subject matter. These choices are in part the result of personal inclination, but they also define what I take to be the major contours of the subject. Unlike previous analysts of the countersubversive tradition, I focus on the center of American politics rather than on the extremes, presidents and other political leaders rather than outsiders, racial and sexual phobias rather than ethnic conflicts and status anxieties, countersubversive mentalities rather than operational programs, and personal projects and unconscious fantasies rather than economic interests and instrumental schemes. The final chapter, a theoretical retrospective, defends these choices by situating my approach to countersubversion against previous studies of the subject. That chapter is placed at the end of the book, for a theory is best judged after acquaintance with its practice.

I have introduced the chapters that follow in the order in which they appear. They also have another order, however, the order in which they were written. Let me conclude this preface with a brief intellectual genealogy.

The four earliest essays, republished with only minor editorial changes, all address political repression and demonology as instruments in the historical construction of an American political identity. "Nonpartisanship and the Group Interest" and "Liberal Society and the Indian Question" represent the two halves of my original work. The orientation of that work shifted in the 1960s from the study of group politics and social movements (methodologically although not politically orthodox within political science) to a radical psychoanalysis of politics that is wholly outside the discipline. "Nature as Politics and Nature as Romance" and "The King's Two Bodies," the next pair of essays, were in effect efforts to heal the split in my own work between politics and psychology by Americanizing it. They analyze the bifurcations between the political and the personal within the American political tradition itself, first in the vocabularies of nature, then in the politics of presidents who aspired to heroic stature.

The remaining chapters, all composed or revised with this book in mind, are efforts at synthesis. The account of political repression asks how American history would look if repression were placed at its center. The final chapter reflects on my approach to political demonology. And the remaining three essays put the divided halves of American political discourse back together again by examining the interpenetration of the personal and the political in dominant political symbols. These chapters address motion pictures. The shift to film may appear to be a flight to culture from the political subjects of labor politics and Indian policy with which I began. But the analysis integrates the political history in my early work with the literary and psychological materials to which I turned. I am trying, against dominant tendencies in the study and practice of American politics, to use cultural documents to connect political action to its makers and its meanings.

Students at Berkeley, in the classroom and in political action, have had a large impact on this book. I also owe more than I can say to the comments and continuing intellectual stimulation of a number of Berkeley friends: Elizabeth Abel, Kim Chernin, Arlie Hochschild, and Lillian Rubin; Norman Jacobson, Hanna Pitkin, and Paul Thomas; Catherine Gallagher and Stephen Greenblatt; Jim Breslin, Kathleen Moran, Carolyn Porter, and the other members of the Friday group; and Ann Banfield. Todd Gitlin, Jim Kettner, Paul Rabinow, George Shulman, and Michael Shute were helpful with particular chapters, and I have also responded to the good advice offered by Jim Clark, Director of the University of California Press, and by T. J. Jackson Lears, Michael Meeker, and Sheldon Wolin. Betsey Scheiner did a splendid job of editing.

Portions of this book were presented before extremely helpful audiences. I should like particularly to thank students at Reed College and fellow panel members and the audience at a Western Political Science Association meeting (for chapter 8); participants in the Christian Gauss seminars at Princeton (for chapters 1 and 7); members of the Northern California Political Science Association and students at the California Institute of Technology (for chapter 1); participants in a panel of the Western Political Science Association and faculty and students at the University of California, Riverside, and at the University of Washington (for chapter 3). Judy Gorman, Emily Hauptmann, and Tony Kenney typed the bulk of the manuscript. I am grateful to Nancy Goldman and the Pacific Film Archive for invaluable help in arranging movie screenings and to the Committee on Research of the University of California at Berkeley for financial assistance.

CHAPTER I

Ronald Reagan, the Movie

"The neatest Christmas gift of all!" says Ronald Reagan.
You can twist it. . . . You can twirl it. . . . You can bend
it. . . . You can curl it. . . . The new revolutionary collar on
Van Heusen Century shirts won't wrinkle . . . ever!

> *Caption accompanying a picture of "Ronald*
> *Reagan starring in Universal International's* Law
> and Order, *Color by Technicolor"*

The year is 1940, Stalin and Hitler have signed their pact, and Europe is at war. Saboteurs are operating inside America as well, blowing up bridges and trains. The House Un-American Activities Committee, investigating sabotage and sedition, subpoenas Joe Garvey, the chairman of the Society of Loyal Naturalized Americans. Garvey speaks with a foreign accent; he insists that the purpose of his organization is simply to preserve American neutrality and keep the country out of war. When asked by HUAC's chairman if his organization's labor racketeering, unlawful assembly, and sabotage are the activities of loyal Americans, Garvey responds that such accusations are "capitalistic" lies. In truth, however, Garvey heads a ring of foreign spies.

One of Garvey's saboteurs has been killed in a train wreck; the Secret Service sends an agent to impersonate him. To test the agent's identity, Garvey's toughs masquerade as policemen and knock him around; they accuse him of being a Wobbly and a Red. When they are satisfied that he is what they have charged him with being, an anti-American subversive, Garvey's men take him to their boss.

America has invented a miraculous defensive weapon that paralyzes electric currents at their source. The inertia projector, as it is called, stops and destroys anything that moves. According to an American admiral, it will "make America invincible in war and therefore be the greatest force for peace ever invented." When Garvey and another foreign spy fly off with the plans for the weapon, the secret agent follows.

1

He turns the inertia projector on the spy plane; the plane stops in mid-air, catches fire, and plummets to the ground.

The American agent has an assistant, Gabby Waters. While the fate of the country hangs in the balance, Gabby's girlfriend has been nagging him to marry her. Where the spies have failed, she is about to succeed in capturing her man when the secret agent and his boss turn the inertia projector on the car taking the couple to the altar. The secret weapon stops the car. As his girlfriend fumes helplessly, Gabby is rescued from female entrapment and "save[d] for the service."

Murder in the Air (1940), the movie I have been describing, is a minor piece in the 1940s politicization of Hollywood. It illustrates several tendencies that emerge in the course of that decade. *Murder in the Air* begins as if its theme is counterfeit money; the movie then shifts to spying and counterfeit identity, initiating the move from crime to countersubversion that characterizes 1940s Hollywood. Collapsing Communists into Fascists, *Murder in the Air* presages the turn from the anti-Nazi films of World War II to the anti-Communist films of the cold war. Male freedom in this movie is threatened by both a nagging woman and a foreign power; merging those dangers and then zapping the woman and the subversives, *Murder in the Air* also looks forward to the sexual politics of cold war movies.

But *Murder in the Air* would remain forgotten, as it has until now, if the man who played the secret agent, Brass Bancroft, were not Ronald Reagan (see Fig. 1.1). The attack on subversion; the merging of Communism and Fascism; the flippancy about matters of life and death, peace and war; the obsession with intelligence agents as the means to national security; and, most striking, the existence of an airborne defensive superweapon that will make America invulnerable—all these look forward beyond World War II to the Star Wars militarization of space and the Reagan presidency. Reagan's explanation for the unfinished security arrangements that allowed terrorists to kill American troops in Beirut—"Anyone that's ever had their kitchen done over knows that it's never done as soon as you wish it would"—could be a quip from the movie. Reagan explained the terrorist success by the "near destruction of our intelligence capacity . . . before we came here," thereby distinguishing the CIA under Carter from the wartime Secret Service. Believing there has never been a time in history "when there wasn't a defense against some kind of threat," President Reagan intervened against his own scientific consultants and normal bureaucratic processes to write out in longhand the paragraphs of his March 1983 speech advocating a ballistic missile defense system that "holds the promise of changing the course of history." "The Strategic Defense Initiative has been labelled Star Wars," the president said two years later. "But it isn't about war. It is about peace. . . . If you will pardon my stealing a film line—the force is with us." In quoting a contemporary movie, was Reagan paying homage to its predecessor? Are we now being ruled by the fantasies of a 1940s countersubversive B movie?[1]

This chapter investigates the making of Ronald Reagan in 1940s Hollywood. The presidential character, I shall argue, was produced from the convergence of two substitutions that generated cold war countersubversion in the 1940s and underlie its 1980s revival—the political replacement of Nazism by Communism, from which the national-security state was born, and the psychological shift from an embodied self to its simulacrum on film. Reagan, I shall suggest, found out who he was through the roles he played on film. By responding to typecasting that either attracted or repelled him, by making active efforts to obtain certain roles and to escape others, Reagan merged his on- and offscreen identities. The confusion between life and film produced *Ronald Reagan*, the image that has fixed our gaze. In a deliberate imitation of the Reagan process, this chapter explores that confusion between life and film to bring the making of this president into view.

I

"Movies are forever" was the theme of the 1981 Academy Awards. President Ronald Reagan, the first Hollywood actor elevated to the presidency, was scheduled to welcome the academy from the White House. "Film is forever," the president was to tell the academy. "It is the motion picture that shows all of us not only how we look and sound but—more important—how we feel." Hollywood movies, Reagan was suggesting, mirror back to us the feelings on the screen as if they were our own, as if we were not given those feelings by the movies themselves. As confirming evidence of the power of film, John W. Hinckley, Jr., imitating the plot of the movie *Taxi Driver*, deliberately shot the president on the day of the Academy Awards. Obsessed with *Taxi Driver*, Hinckley had seen it again and again and had cast himself in the role of its isolated, deranged, and violent protagonist. Like the character played by Robert De Niro, Hinckley became a gun freak. Like him, he determined to win the woman he loved—Jody Foster in Hinckley's fantasy, the character she played in the movie—by assassinating a political leader. Hinckley,

like the De Niro character, failed as a political assassin. But he pre-
empted the Academy Awards and postponed them for an evening. De
Niro, nominated for an Oscar in 1976 for his performance in *Taxi
Driver*, had been nominated again five years later. He had planned to
absent himself from the 1981 ceremonies, but he appeared the night
following the attempted assassination, accepted an award for his performance in *Raging Bull*, and told the audience that *he* loved everybody.
De Niro was testifying that he was not really the character he and
Hinckley had played.[2]

In spite of De Niro's attempt to distance himself from his *Taxi Driver*
role, Hinckley's act reinforced the president's interpretation of the
power of film. Millions of Americans experienced the assassination attempt by watching it over and over again on television. The power of
the film image confirmed the shooting; it also allowed Reagan to speak
to the academy the next night as if the shooting had never happened.
The television audience watching a screen saw a Hollywood audience
watch another screen. One audience saw the other applaud a taped image of a healthy Reagan, while the real president lay in a hospital bed.
Reagan was president because of film, hospitalized because of film, and
present as an undamaged image because of film. The shooting climaxed
film's ingestion of reality. In so doing, it climaxed, in an uncanny way,
Reagan's personal project: the creation of a disembodied self that, by
rising above real inner conflicts, would reflect back to the president and
all the rest of us not only how he looked and sounded but—more important—how he felt and who he was.

At the same time that the assassination attempt dissolved the boundaries between film and real life, it allowed Reagan to exploit another
boundary confusion. "I have come to speak to you tonight about our
economic recovery program," the president told a joint session of Congress several weeks after he was shot. But first he digressed "for a moment" to thank the millions of Americans who had offered him their
"expression of friendship and, yes, love" after the assassination attempt.
"Now let's talk about getting spending and inflation under control and
cutting your tax rates," Reagan continued. "Thanks to some very fine
people, my health is much improved. I'd like to be able to say that with
regard to the health of the economy." The president was identifying the
recovery of his mortal body with the health of the body politic, his own
convalescence with his program to restore health to the nation. Reagan
was presenting himself as the healer, laying his hands on the sick social

body. He was employing a very old symbolism, one that merges the body of a political leader and the body of his realm.[3]

The doctrine of the king's two bodies, as we shall see in chapter 3, developed in the sixteenth century to address the relationship between a ruler's mortal body and his body politic. That doctrine, which marked a shift in the locus of sacred power from the church to the state, derived from the two bodies of Christ. Theologically, the death of Christ's mortal body created a mystic body, the regenerate Christian community. Sixteenth-century political leaders sought, like divine kings, to reabsorb that mystic community into their own personal bodies. American presidents and their publics have also identified the president's welfare with the health of the body politic and have attributed magical, healing power to the presidential touch.[4] But during Reagan's lifetime the locus of sacred value shifted from the church not to the state but to Hollywood. Reagan was born again to embody America through his sacrifice and rebirth on the screen.

It was D. W. Griffith who made Reagan possible as a presence who feels real to himself and his audience because he is seen. As I shall argue in chapter 7, Griffith wanted to collapse the world into film. He—and the mass culture he founded—shifted the locus of the real in America from mythicized history to image by crystallizing demonological images and placing them on film. But Griffith's project was the inverse of the one in Reagan's Hollywood. Griffith saw film as a visionary alternative to the mundane. He was possessed by the newness of film technique, by his own inventive power, and then, in the 1920s, by the artificiality of his movies. Griffith called attention to the filmmaker and his instruments, to the camera eye and the film cut. By contrast, in Kevin Brownlow's words, "the Hollywood aim was to perfect technique and thus render it imperceptible." The Hollywood movie in its classic years—the late 1930s through the 1950s, the years of Reagan's Hollywood career—blended the storyteller with the narrative and disguised the artfulness of film cuts. Dialogue and the moving camera made movies seem mimetic of quotidian reality. Hiding technique naturalized the fantasy nature of film content. For both filmgoers and participants in the making of films, reality lay neither in the process by which the movie was constructed nor in the outtakes on the cutting room floor, but rather in the final cut that eliminated all those shots, scenes, and versions of the plot where something had gone wrong.[5]

Early cinema, whether in Eisenstein's social or in German expres-

sionism's psychological mode (Griffith fathered them both), opened up
an interiorized world. Hollywood naturalism, in which depth of focus
gave the illusion of ordinary three-dimensionality, kept viewers on the
surface of the image. The audience knew it was at a motion picture
theater but was not led to ask whether what it was seeing was real.

The classic Hollywood movie was overdone and improbable and, at
the same time, continuous with ordinary life. Michael Wood has suggested that such films, with their overblown lines of dialogue and their
references to one another, constituted a larger-than-life world of their
own. Hollywood did not relax mundane constraints to obliterate daily
life, however, but to allow its daydreams to take over. The stories and
the methods of these movies broke down the barriers between fantasy
and reality, heroes and ordinary people. Classic Hollywood films put
realism in the service of fantasy, as if movies were mirroring the mundane. They encouraged confusion between "day-dreams," as Martha
Wolfenstein and Nathan Leites call these films, and daily life. For many
people, movies functioned as arenas for role playing, and they were the
place where the role player who was to become president of the United
States discovered his identity.[6]

Griffith had contrasted the masses who worshiped stars to the thinking classes who preferred the artistic standard imposed by a great director. He prophesied the director-artist as the hero of the future, but he
was wrong.[7] The mass viewer would take as hero his or her ideal self,
bigger than life, reflected in the star. And an actor who never reached
the pinnacle of Hollywood stardom would use his confusion between
"day-dreams" and reality to mediate between the mass public and the
image of the ideal.

"It has taken me many years to get used to seeing myself as others
see me," Reagan writes in his autobiography. "Very few of us ever see
ourselves except as we look directly at ourselves in a mirror. Thus we
don't know how we look from behind, from the side, walking, standing,
moving normally through a room. It's quite a jolt." But the actor, says
Reagan, learns to see himself from the outside in as others see him, not
from the inside out. He gives up the "mental picture" of the character
he plays as separate from himself and becomes at once the viewer of the
object and the object seen.[8]

A mirror requires both a referent and its reflection; it is dependent
on outside standards to supply a reality check. Movies have frequently
used a mirror image to create a double of the self, a split of the ideal
self from its dark reflection. But the screen also takes the place of a

mirror. It obliterates the referent: a self who sees himself from all angles fragments and disappears into his image. Self-sufficient, the screen dispenses both with external history and with the historically formed human interior (for which the mirror reflection was often a symbol). When the camera brought Reagan's self inside the screen, to exist as an observed outside, it shattered the distinction between inside and outside to produce "quite a jolt."[9]

"There are not two Ronald Reagans," Nancy Reagan assures us. In her words, "There is a certain cynicism in politics. You look in back of a statement for what the man really means. But it takes people a while to realize that with Ronnie you don't have to look in back of anything." She is describing a man whose most spontaneous moments—"Where do we find such men?" about the American D-day dead; "I am paying for this microphone, Mr. Green," during the 1980 New Hampshire primary debate—are not only preserved and projected on film but also turn out to be lines from old movies. The president knows, in the words of a member of his staff, that "all of us are deeply affected by a uniquely American art form: the movies." Responding to the charge that Reagan confuses the world depicted in movies with the world outside it, the presidential aide explained that cinema heightens reality instead of lessening it. Unwilling to acknowledge the conflation of movies and reality as a uniquely American contribution, the aide insisted that the president knew the difference between cinema and reality because he normally credited the lines he used.[10]

Reagan has, to be sure, deliberately quoted movie lines to make himself the hero of American cultural myths. "Go ahead. Make my day," the president told Congress, promising to veto a tax increase. He was repeating Clint Eastwood's dare in *Sudden Impact* that a hoodlum murder a woman hostage to free Eastwood to shoot the criminal. "Boy, I saw *Rambo* last night," the president said in July 1985 after the thirty-nine hostages held in Lebanon had been released. "Now I know what to do the next time this happens." At other times, however, Reagan has not only hidden from his audience the filmic origins of his words to create the appearance of spontaneity but concealed those origins from himself as well. CBS's "Sixty Minutes" has traced the process by which Reagan first credited the line "Where do we find such men?" to the movie admiral in *Bridges at Toko-Ri*, then assigned that line to a real admiral, and finally quoted it as if he had thought of it himself. The president has inadvertently called his dog "Lassie" in front of reporters. He has told a mass audience about the captain of a bomber who chose to go down with his plane rather than abandon a wounded crew member—"Congressional Medal of Honor, posthumous," concluded Reagan with tears in his eyes—only to have it revealed by a sailor who had seen the film aboard a World War II aircraft carrier that the episode was taken from Dana Andrews's *A Wing and a Prayer*. Reagan knew the Holocaust had happened, he told a gathering of survivors, because he had seen films of the camps. If there are not two Ronald Reagans, we owe his integration to film.[11]

Like earlier countersubversives, Reagan has divided the world between the forces of good and an empire of evil and traced all troubles at home and abroad to a conspiratorial center. Unlike them, however, he seems neither internally driven nor possessed. As many commentators have noted, he combines political punitiveness with personal charm, right-wing principle, and political salesmanship. Speaking like a radio announcer or talk show host (Reagan has been both), he presents political events of his own making as if he were somehow not responsible for them. He represents valued qualities rather than acting on them. Reagan suggests not the producer self who makes things happen but the celebrity who shows them off.[12]

Robert Dallek has explained the disjunction between the form and content of Reagan's politics by invoking the shift in the course of the twentieth century from idols of production to idols of consumption. The hero of production was a hard-working figure, admired for his achievements. The idol of consumption is a celebrity; his (or her) appeal comes from looks, not action. The idol of production made durable goods. The idol of consumption is a salesman or the object he sells. The former idol, like Reagan's rhetoric, acted on the supply side. The latter, like Reagan's tax cut, stimulates demand. The one flourishes in a manufacturing economy, the other in an economy based on service and information. Ordinary Americans can identify with the idol of consumption because he does not exercise authority over them or (like the traditional captain of industry) over employees at the workplace.[13]

The idol of production rose on his merits; the idol of consumption rises through good fortune, from being in the right place at the right time. "A miracle happened," Reagan has said of his first success in broadcasting; it could have happened to anyone. The idol of consumption is the chosen not the chooser, the product not the producer. He inhabits "a world of dependency," writes Leo Lowenthal in his classic study of the heroes of popular biography, "in which the average man is never alone and never wants to be alone." The president who urges a return to a time before Americans were "robbed of their independence" plays on the values of production but does not live them, for he was formed as an idol of consumption.[14]

The idol of production was inner-directed, aggressive, and driven. He valued character, possessing a self-controlled ego that was divided between duty and desire, a superego, and an id. The celebrity displays personality. He pleases others; intimate before the mass audience, he plays at privacy in public. Neither a repressed interior nor an intractable reality exercise claims over the celebrity, for he exists in the eye of the beholder. Since he replaces reality by fantasy, his pleasure and reality principles do not collide. Freed from the reproaches of either the conscience or the unconscious, he gains a reassuring serenity.

But the model of production and consumption is ambiguous. On the one hand, it contrasts superficial appearance with deeper source, a procedure endorsed by my concern with the production of *Ronald Reagan*. From that perspective the consumption idol is a fetish that can be demystified when we examine the process that produced it. On the other hand, the opposition of production to consumption implies a historical displacement of the former by the latter, so that distinctions between the way something looks and the way it really is are increasingly difficult to draw. From that perspective value is created not by work in production but by desire in exchange. The oppositions that traditionally organized both social life and social critique—oppositions between surface and depth, the authentic and the inauthentic, the imaginary and the real, signifier and signified—seem to have broken down. The dispersal of the subject in space, as Fredric Jameson has put it, replaces the alienation of the subject in time, and nostalgia for imitating historical surfaces replaces concern with the actual character of private and public history. From this point of view, Reagan's easy slippage between movies and reality is synechdochic for a political culture increasingly impervious to distinctions between fiction and history.[15]

Ronald Reagan has a synchronic presence whose power is not reducible to its origins, but it has a history as well. Since people are not images, neither Reagan nor any other human being comes into the world as a pure idol of consumption. The category represents an ideal type, an aspiration. Consumption idols respond in part to economic and social imperatives. But they also mark the convergence of the personal and the political, which came together for this president on the movie screen.

The desire to have one's identity scripted on film is not unmotivated.

In this instance, movies allowed Reagan to disown aggression and to enact it at the same time. Called to violence in his films, Reagan acted out movie violence in offhand and derealized forms. His roles taught the actor how to insulate himself from experiencing aggression as his own. He played characters who buried anger in wisecracks, suffered from external attack, and employed violence in self-defense. The actor was directed to show the emotional effects of violence only when he was its victim. Otherwise, watching himself play one of the boys on-screen, Reagan observed a figure with no distinctive, individuating, inward-pointing signs. Buried, disturbing feelings—if there were any—dissolved in the reassurance that *Ronald Reagan* was like everyone else.

Reagan's detachment marks an important departure in the history of American countersubversion. Puritans deliberately twinned themselves with their Indian enemies, for savages were signs of their own fallen natures. War not only punished Indians; it also exorcised the devils within.[16] Subsequent countersubversives—*The Birth of a Nation* and cold war movies will be among our texts—denied the identity between themselves and their shadow sides. Nevertheless, the frenzied doubling in such documents revealed the connections that ideology tried to hide. The monster-hunter repressed his attachment to his prey. The repressed bond resurfaced in countersubversive hysteria. Repressive politics in these classic forms of countersubversion invited the analyst to psychoanalyze repression.

But Reagan's affability, by insulating him from the subversive, seems to exclude the investigator as well. He seems not to register, even in a return of the repressed, the consequences of his wishes and politics. When Governor Reagan refused to visit a mental hospital to see the effects of his cuts in state aid, a psychiatrist suggested that he was under strain. "If I get on that couch, it will be to take a nap," Reagan responded.[17] He seems to have fulfilled Freud's lament (a lament that *The Birth of a Nation* should have dispelled until now) that Americans have no unconscious.

When *The Birth of a Nation* was shown during the 1920s Klan revival, Reagan's father would not let him see it. As a Catholic Jack Reagan was a target of the revived Klan, and he also condemned the racism shown on the screen. Reagan recalled, "In our household my father simply announced that no member of our family could see that picture because it was based on the Ku Klux Klan. And to this day I have never seen that great motion picture classic."[18] The reminiscence praises both

his father's humanitarianism and the racist film Reagan has not had to
see.

The difference between making *The Birth of a Nation* and shutting
it out marks the shift from racial domination to avoidance. As Joel Kovel has written, "The dominative racist, when threatened by the black,
resorts to direct violence; the aversive racist, in the same situation turns
away and walls himself off." Asked at the Great Wall of China if he
would like a great wall of his own, President Reagan responded,
"Around the White House." The joke (and the wall it portended, with
antitank barricades, ground-to-air missiles, and American flags) points
beyond the president's desire for physical safety to his wish for insula-
tion. Traditional countersubversives consciously or unconsciously doubled their political demons. Reagan aspires to a self in which, to recall
Nancy Reagan's words, there would not be two Ronald Reagans, since
the disowned, subversive part would have been lopped off. That wish
for an amputated self was granted in Hollywood.[19]

II

An uncanny slippage between life and film marked Ronald Reagan's
entry into the movies. Other aspiring stars were rebaptized in Hollywood, receiving stage names to replace their own. Reagan had been
baptized Ronald, his mother's choice, but he was always called by the
nickname his father gave him, Dutch. Dutch Reagan came to Hollywood and proposed Ronald Reagan as his stage name. "Ronald Reagan,
Ronald Reagan," repeated the head man, and the others around the
table said it after him. "I like it," the boss decided, and gave Ronald
Reagan back his own name. That Hollywood ceremony freed Reagan
from the name of his father and restored his mother's desire. "That's my
boy," Reagan's mother cried when she saw him in his first movie, *Love
Is on the Air* (1937). "That's the way he is at home. He's no Robert
Taylor. He's just himself." Reagan was playing the role he had left behind to come to Hollywood, that of a popular sports announcer (cf.
Figs. 1.2 and 1.3). His real radio station had fired him under sponsor
pressure and then rehired him; his movie station followed suit. In life,
the sports reporter Reagan invented play-by-play baseball games from
minimal, ticker-tape reports. He made up the sports events for his lis-
teners. Movie audiences could confirm Reagan's filmed on-the-spot reporting because they watched the staged sports events along with him.[20]

Reagan met Jane Wyman on the set of another of his early movies, *Brother Rat* (1938). He dated her in the movie, married her in life, the studio cast them as husband and wife in *An Angel from Texas* (1940), and Warner Brothers and Louella Parsons publicized their romance and happy marriage (cf. Figs. 1.4 and 1.5). "The Reagans' home life is probably just like yours, or yours, or yours," the studio quoted Reagan as saying. "Mr. Norm is my alias," the actor wrote in a 1940s movie magazine, presenting himself as the average American. On camera even when he was offscreen, Reagan seemed to have nothing to hide, no self tucked away from public inspection. Asked what the electorate saw in him on the eve of his 1980 victory, Reagan replied, "I think maybe they see themselves and that I'm one of them."[21]

But, as he hinted in his allusion to "Mr. Norm" as his "alias," Reagan's seamless merging of life and the movies in his first Hollywood years shut out an unacknowledged part of his past. The easy slippage between life and his early films meant, in William James's terminology, that in Hollywood Reagan was only once-born. James's once-born, healthy-minded individual has a happy consciousness. He turns into a divided self, torn between an ideal image and a dark, aggressive side, when he uncovers the loathsomeness within him and the destruction in the world. Reagan suffered death and violence, as we shall see, in his crucial, transformative movies; his film experience paralleled but did not duplicate the Jamesian evolution from a once-born character to a divided self. By keeping his sense of evil doubly removed from his sense of self—removed to the screen and removed from his roles on the screen—Reagan acquired an amputated self rather than a divided one. James's divided, sick soul is born again by recognizing that evil is not paralyzing and all-pervasive and by struggling against sin in the world.[22] Reagan parodied that rebirth by imposing screen fantasies on the world in his battle with Hollywood Communism. We turn now where the president has invited us and trace his self-division and reunification through his roles on the screen.

Murder in the Air anticipates the persona and worldview of the president. It is a long way, nonetheless, from the 1940s to the 1980s, from a B movie actor to the president of the United States. Even as *Murder in the Air* seems to collapse that distance, it exposes it. Ronald Reagan as Brass Bancroft is too brash, too aggressive, too hard-edged. He does not convey reassurance, and he is not a convincing actor. Distorted facial expressions and wooden gestures mar Reagan's performance in *Love Is on the Air*. He is less awkward in *Murder in the Air*, but even though he approaches a naturalistic performance, his cockiness is still exaggerated. Nothing seems to touch him. The shift from the air of radio to that of planes, the shift from love to war, was not sufficient to turn the actor into commander-in-chief. To acquire presidential stature, Reagan had to combine independence and dependence, power and loss, aggression and receptivity. He could not simply do damage to others; he had to appear to have damage done to him. As the hero he played opposite in *The Hasty Heart* (1950) would put it, he "had to be hurt to learn." He had to learn to be seen not simply as the man who sent American boys to die in Lebanon but, like the image in the film clip shown at the 1984 Republican convention, as the mourner identified with those boys, who stands beside their coffins.

Reagan's persona as a B movie crime fighter climaxed in a World War II film, *Desperate Journey* (1942). The movie perfectly exemplifies Béla Balázs's characterization of American World War II films "in which the bloodiest catastrophe in world history is portrayed like an amusing raw-humored manly adventure."[23] Although Reagan, as Johnny Hammond, is trapped behind enemy lines for most of the movie, the war has no internal impact on him. Reagan and the other members of his bombing crew, shot down over eastern Germany, perform miraculous acts of sabotage and escape as they work their way west. Although some crew members are killed, the characters portrayed by Reagan, Erroll Flynn, and Arthur Kennedy remain unharmed. In the climactic scene of mass destruction they steal a German plane, and Reagan, swiveling a machine gun in the bubble of the nose, mows down row after row of Germans as they rush to stop the aircraft from taking off. The slaughter is at once horrifying and painless, because the Germans have been portrayed as buffoons throughout the film. No one really gets hurt in *Desperate Journey*, since by not taking war seriously, the film turns war into a movie.

But even when the rugged individualists that Reagan played in such films were organization men, they were not protective, reassuring figures. Although Brass Bancroft is knocked out and left to drown during his adventures, both he and Johnny Hammond remain emotionally untouched by what they have been through. Since they communicate so little feeling, the viewer does not feel cared for by them. For Reagan to gain presidential stature, he had to acquire a falsely vulnerable objectified self to stand in for the self missing in action. To become a successful idol of consumption, he had to move beyond the rugged individualist American past with which he wished to be identified. He did so by reconnecting through his film roles to the dependence in his personal history in order, finally, to find a substitute for that dependence and play at freedom.

Warner Brothers was quick to spot the dependent side of Ronald Reagan. The studio allowed him to win in B movies, but it made him lose in the feature. Reagan was Bette Davis's playboy boyfriend in *Dark Victory* (1939) (Fig. 1.6). He is mostly drunk on-screen and is never seen without a glass in his hand. Davis is aggressive, Reagan is passive. She begins the movie as his girl and turns to him again in her refusal to face both her imminent death and her love for the fatherly doctor who operated (unsuccessfully) on her. Davis is a wired, cigarette-smoking projectile, a spoiled, independent young woman. Her destiny is to turn into a good girl-wife and to die. Although the film is all too clear about what it wants from women, Reagan is not the beneficiary. Glass in hand, he relinquishes Davis to George Brent (Dr. Steele). Reagan hated playing that scene and refused to do so in the effeminate manner called for by the director.[24] But although his performance is stilted, Reagan's character is not unsympathetic. *Dark Victory* foreshadowed a future in which Reagan could acquire heroic stature not simply by playing a tough guy but by first enacting and then shedding his playboy persona.

Worried that he would be stuck in B movies, Reagan introduced Warner Brothers to the idea of a film about Knute Rockne. Reagan had played football all through his youth; he got his first radio job, he reports, by simulating the end of a game his college had won in the last twenty seconds by using "the old Rockne special." Reagan missed his block in the actual game, as he tells the story, and made it in the radio reconstruction. By pointing to the difference between real game failure and fictional success, the movie actor invoked the daydream in which the ordinary man replays events in his own life to turn failure into success. Reagan was a hero not on the real football field, but first in the radio and then in the Hollywood reenactments.[25]

Reagan had been a real football player, to be sure, but for the movie of Knute Rockne he aspired higher than his college position on the line. He suggested Pat O'Brien for Rockne and himself for the legendary Notre Dame halfback, George Gipp. The studio cast O'Brien willingly but did not think Reagan looked like a football player. He only got the part, with O'Brien's help, after ten other actors failed screen tests and after he showed the studio pictures of himself in his college football uniform. A journeyman actor like Reagan normally had little to say

about his parts, but Reagan initiated *Knute Rockne* because he wanted
to play the Gipper. It is his favorite role, and the president invokes it
again and again.[26]

The part of the Gipper is a small one; Reagan is on-screen for barely
fifteen minutes. "I would give my right arm for a halfback who could
run, pass, and kick," says Rockne, and he trips over the Gipper's feet.
Reagan plays a rangy, good-looking, wisecracking young man who
scores a touchdown on his first run from scrimmage and makes long
gains rushing or passing in game after game. But the football star is an
enigma. "I don't like people to get too close to me" on the field or off,
he tells Rockne's wife. That admission comes in a moment of self-
revelation when, in Rockne's absence and with his wife as mediator,
the father-son love between the coach and his star is declared. As if the
insulated, male, American hero cannot survive that self-revelation, the
Gipper immediately gets a sore throat, Rockne sends him to the hospital, and he dies of viral pneumonia.

But the Gipper lives on—as every American now knows—an inspiration for Notre Dame and the country. Stricken by phlebitis years after
Gipp's death, Rockne also faces defeatism on his team. He is wheeled
to the annual Army–Notre Dame game in a wheelchair; at halftime,
with his players beaten and behind, Rockne repeats the Gipper's dying
words. "Someday when the team is in trouble," Gipp had told Rockne,
"tell them to win one for the Gipper." The inspired team members leap
up and rush onto the field. "That's for you, Gipp!" says the player who
scores the first of the many touchdowns that bring victory to Notre
Dame.

At the 1981 Notre Dame commencement, in his first public appearance after he was shot, President Reagan insisted that the movie line
"Win one for the Gipper!" not be spoken "in a humorous vein." "Do it
for the Gipper," Reagan told the U.S. Olympic athletes in the summer
of 1984. "Win those races for the Gipper!" was how Reagan urged
crowds to vote the straight Republican ticket during the fall campaign.
But the Gipper (as played by Reagan) was dead when those words were
spoken in the movie. If you elect Republicans, Reagan told the crowds,
"Wherever I am, I'll know about it, and it'll make me happy." The president spoke as if, playing the Gipper, he was witness to his own death
and ascension.[27]

After his defeat at the 1976 Republican convention, Reagan quoted
lines he'd memorized as a child: "Lay me down and bleed a while.

Though I am wounded, I am not slain. I shall rise and fight again." Slain as George Gipp, Reagan rose to fight again, to invoke the spirit of the dead hero into whom he had dissolved.[28]

Knute Rockne doubles the theme of regenerative sacrifice by having Rockne catch Gipp's martyrdom. The coach risks his life to attend the football game when he has phlebitis, speaks the Gipper's line from a wheelchair with a blanket over his legs, and dies in a plane crash soon after. A priest tells the mourners at Rockne's funeral, "The spirit of Knute Rockne is reborn in the youth of today."

"It's like seeing a younger son I never knew I had," Reagan jokes when he watches reruns of *Knute Rockne*.[29] The sacrifice of that son knit first the team and then the country together. But whereas Gipp's sacrifice preceded the sacrifice of the film father, Knute Rockne, it gave birth to the actor father, now president, Ronald Reagan. In real history fathers come before sons; in Reagan's film-mediated history the son (George Gipp) produced the father (President Reagan), a father who has replaced his real father by the image of his own younger self.

The sacrifice of Reagan-Gipp, moreover, broke down the boundary not only between son and father, Gipp and Rockne, but also between human body and body politic. By shifting the source of personal identity from the living body of George Gipp to his spirit, Gipp's sacrifice turned the body mortal into the *corpus mysticum*. The Gipper's sacrifice, however, was mediated through film and not religious ceremony. Invoking the Gipper after he was shot, Reagan identified his own recovery with his economic recovery program for the nation. He could claim to embody the nation, exploiting the boundary confusion between the president's body and the body politic, because he had risen from the confusion between life and film.

At the South Bend premiere of *Knute Rockne* in 1940, trainloads of celebrities joined a hundred thousand other visitors to the town. The governors of eight states declared a national Knute Rockne week, and a week of radio broadcasts climaxed with Kate Smith singing "God Bless America" and with Roosevelt's son delivering a personal message from his father. Reagan had played a radio announcer in *Boy Meets Girl* (1938) who broadcast movie premieres from Hollywood theaters. Two years later the actor joined the *Knute Rockne* premiere as one of the stars.[30]

When Reagan and Pat O'Brien attended *Knute Rockne*'s opening at Notre Dame, Nelle Reagan asked her son to take his father with them. Reagan recalls the "chilling fear" he felt at that request, for Jack Reagan was an alcoholic. Reagan had brought his father to Hollywood to handle his fan mail, but that father-son role reversal did not suffice to keep the father under control. Although Nelle assured her son he could trust his father, Jack Reagan and Pat O'Brien went on an all-night drinking binge nonetheless. O'Brien thought Reagan's father hilarious, but Reagan's anxiety about how his father would behave at lunch the next day was not dispelled until the mother superior who had sat next to Jack "informed me that my father was the most charming man she had ever met."[31] Reagan's father and mother introduced anxiety; Pat O'Brien and the mother superior dispelled it. The story points to the personal sources of Reagan's need to move from home to Hollywood and also reveals the failure of *Knute Rockne* to enforce the break.

Knute Rockne inverted Reagan's familial past, replacing an unreliable, dependent father with an idealized, strong one (Fig. 1.7) and transforming forbidden anger at the historical father into the filmed son's sacrifice. That sacrifice was a gift to the father, and Reagan's need to deny the conflicts in his personal history attracted him to the idealized father in *Rockne*. Idealization buried anger, and even though the idealized father was also sacrificed, *Knute Rockne* gave no room for negative feelings against authority. The film in which Reagan reinhabited his past to emancipate himself from it is *King's Row* (1942), the movie that made him a star, which he places at the center of his autobiography and which he has singled out as the film with the deepest personal significance for his life.

III

"My face was blue from screaming, my bottom was red from whacking, and my father claimed afterward that he was white when he said shakily, 'For such a little bit of a fat Dutchman, he makes a hell of a lot of noise. . . .' 'I think he's perfectly wonderful,' said my mother weakly. 'Ronald Wilson Reagan.'"

Blue face, red bottom, white father: "I have been particularly fond of the colors that were exhibited," announces the author, wrapping himself at birth in the American flag. We are on the first page of Ronald Reagan's autobiography, *Where's the Rest of Me?* "In those early days I was sure I was living the whole life of Reagan," Reagan continues. "It was not until thirty years later that I found that part of my existence was missing."

The missing part of Reagan's existence was his legs, and he lost them in *King's Row*. Some people might find that loss troublesome, but it was the making of the actor's career. In his words, "I took the part of Drake McHugh, the gay young blade who cut a swathe among the ladies." Drake romanced the town surgeon's daughter. When a railroad accident knocked him unconscious, the "sadistic doctor" took his revenge. He "amputated both my legs at the hips." Reagan woke in a hospital bed to speak the line that made him a star: "Where's the rest of me?" (See Fig. 1.8.)

Those five words, Reagan reports, presented him with the most challenging acting problem of his career. He had to become a legless man, or the line would not carry conviction. "I rehearsed the scene before mirrors, in corners of the studio, while driving home, in the men's rooms of restaurants, before selected friends. At night I would wake up staring at the ceiling and automatically mutter the lines before I went back to sleep. I consulted physicians and psychologists; I even talked to people who were so disabled, trying to brew in myself the cauldron of emotions a man must feel who wakes up one sunny morning to find half of himself gone." When at last Reagan climbed into bed to shoot the scene, "In some weird way, I felt that something horrible had happened to my body." Trying "to reach for where my legs should be" and twisting in panic, Reagan delivered in a single take the finest shot of his career. "The reason was that I had put myself, as best I could, in the body of another fellow." But Drake McHugh was not simply "another fellow," for Reagan made a discovery about himself in *King's Row*. Reagan learned by playing Drake McHugh "that part of my existence was missing," and so he called his autobiography *Where's the Rest of Me? King's Row* taught Reagan that he was only "half a man" and made him search for what he lacked. But the film that pointed to something missing in the actor also made him a star. Why should the body of a legless man have possessed Reagan so personally and raised him to stardom?[32]

Reagan begins *Where's the Rest of Me?* with his birth, switches to his rebirth in *King's Row*, and then returns to his father. Jack Reagan was a shoe salesman. "He loved shoes. He sold them as a clerk . . . and spent many hours analyzing the bones of the foot." But Jack Reagan failed as a shoe salesman, and his son remembers, at age eleven, coming upon his father "flat on his back on the front porch," "his arms spread out as if he were crucified," passed out from drink. Jack Reagan had lost "another bout with the dark demon of the bottle," and the son had to overcome "the sharp odor of whiskey" to drag his father into the house. Jack Reagan "never lost the conviction that the individual must stand on his own feet," but he could not do so himself. He survived the depression by distributing relief checks for the WPA.[33]

Like many another self-made man, this son who celebrates family had first to escape his own. How, if your father is a failed shoe salesman, do you avoid stepping into his shoes? The answer *King's Row* provided was this: by cutting off your legs. The Christian loses himself as body to find himself as spirit. Reagan was born again in Hollywood by relinquishing "part of myself" in *King's Row*.

King's Row was set, a sign announces at the opening of the film, in "a good clean town. A good town to live in, a good place to raise your children," like Tampico, Illinois, where Reagan was born, or Dixon, where he grew up. "We all have spots we dream of and want to go home to," says the character Reagan plays in *The Hasty Heart*. "For me it's a little place on the Duck River, Dixon, Illinois." But the American family in *King's Row* turns out to consist of sadistic fathers, demonic mothers, and daughters whose dangerous sexual desires place young men in jeopardy.

"The story begins with a closeup of a bottom," writes Reagan, introducing his birth in the first sentence of *Where's the Rest of Me? King's Row* opens on a country idyll, as a young girl and boy disrobe to swim in a pond. "It's not so warm on the bottom," the boy tells the girl, and in the next shot the outline of her naked bottom is visible beneath the water. In the scenes that follow, the girl is given a birthday party to which no one comes; the boy and his best friend swing on the rings of an icehouse with a working-class girl so they can see her underpants; and the boy hears the cries of another friend's father, screaming because a doctor is operating on his legs. Preadolescent sexuality, punctuated by violence to destroy its innocence, introduces and concludes childhood in *King's Row*.

This prologue defines the character of the film that made Reagan a star. *King's Row* is a classic in the American gothic form. The gothic sensibility has Christian roots (to which the label, gothic, points), and it reveals the dark underside of born-again Christianity. American gothic depicts a titanic struggle between the forces of good and evil, in which the world is under the devil's sway. American gothic art is an art of dualism, of haunted characters, violence, and horror. Although it claims to stand for good, it is fascinated by evil. Rebirth carries less conviction in the gothic imagination than the power of blackness does, and the regenerate remain filled with vengefulness against the world that has damaged them. *King's Row* illustrates the shift from the wisecrack-

ing surface of 1930s Hollywood movies to 1940s psychological night-
mares (and its director, Sam Wood, would become obsessed with the
Communist penetration of Hollywood in the years after World War
II).[34]

The main portion of *King's Row* more than fulfills the gothic promise
of the opening scenes. The film's protagonists, played by Reagan and
Robert Cummings, are doubles in a movie of doubles. Both boys are
wealthy orphans, in the course of the movie both lose the relatives who
replace their parents, and both fall in love with doctors' daughters. Parris Mitchell (Cummings) is drawn (in the Tower family) into maternal
insanity, implied father-daughter incest (explicit in the book), and the
power of a father (Claude Rains) who kills his daughter and himself.
Drake McHugh confronts (in the Gordon family) a monstrous mother
(Judith Anderson), a sexually sadistic father, and the loss of his legs.
Wolfenstein and Leites describe the hero and heroine of the typical
1940s movie romance as unbound by family ties. The young protagonists are homeless in such romances and jauntily self-sufficient. Menacing surrogate parents appear only in gothic melodramas, set far from
the familiar world. *King's Row* collapses melodrama into romance. The
boys may be orphans, but (to quote Wolfenstein and Leites) there is no
"escape of children from protracted involvement with their parents."
The children in *King's Row* are trapped in the American family.[35]

The classic American family in *King's Row*, with working father,
housewife mother, and child, is a horror. There is incest in one doctor's
family, sadism in the other. The Family Protection Act, sponsored by the
born-again New Right, would punish departures from the classic American family. *King's Row* locates the desire and necessity for punishment
within that family itself.

Both doctor fathers take vengeance (murder and amputation) for
their daughters' sexual desire. In the movie's iconography, however,
mothers are to blame. The monstrous mothers drive their husbands to
violence or embrace it themselves. They derange fathers and contaminate daughters. Because mature women in this movie endanger men,
the young women Drake and Parris finally marry have benign, aged fathers and no mothers. Daughters who unite love with sexual desire are
punished (Louise Gordon) or destroyed (Cassandra Tower). Randy
Monaghan, the woman Drake marries, can survive because her lover
becomes, as Parris says about Drake and Reagan about himself, "half a
man."[36] The protection men need in *King's Row* is not the protection
of family but protection from women.

Brothers are rivals in the typical American movie romances Wolfenstein and Leites describe.[37] There is no overt antagonism between Parris and Drake, yet the physical youth, Drake, is sacrificed so that his spiritual brother can become whole. The happiness of the intact young man is bought at the price of the legs of his double.

Reagan underscores the connection between *King's Row* and his own youth. He calls the film "a slightly sordid but moving yarn about antics in a small town, something that I had more than a slight acquaintance with." Then he describes the movie's "accident in the railroad yards," in which a moving train that was supposed to be stationary cost Drake McHugh his legs, and a few pages later he reports an escapade in which his brother and he crawled under a train stopped at the town station, getting to the other side just before the train pulled out. Reagan's mother punished him for risking the bodily harm that he was to suffer as Drake. Using the word "antics" to connect his own childhood to *King's Row*, Reagan places himself within the movie by shutting out its horror. He is engaging in acknowledgment by denial.[38]

The Towers and Gordons were hardly replicas of the Reagans. In spite of poverty, paternal alcoholism, and several moves from one town and one shoe salesman's job to another, Reagan remembers a happy childhood. That must be part of the story; yet the son who, influenced by his mother, "could feel no resentment against" his passed-out father[39] is dissociated from his feelings. *King's Row* supplied a target for anger that could be placed outside the self. It provided the negative family from which Reagan had cut himself off. The movie reunited him to his problematic history in order, by amputation, to free him from it.

Why did Reagan need to be free of his father? In her psychological study of the president, Betty Glad addresses the anger young Reagan was not allowed to feel; in his study Robert Dallek emphasizes Reagan's fear of helplessness. Dallek locates the president's political hostility to dependence in his need to separate himself from his dependent father. Reagan himself blames one of his father's drinking bouts on Jack Reagan's indignation over the "narcotic" of welfare; Dallek's analysis illuminates Reagan's resistance to playing the alcoholic role in *Dark Victory*. But Jack Reagan's "dark demon" pointed to both the father's helplessness and the son's in the face of the father. Reagan recalls that his father once "lifted me a foot in the air with the flat side of his boot" when he caught the boy fighting. The boy associated anger with dependence, *Where's the Rest of Me?* suggests, since dependence simultaneously filled him with anger and made him a target. Jack Reagan used his leg to punish the helpless son. Dr. Gordon became the punishing father, amputating the legs of a helpless young man.[40]

By moving from *King's Row* to his father and connecting his youth to Drake McHugh's, Reagan made himself the victim. But Jack Reagan died between the filmings of *Knute Rockne* and *King's Row*. Reagan had married in January 1940, and his first child was born a year later. Within a few months of becoming a father, he lost his own father, who had kicked him but was himself a beaten man. *King's Row* mutilated the actor for any death wishes against his father or feelings of triumph over him. The president has trouble drawing hands and feet; in a doodle of himself in a football jersey, the limbs are missing (as if to merge the Gipper and Drake McHugh).[41] *King's Row* did not end with mutilation, however. By both punishing the actor and giving him a target for anger, the movie allowed him to reexperience and conquer his helplessness.

Drake McHugh feels defeated after his legs are cut off until he discovers who is to blame. "Where did Doctor Gordon think I lived, in my legs?" scoffs Drake when he learns that the doctor amputated his legs not to save his life but to turn him into "a lifelong cripple." Drake's anger at Gordon frees him from self-pity, and he and his wife make their fortune in real estate. At the film's end they move into one of their new houses, in a suburb outside King's Row. In the final image on the screen, Drake, his wife, and his best friend approach their white house on the hill. The two films that made Reagan a star supplied him with an idealized authority he could sacrifice and a sadistic one he could be punished by and then overcome. Freed from the gothic small town, Reagan would reinhabit, as fantasy life for millions, an ideal version of the American past.

Reagan appeals to an American dream past where, in his misquotation of Tom Paine, "we have it in our power to begin the world over again." Drake McHugh resolves the struggle between good and evil by rising above the rooted body; upward mobility, in Reagan's images, saves us from the gothic nightmare of being trapped down below. This nightmare has personal resonance for Reagan, since he suffers from the American pioneer's disease, "a lifelong tendency toward claustrophobia." The boy at the bottom of the football pile, he tells us in his autobiography, "got frightened to the point of hysteria in the darkness under the mass of writhing, shouting bodies." To protect himself from claustrophobia during the filming of *Hellcats of the Navy* (1957), in which Reagan played a submarine commander, he rushed to the periscope between takes to watch the activity in the harbor. Upward mobility moved the actor from the bodies to the spectacle, from the bottom of the pile to the top, and he insists on the need to "restore a . . . vertical structuring of society." Communism, Reagan charges, is "the most evil enemy mankind has known in his long climb from the swamp to the stars." His own long anti-Communist climb reached both movie stardom and the outer space of the Strategic Defense Initiative (Star Wars). In the president's words, "There is no left or right, only an up or down. Up to the maximum of individual freedom consistent with law or order, or down to the ant heap of totalitarianism."[42]

Upward mobility, in rugged individualist rhetoric, frees the self-made man from dependence. Filmed amputation did not, however, emancipate Reagan from his dependent father. It made Drake McHugh helpless and dependent, cared for by a maternal woman as Nelle Reagan had cared for Jack. That result may have constituted a happy ending in film and childhood fantasy, but it came at the price of manhood. Drake has a sexual romance with Randy Monaghan, his working-class Irish girlfriend, before he loses his money and his legs. Drake's poverty, which sends him to the railway station job and places him within an Irish family, brings him closer to Reagan's childhood. But when Drake marries Randy, as the movie makes explicit, he has lost his sexuality. *King's Row* freed Reagan from the father by placing him under female power.

The happy family announced at the beginning of *King's Row* is promised again at the end. But Drake has been swallowed up by the gothic nightmare in between. He will raise no children. Drake's happy family, cut off from the past and the future, can only exist as a dream.

Reagan still inhabits *King's Row*. He made it the center of his autobiography, he watched it again and again with Jane Wyman and their guests, he watches it with Nancy Reagan, and he chose its music as the fanfare for his 1980 inauguration. But the *King's Row* solution created a problem that plagued Reagan (he says in *Where's the Rest of Me?*) for the remainder of his Hollywood career.[43]

IV

Reagan was in the army when *King's Row* appeared. Stationed in Hollywood, he made training, morale, and reenlistment movies for soldiers, defense workers, and the mass public. These movies, whatever their audience, confused entertainment with war. In *This Is the Army* (1943), Reagan played a corporal who stages an army variety show during World War II. His father, portrayed by George Murphy, had put on a soldier's show during the First World War and then lost the use of a leg. Reagan, who had played a legless hero the year before and who would follow Murphy into California politics two decades later, inherits the master of ceremonies role from his film father. Murphy's performers had marched off the stage into the trucks taking them to embark for France. By World War II war itself, as mass, militarized formations, had taken over the stage. The movie ends with a command performance of Reagan's show before the president of the United States.

This Is the Army made war into entertainment; Reagan also made entertainment into war. Although never close to combat, Reagan reports that he participated in "one of the better-kept secrets of the war, ranking up with the atom bomb project." "Everyone who has ever seen a picture based on World War II," writes Reagan, will recognize the briefing in which he played a role. To prepare pilots to bomb Tokyo, Hollywood special effects men built a complete miniature of the city. They "intercut their movies of the model with real scenes taken from flights over Tokyo," thereby creating a series of movies that enacted bombing runs. Reagan narrated the films, and each one concluded "when my voice said, 'Bombs away.'" Reagan's account of his wartime service slips from the Manhattan project to the moving picture theater, from real war to a mock-up of war. To make himself a participant, Reagan breaks down the distinction between real bombs and simulated bombing runs. As a result, none of the explosives in his account, from the bombs he narrates to the atom bomb, fall on real targets. When Reagan told crowds in his first campaign for governor that he served as an adjutant at an Air Force base, he did not mention that it was in the film community.[44]

As if to compensate for taking care of Reagan during the war, Hollywood cast him in a series of postwar films that placed him in the wrong kind of danger. Before *King's Row* Reagan had played the young Custer in *Santa Fe Trail* (1940) and, in *International Squadron* (1941), a carefree RAF pilot who atones for his costly nonchalance by dying on a heroic mission. These roles, which he got from his success as the Gipper,[45] joined heroism to sacrifice. But *King's Row* typecast the actor as a figure vulnerable not in combat but in romantic entanglements. The American playboy cannot be truly manly because his involvements are with women and masculinity is realized in relations among men. Reagan hoped that the trajectory from *Dark Victory* through *King's Row* would free him from female entanglements and prepare him to play a cowboy. But Warner Brothers drew a different box office lesson from the actor's Hollywood career. The characters Reagan played after the war were invaded by illness and by women.

Reagan wanted a big-budget Western for his first postwar film. The studio cast him instead in the black-and-white *Stallion Road* (1947). The movie "opened the door to finding another part of me," writes Reagan. He bought the horse he rode in the movie, changed its name to the name it bore in *Stallion Road* (Tarbaby), and imitating the character he played, acquired a horse ranch. But Reagan did not portray a western hero in *Stallion Road*. A veterinarian instead, he develops a serum that saves cattle from an anthrax epidemic and then catches the disease himself. Given up for dead, he is nursed back to health by Rory Teller (Alexis Smith). In *Night unto Night* (1949) the Reagan character, John, has epilepsy. He has lost the will to live and plans suicide but is saved by Ann's (Viveca Lindfors's) love. In *The Hasty Heart* (1950) (was it better or worse?) Richard Todd played the soldier dying of a fatal disease and Reagan was reduced to feigning illness in order to remain at his side; Todd won the Academy Award nomination. As Grover Cleveland Alexander in *The Winning Team* (1952), his last Warner Brothers film, Reagan makes a comeback from epilepsy. In *Tennessee's Partner* (1955), his penultimate Hollywood movie, Reagan's character is an unworldly cowboy humiliated by a woman, who dies saving the life of his best friend.[46]

Reagan did not always sicken or die in his postwar films, but women invariably gave him trouble. He and Shirley Temple fall in love in *That Hagen Girl* (1947). The Reagan character is old enough to be the girl's father and, rumor has it, is. Reagan is harassed in *Louisa* (1950) by his mother's romances with two elderly men. To simulate a home for a chimpanzee in *Bedtime for Bonzo* (1951), he hires a nurse to masquerade as his wife. Reagan plays a professor of psychology whose father was a criminal and who wants to prove (as if he were the chimp) that environment can triumph over heredity. Reagan also plays a professor in *She's Working Her Way Through College* (1952); this time his wife suspects him of being infatuated with the show-girl in his class (see Fig. 1.9). In *The Voice of the Turtle* (1947) and *John Loves Mary* (1949), Reagan plays a World War II veteran innocently caught between two women. Only in *The Girl from Jones Beach* (1949), where Reagan is a magazine illustrator who cuts up the bodies of twelve girls to make one perfect figure, does his character take charge of women. But he broke his tailbone on the set of that movie; he blames Eddie Arnold for bumping into him and knocking him down while Arnold was ogling the girls.[47]

These romantic comedies, with their erratic women and emasculated leading man, exemplify the domestic anxieties on the postwar Hollywood screen. The films also—to recall the president's words—tell us something not simply about how Reagan looked to casting directors but about how he felt as well. Resenting accusations that he "never got the girl" in his movies, Reagan once listed all the heroines he got. "I always got the girl," he insisted, but as he knew at the time, the issue was not whether he got the girl but how. His list included girls he got by losing his legs, by nearly dying of epilepsy and anthrax, and by undergoing other forms of humiliation. He got the girl, like his father, by being dependent. Reagan did not like making these movies and left Warner Brothers because of them. "I . . . put my foot down. Then the studio put its foot down—on top of mine" is the way he put it. Reagan found the roles particularly disturbing because they mirrored his private life.[48]

Soon after he caught anthrax in *Stallion Road*, Reagan came down with viral pneumonia. That disease, which killed George Gipp, almost killed him, and Reagan reports lying in his hospital bed and wanting to die. Jane Wyman was several months pregnant and, under the strain from Reagan's illness, she gave premature birth to a stillborn baby. The next year, 1948, she filed for divorce. "I was notified I was going to be a bachelor again," writes Reagan, and "I came home from England and broke my leg in half a dozen places." As he had with viral pneumonia, Reagan spent weeks in bed. "Free of any responsibility," in "my warm cocoon," Reagan was imitating Drake McHugh. Even when he was on his feet again, the actor did not enjoy his bachelor years. "I was footloose and fancy-free," Reagan recalls, "and I guess down underneath miserable."[49]

Reagan wanted domesticity, but Wyman preferred a more glamorous life. She "couldn't stand," she complained, "to watch that damn *King's Row* one more time."[50] Wyman's career was rising while Reagan's was in decline. When she won an Academy Award for her role in *Johnny Belinda* (1948), Reagan quipped, "I think I'll name Johnny Belinda as the co-respondent." Their separate careers, as Reagan saw it, had taken his wife from him. Reagan's career diverged from Wyman's, however, not because they both made movies but—and this is the reason other than watching *King's Row* she gave for leaving him—because he was turning from movies to anti-Communist politics.[51]

"An actor spends half his waking hours in fantasy," Reagan writes in his autobiography. "If he is only an actor, I feel, he is much like I was in *King's Row*, only half a man." No line better speaks to an actor's condition, writes Reagan, than "Where's the rest of me?" It explains why he left Hollywood. As an actor Reagan had lost his "freedom." He was "a semi-automaton, 'creating' a character another had written." Deciding to "find the rest of me . . . I came out of the monastery of movies into the world."[52] Warner Brothers would not let Reagan play the traditional hero on-screen. The studio deprived him of the idealized self he wanted to enact and gave him parts that exposed his weakness instead. When Reagan shifted from film to reality, however, he cast reality in terms of make-believe. By standing up for America in another Hollywood drama, he sought to end Communist influence in the movies.

V

In 1946, five years after Drake McHugh asked, "Where's the rest of me?" writes Reagan, "under different circumstances than make-believe, I had to ask myself the same question." Reagan answered it by leading the fight against "the Communist plan . . . to take over the motion picture business." "We had a weekly audience of about 500,000 souls. Takeover of this enormous plant and its gradual transformation into a Communist grist mill was a grandiose idea. It would have been a magnificent coup for our enemies." The actor emerged from his hospital bed and his filmed humiliations to enter the cold war. Reagan, as he tells it, recovered his legs in the struggle to prevent a Communist takeover of Hollywood.[53]

"Russ Imperialism Seen by Veteran," ran the headline over a 1950 story in the *Los Angeles Times*. "A former captain of the Army Air Force," as the story identified him, "Reagan portrayed the screen as the great purveyor of information about the American way of life. He said it was this that Red Russia cannot match, so it tried to take over. When it failed, he said, it tried various schemes to ruin the industry. 'The Russians sent their first team, their ace string, here to take us over,' he said. 'We were up against hard-core organizers.'"[54]

The fantasy of Communists taking over Hollywood was delusional, the stuff of a Hollywood movie. But two factors gave credence to that delusion and made it continuous with mundane life. The first was the presence of significant numbers of Communists in the motion picture business in the 1930s and 1940s. They influenced no movies, but they were not imaginary. The second was the widely shared belief in their conspiratorial power.[55]

From 1935 to 1950, Hollywood may have been the most politicized community in America. Communists, other leftists, and liberals worked together in the popular front; they were united by the depression, by their hatred of Fascism, and by their loyalty to Franklin Delano Roosevelt. Warner Brothers, known as the working man's studio, was the most pro-Roosevelt place to work in the industry. Reagan participated in progressive politics, and FDR was his hero. He joined the American Veterans Committee and HICCASP (The Hollywood Independent Citizens Committee of Arts, Sciences, and Professions), popular-front organizations in which Communists were active.[56]

Communists influenced no movies. Most Hollywood Communists were screenwriters, and their rare efforts to infiltrate progressive lines of dialogue were pathetic and futile. Warner Brothers produced a pro-Soviet film during World War II to give Roosevelt a movie that created sympathy for his Russian ally. Jack Warner made *Mission to Moscow* because of his ties to FDR, not because of the hidden influence of the screenwriter, Howard Koch. But Jack Warner led the search for hidden Communists when anti-Fascism turned into anti-Communism, and he blacklisted Koch.[57]

Although Communists had no power over motion pictures, they were active in the Conference of Studio Unions (CSU), which battled with the studios and with the International Association of Theatrical and Stage Employees (IATSE) from 1945 to 1947 for control of the studio crafts. When the House Un-American Activities Committee began investigating Communist influence in Hollywood in 1947, fears of a Communist takeover spread throughout the industry. In part those fears rationalized management's position in the industrial conflict. In part anti-Communist hysteria displaced anxiety over political interference from the proximate source, Washington, to Moscow. In part Hollywood was taken over by the cold war. But whatever the sources of the anti-Communist obsession, it was normalized by being so widely shared.[58]

Roy Brewer, president of IATSE, told HUAC in 1947, "The one potent force that stood between complete control of the industry by the Communists and their defeat at the crucial point in 1945 were the A.F. of L. unions" (Brewer was Reagan's close friend in the late 1940s; after Reagan became president, he appointed Brewer to a federal job). Sam Wood, who had directed *King's Row*, formed the Motion Picture Association for the Preservation of American Ideals to fight Communist subversion. Wood carried a black book everywhere to write down the names of Communists whenever he found out about them. Wood's obsession deranged him, his daughter thinks, and contributed to his early death. The director internalized trouble that other anti-Communists—liberals and conservatives, management and labor—successfully extruded onto Reds.[59]

Reagan remained a New Deal liberal when he turned against the Communists. He was a founder and national board member of Americans for Democratic Action, formed in 1947 as a liberal, anti-Communist organization. He campaigned for Harry Truman and Hubert Humphrey in 1948 by attacking Wall Street as well as the Soviet Union.[60] Reagan's cold war liberalism did not, however, make him soft on Communism, for liberals shared the universal hysteria. The actor was not pressured either to see his fear of subversion as one perspective among many or to repress acceptable political alternatives; his was the only legitimate point of view. Reagan's demonology was not marginal, a sign of personal disturbance. It was the norm.

It was a norm, moreover, that spread from Hollywood around the country. HUAC's investigation of the motion picture industry, along with the Truman doctrine and the Hiss case, formed the consciousness of cold war America before the Rosenbergs and Joe McCarthy were household names. The hot war against Hitler and Japan slid easily into the cold war against Stalin and Asian Communism in the consciousness that formed Reagan's politics in the 1940s and that he brought to Washington. "The real fight with this new totalitarianism belongs to the forces of liberal democracy," he wrote in 1951, "just as did the battle with Hitler's totalitarianism."[61] World War II signifies for Reagan more the first act in the struggle against Communism than the extermination of the Jews. Hence he used the fortieth anniversary of V-E day in 1985 to shore up the German-American anti-Soviet alliance by visiting Bitburg cemetery and equating Jewish victims of the Holocaust with the German soldiers buried there. Both, said Reagan, were "victims" of "the awful evil started by one man."[62]

Reagan's enlightenment about Communism in postwar Hollywood defines the founding moment of the politics in which we now all live. The president brought with him to Washington other men who had participated in intelligence work during World War II and then shifted to the anti-Soviet fight. There was a romance of World War II in 1940s America, denied to countries on whose soil the war was fought. President Reagan has revived that romance, filtered it through Hollywood, and frozen it at the moment when Nazis turned into Communists (in theory—while real ones went to work for American intelligence). Reagan learned that Communists were "monsters," he told Robert Scheer in 1980, "when they were trying to take over Hollywood." He learned then what he still believes, that "the Soviet Union was the mother lode, the center, which controlled subversives around the world."[63]

Isolationist Republicans shared Reagan's view of Soviet influence, but while they tried to withdraw from the alien world (at least in Europe), Reagan wanted to transform it. As a cold war Democrat, he never shared the parochial conservative opposition to increased military spending and a global, interventionist foreign policy. Reagan, unlike provincial conservatives, was and remains a statist. To combat Communist penetration, from 1940s Hollywood to 1980s Washington, Reagan has supported a militarized surveillance state.

Hollywood anti-Communism, as Reagan understood it, restored his independence by freeing him from make-believe. But Communist influence was not the only fantasy Reagan took with him from the movies; he took the fantasy of independence as well. Reagan wore a gun during his battle against the Communists to protect himself from Red reprisals. As he put it, "I mounted the holstered gun religiously every morning and took it off the last thing at night." Pioneer heroism and Indian war had moved from American history into Hollywood fantasy. "We are for the free enterprise system," Reagan told the Los Angeles Rotary Club in 1948. "We have fought our little Red brothers all along the line." Reagan meant Communists, but his phrase evoked Indians. Shifting from one red enemy to another, Reagan brought frontier individualism back into history again.[64]

Reagan is fond of quoting Sterling Hayden's testimony before HUAC that the Communists were taking over Hollywood until "we ran into a one-man battalion named Ronnie Reagan." But the lone man in Hollywood was actually a victim of corporate, countersubversive cooperation. HUAC, the motion picture industry, the unions, and private agencies like the American Legion all worked together, blacklisting those people who refused to name names. As president of the Screen Actors Guild, the one-man battalion joined a surveillance network that, as we shall see in chapter 2, imitated the enemy it was designed to destroy.[65]

Reagan was drawn to the Screen Actor's Guild, he writes in his autobiography, because it was an avenue to the stars. When he walked into the union boardroom, he "saw it crowded with the famous men of the business. I knew that I was beginning to find the rest of me." The statement unwittingly replaces the legs that rooted him to his failed father with the support of famous men. Reagan rejected the Left, he told Tom Hayden, when he discovered that it operated through secret caucuses in large, popular-front organizations. He had given the same testimony before HUAC decades earlier. Reagan innocently lent his name to a charitable cause, he told the committee, only to find out that the Communists were using him. The discovery that he was being "spoon-fed and steered" transformed him from innocent victim to one-man battalion.[66]

But Reagan prefers playing the one-man battalion to living it. "He simply looks to someone to tell him what to do," says his former campaign manager, John Sears. "He can be guided." Reagan agrees. When press spokesman Larry Speakes stepped in front of him to ward off a reporter's question about the reappointment of Anne Burford, the president quipped, "My guardian says I can't talk." Asked on another occasion if he thought of Michael Deaver, the aide closest to him, as a son, Reagan replied, "Gee, I always thought of him more as a father figure." Reagan has found the support his father had received but not given him at home.[67]

The process of relying on behind-the-scenes support, which he made part of himself, climaxed during the Hollywood inquisition. Refusing to be manipulated as a front for the Communists, Reagan fronted instead for the powerful men in Hollywood who led the fight against Communist influence. He found the rest of him by playing a one-man battalion and hiding the rest of him, which guided that battalion, behind the scenes. Replacing the personal with the political, Reagan helped orchestrate a blacklist whose existence he denied.

"There was no blacklist in Hollywood. The blacklist in Hollywood, if there was one, was provided by the Communists," Reagan told Robert Scheer in 1980. But as president of the Screen Actors Guild from 1947 to 1952 and member (and president for one year) of the Motion Picture Industry Council, Reagan enforced the blacklist. He supported a provision in the guild constitution barring Communists from membership. He acted as an informant for the FBI, naming actors and actresses who "follow the Communist party line." Reagan told the actress Gail Sondergaard, after she took the Fifth Amendment before HUAC, that the union opposed a blacklist. "On the other hand, if any actor by his actions outside of union activities has so offended public opinion that he has made himself unemployable at the box office, the Guild cannot and

would not force any employer to hire him." Reagan refused to defend
Sondergaard because she would not become an informer. But he met
with repentant ex-radicals to help them cooperate with HUAC, name
names, rehabilitate themselves, and continue to work in the movies.[68]

When he joined the fight against Communism, Reagan put the Reds
in Drake McHugh's place, for they became the sacrificial victims. By
casting Communists from the body politic, Reagan directed his violence
away from authority and outside the family circle. But whereas he presented the shift from Drake McHugh to anti-Communism as restoring
his personal legs, he actually acquired institutional support to substitute
for his family of origin. Reagan displaced his dependence onto others—
those ruled by the monstrous "mother lode"—and punished them for
his desire.

VI

Anti-Communism gave Reagan an explanation for and an alternative
to his declining Hollywood career. It also, he tells us, supplied him with
a new wife. Reagan met Nancy Davis when, as president of the Screen
Actor's Guild, he established that she was not the Nancy Davis on a list
of Communist sympathizers. "That's the girl I've decided to marry,"
Drake McHugh says of the surgeon's daughter. But the surgeon cuts off
his legs, and he ends up with a working-class woman instead. Reagan
learned on their first date that Nancy's father "was one of the world's
truly great surgeons"; the actor was on crutches because he had broken
his leg. Reagan had lost Bette Davis in *Dark Victory* to a neurological
surgeon old enough to be her father. He married the daughter of a neurological surgeon, a woman who, unlike Jane Wyman, would subordinate her career to his. As a board member of the Screen Actors Guild,
Wyman had introduced Reagan to the union. Guild president Reagan
appointed and reappointed Nancy Davis to the board. "My life began
when I got married. My life began with Ronnie," says Nancy Reagan.
"If Ronnie were a shoe salesman, I'd be out selling shoes." A 1950s
photograph shows Reagan in his new, all-electric home, his wife seated
on the floor at his feet.[69] Reagan had traded in subordination to Knute
Rockne as the Gipper for humiliation by the showgirl as the professor.
Now his wife was the lower half of him (cf. Figs. 1.7, 1.9, and 1.10).

Reagan had once been, as he put it, "a near-hemophiliac liberal. I
bled for 'causes': I had voted Democratic, following my father, in every
election." He left behind Jack Reagan's politics when he married Loyal

Davis's daughter, and he adopted the punitive, right-wing politics of the surgeon. Backed by the Movie Corporation of America (MCA), Reagan hosted the *GE Television Theater* in the 1950s, and *TV Guide* called him "the ambassador of the convenience of things mechanical" to America. Reagan spoke for General Electric around the country against "the most dangerous enemy ever known to man," whose advance guard inside America was FDR's welfare state. As he attacked state socialism, Reagan profited from his ties to MCA, GE, and Twentieth-Century Fox to (like Drake McHugh) make his fortune in real estate. Together his new politics, his new wealth, and his new family made him whole. His autobiography ends with Clark Gable's reminder, "The most important thing a man can know is that, as he approaches his own door, someone on the other side is listening for the sound of his footsteps." No passed-out father is in front of this doorstep, blocking access to mother and home. The actor has his legs back; his last sentence is "I have found the rest of me."[70]

Reagan's integration was not complete, however, for he had reentered the real world as the enemy of his own and his father's political past. Reagan had often ended his speeches for GE with the phrase Roosevelt had made famous, "rendezvous with destiny." He used those words again in the 1964 speech for Goldwater that catapulted him onto the national political stage. But Reagan failed to acknowledge his indebtedness to Roosevelt in the 1950s and 1960s. To recover all the rest of him, he discovered as he approached the White House, he had to incorporate FDR as well. "We have to be willing to be Roosevelt," asserted Reagan's adviser Richard Whalen during the 1980 primary campaign. Quoting FDR twice in his speech accepting the presidential nomination, Reagan cloaked himself in Roosevelt's mantle. At a time of economic and spiritual crisis comparable to the Great Depression, Reagan promised to restore the old Roosevelt coalition of middle-class, blue-collar, ethnic, and southern white Protestant voters and renew confidence in America.[71]

Reagan's election in 1980 was the first defeat of an elected presidential incumbent since Roosevelt beat Hoover, and by a comparable landslide. Carter and Hoover were the two engineer presidents, out of touch with the country's political coalitions and with its emotional life. Carrying his party into power with him, Reagan promised to end the paralysis of American life. Like Roosevelt, he won landslide reelection to a second term, in a contest that not only confirmed the new directions in which the president was taking the country but may also have consummated the first lasting electoral realignment since FDR's second term.

Reagan had prepared himself to follow Roosevelt, for FDR was the young Reagan's first political hero. He learned passages of FDR's First Inaugural by heart, developed a convincing impersonation of the president, and began to use Roosevelt's words and gestures in the 1950s in his political presentation of himself. "Roosevelt gave back to the people of this country their courage," said President Reagan. He was "an American giant," "one of history's truly monumental figures." Like Roosevelt, said Reagan in 1982, he was trying to save our system, not destroy it. But Roosevelt had merely offered government relief to middle- and working-class "forgotten Americans" like Jack Reagan. Ronald Reagan promised these same "forgotten Americans" "the ladder of opportunity." The patrician Roosevelt did not offer that ladder, did not need it, and could not climb it. FDR had no legs.[72]

Roosevelt, like Reagan, lost his legs on the road to the White House. His biographers picture him before he got polio as a rich playboy who did not take life seriously. He acquired presidential stature in the struggle against his affliction. The figure of the brave, crippled president entered popular culture in the 1930s, surely influencing the images of Knute Rockne in a wheelchair and Drake McHugh. But FDR-as-cripple was also a stock figure of right-wing caricature, for Roosevelt never got back the use of his legs. Reagan promises not merely to imitate his father's hero but to surpass him.

Reagan did not slay his father and rise above him, however. Rather, by identifying with his father's wound and his mother's denial, he inherited both the father's need for support and the mother's cheerful blindness to internal trouble. Reagan's first marriage and his postwar movie roles had called attention to his dependency needs without gratifying them. His new marriage and new politics provided upward mobility based neither on the rugged independence of the self-made hero nor on ties to an actual past but based rather on corporate and domestic support. Even though he was fearful that dependence exposed the self to aggression, Reagan did not relinquish the need for care; he became an idol of consumption by finding caretakers he could trust. The president was silent in response to a reporter's question on arms control until he repeated aloud his wife's whisper, "Doing all we can."[73] Reagan has realized the dream of the American male, to be taken care of in the name of independence, to be supported while playing the man in charge.

The president would have us believe that, having recovered his legs, he rules as the healed Drake McHugh. Reagan used the image of his own healing body to promote his economic recovery program. "Vote against me and you will cut me off at the knees," he often tells Congress. He bought a new pair of boots after his 1981 Congressional budget victory, and he signed the bill sitting at his desk with his leg held high in the air. Asked what he would do after the signing ceremony, the president replied, "Go out and cut the brush!" "Well, don't cut your leg off," joked a reporter. *"Where's the Rest of Me?"* interjected the president's wife. "You shouldn't have mentioned that," said the president.[74]

But Reagan is more than Drake McHugh with his legs back. He embodies national fears of helplessness and dependence in order to overcome them by punishing the enemies responsible for American weakness. It was by taking vengeance for evil that he found the rest of him, according to his autobiography. The man who married the surgeon's daughter as he recovered the rest of him combines Drake McHugh with Dr. Gordon.

New Deal liberals like Thurman Arnold invoked political doctors to legitimate the welfare state. Dr. New Deal was Roosevelt's term for a government that cared for its people. But Dr. New Deal, complains Reagan, addicts the patient instead of curing him: "President Roosevelt started administering medicine to a sick patient, but those people who then gathered around and became the structure of government had no intention of letting the patient get well and cut[ting] him off the medicine." Reagan wants to cut the patient off. He presents himself not as a pill doctor but as a surgeon.[75]

Reagan compares "cutting back on the runaway growth of government" to "performing surgery on a patient to save his life." (Surgeons find it hard, by contrast, to operate on Democrats and "separate demagogic from solid tissue, without causing the death of the patient.") To stop the "spreading cancer" of welfare, Reagan applies the "welfare ax." "Reagan readies the ax," *Newsweek* proclaimed early in the president's first term; *Time* put the ax on its cover. "The howls of pain will be heard from coast to coast," Reagan promised, as *Time* praised his ability to "inflict pain . . . with nerve and verve." Reagan and Budget Director David Stockman, operating against what Stockman called the "fiscal hemorrhage," plunged an ax into the 1981 budget in front of the television camera. Four years later Reagan and Alabama senator Jeremiah Denton posed holding aloft a "tax ax." Reagan also promised to "amputate" unnecessary government programs. The president would wield the ax and not be its victim, he insisted. Being a lame duck would not

hinder his efforts to cut government spending, he told cabinet members
at their first meeting after his reelection. "I'll put a cast on that lame
leg, and that will make a heck of a kicking leg." To prove independence,
not so easy in a corporate world, Reagan punishes those dependent on
him.[76]

Reagan's surgical metaphors capitalize on the slippage between personal bodies and the body politic. The president wants that slippage to
go in both directions, so that he can embody punishment and still claim
that his programs have hurt no one. Speaker of the House Tip O'Neill,
by contrast, complained that the Democratic substitute for the 1981
budget was like "cutting your legs off at the knees instead of the hips."
"It's like being told to amputate your own leg," agreed a House Education and Labor Committee aide. Although the Democrats want to call
attention to the ordinary human beings hurt by Reagan's budget cuts,
by adopting Reagan's metaphor they turn themselves into the victims.
They thereby reinforce Reagan's self-image as the surgeon who causes
symbolic pain and not real suffering.[77]

Reagan's glorification of American life goes with his refusal to inhabit it. The people in his celluloid world—like the Van Heusen shirt
collar in the advertisement that introduced this chapter—can be twisted
and twirled, bent and curled, without suffering damage, and since no
real harm comes to anyone, the president appears benign. He is cut off
from the effects of his political programs. To represent toughness it is
best to operate in a symbolic universe protected from the real-world
obstacles that might threaten that toughness or expose its punitive character. Symbolizing toughness and staying out of touch, far from being
contradictory, are mutually reinforcing. But Reagan's dream of law and
perfect order, deforming the world as it is to preserve it as a wrinkle-
free ideal, has punishing consequences for sensate human beings down
below.

The president's uncanny mixture of invoked and derealized violence
reaches a climax in his thoughts on Armageddon. The gothic sensibility
looks forward to Christ's second coming but is obsessed by judgment
day. It dwells less on the peaceable kingdom than on divine vengeance.
Asked if he were concerned to preserve the wilderness for future generations, then-Secretary of the Interior James Watt replied, "I do not
know how many future generations we can count on before the Lord
returns." Watt's version of born-again Christianity, radically splitting
our sojourn on earth from eternal life, justifies destroying the natural
world. Reagan himself has said more than once that he believes literally

in scriptural forecasts of a climactic struggle between the forces of light and darkness, that he expects that showdown to occur "in our generation," that such events as the Communist takeover of Libya fulfill biblical prophecies, and that he expects the final conflict to break out in the Middle East.[78]

These musings take operational force from the administration's belief in a winnable nuclear war. "Reagan Enjoys Doomsday Ride" was the headline when the president rose above the earth, participating in the planning to survive nuclear combat by defeating Soviet efforts to "decapitate" C^3I (the American center of command, control, communication, and intelligence). Although Reagan has imagined the coming of the biblical Armageddon and "kind of thinks the Soviets are going to be involved in it," he insists that "I have never seriously warned and said that we must plan according to Armageddon." But he acknowledges conversations with "theologians" for whom the American-Soviet struggle is evidence "that the prophecies are coming together that portend" judgment day. Reagan's cheerfulness collapses the last judgment into the millennium. By musing on world destruction and then denying he has done so seriously, the president is normalizing the end of the world.[79]

Jerry Falwell, one of the theologians to whom Reagan referred, told his television audience in 1980 that the apocalypse prophesied in Revelations and the Book of Daniel was at hand. The Jews have returned to Israel, Falwell explained, as foretold in the Bible. A war will break out in the Middle East, and the Russian beast will invade. (To make the last judgment real to his audience, Falwell showed movies of himself inspecting the projected battlefield.) The Antichrist will unleash a nuclear war, Falwell went on to say, and 400 million people will die. The saved will not suffer, however. Uprooted from the earth, they will escape the violence that is to be visited on those down below "and meet Christ in the air."[80]

VII

When D. W. Griffith lost his hold on film, as we shall see, his movies came back to haunt him. Reagan rose above film by taking his Hollywood identity to Washington. The Communists failed to capture Hollywood, he writes in his autobiography, but they initiated a series of costly studio strikes that caused the decline of Hollywood as the entertainment capital of the world. Reagan does not regret that decline for himself, he implies, for he writes that he only became whole when he stopped making movies. But the autobiography's final chapters comprise an elegy for a vanished Hollywood, suggesting that Reagan rescued the movie set by transferring it to Washington. Reagan's presidential identity did not develop completely outside film, in anti-Communism, remarriage, and the attack on the welfare state. After he left Warner Brothers the actor starred in several movies that form a bridge to the president.[81]

These films were not box office successes, and they did not save his movie career. Perhaps that career ended because Reagan made World War II and cold war films in the 1950s when the country wanted relief from politics. Perhaps Reagan faced tougher competition from Hollywood stars than he did from political leaders, once the New Deal political system broke down. Perhaps Americans want something different from politicians than from stars, something more reassuring and more like themselves. Does failure in Hollywood succeed in politics by breaking down the disjunction between image and life more effectively than the bigger-than-life stars of the classic Hollywood movie can do? However we account for the disjunction between Hollywood decline and political triumph, we can watch Reagan become president in his final films.

Reagan left Warner Brothers so he could choose his own roles. He wanted to make Westerns, and his first post–Warner Brothers film was *The Last Outpost* (1951). While fighting Communists offscreen, he fought Indians in front of the camera. Just as the Communist threat, Truman supporters hoped, would unite Democrats and Republicans, so the Apache danger in *Last Outpost* makes allies out of Union and Confederate soldiers. In *Cattle Queen of Montana* (1954) Reagan saves Barbara Stanwyck from Indians (see Fig. 1.11); the local reds are being manipulated by a white outlaw. Reagan plays a gunslinging sheriff in *Law and Order* (1953) who brings peace to a western town. He also made a Western set in Central America; an adventure movie with an anti-Communist backdrop set in Hong Kong; and the cold war parable *Storm Warning* (1951; see chapter 8), in which the Ku Klux Klan stands in for the Communist party.[82]

Recalling his lawman persona, Reagan told an audience, "I once played a sheriff who thought he could do the job without a gun. I was dead in twenty-seven minutes of a thirty-minute show." The president also quotes Dirty Harry and Rambo. But when he invokes his own movie roles, he wants to be seen as the Gipper. Reagan mimed a cowboy firing his six-shooters after American planes shot down Libyan jets in 1981, but he did so in front of his aides and not the television cameras.[83]

None of the movie stills chosen for *Where's the Rest of Me?* place Reagan on horseback; all three photographs put him in bed. He is without legs in *King's Row*, in the company of his wife and his best friend (Fig. 1.12). He has died in *Knute Rockne* and is being blessed by a priest and the Rocknes (Fig. 1.13). He is sitting back-to-back with Richard Todd, who will soon die of a fatal disease in *The Hasty Heart* (Fig. 1.14). These stills evoke redemptive suffering. They connect Reagan to victimhood, not aggression, and the merging of the two will bring his movie career to a close.

Reagan plays Web Sloane, an army intelligence officer, in *Prisoner of War* (1954). He allows himself to be captured by the North Koreans to expose the brainwashing and torture in Communist POW camps. But after volunteering for danger, Web avoids it. He pretends to cooperate with the Communists to gather evidence against them. Although the movie audience is in on the secret (that Web is a loyal American), it nevertheless watches other Americans starved and hideously tortured while Web grows fat. Extended masochistic scenes of torture establish the Americans as victims, but Web is not one of them. Sinister, dehumanized Asian torturers, stereotypes that merge racism and anti-Communism, recur in movies from World War II on. But the Korean War never enjoyed the filmic popularity of its predecessor, and the peace treaty had been signed by the time *Prisoner of War* was released. No one went to see it. Reagan defends *Prisoner*'s documentary accuracy, wishes the film were more widely viewed, and blames liberals for its bad box office.[84] But the disturbing images of torture and identity confusion unsettle Reagan's aura of innocence more than the film intended.

Reagan's movies played with hidden identity from the beginning (*Accidents Will Happen* [1938] and *Murder in the Air*) to the end of his career (*Cattle Queen of Montana* and *Prisoner of War*). He portrayed characters who joined criminal or subversive organizations in order to expose them, allowing the innocent actor to participate in forbidden activities. Although the theme of identity confusion was appropriate for an actor who found his identity through film, the process threatened to raise doubts about who Reagan actually was.

Cold war ideology, as we shall see, required America simultaneously to imitate practices attributed to the enemy and to demonize the subversive in order to defend against the resulting breakdown of difference.

But looked at from outside the demonological system, the mirroring process blended the subversive into his countersubversive reflection. President Reagan defends the motion picture itself for an analogous blurring process, for mirroring back our identities and telling us who we are. The desired self in that transfer is the one on the screen, for it is the self one wants to be, the commodity that acquires value from the viewers' desire. Therefore, the movie self, like the countersubversive, points to the definition of identity in doubling and to the absorption of identity in exchange.

Throughout his entire Hollywood career, in over fifty movies, Ronald Reagan was never cast as the heavy. Reagan's image was so secure that he could play a foreign spy (Steve Svenko, alias Fred Coe) in *Murder in the Air* or the American turncoat in *Prisoner of War* and still seem Ronald Reagan, the innocent. There is, however, a danger of slippage between good and evil in such masquerades. As I will argue in chapter 8, cold war science fiction addressed anxieties about the loss of the self to its simulacrum, in contrast to cold war political films, which inadvertently undercut the distinction between subversive and countersubversive. Appropriately, it was a director of science fiction films who imagined the takeover of Reagan's identity. In 1964, the year Reagan entered national prominence in his Goldwater speech, Don Siegel cast him in *The Killers* as a criminal masquerading as a respectable businessman. Siegel had directed *Invasion of the Body Snatchers* in 1956. In that movie pods possess innocent townspeople; since the viewer cannot tell the person from his or her pod, *Body Snatchers* questions whether the original character was really benign. In Reagan's previous masquerades, the good Reagan was always visible beneath the bad; in *The Killers* Siegel turned that image inside out. Reagan masterminds a robbery, uses Angie Dickinson as bait to lure an innocent racing car driver into the plot, and secretly has the driver killed. In what would become the movie's most lasting image because of the actor's emerging political career, Reagan dons a police uniform to rob a payroll truck.

The Killers was Reagan's last film. Strictly speaking it was not a Hollywood movie, since Siegel made it for television. When it was judged too violent for family living rooms, it was shown in motion picture theaters instead. *The Killers* may have been only a movie. But Reagan regrets making it,[85] for he does not want to be seen as orchestrating killings while wearing an all-American mask.

Seven years before *The Killers*, in his final Hollywood motion picture, Reagan also played a man who comes under suspicion of murder.

He portrayed a submarine commander accused of making military decisions for personal motives. This time the doubts about the actor's innocence are resolved by making him a victim. In *Hellcats of the Navy* (1957) Reagan successfully turned Dr. Gordon into Drake McHugh. I shall end where I began, with a World War II film.

Hellcats opens with frogmen leaving a sub to bring back Japanese mines. Reagan (as the captain, Casey Abbott) submerges his vessel to escape a Japanese destroyer, thereby abandoning one frogman who has not yet returned. The frogman was romancing Abbott's former girlfriend, and the ship's lieutenant, Don Landon, thinks that is why the captain left him behind to die. Nurse Helen Blair, the woman in question, is played by Nancy Reagan (Fig. 1.15).

Abbott won't risk the sub to save his rival. He risks it instead to chart a path through the underwater mines. The ship is sunk and sixty men die, riddled with bullets or trapped below. Landon accuses his captain of endangering the submarine for personal glory. But it is Landon not Abbott, the film tells us, who is confusing personal needs with military necessity.

Abbott is trapped in a cable outside the sub in the movie's climactic scene. A Japanese destroyer is approaching, and Landon must decide whether to submerge the vessel. The men on the ship are your responsibility, Abbott tells Landon, advocating his own death. Like Abbott before him, Landon must be mature enough to sacrifice a rival for reasons not of personal hostility but national security. Miraculously, however, when the ship resurfaces Abbott is still alive. He has freed himself from the cable at the last minute. Although the conscious mind knows that Abbott survived by not submerging with the sub, the imagery suggests death and resurrection.

Abbott had broken off his romance with Helen Blair to protect her from the risks of war. But she never stopped loving him, remaining loyal in the face of the suspicion that he deliberately killed the man who took his place. By reenacting his rival's sacrifice, Abbott frees himself from the charge of bad motives; he is now united with the men who died under his command. Since Abbott is above suspicion, he can have a personal life. At the movie's end he and Helen Blair prepare to wed. Reagan's final Hollywood movie, mixing life and film to the end, supplied him with the perfect marriage of military and familial authority. It is not the commander-in-chief (Fig. 1.16) who is contaminated by bad motives, says the film, but subordinates (Landon the junior officer, Rogin the critic) who cannot accept his authority.[86]

The Nancy Reagan film shown at the 1984 Republican convention cut from shots of her among children and drug abusers to a scene from *Hellcats of the Navy*. Nancy Reagan, who had cried real tears while filming that scene, repeats her faith in the commander as he leaves on his climactic voyage. In cutting from life to the movie, the Republican National Committee may seem to have exposed the manufactured nature of its real-life image of the president's wife. But another film event suggests that the media men deliberately dissolved the boundary between life and image to offer us the reassurance of film. The president reelected in 1984 does not promote the telescreen as an instrument of surveillance and personal invasion on which big brother is watching you. Instead he offers freedom from public and private anxieties by allowing you to watch big brother. When Nancy Reagan spoke at the convention following the film of her life, Ronald Reagan watched her on television from their hotel suite. "Make it one more for the Gipper," she urged, and the mass television audience (including him) saw her tiny figure turn with arms raised in support of an enormous image on the screen behind her, larger than her and larger than life (see Fig. 1.17). On camera in the hotel room, the image watched itself wave back, forming the truncated head and shoulders of her husband, the president of the United States.[87]

CODA

Talks were stalled at the 1985 Geneva Summit, as the White House tells the story, because of staff interference between the two heads of state. Reagan was particularly irritated with Georgi Arbatov, the leading Soviet Americanist, for describing him as a B-movie actor. "Do one thing for me," Reagan told Gorbachev as the two men walked alone. "Tell Arbatov they weren't all B movies." Gorbachev was prepared. "The one I liked was the young man without the legs," he responded, and he asked Reagan what it was like to see himself in his old films. Reagan, now on familiar ground, used the line he had used so often before, "It's like seeing the son you never had"—the imaginary son who had grown up to be president.[88]

That colloquy, according to the White House, broke the ice between the two world leaders. Thanks to the personal relationship Reagan and Gorbachev established, the Russians agreed to a joint Soviet-American statement that did not repudiate Star Wars. One old movie, *King's Row*, had paved the way for SDI (named for another movie) to go into pro-

duction. But George Lucas, the creator of *Star Wars*, insisted that the
title was his private property. A group calling itself High Frontier was
airing television commercials promoting Star Wars. "I asked my daddy
what this Star Wars stuff is all about," says a little girl's voice, as red-
colored missiles fly toward and bounce off an invisible shield. "My daddy's smart," says the little girl. The commercial associates the girl's
daddy with the American president, us citizens with children in need of
reassurance. The president of the United States is virtually alone, however, in claiming that Star Wars could actually provide a perfect defense
like the one pictured on the television screen. Lucas, unwilling to be
credited with Reagan's political fantasy, sued to remove his name from
the product. But Judge Gerhard Gesell, sitting in federal court, decided
the case against the filmmaker. *Star Wars* was a trademark, ruled the
judge. It did not belong to its producer but to any consumer who
wanted to use it. Star Wars was in the public domain.[89]

1.1. Reagan as Brass Bancroft, *Murder in the Air* (1940)

1.2. Reagan as a radio announcer, WHO

1.3. Reagan as a radio announcer, *Love Is on the Air* (1937)

1.4. Ronald Reagan and Jane Wyman, *Brother Rat* (1938)

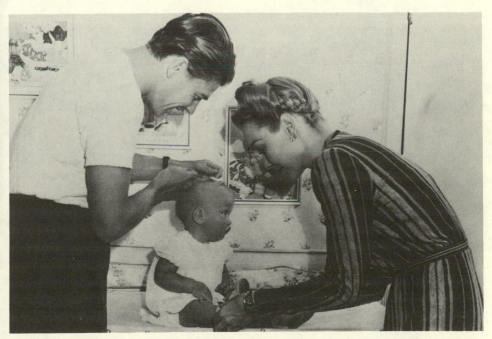

1.5. Ronald Reagan and Jane Wyman at home

1.6. Reagan and Bette Davis, *Dark Victory* (1939)

1.7. Ronald Reagan and Pat O'Brien, *Knute Rockne, All American* (1940)

1.8. "Where's the rest of me?"

Ronald and Nancy Reagan,
circa 1954, relax
in the living room
of their
GE all-electric home.

1.9. Reagan and the show-girl, *She's
Working Her Way Through College*
(1952)

1.10. Ronald and Nancy Reagan at home

1.11. *Cattle Queen of Montana* (1954)

1.12. Ronald Reagan, Robert Cummings, and Ann Sheridan in *King's Row* (1942)

1.13. The Gipper's death scene, *Knute Rockne*

1.14. Reagan and Richard Todd, *The Hasty Heart* (1950)

1.15. Ronald and Nancy Reagan, *Hellcats of the Navy* (1957)

1.16. Ronald Reagan as commander-in-chief, *Hellcats of the Navy*

1.17. Ronald and Nancy Reagan, the Republican National Convention, 1984

CHAPTER II

Political Repression in the United States

Most treatments of the countersubversive mentality, as we shall see in chapter 9, disconnect demonology both from major American social divisions and from institutionalized political repression. Most versions of American history, by a complementary set of choices, chart a progress toward freedom and inclusion. To link countersubversive thinking to political repression is to write another history. Such an account hardly stands in for American history as a whole. But if certain familiar patterns recede into the shadows, neglected, dark areas emerge into light.

At the same time, the subject of political repression must not be confined to the suppression of already legitimate political opposition. A history of American political suppression must attend to the repression of active, political dissent. But it must also direct attention to prepolitical institutional settings that have excluded some Americans from politics and influenced the terms on which others entered the political arena. An account of American political suppression must acknowledge the suppression of politics itself. It must notice the relations between politics and private life. Countersubversive ideologies, psychological mechanisms, and an intrusive state apparatus all respond to the fear of subversion in America. We begin with the controls exercised over peoples of color.

I

"History begins for us with murder and enslavement, not with discovery," wrote the American poet William Carlos Williams. He was calling attention to the historical origins of the United States in violence against peoples of color. He was pointing to America's origins in the origins of a capitalist world system. Indian land and black labor generated a European-American-African trade in the seventeenth century and contributed to the development of commodity agriculture, industrial production, and state power in Europe and the Americas. Karl Marx wrote, "The discovery of gold and silver in America, the extirpation, enslavement, and entombment in mines of the aboriginal population, the beginning of the conquest and the looting of the East Indies, and the turning of Africa into a warren for the commercial hunting of black-skins, signalized the rosy dawn of capitalist production. These idyllic proceedings are the chief momenta of primitive accumulation."[1]

By primitive accumulation Marx meant the forcible acquisition by a mixture of state and private violence of land and labor to serve the accumulation of capital. Primitive accumulation made land, labor, and commodities available for the marketplace before the free market could act on its own. The suppression, intimidation, and control of peoples of color supplies the prehistory of the American history of freedom. People of color were important, moreover, not only at the origins of America but also in its ongoing history—through westward expansion against Indians and Mexicans, chattel slavery and the exclusion of emancipated blacks from political and economic freedom, and the repressive responses to Hispanic and Asian workers. The American economy exploited peoples of color, but American racial history is not reducible to its economic roots. A distinctive American political tradition that was fearful of primitivism and disorder developed in response to peoples of color. That tradition defines itself against alien threats to the American way of life and sanctions violent and exclusionary responses to them.

Indians in early America, emblematic of chaos, were not seen through New World lenses. They rather came to embody the masterless men who appeared in Europe with the breakdown of traditional society. "Liv[ing] without government," in the words of one early report, and freed of the restraints of family, church, and village as well, the idle, wandering savages were depicted as engaging in incest, cannibalism, devil worship, and murder. Some European-Americans, to be sure, depicted savages not as monstrous but as noble. Traders, promoters of commercial ventures, settlers no longer threatened by powerful tribes, and humanists drawn to a classical or Christian golden age all imagined peaceful primitives enjoying a state of innocence. But the noble savage and his dark double were joined. Both images of primitivism appropriated Indians for white purposes. Both made the Indians children of nature instead of creators and inhabitants of their own cultures. Both ignored Indian agriculture and depicted a tribalism that menaced private property and the family. Neither the noble nor the devilish savage could coexist with the advancing white civilization. Both images rationalized the dispossession of the tribes.[2]

Indians did not use the land for agriculture, explained Massachusetts Bay governor John Winthrop. Since the wandering tribes failed to "subdue and replenish" the earth, white farmers could acquire their land. Winthrop's principle of expropriation was an accepted tenet of international law by the early eighteenth century. It did not justify the individual acquisition of farming plots, however, but rather state action. First the colonies and the mother country, then the independent states, and finally the federal government expropriated land by making treaties with Indian tribes. George Washington, justifying the treaty method, defended

> the propriety of purchasing their lands in preference to attempting to drive them by force of arms out of our country, which, as we have already experienced, is like driving the wild beasts of ye forests, which will return as soon as the pursuit is at an end, and fall, perhaps upon those that are left there; when the gradual extension of our settlements will as certainly cause the savage, as the wolf, to retire; both being beasts of prey tho' they differ in shape.[3]

Indians were animals, but fortunately they were men as well. As men they could make contracts, accept money, and consent to the loss of their land. Treaties presented a fiction of Indian freedom to disguise the realities of coerced consent, bribery, deception about boundaries, agreements with one faction enforced on an entire tribe, and the encouragement of tribal debts—real and inflated—to be paid off by the cession of land.

The policy of Indian removal conceived by Thomas Jefferson, employed in his and succeeding administrations, and forced upon the southern Indians by Andrew Jackson, offered Indians the freedom to move west if they relinquished their ancestral holdings. Although removal treaties (discussed in chapter 5) were forced upon the tribes, the treaty method allowed Indian expropriation to proceed under the color of law. It engaged Indians in consent to their own subjugation.[4]

The federal government abrogated tribal treaty-making rights in 1871. In return for depriving Indians of their collective freedom, the government promised individual freedom. The government had begun to offer freedom to individual Indians early in the nineteenth century to atomize tribes and subject their members to market pressures and state laws. The most important individual freedom offered Indians was freedom from communal land ownership. Some tribal leaders in antebellum America believed that individual allotments were the only way to preserve Indian land, but widespread fraud and intimidation quickly transferred Indian freeholds to white land companies. The Dawes Severalty Act of 1887, which Theodore Roosevelt praised as "a mighty pulverizing engine to break up the tribal mass," offered Indians the opportunity to become free Americans; the freedom that they actually acquired was the freedom to alienate their land. Railroads, mining interests, cattlemen, and land corporations acquired the land allotments granted Indians. Between 1887 and 1934 the tribes lost an estimated 60 percent of their holdings. In 1983 Secretary of the Interior James Watt proposed to grant Indians "freedom" from their "socialistic" dependence on the federal government and on their tribes; Indian spokesmen, in response, denied they were Reds. The freedom offered Indians, from Jackson to Watt, has undermined communal loyalties as sources of political resistance.[5]

American Indian policy from the beginning combined freedom with coercion, the method of the marketplace with the method of the state. Government has shown two faces to the tribes, one of violence, the other of paternal guardianship. Consider the acquisition of land. Whites claimed Indian land not only by right of treaty or proper use but also as the fruits of a just war. Conflicts over land and living space produced a series of Indian wars, beginning with Virginia's war against the Powhatan Confederacy in 1622 and with the New England Pequot War of 1636–37. White expansion provoked most of these wars; savage atrocities were cited to justify them. Wars over living space produced civilian casualties on both sides; but whereas Indian violence was attributed to primitive ferocity, the systematic destruction of Indian crops and villages was defended as a matter of deliberate policy. White victories, it was said, proved the superiority of civilization over savagery. Indian wars were important in the colonies and during the Revolution. They also promoted American continental expansion from the War of 1812 to the closing of the frontier. More than two hundred pitched battles were fought in the West during the Gilded Age, and there was also periodic guerilla warfare in outlying regions.[6] The history of Indian war ended at Wounded Knee, South Dakota, in 1890 with the massacre of two hundred Sioux men, women, and children, including the old warrior, Sitting Bull, after a ghost dance ceremony.

Indians displaced by treaty or defeated in war were offered "paternal guardianship." Indian tribes were "in a state of pupilage," ruled the Supreme Court in *Cherokee Nation* v. *Georgia* (1831); "their relation to the United States resembles that of a ward to his guardian." Since the Cherokees were not a nation, they could not maintain an action in court to protect their autonomy. As the equals of whites, Indians had the freedom to lose their land; as the wards of a paternal government, Indians were confined. The government adopted a reservations policy before the Civil War and enforced it on the western tribes in the late nineteenth century. Confined to reservations, tribes were dependent on government food, clothing, and shelter. Although they were held in protective custody, their land continued to be subject to encroachments from cattle, agricultural, and mineral interests.

Confinement was seen not simply as the opposite of Indian freedom but as the preparation for a new kind of liberty. "Civilized and domesticated," reservation Indians were to be freed from their tribal identities and remade as free men. "Push improvement on them by education, alienation, and individuation," urged an Osage agent in the late nineteenth century. Indian agents encouraged commodity agriculture, ignoring unsuitable topographical and cultural conditions and the presence of rapacious whites. Compulsory government boarding schools regimented children in barracks far from their parents' homes, forced them to abandon tribal dress, and punished them for using their native tongue.[7]

When antebellum Indian Commissioner Thomas McKenney had evoked "their helplessness and their dependence on the President as their father," his intention was more than benevolent description. McKenney wanted to make Indians over into the "children" he described. The passionate, profligate savages imagined at the beginning of American history had given way by the end of the nineteenth century to dependent Indians whose helplessness was the condition of their improvement. Amerigo Vespucci had depicted lascivious savages whose "women, being very lustful, cause the private parts of their husbands to swell up to such a huge size that they appear deformed and disgusting." Four hundred years later a leading Indian reformer, Merrill E. Gates, explained, "We have, to begin with, the absolute need of awakening in the savage Indian broader desires and ampler wants. . . . In his dull savagery he must be touched by the divine angel of discontent. . . . Discontent with the teepee and the starving rations of the Indian camp in winter is needed to get the Indian out of the blanket and into trousers— trousers with a pocket in them, and with *a pocket that aches to be filled with dollars*." (Italics are in the original.) The progress from sex to money had replaced the swollen private parts of Vespucci's Indian with the aching, empty pockets of Gates's.[8]

Aspirations to turn native Americans into passive receptacles for white desires were not wholly fulfilled, however. Reservation tribes maintained some autonomy, thanks in part to varying mixtures of accommodation and resistance and in part to federal recognition (beginning with the New Deal) of Indian rights. Assaults on Indian land, water, and minerals continue, nonetheless, often with the cooperation of the Bureau of Indian Affairs. Dillon S. Myer, for example, as head of the bureau under President Truman, denied tribes the right to hire lawyers to defend themselves against predatory whites. The commissioner accused Felix Cohen, the leading American authority on Indian law and an opponent of Myer's policies, of being a Communist sympathizer.[9] The Eisenhower administration sought to abolish reservations altogether, and although that effort was only partially successful, it shifted considerable land from Indians to whites. Today Indian tribes remain what *Cherokee Nation* v. *Georgia* defined them to be: "domestic, dependent nations" within the United States.

The dispossession of Indians did not happen once and for all in American history. America was continually expanding west, and while doing so it decimated, removed, or confined one tribe after another. That history had major consequences not only for Indian-white relations but also for American history as a whole. It defined America from the beginning as a settler society, an expanding, domestic, imperial power. Expansion guaranteed American freedom, so it was believed, protecting Americans from the crowded conditions and social class divisions of Europe. Although Indian wars actually exemplified state violence, they fed an opposite myth—the myth of the self-made man. Masterless Indians had challenged European institutional restraints at the beginning of American history. Early settlers made Indians a threat to community. By the Age of Jackson, Americans celebrated their own independence, which Indian tribalism threatened to confine. White Amer-

icans contrasted their own freedom, disciplined by self-restraint, with
the subversive, idle, and violent freedom of the Indians. The self-reliant
American gained his freedom, won his authority, and defined the American national identity in violent Indian combat in the West.[10]

With the perceived closing of the continental frontier in the 1890s,
the policy of Manifest Destiny was extended to Asia. The suppression
of the Philippine independence movement after the Spanish-American
war caused hundreds of thousands of deaths. America was, according
to those who carried out and defended its Philippine policy, continuing
its conquest over and tutelage of primitive tribes. Indian policy also set
precedents for twentieth-century interventions in Latin America. The
country's expansionist history against savage peoples of color culminated rhetorically and in practice in the war in Vietnam. Counterinsur-
gent, savage warfare returned in the 1980s to the New World, Central
American arena where it had always prospered, as the United States
supported death squads in San Salvador and terror bombing and a
scorched earth policy in the El Salvador countryside, the torture and
murder of Guatemalan Indians, and terrorist attacks by "freedom fighters" on the people and government of Nicaragua. Calling the Nicaraguan contras "the moral equal of our Founding Fathers," President Reagan laid claim to a tradition for which other citizens of the United States
might wish to make reparation.[11]

Indian policy also had domestic implications. Indians were the first
people to stand in American history as emblems of disorder, civilized
breakdown, and alien control. Differences between reds and whites
made cultural adaptation seem at once dangerous and impossible. The
violent conquest of Indians legitimized violence against other alien
groups, making coexistence appear to be unnecessary. The paranoid
style in American politics, as Richard Hofstadter has labeled it, goes
back to responses to Indians. The series of Red scares that have swept
the country since the 1870s have roots in the original red scares. Later
countersubversive movements attacked aliens, but the people who originally assaulted reds were themselves aliens in the land. Responses to
the Indians point to the mixture of cultural arrogance and insecurity in
the American history of countersubversion. The identity of a self-making people, engaged in a national, purifying mission, may be particularly
vulnerable to threats of contamination and disintegration. The need to
draw rigid boundaries between the alien and the self suggests fears of
too dangerous an intimacy between them.[12]

Just as fears of subversion moved from Indians to other social groups, so did techniques of control. The group ties of workers and immigrants were assaulted in the name of individual freedom. State violence, used to punish Indians who allegedly preferred war to labor, was also employed against striking workers. A paternal model of interracial relations developed in slavery as well as in Indian policy. Finally, Indians shared their status as beneficiaries of meliorist confinement with the inmates of total institutions. These arenas—slavery, the asylum, labor relations, and radical dissent—form the major loci of American political suppression.

II

The early repressive labor system in the colonies, with restrictive terms of indenture for both white and black workers, gave way by the eighteenth century to freedom for whites and slavery for blacks. That division had less significance in the North, which lacked a large, propertyless proletariat, than in the South. Slavery secured a labor force for southern plantations. It overcame the twin threats of interracial, lower-class solidarity and class war between propertied whites and land-hungry white servant workers. A slave labor system restricted to blacks could not have developed without preexisting invidious racial distinctions. But slavery intensified racism. Racialist thinking simultaneously justified black enslavement and forged racial bonds across class lines among whites.[13]

Both blacks and Indians, in racialist thought, posed primitive threats to the social order. But those threats differed, in keeping with the contrasting white desires for Indian land and black labor. Indians, on the margins of white settlement, posed the subversive threat of freedom; that threat was met by the displacement, elimination, or confinement of the tribes. Blacks, upon whose labor whites depended, posed the subversive threat of reversing the relations of dependence. Indians offered escape from political, social, and familial institutions; blacks threatened social and sexual upheaval.[14]

Slavery, a labor system, constituted the fundamental social relationship between whites and blacks. But law and cultural myth transformed white domination into a black sexual threat. The first statements and acts that distinguished between individuals purely on the grounds of ancestry had to do with interracial sex and with determining the status of mixed offspring. By defining children of interracial unions as black and therefore slaves, legal enactments guaranteed a slave labor force.

Other slave societies, with small white settler populations, created a special caste of mulattoes; human beings in the United States had to be either white or black. Although this absolute bifurcation had practical origins, it also derived from northern European, Protestant cultural phobias.[15]

Thomas Jefferson warned that the slave who engaged in interracial sex was "staining the blood of his master." Jefferson feared the black man's desire for the white woman, reversing the actual direction of interracial sexual exploitation under slavery. Women were identified with blacks in the seventeenth century as sources of dangerous, sexual passion. Prohibitions against sex between black men and white women helped keep the women within a patriarchal, family-centered society. As fears of female sexuality went underground in the later eighteenth century, black men were alleged to threaten white women by what they wanted from them, not by what they shared with them. The repressive effect was the same. "Mulattoes are monsters," warned the nineteenth-century Mississippi defender of slavery, Henry Hughes. "Amalgamation is incest." Hughes's association of miscegenation with incest suggests that he feared blacks not because they were so alien to whites but because they were all too close to them.[16]

Slaves were excluded from the political process in antebellum America. Fears that they would enter politics in a revolutionary way, through slave uprisings and mass murder, led to harsh southern slave codes. These codes forbade teaching slaves to read or write and prohibited slaves from congregating for social or religious purposes without the presence of a white or from leaving their plantations without a pass. Southern states made manumission difficult or impossible. Slave marriages enjoyed no legal protection, and slaves had no recourse against being bought or sold. A paternalist ideology claimed that the plantation was a family and made the master entirely responsible for the welfare of his slave children. Slave codes were enforced intermittently, to be sure, and the life of southern blacks was not defined solely by them; many planters, moreover, took seriously their paternal obligations. But even on its own terms paternalism attended to slaves only by depriving them of the right to speak and act for themselves. In combination with the slave codes, planter paternalism deprived slaves of all legal protection. Slave patrols of armed white men maintained racial order. In real or imagined times of trouble, these patrols or other white mobs took racial matters into their own hands.[17]

Free blacks did not fare much better than slaves, either in the North or in the South. Southern states tried to expel free blacks; many had no legal residence. Northern states prohibited blacks from voting, serving on juries, or testifying in court and deprived them of civil rights as well. Northern mobs rioted against free blacks, destroying neighborhoods and killing men, women, and children.

Slavery not only denied freedom to blacks; it also decisively influenced the history of freedom for whites. Americans fought a revolution in part to protect property created by slave labor, and the profits from that labor financed the revolutionary alliance with France. In addition, the vast majority of propertyless workers in revolutionary America were in chains, racially divided from the mass of free whites. White Americans could demand the end of their enslavement (as they called it) to Britain without fearing, as their European counterparts did, that propertyless workers would demand their natural rights as well.[18]

Slavery also guaranteed white freedom in the antebellum South. "In this country alone does perfect equality of civil and social privilege exist among the white population, and it exists solely because we have black slaves," declared the *Richmond Enquirer* in 1856. "Freedom is not possible without slavery." The South was a herrenvolk democracy, in which political and social equality among whites rested on the subjugation of blacks and in which the aspiration to acquire slaves made ambitious yeomen into imitators rather than adversaries of the planter class. The racial division mitigated tensions between the paternalist and premodern plantation on which the southern elite lived and the individualist and formally democratic order outside its gates.[19]

The Denmark Vesey slave conspiracy of 1822, the Nat Turner rebellion a decade later, and the beginnings of abolitionist agitation in the early 1830s all fed southern fears of racial rebellion. The resulting restrictions imposed on slaves underlined the dependence of white southern freedom on black slavery. But the fear of antislavery agitation drastically curtailed political and intellectual freedom for southern whites as well. It was illegal to argue in southern states that slavery was an illegitimate form of property or to advocate its abolition. The federal government acquiesced in the censorship of southern mail to prevent the circulation of antislavery literature. Mob violence intimidated the occasional antislavery editor, and the fear of subversive ideas spread beyond antislavery to inhibit intellectual and cultural expression more broadly.[20]

The defense of slavery also restricted political freedom in the nation as a whole. Congress adopted a gag rule in 1836 to prevent discussion of antislavery petitions. Antiabolitionist mobs, more often than not led by local gentlemen of property and standing, invaded abolitionist meetings and destroyed abolitionist newspapers. In Alton, Illinois, in 1837, a mob murdered the abolitionist editor Elijah Lovejoy.[21]

The abolition of slavery, in spite of proslavery fears, led to neither political nor social freedom for blacks. A new, quasi-peonage system replaced slavery as the dominant form of labor in southern agriculture. Sharecropping arrangements, tenant farming, and a crop lien credit system tied black agricultural workers to planters and merchants. Black convicts, often imprisoned without due process, worked southern mines and built and repaired southern roads. The Ku Klux Klan terrorized blacks during Reconstruction, when they enjoyed a small measure of political power. Jim Crow laws developed to enforce social segregation, and lynchings and mob violence punished real or imaginary black assertions of freedom.

Black efforts to acquire political power climaxed at the end of the nineteenth century in southern Populism, an interracial alliance of black and white farmers. Physical intimidation, electoral fraud, and racial fears all played a part in its defeat. That defeat was followed by the total disenfranchisement of blacks. Suffrage restrictions excluded many poor whites as well. The specter of black power and the political exclusion of blacks created a system of one-party politics in the South. That politics was characterized by low participation; shifting, personally based factions; demagogic appeals; and the emergence of leaders hostile not just to racial equality but to a variety of ideas that were labeled un-American.[22]

A pseudoscientific racist ideology, justifying black subordination and stigmatizing non-Teutonic European immigrants as well, developed in postbellum America. Imperial democrats like Theodore Roosevelt and Woodrow Wilson merged tutelary visions of the white man's burden abroad with justifications of racial inequality at home. Blacks were deprived of political power and suffered from economic discrimination in the North as well as the South, but no legal, state-enforced system of segregation developed in the North. A formal commitment to racial equality was enshrined in the Fourteenth and Fifteenth Amendments to the Constitution. Courts used the Fourteenth Amendment for seventy-five years to protect corporations instead of blacks. But a series of rulings against discrimination culminated in 1954 in *Brown v. Board of Education of Topeka*, which outlawed legally segregated schools. The decision set in motion a movement for black political and civil rights, the intimidation of which belongs with a discussion of the politics of the 1960s.[23]

The 1790 naturalization law, one of the first acts of the new federal government, prohibited nonwhite immigrants from becoming naturalized citizens. That act expressed desires for a homogeneous population, the consequences of which have reached beyond racial exclusion. Peoples of color, nonetheless, have felt the legal effects of such desires with particular force. Hispanics and Asians who came to work in the United States or who lived on land seized by the expanding nation were denied full civil and political rights well into the twentieth century. Most worked in labor-repressive systems in the farms and mines of California and the Southwest. Anti-Chinese agitation played a central role in California politics from the 1870s through the Progressive period. In perhaps the greatest single deprivation of rights in all American history, 110,000 Japanese-Americans were rounded up and interned in "concentration camps" (as President Franklin Roosevelt called them) during World War II. The Japanese were, according to the army official who recommended their incarceration, an "enemy race." Earl Warren, then the California attorney general, explained that he knew methods to "test the loyalty" of individual Caucasians. "But [he complained] when we deal with the Japanese we are in an entirely different field, and we cannot form any opinion that we believe to be sound." The Supreme Court upheld forcible Japanese internment in *Korematsu* v. *U.S.* (1943) on national emergency grounds. President Harry Truman rewarded Dillon S. Myer for directing the War Relocation Authority by appointing him Commissioner of Indian Affairs in 1950.[24]

American history is normally seen as a history of freedom rather than suppression. American racial history suggests that the suppression of peoples of color outside the normal political system has supported the freedom of the people within it. But the connections—real or imagined—between Indians and masterless Europeans, black and white workers, black sexuality and white women, all call into question any simple notion that whites were granted political rights while peoples of color were denied them. A fear of subversion has converted conflicts of interest in race relations into all-encompassing, psychologically based dangers to personal and national identity. That same fear of subversion underlies the nonracial history of American political repression.

III

The Alien and Sedition Acts of 1798 nearly abolished freedom of speech and the press in the new nation. The Sedition Act made criminal "any

false, scandalous and malicious" writings or utterances against the government that were intended to defame government officers or excite
against them the hatred of the people. The Alien Acts increased the period of residency prior to citizenship to fourteen years, authorized the
president to deport any alien he considered dangerous to domestic
peace, and empowered him to expel citizens of a country at war with
the United States. These acts were the culmination of a dominant strand
of thought in eighteenth-century America hostile to political liberty.[25]

The English common law of seditious libel, valid in the colonies, punished criticism that lowered the government in public esteem and threatened to disturb the peace. Defenders of free expression in the colonies,
before and during the Revolution, never attacked the concept of seditious libel at its roots. They did oppose prior restraints on the press,
which the First Amendment eventually prohibited. They also demanded
that jury trials be held in seditious libel prosecutions and that truth be
allowed to stand as a defense. There is no evidence that the authors of
the First Amendment intended to abolish the common law of seditious
libel. The Alien and Sedition Acts themselves instituted no prior restraint, called for trial by jury, and permitted truth as a defense. Hence
their supporters could well have found the acts consistent with the First
Amendment.

American revolutionaries had attributed colonial factionalism to the
British Crown. Once that alien presence was removed from American
life, it was thought, factional conflicts would disappear. No theory justified an institutionalized opposition to popularly based government.
Trial by jury and truth as a defense protected Americans who attacked
the Crown; they offered no refuge for those critical of locally popular
governments. Only one case brought under the Alien and Sedition Acts
ended in acquittal.

The Alien and Sedition Acts refused to countenance the existence of
a legitimate political opposition. Jeffersonian Republicans, targets of
the acts, developed in response the first theory of free expression in
America to repudiate seditious libel. The Jeffersonians rejected the distinction between ordered liberty and license, the distinction upon which
earlier defenses of free speech had rested. The need to show the truth of
an idea, they argued, inadequately protected freedom of opinion. Madison, in *Federalist* 10, had already insisted that factions could not be
suppressed without destroying liberty. His 1800 report to the Virginia
House of Delegates argued that popular governments, unlike hereditary
monarchies, could not be libeled. A system of popular rule required

freedom to criticize the government, wrote Madison. The defeat of the
Federalists in 1800 established the legitimacy of political opposition in
America.[26]

Legitimate opposition was still to be distinguished from illegitimate
opposition. President Jefferson himself countenanced seditious libel
prosecutions in the states. State action to suppress dissent, derived from
the law of seditious libel, would come to play a major role in the twentieth century. Modern governments seeking to suppress sedition would
also draw on the tradition enshrined in the other half of the Alien and
Sedition Acts, the belief that blamed aliens for sedition.

Federalists had charged that agents of the French Revolution, in combination with a secret order of Freemasons and Bavarian Illuminati,
were conspiring to destroy American independence. The Illuminati conspiracy, a fantasy of the Federalist imagination, justified the Alien and
Sedition Acts. Although state laws were rarely passed to suppress such
foreign threats in antebellum America, conspiratorial fears still dominated politics. Americans mounted a series of crusades against Catholics, Masons, the Mormon church, the "monster-hydra" bank of the
United States, the abolitionists, the slave power conspiracy, and the demon rum.[27]

Aside from those demons connected to Indian dispossession and slavery, the Catholic church was the most important continuing target of
antebellum countersubversion. "Three-fourths of the foreign emigrants
whose accumulating tide is rolling in upon us, are, through the medium
of their religion and priesthood," wrote the Reverend Lyman Beecher,
"entirely accessible to the control of the potentates of Europe, as if they
were an army of soldiers, enlisted and officered, and spreading through
the land." Members of this Catholic conspiracy, according to the inventor of the telegraph, Samuel F. B. Morse, stood "in regular steps of slave
and master." (Morse was the son of the Reverend Jedidiah Morse, who
had introduced the fantasy of a "secret revolutionary conspiracy of Illuminati" into America.) The Catholic church, like other targets of
countersubversive fantasies, combined total order with sexual license.
Maria Monk's *Dutiful Disclosures of the Hotel Dieu Nunnery of Mon-
treal* (1836), which charged that nuns and priests lived in criminal intercourse and baptized and strangled their babies, was endorsed by the
Protestant religious press and became a national best-seller. The domination exercised within Catholic orders, countersubversives believed,
threatened to spread throughout society. "The serpent has already com-
menced his coil about our limbs, and the lethargy of his poison is creep-

ing over us," warned Morse. "We must awake or we are lost." Fears of
a Catholic conspiracy continued to play an active role in American politics through the 1920s, when the anti-Catholic Ku Klux Klan mobilized
millions of followers.[28]

The fear of alien conspiracies led to blaming problems in American
life on forces operating outside it. Conspiracy hunting turned political
differences into absolute struggles between good and evil. Antebellum
crusades had millennial, Protestant roots. They also reflected the dark
side of American individualism. In mobile, antebellum American society, individuals influenced others to advance themselves and hid their
real identities behind confidence-inspiring facades. Pervasive role-play-
ing generated suspicions of hidden motives, as individuals tried simultaneously to influence others and to protect themselves from invasion.
Countersubversives imagined secret centers of power that issued direc-
tives and constrained individual freedom. Conspiracies like the ones exposed by Maria Monk threatened simultaneously to disorganize the vigilant self and to fulfill its hidden desire to dominate.[29]

Efforts to stigmatize aliens were often more than rhetorical. Mobs
not only assaulted abolitionists and free blacks; they also attacked Catholic neighborhoods and destroyed Mormon communities. The mob that
burned a Roman Catholic convent in Charlestown, Massachusetts, in
1834 had been stirred by the fiery sermons of Lyman Beecher. Beecher
attacked popery as the enemy of religion and republicanism, exhorting
his audience to action against it.[30]

But those like Beecher, who were concerned with alien dangers before the Civil War, relied most heavily neither on state laws against dissent nor on mob action. They sought instead to build institutions and
form characters that would domesticate American freedom. The anti-
Masonic impulse in Rochester, New York, for example, was coopted
and transformed into a method of evangelical, Protestant discipline. The
wives of manufacturers and other middle-class women, visiting and con-
verting the poor, substituted orderly institutions of work, worship, and
domesticity for secret centers of vice. In attracting sober workers to the
church, evangelicals reformed working-class factories and neighborhoods.[31]

The men and women who invented the asylum and reformed the
family proposed to work on the interior of the self. Their efforts dovetailed with the pressures to conformity Tocqueville observed on his trip
to America. The tyranny of public opinion, the ideology of domesticity,
and the creation of the asylum all limited political dissent in scarcely

measurable ways. Insofar as they succeeded, they did not simply intimidate political opposition already formed but inhibited the formation of new opposition. Our subject now is the suppression of politics at the prepolitical level, through the transformation of potentially political discontent into problems of personal life.

The removal of external British authority created a crisis of order for elites in the new nation. "We have changed our form of government," explained the Philadelphia physician Benjamin Rush, "but it remains yet to effect a revolution in our principles, opinions, and manners to accommodate them to the forms of government we have adopted." One solution (which Rush himself favored in the Pennsylvania constitutional debates of 1776) was to maintain a restricted suffrage and keep those who might threaten property and order out of electoral politics. But suffrage was already widespread before the Revolution. By the Jacksonian period all states except Rhode Island and South Carolina had universal white manhood suffrage.[32]

Suffrage restriction continued to deny a political voice to women and peoples of color. Susan B. Anthony and fifteen other women were arrested for voting in the 1872 presidential election and charged with violating a federal law. Picketers from the Women's party in Washington, D.C., were assaulted by mobs, arrested, and jailed during World War I for attacking the effort to "make the world safe for democracy" in a country that denied half its citizens the vote. Although women received the franchise in some states in the late nineteenth and early twentieth centuries, they were not granted voting rights in the nation as a whole until the Nineteenth Amendment was ratified in 1920.[33]

Nineteenth-century women were denied not only the vote but also control of their own property and entrance to many professions and trade unions. An ideology of domesticity justified restricting woman's sphere to the home. The proponents of domestic ideology (such as Lyman Beecher's daughter Catharine) offered women the power to shape their husbands and sons in the family in return for relinquishing direct claims to exercise power in society. Some women (such as Catharine Beecher's sister, Harriet Beecher Stowe) employed domestic values against antifamilial social practices; slavery and alcoholic intemperance were the most prominent targets. But women who entered public life directly were said to unsex themselves and unman men. Instead, domestic ideology made women the instruments of morality and social control in order to confine others.[34]

Domestic ideology offered the family as both a refuge from and a solution to social disorder. The turn to the family did not so much enrich private life, however, as socialize it. Denying the truly private character of the home, domesticity made the family less a haven for protecting eccentricity than an arena for forming and standardizing personality. Enlisting the child's desire for love and threatening him with the loss of love, the mother would influence the child to internalize morality. Characters formed by regulated affection in the home could safely enter the world. This retreat to the family encouraged the displacement onto politics of discontents originating in domestic life (but forbidden to be traced to their source). At the same time, domesticity dissolved political into personal problems. By locating social troubles and their solution in the family, domestic ideology shifted attention from the public arena into the home. It thereby took its place as part of the second method (after suffrage restriction) that Rush had proposed to domesticate political freedom, the method of internalizing authority.

The internalization of authority in antebellum America had four components: a shift away from ceremonial public places into private but standardized interiors; a redefinition of political, social, and cultural conflicts as problems of crime and disease; loving confinement as the method of punishment and reform; and the creation of a self-controlled interior, resistant to corrupting temptations from the body and the world. Benjamin Rush, friend of John Adams and other revolutionary leaders, was the founder of the new discipline. Rush was a leading prison reformer and opponent of public executions; the father of the mental hospital; a promoter of public schools; and, as the American who discovered the dangers posed to the vigilant self by liquor and masturbation, the guiding spirit behind the nineteenth-century movements against alcoholic consumption and self-abuse.

Rush did not confine his reform efforts to whites. An opponent of slavery before the Revolution, the doctor responded to claims of Negro inferiority by attributing black racial qualities to disease. Jefferson compared the desire of black men for white women to the desire of male orangutans for female blacks. Rush rejected the view that the color of blacks had been produced by intercourse with orangutans; he attributed it to leprosy instead. Linking blacks to sexuality, immorality, and crime 'invit[es] us to tyrannize over them," Rush explained. "Disease," by contrast, "has always been the signal for immediate and universal compassion." And Rush thought he saw signs for a cure.[35]

The effort to rescue blacks by making them leprous did not have wide appeal in post-Revolutionary America. But in medicalizing social tensions among whites and offering remedies to stop the contagion, Rush initiated a lasting set of reforms. Rush proposed to convert men into "republican machines. This must be done if we expect them to perform their parts properly, in the great machine of the government of the state." Such "good citizens" would exercise their freedom in a self-controlled way. Rush preserved the distinction between liberty and license when he moved it from state enforcement into the individual conscience. New institutions were to form that conscience. For the middle class, as domestic ideology signaled, the most important of these institutions was the nuclear family, and it was supplemented by the school. Those falling out of the middle class—or never in it to begin with—were to be confined and reformed in asylums: schools, prisons, hospitals, and factories. Their purpose, Rush explained, was to "render the mass of the people more homogeneous, and thereby fit them more easily for uniform and peaceable government."[36]

Asylums responded to the perceived breakdown of a deferential order in post-Revolutionary America. They housed those masterless men and women liberated by the marketplace, political freedom, and geographic mobility and no longer ordered within the traditional structures of kin group, church, and community. Some asylums, such as the mental hospital, offered protection from the outside pressures of a mobile, acquisitive society. Others, such as the prison and the paternally organized factory, contained the threat posed by the "dangerous classes" of urban immigrants and the poor. Just as the reservation would confine and reform the "perishing classes" of savages, so the urban "dangerous classes" were offered the prison.

Rush opposed public executions because they stimulated crowds not to obedience but to disorder. Physical violence not only provoked mob violence in return but also failed to reform the criminal. Whipping offenders subdued their bodies, according to prison reformers, but failed to reach their hearts. Instead of whipping the wrongdoer and setting him loose (the normal practice in the eighteenth century), the new prisons confined criminals behind walls. Like the home, the asylum provided a place of refuge and replaced physical force by disciplined love. In keeping with developing domestic practices, greater privacy for the inmate was combined with surveillance over him and attention to his interior. English and American reformers advocated removing the chains from the prisoner and enlisting him in his own cure. Isolated from the bad influences of one another, regimented, observed, and subjected to a regularized authority, criminals would learn to love society.

Although in practice the prison sacrificed the regeneration of the criminal to his confinement, in theory it offered a perfect marriage of the two methods that were coming to dominate the American practice of control: concentrated state coercive power and the creation through interior reform of a free man.

Tocqueville and Gustave de Beaumont, who came to America to study the new prisons, observed that "while society in the United States gives the example of a most extended liberty, the prisons of the same country offer a spectacle of the most complete despotism." That paradox reflected the rise of total institutions in response to fears of extended liberty. But a deeper commonality lay underneath the contrast. Both the society and the prison wiped out traditional loyalties that bound people together. The spread of freedom in a society of such extended liberty required the formation of selves who would not abuse that liberty. Both the mobile society and the total institution isolated the self and invaded his or her interior. Individuals fearful of incurring disapproval, wrote Tocqueville, and deprived of support from traditional subcultures and kin groups, would not risk isolating themselves from the democratic mass. They would not develop the freedom of opinion to entertain subversive ideas. Tocqueville explained, "Despotism, to reach the soul, clumsily struck at the body, and the soul, escaping from such blows, rose gloriously above it. Such is not the course adopted by tyranny in democratic republics. There the body is left free, and the soul is enslaved."[37]

In Tocqueville's analysis the task of enforcing the distinction between liberty and license, which once belonged to the state, moved simultaneously within the individual conscience and out into public opinion. Those who stepped beyond the bounds of legitimate controversy faced not so much punishment by the state as estrangement from the social mass. The institutional structures that domestic and asylum reformers favored molded characters vulnerable to the social pressures that Tocqueville described.

Reformers and institution builders in the twentieth century reacted against the regimented isolation of inmates in the nineteenth-century prison. Progressives proposed to attend to the life history of the individual case and to turn the prison into a protocommunity. They shifted attention from the crime to the criminal and from guilt or innocence to sickness or health. But since confinement itself remained intact, the consequence was to extend surveillance inside and outside the prison walls. The parole system tracked inmates after their release. Juvenile courts investigated offenders before they were institutionalized. The young, the welfare recipient, and the mentally ill surrendered legal rights to members of the helping professions. Those incarcerated in "moral hospitals," as Denver judge Ben Lindsey called the asylums, did not need protection from authority.[38]

A therapeutic approach to social problems affected the treatment not only of crime, poverty, and mental disturbance but also of political conflict as well. Reform practice turned conflicts of interest into problems of personal and social adjustment. Its soft form of coercion competed in politics and in crime with a punitive, law-and-order methodology. Both dissolved the distinction between political and personal disturbance, the one in the name of therapy, the other in the name of punishment. The criminalization of political differences, the collapse of politics into disease, the spread of surveillance, and the stigmatization of dissenters as social pariahs have all played important roles in the suppression of radical politics. They have done so not merely through the pressures of public opinion, as in Tocqueville's analysis, but through the armed force of the state.

IV

Antebellum politics had at its center the repression of Indians and blacks; workers took their place after the Civil War. The rhetoric of a struggle between savagery and civilization moved from the frontier West to urban America, from Indian conflict to class war. Late nineteenth-century newspapers warned at the same time, as Richard Slotkin has shown, against the "Hostile Reds" on the frontier and the "Red Spectre of the Commune" in American cities. They conflated the idle, disorderly free blacks in the South with the northern, urban proletariat. These confusions helped justify both search-and-destroy missions against western Indians and violence against blacks, and they also promoted the suppression of working-class discontent.[39]

Racial mythologies continued to dominate American culture and politics in the industrial age at the expense of peoples of color, but pseudoscientific racial theories were now extended to European immigrants as well. That signaled the new, central importance in postbellum America of ethnocentric, class war. A series of Red scares, one in the 1870s, one in 1886, and one in 1919, marked the half-century between 1870 and 1920. Each located subversive political ideas within an alien, immigrant working class.

The modern history of countersubversion began with the Red scare of 1873–78. It arose in response to the Paris Commune abroad and to a major depression and radical labor protest at home. "Today there is not in our language, nor in any language, a more hateful word than communism," proclaimed a professor at the Union Theological Seminary. Cities built armories to protect themselves against working-class uprisings, states revived militias, and police attacked strikers and unemployment demonstrators. Hundreds of thousands of unemployed, roaming the country in search of work, generated a "tramp" scare.[40]

The dean of the Yale Law School announced in a paper delivered at the 1877 meeting of the American Social Science Association, "As we hear the word *tramp*, there arises straightaway before us the spectacle of a lazy, incorrigible, cowardly, utterly depraved savage." Tramps, like Indians before them, were wandering, masterless men. Participants in the tramp scare blamed the industrial capitalist threat to homogeneous, ordered communities on the wandering victims. The breakdown in social order was real. It stemmed, however, not from savages and Communists but from centralized corporations and their need for a national market in labor and other commodities. Social breakdown climaxed in the nationwide railway strike of 1877 (called "nothing more nor less than French Communism" by an official of President Hayes's administration), in which strikers fought with police and mobs seized and burned the Pittsburgh railway yards.[41]

The first anti-Red political trial with nationwide significance took place in Chicago in 1886. It was a response to mass working-class support for the Knights of Labor, a strike against Jay Gould's railroad system, and a national movement for the eight-hour day. When mounted police ordered an anarchist demonstration in Haymarket Square to disperse, someone threw a bomb. It injured seventy policemen and killed one. Eight Chicago anarchists, some neither present at the rally nor known to one another and none connected to the bombing, were found guilty of conspiracy to commit murder. Four were executed. (One killed himself in jail, and the remaining three were pardoned in 1893.) The Haymarket anarchists were convicted for radical ideas and violent talk. Their trial, which was conducted in an atmosphere of national hysteria, destroyed not only the Chicago anarchist movement but the Knights of Labor as well. For the next forty years industrial unions organizing unskilled workers were the targets of state and state-sanctioned violence.[42]

The most significant state labor repression in the next half-century was the repression of the Pullman boycott and nationwide railway strike of 1894. Attorney General Richard Olney, a former corporate lawyer who sat on the board of one of the struck railways, obtained a federal injunction that effectively outlawed union activity. The injunction permitted individual workers to leave their jobs, because to force them to work would violate their freedom of contract. But in a massive prohibition of freedom of speech and assembly, workers and union leaders were forbidden to convince others to quit work. The injunction safeguarded the same private freedom that was offered to Indians who abandoned their tribal ties. It outlawed political freedom, the freedom of community members to speak and act together. American Railway Union leaders were arrested for violating the injunction; the union's president, Eugene Victor Debs, went to jail.[43]

States continued to suppress labor's free speech and assembly in the twentieth century and to meet organizing efforts with violence. Western miners suffered from a particularly bloody history of state and corporate violence. When the anticapitalist Industrial Workers of the World (IWW) was formed in 1905, western miners and woodworkers provided its major support. Local officials jailed IWW organizers for making public speeches, a practice that led to free-speech fights in such western cities as Spokane, Washington; Fresno and San Diego, California; and Minot, North Dakota. Wobblies arrested for exercising their rights of free speech filled the local jails; their nonviolent civil disobedience often generated violence in return.[44]

Hostility to the IWW and to subversive ideas climaxed in the Red scare during and after World War I. In the second great Chicago conspiracy trial, thirty years after Haymarket, 101 Wobblies were convicted of conspiring to obstruct the war. Many were guilty simply of membership in the IWW. Others were convicted on the basis of statements made before the United States entered the fighting.

The Espionage and Sedition Acts of 1917–18 made it a crime to speak or act against the war. Even if aliens remained silent and inactive, they were subject to summary arrest. Socialist congressman Victor Berger, appealing his conviction under the Espionage Act, was barred from taking his congressional seat by a vote of 311–1. Debs, who had become a Socialist party leader after the suppression of the Pullman strike, was sentenced to ten years in prison for making an antiwar speech. The U.S. Post Office conducted a campaign of censorship against the Socialist party and the IWW, removing their publications from the mail.[45]

State governments also passed laws outlawing opposition to the war and forbidding expressions of revolutionary disloyalty to the American form of government. The Supreme Court upheld convictions under state criminal syndicalism laws, ruling that states could punish revolutionary words spoken with malicious intent that might have a tendency to provoke violence in the future. These rulings revived the doctrine of seditious libel.

War intensified the hysteria over disloyalty in America, but the Red scare reached its greatest heights after the war was over. America in 1919, reported a British journalist, "was hag-ridden by the spectre of Bolshevism. It was like a sleeper in a nightmare, enveloped by a thousand phantoms of destruction." The assault against subversion climaxed in two events: the suppression of the 1919 steel strike and a series of Justice Department raids that rounded up thousands of allegedly subversive foreigners for deportation. The Red scare ushered in the nativist mood and the obsession with 100 percent Americanism that dominated the politics of the 1920s.[46]

Political interventions helped destroy the Knights of Labor, the American Railway Union, the IWW, and the organizing efforts among steelworkers. State violence denied public space to workers and inhibited broadscale political expression. It helped engender, instead, the fragmented and privatized pluralism of the American Federation of Labor. The conservative craft unions of the AFL survived and grew between 1886 and 1920. Nevertheless, the entire labor movement enjoyed little better than an outlaw status before 1935. The repression of labor was more violent and severe in America than it was in any other western, industrializing country. The Supreme Court, in *In Re Debs* (1891), legalized the use of court injunctions to break strikes; employers enjoyed injunctive relief from strikes that damaged "probable expectancies" of future profit rather than existing real property. Unions were subject to conspiracy prosecutions for boycotting nonunion goods, for having large numbers of strikers present at plant gates, and for inducing workers to break contracts that committed them not to join unions. Courts protected the individual "freedom of contract" of workers at the expense not only of worker collective action but also of political efforts to regulate the conditions of employment. Wage, hour, and child-labor laws were all ruled unconstitutional.[47]

State violence, which controlled peoples of color before the Civil War, repressed postbellum working-class and radical protest. State militias and federal troops were used to break strikes; strike breaking became, with the end of the Indian wars, the most conspicuous function of the regular army. Violence, killings, and massive arrests occurred during strikes. The national state shared its monopoly over legitimate force with corporations and detective agencies. These private bodies conducted surveillance and employed armed men. The conferring of state functions on private groups, a general feature of American politics, played an important role in labor conflicts through the 1930s. Together, state and private action deprived workers before the New Deal of their right to organize.

The 1935 Wagner Act, called labor's Magna Charta, made employer interference with the right to organize into an unfair labor practice. One historian has labeled the act "perhaps the most important civil liberties statute ever passed by Congress."[48] Three years earlier the Norris–La Guardia Act had outlawed the use of the labor injunction. The Supreme Court, in *Thornhill* v. *Alabama* (1940), extended First Amendment protection to peaceful picketing in labor disputes. Later courts restricted the scope of *Thornhill*, and the 1947 Taft-Hartley Act removed some of the legal protections for union organizing activity. The percentage of the workforce organized into unions has declined in the past forty years, as the labor movement has lost its central place in the Democratic party and been reduced to narrow, interest group status. Nevertheless, since the 1940s organized labor has been accepted as a legitimate interest in American society.

The organization of industrial workers into the Congress of Industrial Organizations (CIO) and the ties of CIO unions to the welfare state and the Democratic party began to eliminate working-class activity as the target of countersubversion. Labor struggles remained important, however, at the origins of the post–World War II Red scare. Communists and their allies controlled several CIO unions. Those unions supported the war and were allied with the Democratic party. When the beginnings of the cold war ended that alliance, the government and its union supporters moved to destroy left-wing labor. The Taft-Hartley Act deprived unions whose officers refused to sign anti-Communist loyalty oaths of the protection of the National Labor Relations Board. The CIO expelled those unions in 1948. Labor-management conflict in the motion picture industry also contributed to the postwar Red scare by helping to generate the Hollywood blacklist. Once the domestic cold war was fairly launched, however, labor was not its central target.

Earlier Red scares developed out of class conflicts between labor and capital in which the state served mostly as the agent of the capitalist class. The Soviet Union replaced the immigrant working class as the source of anxiety in the decades after World War II. The combat between workers and capitalists was supplanted by one between Moscow's agents (intellectuals, government employees, students, and middle-class activists) and a state national-security apparatus.

Both the postwar Soviet Union and the radical labor movement of an earlier period posed genuine threats to dominant interests in American society, although the nature and extent of those threats are a matter of controversy. There were also real conflicts of interest between white Americans and peoples of color. But the countersubversive response transformed interest conflicts into psychologically based anxieties over national security and American identity. Exaggerated responses to the domestic Communist menace narrowed the bounds of permissible political disagreement and generated a national-security state.

V

The cold war marks the third major moment in the history of countersubversion. In the first moment whites were pitted against peoples of color. In the second Americans were pitted against aliens. In the third, which revolves around mass society and the state, a national-security bureaucracy confronts the invisible agents of a foreign power.

Throughout American history the subversive has threatened the family, property, and personal and national identity. But three shifts—from visibility to invisibility, from the body to the mind, and from the American individual to the national-security state—distinguish the first Red scares from their cold war descendant. First, subversives were alien in earlier Red scares, and they looked visibly different from Americans. Communists in 1950s mass society were indistinguishable from everyone else. Second, as the visible differences that stigmatized subversives disappeared, it became all the more important to discover who was under foreign control. Instead of standing simply for savagery and disorder, the subversive was the instrument of an alien order. That combination was not new in itself; it harked back to claims that foreign powers controlled American Indians and that the pope directed American Catholics. But the shift in emphasis from the deranged subversive body to the calculating alien mind justified the third departure in countersubversive history, the rise of the national-security state.

In July 1919, without congressional authorization, the attorney general's office created the General Intelligence Division (GID) within the Justice Department. Its purpose was to infiltrate and collect information on radical organizations. The GID borrowed the techniques of labor espionage and surveillance employed by private corporations and detective agencies. It was headed by J. Edgar Hoover, a twenty-four-year-old former cataloguer in the Library of Congress, who had moved to a clerkship in the Justice Department's Enemy Alien Registration unit. Hoover boasted of his role in breaking the 1919 steel strike. He and Attorney General A. Mitchell Palmer supervised the alien raids of 1919–20.[49]

Hoover also made a series of sensational charges against alleged radicals. Blaming subversives for the 1919 race riots (and thereby not only imagining conspiracies that did not exist but also making blacks the perpetrators rather than the victims of the outrages), Hoover attacked black leaders for being under Bolshevik influence. He charged them with being "openly, defiantly assertive" of their "own equality or even superiority." Hoover established files on alleged subversives. He investigated and tried to discredit people who opposed his actions, like the noted civil libertarians Zechariah Chafee, Jr., and Felix Frankfurter.

Attorney General Harlan Stone terminated the GID in 1924, the year he reorganized the Federal Bureau of Investigation. Stone placed Hoover in charge of the entire FBI and ordered the FBI to limit its investigations to actual violations of federal law. In violation of Stone's memorandum, the FBI continued to collect information on radical labor and political organizations. Moreover, Hoover's appointment meant that the United States was unique in combining criminal detection and political surveillance in a single agency. Stone placed in charge a man trained in political countersubversion rather than law enforcement. Hoover's rise to head the FBI confirmed the confusion between crime and radical dissent at the heart of the American fear of subversion.[50]

Franklin Roosevelt secretly rescinded Stone's restrictions on the FBI in 1936, reactivating it as a political surveillance agency. But although Roosevelt occasionally used Hoover for intelligence against his own political adversaries, he was not aware of the large-scale expansion in bureau activities that began under his presidency. Hoover was creating a secret political police to infiltrate, influence, and punish dissenting political speech and action.[51]

Other branches of the federal government also developed countersubversive instruments. The House of Representatives created a committee to investigate un-American activities in 1938. In 1940 Congress passed the Smith Act, making it a crime to advocate, or conspire to advocate, the overthrow of the government by force or violence. Congress attached this prohibition to the Alien Registration Act, perpetuating the association of aliens and sedition.

Nazism provided the occasion for the emergence of the national-security apparatus. Communists, who were to be its major targets, actually helped develop the countersubversive ideological rationale. The first prosecutions under the Smith Act, welcomed by the Communists, were of leaders of the Trotskyist Socialist Workers party. Within a few years the Communist party would be the target of Smith Act prosecutions. In the period after World War II, as in the decades before it, Communists and their alleged sympathizers have been the major targets of the suppression of political dissent.[52]

In March 1947 President Harry Truman announced he was sending military aid to Greece and Turkey to defend their regimes against Communist attacks. In that same month the president established a new government-loyalty program. Declaring Communism a domestic as well as a foreign menace, he set the stage for the Red scare of 1947–54. All present and prospective government employees were to undergo investigations of their loyalty, with each government agency establishing its own loyalty review board. How was loyalty to be established? Loyalty boards gave great weight to past beliefs and memberships. They asked questions about political views and social practices. Such questions included, "Do you ever have Negroes in your home?" "Do you read Howard Fast? Tom Paine? Upton Sinclair?" Loyalty boards relied heavily on information supplied by anonymous informers, who included former Communists, FBI infiltrators, and ordinary citizens who claimed to have derogatory knowledge of those against whom they informed. Accused employees were not entitled to hear the specific charges against them or to know the names of government informers. The burden of proof lay on the accused individual, who had to establish not only that he or she had been loyal in the past but also that there were no reasonable grounds to expect disloyalty in the future.[53]

An estimated 13.5 million workers, 20 percent of the labor force, were subject to loyalty programs in government and sensitive private industry.[54] Other nations facing greater political instability instituted no elaborate loyalty tests for government employment. The historic American fear of subversion was spawning a government bureaucracy, whose growth marked a sharp, institutional break with the past.

The criteria for determining loyalty included past or present membership in any organization designated as subversive by the attorney general. The attorney general's authority to issue such a list, wrote civil libertarian Alan Barth, gave him "perhaps the most arbitrary and far-reaching power ever exercised by a single public official in the history of the United States." The attorney general's list played a major role both inside and outside the government. "Its aim," explained Attorney General Tom Clark, was "to isolate subversive movements in this country from effective interference with the body politic." The attorney general could proscribe any organization and thereby deprive individuals who had once belonged to it of government employment. The list was also used to deny employment to individuals in the private sector and to stigmatize political opponents.[55]

The Truman and Eisenhower administrations moved against alleged subversives in society as well as in government. Communist party leaders were arrested and convicted under the Smith Act. The government denied passports to anyone whose travel was "not in the interests" of the United States, including the black singer and actor Paul Robeson. Hundreds of aliens were arrested for deportation in early 1948 alone, and prominent resident aliens like Charlie Chaplin were denied reentry. The State Department also moved to deport naturalized citizens. When Rose Chernin resisted such efforts as head of the Los Angeles Committee for the Protection of the Foreign-Born, the government tried to deport her, too. During the years of the cold war and the Korean War, the Supreme Court excluded Communists and Communist-sympathizers from the protections of the Bill of Rights. But in *Yates* v. *U.S.* (1957) the Court ruled that those convicted of conspiracy to advocate the overthrow of the government by force must be shown to have urged others "to do something rather than merely to believe in something." That decision, which freed Rose Chernin and other Communist leaders convicted with her, effectively ended prosecutions under the Smith Act.[56]

National-security agencies of the government greatly expanded their activities under Presidents Truman and Eisenhower. The FBI perfected its two major countersubversive weapons, surveillance and files. By 1960 the bureau maintained 430,000 files on individuals allegedly connected to subversive activities. Private citizens cooperated with the bureau in reporting suspicious behavior. Harvard professor Henry Kissinger opened a letter sent to a participant in his international relations seminar and communicated its contents to the Boston FBI office. The FBI also kept an index of those who posed a danger to national security and who should be rounded up during a national emergency. The index contained the names of writer Norman Mailer and of Senator Paul Douglas, a liberal Democrat and anti-Communist.[57]

The FBI relied heavily on wiretaps and bugs. Eisenhower's attorney general, Herbert Brownell, authorized break-ins to install wiretaps. Brownell boasted that FBI investigations covered "the entire spectrum of the social and labor movement" in the country. Under the COMIN-FIL program, the bureau did not wait to act until it had evidence of Communist activity; rather it infiltrated any organization where it suspected it might find Communists.[58]

Hoover kept files on the private lives of congressmen and other prominent Americans. He used information from those files to intimidate or discredit people critical of the FBI. Fear of reprisals helps explain Hoover's political untouchability during the half-century he headed the bureau. His mass and elite popularity also stemmed from the American obsession with Communism and with the equation of the fight against Communism with the fight against crime.

The transformation of political dissent into criminal disloyalty was fed by sensational accusations of espionage in the late 1940s against Alger Hiss, Judith Coplon, and Ethel and Julius Rosenberg. Congressman Richard Nixon, who rose to national prominence through the Hiss case, described it as "a small part of the whole shocking story of Communist espionage in the United States." Hiss, accused of transmitting confidential state department documents, was convicted of perjury. The Rosenbergs were executed for, in Judge Irving Kaufman's words, "putting into the hands of the Russians the A-bomb." Judge Kaufman accused the Rosenbergs of responsibility for Communist aggression and American deaths in Korea. Hiss and the Rosenbergs may well have passed confidential information to the Russians; their guilt is still in dispute. But the Rosenbergs neither gave the Soviet Union the atomic bomb nor caused the Korean War. Their highly publicized trial and unprecedented death sentences helped to justify the governmental obsession with national security and to identify opposition to American policies in the cold war with criminal, treasonable disloyalty.[59]

Truman and his anti-Communist, liberal supporters distinguished the Communist party from legitimate political oppositions. The Communist party, they argued, was an international conspiracy to overthrow American government, taking orders from a foreign power. Soviet expansion into Eastern Europe, the Berlin blockade, and the invasion of

South Korea required, in their view, a firm American response. Anti-communist liberals rightly called attention to Soviet expansion, to the monstrous crimes of the Russian state against its own people, and to Moscow's direction of the American Communist party. Some members of the party were probably spies and murderers, just as some agents of the American state were. But the assault on Communists and Communist sympathizers focused not on actual crimes but on memberships, beliefs, and associations. It thereby spread by its own logic to so-called fellow travelers, people who associated with Communists, shared their beliefs, and might secretly be responsive to party direction.

The Truman administration initiated the postwar anti-Communist obsession, but its logic turned it against those who had given it birth. Congressional Republicans found the Democratic administration itself sympathetic to Communism. Senator Joseph McCarthy of Wisconsin was the most prominent Republican to accuse Truman of "coddling" Communists. Accusations by McCarthy and other Republicans intensified the pressures on government employees for political conformity.[60]

Congressional committees investigated the political associations of private citizens and government employees. Individuals were forced to name the names of their alleged Communist associates, take the Fifth Amendment against self-incrimination, or go to jail for contempt of Congress. The major function of these degradation ceremonies was neither to discover crimes nor to make new laws but, rather, to stigmatize individuals, proscribe political ideas, and turn community members against one another. Like the effort to break up Indian tribes and like the labor injunction, the ritual of naming names atomized political association. As Tocqueville had foreseen, isolated individuals faced the opprobrium of public opinion. They also faced reprisals from private employers and from the state.[61]

Senator McCarthy gave his name to the atmosphere of suspicion and political fear that dominated America from 1947 until after the end of the Korean War. McCarthy's use of the Red scare against both the Truman and Eisenhower administrations led scholars to call the domestic Red scare McCarthyism and to interpret McCarthyism as popular hysteria against responsible, elite policymakers. Such views ignored McCarthy's institutional support—in the Republican party, in Congress, and among local elites.[62] Labeling the Red scare McCarthyism also deflected attention from the origins and continuation of countersubversive practices within the executive branch; from the growth of a national-

security bureaucracy; and from the association of Red scares with liberal, Democratic presidents. Democratic chief executives, from Andrew
Jackson to Lyndon Johnson, forged a strong, personal presidency and
carried out a messianic, expansionist foreign policy. From the 1830s to
the 1960s they were the major presidential sources of Red scares.

In understanding the power of the countersubversive imagination in
American political life, it is essential to attend to mass fears of Communism and to the tyranny of public opinion and pressures for political
conformity. Red scares cannot be reduced to mass hysteria, however.
Similarly, advertising and the mass media and their impact on political
demonology do not simply reflect popular desires. Mass opinion has
institutional sources. Hollywood, discussed in chapters 1 and 8 of this
volume, was one center of opinion formation during twentieth-century
Red scares; Madison Avenue was another. Insofar as the mass public is
concerned, the significance both of movies and of advertising from the
1920s until the present lies less in mass countersubversive political mobilization and more in the displacement of politics by private life.

Advertising, which came of age in the 1920s, responded to the political turmoil of the postwar years. Influenced in part by the consumer-
oriented political reforms of the Progressive period, advertisers proposed to replace workers-as-producers, who engaged in class conflict,
with workers-as-consumers. Mass society would replace class society,
since goods bound together people at antagonistic ends of the political
spectrum.[63]

The political concerns of some advertising executives dovetailed with
more widely shared reliance on consumer goods to promote personal
happiness. The exploitation of the psychological function of commodities had much in common with therapeutic approaches to politics. The
language of self-fulfillment in both arenas promoted personal dependence, in the one case on the institutions of the helping professions, in
the other on new products that could cure personal anxieties.[64]

Advertisers proclaimed not consumer dependence but consumer democracy. Through purchases, buyers were "constantly participating in
. . . their industrial government," claimed department store magnate
Edward Filene. "The masses of America have elected Henry Ford. They
have elected General Motors," said Filene, "and all the other great industrial and business leaders of the day." By presenting the corporation
as a source of goods for sovereign consumers rather than a structure of
market or workplace power, Filene legitimated private concentrations

of power and directed voter-consumers away from political challenges to the corporation. The ads and surveys that determined consumer preferences, explained market researcher Edward Bernays, marked a "Declaration of Independence" from traditional democratic ideas. Such arguments moved in post–World War II America from advertising into the political arena itself. Social scientists who had engaged in market research or were adapting its survey techniques defined political democracy on the model of consumer democracy. Arguing that direct public participation was dangerous, they restricted democracy to offering the masses a choice between elite institutions.[65]

The advertising industry, which reached its maturity in the 1950s, promised a suburban utopia of pacified private life. The Red scare enforced that utopia. Both advertising and countersubversion stigmatized un-American activities. External coercion and internal influence worked together, as they had in Indian policy and asylum reform, to domesticate the self and make it safe for political freedom.[66]

But the 1950s American dream contained within it the seeds of its own disintegration. The optimism about private life that Hollywood and the advertising industry had helped to create formed a generation that would turn to political action to fulfill personal desires. Responding to the dominant culture's subordination of politics to personal life, the New Left made the personal political. New Left activists entered political life as the anti-Communist politics of the cold war were culminating in Vietnam. Expansion against Asian Communists generated opposition from the "new barbarians" (as their critics called them) in America.[67] This symbolic reenactment, at home and in Asia, of the conflict between civilization and savagery coalesced with a black protest movement in which the original New Left cadres had been formed. The racial politics of American history, in a massive return of the repressed, took over the country in the 1960s, producing in response a massive state repression of political dissent. That repression climaxed in presidential usurpations of power and in the only resignation of an American president. In the 1980s the Reagan administration has avoided the political opposition that brought Nixon down because it has benefited from comparisons with the perceived haplessness of Ford and Carter and because it has concentrated its intimidation on the margins and beyond the borders of the United States.

The end of the Korean War, the Senate censure of Joseph McCarthy, and Supreme Court decisions in several civil liberties cases all reduced political suppression in the latter 1950s. The Court declared the attorney general's list illegal and in *New York Times Co.* v. *Sullivan* (1964) ruled that prosecutions for seditious libel violated the First Amendment. The national-security surveillance bureaucracy was still firmly in place, however, and the rise of the civil rights and New Left movements in the early 1960s triggered a broad campaign of intimidation.[68]

In 1962 the FBI placed Martin Luther King, Jr., leader of nonviolent mass protests against southern segregation, on its list of those to be arrested in a national emergency, and Hoover began a campaign to discredit him. Accusing King of being under Communist influence, Hoover obtained Attorney General Robert Kennedy's permission to tap his phone. The FBI already had under surveillance the National Association for the Advancement of Colored People. At the same time, the FBI refused to protect the civil rights of people whose legal protests against segregation resulted in police and mob violence against them. The rise of a mass movement against the war in Vietnam, after Johnson's election in 1964 and his escalation of the war, led to a vast expansion of the government's political intimidation.[69]

The decade from 1965 to 1975, marked by antiwar and student protests, urban black ghetto uprisings, and impeachment proceedings against Nixon, was the most turbulent period of the century. Presidents Johnson and Nixon believed that Moscow was behind the antiwar movement. Johnson's vice president, Hubert Humphrey, charged that the "international Communist movement" had "organized and masterminded" demonstrations against the draft. Under Johnson the CIA developed an illegal domestic surveillance network; its existence was denied under oath by Director Richard Helms, who had set it up. Between 1967 and 1971 army intelligence collected information, as the Senate Intelligence Committee later reported, on "virtually every group seeking political change in the United States." The FBI vastly expanded its surveillance activities, including break-ins. The bureau expanded its COINTELPRO program which went beyond infiltrating dissident groups (COMINFIL) to actively disrupting them.[70]

Under COINTELPRO, FBI agents forged letters, set political associates and marital partners against one another, got people fired, and instigated violence. A staff report of the Senate Intelligence Committee called COINTELPRO a "sophisticated vigilante operation aimed squarely at preventing the exercise of First Amendment rights of speech and association." Political activists could not be sure whether those with

whom they worked were comrades, informers, or provocateurs. COIN-
TELPRO, according to one confidential FBI document, would "en-
hance the paranoia endemic in these circles, and will further serve to get
the point across that there is an FBI agent behind every mailbox."[71]

The techniques of political repression had changed dramatically by
the post–World War II period. Brutal and public in the last decades of
the nineteenth century, intimidation was carried on by private as well
as public bodies. It became bureaucratized and more centered in a state
apparatus during the Red scares following both world wars. As state
surveillance intensified after World War II, violent intimidation de-
creased. Political repression went underground, intimidating by its invisibility. Surveillance worked by concealing the identity of its actors
but letting the existence of its network be known. Like warders in Jer-
emy Bentham's model prison, the panopticon, the surveillants planted
in subversive organizations could see without being seen. The political
activist, like Bentham's or Rush's prisoner or Tocqueville's democratic
man, was always to wonder whether he or she was being observed. The
state was carrying on a hidden war against the bonds of trust that make
political opposition possible.

National security supplanted un-American activities during the cold
war as the major justification for suppressing political dissent. At the
same time that it increased political surveillance, the national-security
bureaucracy expanded its system of classifying government documents.
By keeping its policies and political disputes secret, the state took politics out of the public realm. To publicize confidential government proceedings was, under those circumstances, not to engage in political
controversy but to endanger the national security. The Nixon administration thus prosecuted Daniel Ellsberg for making public the Pentagon
papers. This classified set of materials on American involvement in Vietnam contained nothing to endanger the national security but much to
endanger the justifications for the continued prosecution of the war.

Public prosecutions played an important role in the suppression of
political dissent. The Johnson administration prosecuted the pediatri-
cian Benjamin Spock, Yale chaplain William Sloane Coffin, and other
antiwar leaders for counseling opposition to the draft. Spock was pro-
scribed from advising the young men who had been raised on his child-
care book. The Nixon administration initiated the third great Chicago
conspiracy trial. In an eerie reenactment of the Haymarket affair, it
prosecuted eight leaders of the antiwar movement—some of whom had

never met—for conspiracy to riot. The indictment made antiwar activists responsible for the police violence that had erupted against protesters at the 1968 Democratic convention.[72]

Violence, which had receded during the cold war, reemerged as a weapon of political punishment during the war in Vietnam. Law enforcement officers killed a black student at Jackson State, South Carolina, in 1967 and four Kent State, Ohio, students three years later. Urban police departments used agents provocateurs against militant, northern black ghetto organizations. Chicago police, with FBI cooperation, raided Chicago Black Panther headquarters and killed two leaders of the party.[73]

Although political repression helped destroy the Panthers, it broadened opposition to the government and its war in Vietnam. Repression helped split the protest movement into a violent fringe on the one hand, enraged at and isolated from American life, and a vast, more amorphous, liberal opposition on the other. The Nixon administration's public statements stigmatized opponents of its Vietnam policies as members of the violent fringe. The administration's covert operations moved against the large, respectable antiwar movement as well. Nixon also tried to intimidate long-established American political institutions. He even antagonized the traditional centers of countersubversion, the FBI and the CIA, by trying to centralize their operations in the White House. The significance of Nixon's activities and the ultimate cause of his downfall lay in his systematic application to politics of techniques long accepted for use against alleged subversives. By his surveillance and intimidation of political opponents and the press, Nixon recreated the hostility to legitimate opposition that lay behind the Alien and Sedition Acts.[74]

Nixon's resignation was followed by the end of the Vietnam War and the political turmoil that surrounded it. The suppression of political opposition that climaxed under Nixon had, it was widely felt, endangered the constitutional fabric of the nation. Gerald Ford's attorney general, Edward Levi, promulgated rules limiting the FBI to law enforcement and bringing its actions under the law. FBI officials were convicted of authorizing illegal burglaries. Former CIA director Helms, indicted for perjury, pleaded nolo contendere to a lesser charge; he received a suspended sentence and a fine of two thousand dollars. The House and Senate Internal Security Committees were abolished, and Congress established an Intelligence Oversight Committee.[75]

Neither the national-security bureaucracy nor the rationale for countersubversion was subjected to fundamental challenge, however. The Supreme Court ruled in 1980 that former CIA agent Frank Snepp violated the terms of his employment by failing to clear his book manuscript with the agency. Snepp disclosed no classified information; the Court's decision implied that anyone who worked in the national-security bureaucracy permanently waived his First Amendment right to publish without prior restraint.[76]

Ronald Reagan extended the Snepp principle in his 1983 "Presidential Directive on Safeguarding National Security Information." Officials who handled sensitive, classified material, according to the executive order, would have to submit to lie detector tests and agree not to say or write anything on national-security matters, even after leaving the government, without first getting official clearance. That rule would allow an administration to censor critics who had once worked for the government and who differed with it on matters of defense, foreign policy, or internal dissent. These provisions were shelved after a public outcry, but officials are still being required, under another portion of the directive, to acknowledge in writing that they face legal penalties for unauthorized disclosures for the rest of their lives.[77]

The government has also acted to prevent aliens with dangerous opinions or associations from entering the United States. America has been protected from such figures as Isobel Allende, widow of the murdered president of Chile; George Woodcock, anarchist historian; and Farley Mowat, author of *Never Cry Wolf*. The Justice Department is prosecuting Sanctuary workers for criminal conspiracy to import illegal aliens, because the Sanctuary Movement is offering a refuge inside the United States to Central American victims of U.S.-sponsored state terrorism. And in *Regan* v. *Wald* (1984) Supreme Court Justice Rehnquist, ruling in the name of national security, gave the executive branch broad authority to curtail the rights of American citizens to travel abroad.[78]

The Reagan administration has also issued new FBI guidelines that, unlike the Levi rules, permit surveillance without evidence of crime. The new rules allow the infiltration of "violence-prone" groups that engage in the "advocacy of" criminal acts or have the "apparent intent" to commit crimes. Perhaps acting under these guidelines, perhaps disregarding them, the FBI spied in the early 1980s on such peaceful antiwar groups as the Physicians for Social Responsibility. The president also granted the CIA authority to conduct surveillance within the United States.[79]

The alleged menace of international terrorism provides the rationale for these executive actions. The Soviet state is accused of directing small bands of terrorists, mostly from the Third World, to commit acts of political violence. This theory of international terrorism not only permits the American government to sponsor its own acts of surveillance and state terror. By merging savages (from the first moment in American political demonology), revolutionaries (from the second), and Soviet agents (from the third), the theory of international terrorism also encapsulates and brings up to date the entire history of American counter-subversion.

CHAPTER III

The King's Two Bodies

Lincoln, Wilson, Nixon, and
Presidential Self-Sacrifice

I

"The king has in him two Bodies," wrote the Elizabethan jurist Edmund Plowden, "*viz*, a Body natural, and a Body politic. His Body natural . . . is a Body mortal, subject to all infirmities that come by Nature or Accident. But his Body politic is a Body that cannot be seen or handled . . . and this Body is utterly void of Infancy, and old Age, and other natural Defects and Imbecilities."[1] The doctrine of the king's two bodies pointed politics in two directions. On the one hand, it separated person from office and made the realm independent of the body mortal who governed it. The language of the king's two bodies identified a body politic subject not to royal prerogative but to rule of law. Having served this function, it disappeared from modern political discourse. From this perspective, such residues in our vocabulary as body politic and head of state seem merely vestigial in a modern legalism that clearly distinguishes occupant from office, subordinates person to law, and addresses the contractual relations of separate, single individuals.

On the other hand, the image of the king's two bodies could take the

An early version of "The King's Two Bodies" was presented as an illustrated lecture to the conference "The American Hero: Myth and Media" at the Institute of the American West, Sun Valley, Idaho, June 1977. On that and subsequent occasions, there were many helpful contributions. I am particularly indebted to Fawn Brodie, Francis Carney, Kim Chernin, J. David Greenstone, Charles Hersch, Greil Marcus, Nad Permaul, Robert Rydell, and Nancy Shinabargar.

chief executive in the opposite direction, not separating physical person from office but absorbing the realm into the officeholder's personal identity. Crowned, robed, and anointed, the king acquired a royal body (Fig. 3.1). Unlike other mortals, he had a "Body . . . utterly void of . . . natural Defects and Imbecilities." Far from gaining independence from its occupant, the office gave transcendent importance to the person. It placed him above the law. It transformed rational, independent citizens into limbs of a body politic, governed by their head. Since the king's body politic was immortal, the king who lost his crown lost his immortal body. From this perspective, the doctrine of the king's two bodies offers us a language in which confusions between person, power, office, and state become accessible. It alerts us to how certain chief executives found problematic their bodies mortal and the human families and dwelling places that housed them; how they sought transcendent authority and immortal identity in the White House, absorbing the body politic into themselves; how they committed massive violence against the political institutions of the fathers and the lives of the republic's sons; and how their own presidential death consummated or shattered their project.

The American Revolution freed the colonies from the king's royal body. Revolutionaries rejected the loyalist claim that the Crown was "chief head, and the *subjects . . . the members*" of the "body politic." "In America," said Tom Paine, "*the law is king.*"[2] America celebrated its bicentennial by overthrowing a president who, promising a "second American revolution," cast himself as king. "When the President does it," Richard Nixon explained, "that means that it is not illegal."[3]

"In absolute governments," Paine had written, "the king is law." Nixon had, like George III, "a monarchical view of his powers," commented Daniel Ellsberg. Archibald Cox heard in Nixon's words the echo of Louis XIV's "I am the state." Nixon had, Cox implied, laid claim to the king's royal body and merged his personal identity with the body politic.[4]

Richard Nixon, who knew his enemies called him king, did not turn to Louis XIV in self-justification. He quoted Abraham Lincoln instead, and quoted him with fair accuracy: "Actions which would otherwise be unconstitutional, could become lawful if undertaken for the purpose of preserving the Constitution and the nation."[5] Lincoln was looking back, like Nixon, on a war presidency. He had presided, as Nixon told journalist David Frost, over an unpopular war that had sown civil strife at home. He had personally and without congressional authorization conscripted an army; suppressed opposition newspapers; suspended the writ of habeas corpus and supervised the arrests, without due process of law, of thousands of opponents of the war; and, in what Charles Beard called "the most stupendous act of sequestration in the history of Anglo-Saxon jurisprudence," expropriated (his word was "emancipated") millions of dollars of private property.[6]

Lincoln, as Nixon also knew, was reviled as "dictator" and "despot" for these acts. He was, worse yet, a king without kingly stature. He was called, in language Nixon also heard applied to himself, "a huckster in politics," "the most dishonest politician that ever disgraced an office in America."[7]

Nixon had long been interested in Lincoln. He read *Abraham Lincoln: Theologian of American Anguish* in his own final, presidential days. As Nixon cloaked himself in Lincoln's mantle, as he appropriated Lincoln's suffering to dignify his own, he must also have sensed something else. Assassination, the act that punished Lincoln for his violations of law, raised him to historical greatness. Without punishment, no redemption. Nixon was in the habit, he told Frost, of visiting Lincoln's sitting room when he had important decisions to make. The night before his own, self-inflicted political assassination, he took Henry Kissinger into Lincoln's White House sitting room. In tears "we knelt down in front of that table where Lincoln had signed the Emancipation Proclamation. Where I used to pray. And then we got up." The next day President Ford, celebrating our "government of laws and not of men," once quoted and once paraphrased Lincoln. He offered Nixon's sacrifice to "bind up the internal wounds of Watergate." In the Nixon-Ford political theater, Nixon played not King Richard but Abraham Lincoln.[8]

Lincoln's sacrifice, in the American mythology we shall address in a moment, made him our political Christ, and it is appropriate that the doctrine of the king's two bodies derived from the two bodies of Christ. The king augmented his human body with a royal body; he aggrandized his mortal person with the immortal body politic. Christ's human body also joined his *corpus mysticum* in a dual unity, two bodies in one. King and Christ both shattered old forms of law. But Christ appeared at the transformational moment when existing law no longer expressed communal spirit. His kingship freed the community from ossified legalism and gave it new life. Christ's transfiguration served transcendent vision, not personal identity. The proof lay in his sacrifice. Crowned with thorns, Christ sacrificed his body mortal (Fig. 3.2) and gave birth to his mystical body, the regenerate community. The living king absorbed the realm into himself; the reborn Christ gave birth to the community and was taken back into it.

"All true Christians are of one body in Christ," John Winthrop told the Puritans on board the *Arabella*. "Love is the fruite of the new birth," said Winthrop. It forms "the ligamentes . . . which knitt these parts together."[9] Ford's call for "brotherly love" after Nixon's resignation faintly echoed this founding document of American community. For Abraham Lincoln and Woodrow Wilson, "Calvinist saviors who failed,"[10] and for the president who modeled himself after them, the stakes were higher. All three imagined themselves as founders, radically transforming the constitutional basis of the nation. The founding instrument for each of them was war. The White House, for all three, turned body mortal into body spiritual and conferred the power to create and destroy. Would they, in punishment for their lawless ambition, die the unsanctified tyrant's death? Would they be stripped of their royal bodies, or redemptively sacrificing their mortal lives, would they regenerate the body politic?

II

Lincoln characterized his presidency, Nixon reminded us, by the violations of law necessary to save the Union. But his speech to the Young Men's Lyceum at the outset of his political career warned against the tyrant who would violate the law and destroy the Union.

Our "fathers," said Lincoln of the men who made the Revolution, founded a "temple of liberty." The sons, mere "legal inheritors of these fundamental blessings," had to maintain it. The great man, however, "*denies* that it is glory enough to serve under any chief." He will not be satisfied "supporting and maintaining an edifice that has been erected by others"; for him the temple of liberty is a prison. "Towering genius disdains a beaten path. . . . It sees *no distinction* in adding story to story, upon the monuments of fame, erected to the memory of others. . . . It thirsts and burns for distinction; and, if possible, it will have it, whether at the expense of emancipating slaves, or enslaving free men."

The fathers fought for the liberating doctrines of the Declaration of Independence, said Lincoln; to protect the Union from "an Alexander, a Caesar, or a Napoleon," the sons must confine themselves within the constitution and the laws. "Let each man remember that to violate the law is to trample on the blood of his father. . . . Let reverence for the laws . . . become the political religion of the nation; and let [everyone] sacrifice unceasingly upon its altars."[11]

The Lyceum speech, Edmund Wilson first suggested, was Lincoln's warning against himself. The young Lincoln, wanting to keep slavery out of American politics, feared that a "Caesar" would bring down the fathers' "political edifice . . . at the expense of emancipating slaves." The threat of slave expansion, said Lincoln two decades later, showed that the sons had inherited from the fathers a "house divided." Blaming the South for introducing the slavery controversy into politics, Lincoln now appealed beyond constitutional legal machinery to the revolutionary Declaration of Independence. Its promise of equality, "temple of liberty" notwithstanding, had still to be redeemed.[12]

As antislavery opposed the tyranny of master over slave, so it freed sons from the political edifice of the revolutionary fathers. The arguments of "kings," Lincoln charged, enslaved men to labor for others forever. The principle of "equal privileges in the race of life" promised that "every man can make himself." The Declaration of Independence thus emancipated children from the houses of their human fathers. It also united the foreign and native-born. In a nation of immigrants, Lincoln explained, descent from actual fathers divided Americans. The Declaration of Independence, "father of all moral principle," united them. Antislavery principles, Lincoln claimed in the 1850s, prevented generational, ethnic, and class conflict. An American did not have to "pull down the house of another" to rise; he could "build one for himself." In the "House that Jack Built" Republican campaign broadside of 1860, "the rails that old Abe split" built the fence that enclosed the field through which passed the road on which traveled the team drawn by the boy who would fill the White House. Lincoln was "living witness," he told an Ohio regiment, that "any one of your children" may come "temporarily to occupy this big White House . . . as my father's child has."[13]

The house, like the body, is the dwelling place of the spirit. Lincoln seems to move from images of confinement and destruction to liberation and opportunity, arriving finally at the locus of the president's *corpus mysticum*, the temple of liberty, the White House. "They have him in his prison house," Lincoln said of the slave. "They have closed the heavy iron doors upon him . . . and now they have him, as it were, bolted in with a lock of a hundred keys." The hope of opening doors for the slave, however, shattered the house of the fathers and brought civil war. Lincoln imagined himself, in the Lyceum speech, as a "sacrifice" on the "altars" of "the temple of liberty." He replaced himself (in his Civil War words to a bereaved mother) with the "sacrifice upon the altars of freedom" of hundreds of thousands of America's "sons." "I dared," he said at the end of his life, "to dream this vision of the White House—I the humblest of the humble—born in a lowly pioneer's cabin in the woods of Kentucky. My dream came true, and where is its glory? Ashes and blood. I . . . have lived with aching heart through it all, and envied the dead their rest on the battle fields."[14]

Antislavery took Lincoln to the White House. No mere servant of personal ambition, his vision spoke to desires for liberation deeply embedded in the culture and in Lincoln himself. Lincoln embodied the wish to be free. But Lincoln's power, he seems to have felt, was a source of devastation. Restoring the freedom of the father's principles to the Union, he had covered the republic in ashes and blood. This voice of accusation imposes no judgment on Lincoln from the outside; it is the voice spoken by Lincoln himself. The president, not merely his critics, magnified his responsibility. As the nation approached and fought its civil war, Lincoln assumed the burden of its suffering.

American culture offered Lincoln two symbolisms with which to give meaning to his power, one classical, the other Christian. Since the Revolution, Americans had seen their fate prefigured in the decline of republics of antiquity; they, like Lincoln, feared the rise of a presidential "Caesar or Napoleon." John Wilkes Booth, repeating Brutus's "*Sic semper tyrannis*" as he shot the king, paired himself with Lincoln in classical tragedy. But Booth imposed no meaning on Lincoln's life and death that the president did not share. Caesar, Lincoln said, had been created to be murdered by Brutus, Brutus to murder Caesar.[15] The actor Booth played Richard III during the war, and the lines on the playbill—"Let them not live to taste this land's increase, That would with treason wound this fair land's peace"—pointed to Lincoln. As if twinned with Booth, Lincoln recited to White House gatherings Richard III's soliloquy when he was, the president explained, "plotting the destruction of his brothers to make room for himself." Unable to sleep, Lincoln took long walks at night against the advice of those concerned about his safety. On those walks he carried *Macbeth*. Returning from Richmond after the Confederate surrender, Lincoln recited Macbeth's speech ending,

> Duncan is in his grave;
> After life's fitful fever he sleeps well;
> Treason has done his worst: . . . nothing
> Can touch him further.

The president who envied the dead their rest on the battlefields quoted the tyrant who could "sleep no more" and who envied the sleep of the murdered king.[16]

Lincoln seems to have asked himself whether he, who sacrificed fathers' constitution and sons' lives to gain the White House, was any more than a classical tyrant. Booth killed Lincoln as a king justly laid to rest for his insatiable, murderous ambition. On that classical reading, the killing of the king restored law and punished transgression. But although Nixon may be remembered as King Richard, Lincoln is not. Classical drama consigned Lincoln to a life full of sound and fury, signifying nothing. But Lincoln could also draw upon a Christian interpretation of the war, which rescued the nation from so bleak a tragedy and gave redemptive meaning to its suffering.

"Neither party expected for the war the magnitude, or the duration, which it has already attained," Lincoln said in his Second Inaugural Address. "The Almighty has His own purposes. 'Woe unto the world because of offenses . . . but woe to that man by whom the offense cometh!' . . . If God wills that [this terrible war] continue, until all the wealth piled by the bondman's two hundred and fifty years of unrequited toil shall be sunk, and until every drop of blood drawn with the lash, shall be paid by another drawn with the sword, as was said three thousand years ago, so still it must be said, 'the judgments of the Lord, are true and righteous altogether.' "[17] Lincoln made the war God's judgment on America for the sin of slavery. Such a reading, however, did not free Lincoln from responsibility; it magnified it. He had become the instrument of God's vengeance.

"We are coming, Father Abraham," shouted the crowds greeting Lincoln at the dedication of the Gettysburg cemetery. They chanted the words of the Union recruiting song (sung to the tune of "The Battle Hymn of the Republic"), "We are coming, Father Abraham, 300,000 more . . . to lay us down for freedom's sake, our brother's bones beside." Secretary of War Edwin Stanton, after the assassination, called the Gettysburg Address the "voice of God speaking through the lips of . . . Father Abraham." This sanctimony should not obscure the meaning of the song, the chant, the name. Father Abraham was an Old Testament patriarch, "tramping out the vineyards where the grapes of wrath are stored." The chanting soldiers were willing Isaacs, offering themselves for sacrifice.[18]

God removed the biblical Isaac from the altar and substituted a ram. An Old Testament reading, moreover, as Dwight Anderson has pointed out, could not account for the death of Father Abraham himself. God's sacrifice of his son, Jesus, prefigured in the story of Abraham and Isaac, washed human sins white in the blood of the lamb and brought forth a new birth. "The fruite of the new birth" was the *corpus mysticum*, the regenerate community. Lincoln's first speech against slave expansion, in 1854, began to prepare such an understanding of civil war. Shifting from classical to Christian imagery, Lincoln warned, "Our republican robe is soiled, and trailed in the dust. Let us repurify it. Let us turn and wash it white, in the spirit, if not the blood, of the revolution." The Emancipation Proclamation—issued in "the year of our Lord one thousand and eight hundred and sixty-three, and of the independence of America the eighty-seventh"—fulfilled the revolutionary "spirit." Gettysburg offered the nation "a new birth of freedom."[19]

Sins are washed white in the blood, not the spirit, of the lamb, however, and Gettysburg was no mere spiritual purification. The "blood of the revolution," Lincoln claimed in the Lyceum speech, created a "living history" in every family—"in the form of a husband, a father, a son, or a brother . . . a history bearing the indubitable testimonies of its own authenticity, in the limbs mangled, in the scars of wounds received." As the revolutionary heroes disappeared, those "giant oaks," said Lincoln, must be replaced as "the pillars of the temple of liberty" by "other pillars, hewn from the solid quarry of sober reason."[20] This legal, passionless, bloodless political religion failed to reach into the hearts of men; it failed to hold the Union together. The sacrifice on the altars of the fathers for which Lincoln had called was the sacrifice of passion; the ritual over which he presided was blood sacrifice. The "ligamentes . . . which knitt together" were the "limbs mangled" at Gettysburg and the other battlefields of war.

Lincoln shifted in the last paragraph of the Second Inaugural from the God of wrath to the New Testament God of love. He urged "charity." He wanted to "bind up the nation's wounds." (He had told Stanton he would end the war on the "Christian principle of forgiveness on terms of repentance.") Assassinating "the forgiver," as Herman Melville called him, Booth completed Lincoln's Christian reading of the war. On Good Friday, 14 April 1865, the "parricides" (Melville) who killed Father Abraham transformed him into Christ. "It is no blasphemy against the son of God," asserted a Connecticut parson, "that we declare the fitness of the slaying of the second Father of our Republic on the anniversary of the day on which He was slain."[21]

The Lyceum speech ended with an appeal that until "the last

trump[et] shall awaken our WASHINGTON," Americans not "desecrate his resting place." Nonetheless, Lincoln's attack on slavery, Democrats charged, betrayed "our fathers who framed the government under which we live." Lincoln felt the force of that charge; denying it, he repeated it over and over again. He left Springfield for his Washington inauguration, he acknowledged, not merely as inheritor and maintainer of the edifice of the fathers but "with a task before me greater than that which rested upon Washington." That task, he explained at Independence Hall, was to preserve the fathers' Union while also reaffirming the fathers' moral commitment against slavery. Lincoln had to save the "mother land" without sacrificing the principle of the Declaration of Independence "that in due time the weights should be lifted from the shoulders of all men, and that *all* should have an equal chance." In the Lyceum speech the weight of the edifice lay on the sons as the price of Union; now Union and freedom must live or die together. Lincoln continued, "If this country cannot be saved without giving up that principle—I was about to say that I would rather be assassinated on this spot than to surrender it."[22]

That "wholly unprepared speech," as Dwight Anderson discovered, prefigured not only Lincoln's assassination but the meaning the nation would give it. Refusing to sacrifice Union or principle, he imagined sacrificing himself instead. Lincoln appeared in the 1860 cartoon *When Washington Was the Sole Standard* as one of four small combatants at the feet of parentally disapproving Washington and the Goddess of Liberty. The cartoon (Fig. 3.3) made the four contestants in the Presidential campaign into interchangeable, petty threats to the Union. *Lincoln's Apotheosis*, the carte de visite found in some version in nearly every American home album after the assassination,[23] shows Liberty's daughters carrying her son heavenward to his final "resting place" at Washington's bosom (Figs. 3.4 and 3.5). The open arms of Washington the father also form the cross that has crucified the son (Fig. 3.4). Lincoln did not achieve "distinction" by overthrowing Washington, as the Lyceum speech feared. The sacrificed son atoned for his transgressions. Caesar's laurel halo and Christ's crown of thorns merge together (Fig. 3.5) as the father of his country welcomes Lincoln into heaven.

The Federal Phoenix (1864), an anti-Lincoln cartoon, pictured Lincoln rising from the ashes of the Declaration and the Constitution. Far from being destroyed, however, the "home of freedom" rose, as Lincoln promised, "disenthralled, regenerated, enlarged, and perpetuated" from the "ashes and blood" of civil war. Lincoln presided over the birth of a nation. He was, in D. W. Griffith's words, "the savior, if not the real creator of the American Union." "The mystic chords of memory stretching from every battlefield," Lincoln's First Inaugural announced, "will yet swell the chorus of the Union." The prophecy alluded to the battlefields of revolution; it was fulfilled in the battlefields of civil war. Lincoln was the war's climactic casualty. His own "limbs mangled" at Ford's Theater "knitt . . . together" the *corpus mysticum*. His own bleeding body bound up the nation's wounds. Carried slowly by train on a twelve-day funeral procession through the North, Lincoln's body merged with the mystic body of the Union—the "great body of the republic," as Lincoln had called the American land, where "one generation passeth away, and another generation cometh, but the earth abideth forever." Alexander Stephens, Confederate vice president, said, "With Lincoln, the Union rose to the sublimity of religious mysticism."[24]

This reborn, mystically sanctified Union was not, however, the fathers' contractual association. Lincoln transformed the Union in order to save it. The heroine of *The Birth of a Nation*, Elsie Stoneman, "began to understand why the war, which had seemed to her a wicked, cruel, and senseless rebellion, was the one inevitable thing in our growth from a loose group of sovereign states to a united nation." For Woodrow Wilson, with whose words Griffith supported his film, Lincoln helped move America from a divided, self-interested contractual association to a unified, spiritual, organic state.[25] He located in the presidency unprecedented power over life and death and over due process of law.

Lincoln believed in his youth that there were "no miracles outside the law." But mere obedience to the law provided America with neither a unifying redemptive purpose nor a transcendent political hero. "The epic that Lincoln lived and directed and wrote" offered another pattern.[26] Rebirth required violent transgression, transgression called forth guilt, and guilt generated atonement. The great man, inspired by a vision of human freedom, shattered the political edifice of the fathers, personified the nation's guilt, and became its sacrifice. America rose from sanctified deaths to a new birth of freedom, the hero to political immortality. The obscure pioneer had risen from splitting the "giant oaks . . . under which his youth had been passed"[27] to his own stone temple and a place "greater than . . . [that of] Washington." What would Lincoln's model mean for Woodrow Wilson, the man Nixon called the greatest president of the twentieth century?

III

Richard Nixon said Woodrow Wilson was his "patron saint." He worked at Wilson's desk while he was vice president; once elected president, he had Lyndon Johnson's desk moved out of the oval office and Wilson's moved in.[28] Nixon prepared his presidential death at Lincoln's desk; he lived his presidential life at Wilson's.

Wilson was the greatest president of the twentieth century, Nixon told Garry Wills, because of his vision of America's world role. Over that vision, Dwight Anderson has shown, Lincoln cast his shadow. As Lincoln revived revolutionary principles by emancipating slaves during the Civil War, Wilson would lead "the attempt to emancipate the world" during World War I. As the revolutionary fathers founded a union of American states, Wilson would found an international League of Nations. "As we once served ourselves in the great day of our Declaration of Independence," said Wilson, we would now "serve mankind."[29]

Wilson first projected America into world leadership in 1901, in a speech defending the bloody suppression of the Philippine independence movement. Speaking on the 125th anniversary of the battle of Trenton, Wilson recalled the revolutionary "dreams of our youth" for the coming century of American "maturity." "The battle of Trenton was not more significant than the battle of Manila," Wilson insisted. America's emergence as a world power transformed "a confederacy" into "a nation" and constituted a "new revolution." "A new age is before us," Wilson wrote a friend, "in which, it would seem, we must lead the world."[30]

America suppressed the Philippine struggle for colonial independence in the name of its own revolution. This paradox was not lost on Wilson. "Liberty is the privilege of maturity, of self-control, of self-mastery," he explained. "Some peoples may have it, therefore, and other may not. . . . Training under the kings of England" prepared the American colonies for self-government; we would now do for the Filipinos what the kings of England had done for us; "they are children and we are men in these great matters of government and justice."[31]

American leadership meant presidential leadership. The vision of America's world role that Nixon owed to Wilson was a vision of presidential power. Presidential control over foreign policy was "absolute," wrote Wilson. The central importance of foreign policy would return the president to the preeminence from which congressional government had displaced him. Presidential power, moreover, would not be confined to foreign affairs. The Filipino "children" required leadership because they were not "knit together" into a "community of life." But America, too, was torn apart by class and ethnic conflict. "The masters of strikes and the masters of caucuses" placed petty, selfish interests over "civic duty." A president who rose to authority in world leadership would weld America into an "organic" nation at home.[32]

The revolution Wilson imagined in the name of the fathers, like the one Lincoln consummated, transformed the constitutional basis of the nation. The founders, wrote Wilson in *Constitutional Government*, created a "mechanical" government of checks and balances. But "governments are living things and operate as organic wholes. . . . No living thing can have its organs offset against each other as checks, and live." Wilson rejected the contractual legalism of the constitutional fathers. The Whigs, pointing to Andrew Jackson's violations of law, had labeled him King Andrew I. Jackson, refusing to enforce a Supreme Court decision, understood, in Wilson's words, that "the constitution of the United States is not a mere lawyer's document; it is a vehicle of life." As a living thing, the state required a single agent of direction. "Leadership and control must be lodged somewhere," wrote Wilson, and they are lodged in the president. The convention picks him out "from the body of the nation." Transforming a mechanical government of checks and balances into an organic unity, the president won the nation's applause, for "its instinct is for action, and it craves a single leader." Wilson imagined the president as the head of a living body politic. His chief executive did not bargain with other citizens and officeholders. Instead, he controlled the limbs of the presidential body, acquiring authority problematic in the unsanctified world of separate, self-interested individuals. Wilson was proposing a modern version of the doctrine of the king's two bodies.[33]

Wilson the political scientist made extravagant claims for presidential leadership over "children" abroad and citizens at home. These claims transformed the founders' constitutional "machine" into a body politic brought to life by its head. Wilson the presidential candidate seemed to sense the dangerous self-inflation such a doctrine implied. He was no "guardian," he said, treating Americans as "children" or "wards" and claiming to know what was best for them; rather, "we need some man who has not been associated with the governing classes to stand up and speak for us." Wilson was not, he insisted, a "political savior" from the "governing classes." He modeled himself instead on "a leader who understood and represented the thought of the whole people, . . . that tall gaunt figure rising in Illinois, . . . the immortal figure of the great Lincoln."[34]

Who but a "political savior" would imitate the "immortal . . . Lincoln"? Wilson's hubris seemed to worry him. Immediately after boasting that he had emancipated New Jersey from "slavery" to political bosses, he delivered a warning against great orators reminiscent of Lincoln's warning against himself in the Lyceum speech. "Don't you know," said Wilson, "that some man with eloquent tongue could put this whole country into a flame? Don't you know that this country from one end to the other believes that something is wrong? What an opportunity for some man without conscience to spring up and say: 'This is the way. Follow me'—and lead in the paths of destruction!"[35]

Like Lincoln, Wilson followed his warning with an appeal to "reason rather than passion"; he promised "not a bloody revolution . . . but a silent revolution." These echoes are reminders not of the reason and spirit that Lincoln and Wilson espoused but of the passion and bloodshed of war. Like Lincoln, Wilson sensed destructive danger deep within himself that was inseparable from his transforming public vision. "I am carrying a volcano about with me," he once wrote. How would Lincoln's example save such a man, soon to lead the country into war, from fulfilling his own prophecy of conflagration?[36]

In 1916 President Wilson dedicated a Lincoln memorial at the site of the log cabin where Lincoln was born. Much like Lincoln himself, Wilson celebrated not the log cabin home but Lincoln's ability to escape it. "Every door is open," Lincoln's life showed, "for the ruler to emerge when he will and claim his leadership in the free life."[37] This celebration of Lincoln's "race of life" quickly turned, however, into a mournful evocation of homelessness. "Lincoln was as much at home in the White House as he was here," said Wilson. "Do you share with me the feeling, I wonder, that he was permanently at home nowhere?" Disembodied from any particular place—"the question *where* he was, was of little importance"—Lincoln was not "a man," Wilson would "rather say," but "a spirit." The price he paid was loneliness. "That brooding spirit had no real familiars. I get the impression that it never spoke out in complete self-revelation, and that it could not reveal itself completely to anyone. It was a very lonely spirit that looked out from underneath those shaggy brows."[38]

Wilson had already written of the "extraordinary isolation" the American system imposed upon the president. His evocation of Lincoln brought person and office together. "There is a very holy and very terrible isolation," said Wilson, "for the conscience of every man who seeks to read the destiny in affairs for others as well as for himself, for a nation as well as for individuals." Loyal to no particular friend, place, or body, Lincoln became in his melancholy isolation the embodiment of the people as a whole. Loyal to no interested self, he did not sacrifice the nation to personal ambition.[39]

America was unique among nations, Wilson explained to a group of newly naturalized immigrants. In other nations one's loyalty was to "the place where you were born." In a nation of migrants and immigrants, loyalty must be to "the place where you go." Other nations were like families, partial to their own members. But even though the American may remember "with reverence his mother and his father," his "purpose is for the future." Americans melted their differentiating, familial loyalties into universal ideals. Wilson knew this from his own experience. Although "born and bred in the South," he paid tribute "with all my heart to the men who saved the union." Giving up his "home" for his "heart," Wilson embodied the American people.[40]

In his early, conservative language, Wilson had given leaders authority over "children" and "wards"; he had spoken of the slow, organic growth to maturity and quoted Edmund Burke.[41] As he approached and occupied the White House, the president's organic metaphors shifted. Instead of evoking tradition and familial authority, Wilson absorbed the people into his own mystic body, himself into the spiritual body of the nation. This merging of self into communal body reached its climax after World War I in Wilson's struggle to found a new world order. Speaking in defense of his League of Nations he explained, "When I speak the ideal purposes of history I know that I am speaking the voice of America, because I have saturated myself since I was a boy in the records of that spirit. . . . When I read my own heart . . . I feel confident it is a sample American heart." Wilson toasted George V of England speaking as the equal of kings: "You and I, sir—I temporarily—embody the spirit of two great nations." Like Lincoln's occupancy of the White House, Wilson's embodiment was temporary; "and whatever strength I have, and whatever authority, I possess only so long and so far as I express the spirit and purpose of the American people."[42]

There is, as Wilson had said of Lincoln, a "holy and terrible isolation" in the claim to read the destiny for others in oneself. Wilson needed, as he had told the immigrants in 1915, "to come and stand in the presence of a great body of my fellow-citizens . . . and drink, as it were, out of the common fountains with them." He told the Boston crowd greeting him on his first return from Europe how "very lonely [he has] been. . . . It warms my heart to see a great body of my fellow citizens again." Domestic opposition to the league threatened to isolate Wilson and call his motives into question. Traveling around the country to "drink . . . of the common fountains" with the people, Wilson insisted that the league "has nothing to do with my personal fortune— my personal ambition." He told the Pueblo, Colorado, audience how "very lonely" he would have felt in Paris if "I thought I was expounding my own ideas. . . . Don't you remember that we laid down fourteen points. . . . They were not my points." Wilson dissolved his identity into America, he implied, to counteract his "personal pride," which isolated him from "the body of my fellow citizens" and engendered a loneliness that only fusion with American crowds could cure.[43]

The leader was lonely, Wilson said of Lincoln, because he could not share his deepest feelings. Public communion provided reassurance that those feelings were admirable, not violent and self-aggrandizing. Should Wilson lose public support, his "terrible isolation" would expose him in all his fatal pride. He would fulfill his own prophecy of the man "with eloquent tongue, . . . without conscience" leading "in the paths of destruction."

"This strange child of the cabin," as Wilson depicted Lincoln, "kept company with invisible things, was born into no intimacy save that of its own . . . thoughts."[44] Counterposing "invisible" spirit to self-interest, place of birth, and physical "intimacy," Wilson echoed Plowden's "Body that cannot be seen or handled" and soared above the world. As if invoking "that tall, gaunt figure rising in Illinois," a cartoon response to Wilson's invasion of Mexico in 1914 pictured the spectral "professor" rising above the blood-red ink he spilt on the map of Mexico (Fig. 3.6).

The cartoon that criticized Wilson's imperial vision resembled the portrait of the president that hung in the library of the home to which Wilson retired from the White House (Fig. 3.7). Stanislav Rembski's painting made the president more spectral than spiritual. It superimposed Wilson on a map of Europe, and his long, skeletal fingers accentuate his ghostly presence. Wilson looks more like a specter haunting Europe than like its liberator.

Disembodied spirits, after all, have real consequences, and Wilson counted on it. He knew that Americans had selfish interests that set them against one another. Soon after he was inaugurated, he called on the people to repudiate these interests. "The days of sacrifice and cleansing are at hand," Wilson proclaimed on 4 July 1913 in a speech at Gettysburg commemorating the fiftieth anniversary of the battle. The national tasks there consecrated were yet to be completed, Wilson announced. He spoke not of American ends but of the means of war.

"War fitted us for action, and action never ceases. I have been chosen leader of the nation. . . . Whom do I command? The ghostly hosts who fought upon these battle fields long ago? . . . I have in mind another host. . . . That host is the people themselves. . . . The recruits are the little children crowding in. . . . Come let us be comrades and soldiers yet to serve our fellow men."[45] War was a metaphor in this call for domestic reform. "The dictate of patriotism to sacrifice yourself" spoke to the subordination of self-interest. But the New Freedom at home failed to overcome selfishness. It failed to make people "drunk with the spirit of self-sacrifice." Within a few years the "brothers and comrades" evoked at Gettysburg became "comrades and brothers" in war. The "little children crowding in" went as "recruits" to real deaths in France. Like Lincoln before him, the president in "command" of that "host" had to come to terms with his battlefield dead. "Again and again, my fellow citizens," Wilson told the crowd at Pueblo, "mothers who have lost their sons in France have come to me and, taking my hand, have not only shed tears upon it but they have added, 'God bless you, Mr. President!' Why, my fellow citizens, should they pray God to bless me? I ordered their sons overseas. I consented to their sons being put in the most difficult parts of the battle line, where death was certain. . . . Because they believe that their boys . . . saved the liberty of the world."[46]

"This sacrifice," Wilson said again and again, required the establishment of a new world order. The boys who died in France merged with "the children" they died to save. Children in their mothers' arms brought tears to Wilson's eyes, "because I feel my mission is to save them." Wilson woke at night, he said, to hear "the cry, the inarticulate cry of mothers all over the world." These were at once the mothers who had lost their sons and those whose sons would die unless the league was born.[47]

Invoking dead and unborn children in his last speeches, Wilson transcended the physical world. He did not "command," he had said at Gettysburg, "the ghostly hosts who fought upon those battle fields long ago." World War I gave Wilson command over his own spectral army, "those dear ghosts that still deploy upon the fields of France. . . . Coming across sea in spirit of crusaders," the American boys were disembodied before they died. "Possessed by something they could only call religious fervor," they were "fighting in dream."[48]

Wilson did not invent the image of ghostly crusaders in battle. He saw it in his favorite movie. Wilson's *History of the American People* had sympathetically described the "ghostly visitors" whose "invisible Empire" restored racial order to the South. The "silent visitations" of this "mysterious brotherhood" materialized on the screen in *The Birth of a Nation*. Donning white masks, robes, and black crosses, the Knights of Christ transfigured bodies natural into holy unanimity. Wilson's "crusaders" subliminally invoked the midnight rides of the Ku Klux Klan[49] (see Fig. 7.5).

Civil war did not, in Griffith's movie, bring forth the birth of the nation. Lincoln was the martyred hero of the first half of the movie. But assassination aborted, in Wilson's words, "Lincoln's idea of a spiritual as well as a physical restoration of the Union." America was reborn in the triumphant ride of the Ku Klux Klan against the threatening dark bodies of the black race. The movie's closing title, celebrating union, paid homage to this achievement of the Klan. Griffith quoted Daniel Webster's "immortal" words, as Wilson had called them, words that "almost create the thoughts they speak," words that "called a nation into being: 'Liberty and Union, now and forever, one and inseparable.'" *The Birth of a Nation* provided Griffith and Wilson a bridge from southern, parochial loyalties to nationalism and—by way of the Philippines and the war to end war—internationalism.[50]

The Birth of a Nation, called *The Klansman* when first released, should remind us of Wilson's violence, of his antipathy to Slavic immigrants and people of color, and of the attack on subversive and hyphenated Americans that climaxed his holy war. The "hyphen," said Wilson in his speeches for the league, was "the most un-American thing in the world." Symbol of the immigrant's loyalty to his home instead of the American heart, it "looked to us like a snake. . . . Any man who carries a hyphen about with him carries a dagger that he is ready to plunge into the vitals of the Republic."[51]

Birth should remind us, however, of Wilson's dream of peace as well as of his Red scare. Released in 1915 and seen by millions before Wilson took America into the war to end all wars, the movie's penultimate title asks, "Dare we dream of a golden day when bestial war shall rule no more? But instead—the gentle Prince in the hall of Brotherly love in the city of Peace." Following these words, the god of war on a raging beast fades into a white-robed Christ, hovering over paradise. "The American people," Wilson promised in the last words he spoke to them, "have accepted the truth of justice and of liberty and of peace. We have accepted that truth, and we are going to be led by it, and it is going to lead us, and through us the world, into pastures of quietness and peace such as the world never dreamed of before." Wilson then reboarded the train taking him through the West and collapsed of a stroke.[52]

Lincoln, "at home nowhere," entered the hearts of his countrymen on the funeral train carrying him through "the great body of the republic." Wilson, seeking renewed communion with the people on his own train journey, underwent a self-inflicted passion. Christ had failed to make his ideals practical, Wilson told the Versailles peace conference. "That is why I am proposing a practical scheme to carry out His aims." This imitation of Christ became an imitation of atonement. Brought to tears by children in their mother's arms, dreaming of the mothers' inarticulate cries, Wilson was not simply the savior of children; he identified himself with the children he had sacrificed. Finally to demonstrate he served not his own ambition but his "clients . . . the children," Wilson was willing to sacrifice himself. "If I felt that I personally stood in the way of the settlement," he promised, "I would be glad to die that it might be consummated." Doctors advised Wilson that the train journey endangered his health, but he insisted on continuing. "Even though in my condition it might mean the giving up of my life," he explained, "I would gladly make the sacrifice to save the treaty."[53]

In Wilson's earliest childhood memory, he stood at the gate of his father's house; he heard that Lincoln had been elected president and that there would be war. Wilson proudly remembered his father's Confederate loyalties. But Lincoln freed Wilson from his father's "home" and showed him the path to the American "heart." Now, in grand self-abnegation, Wilson reached the climax of his imitation of Lincoln. He and Lincoln seemed to fear that freeing the creative self from the house of the fathers mobilized tremendous destructive power; its objective correlative was war. "Salvation" for the "volcano" within him, Wilson had written his fiancée, lay "in being loved." But violence separated the war president from his country's love. Wilson feared that his aggression had threatened the republic and sent its sons to their graves; but violence became redemptive if it consumed the self as well. Rejoining weeping mothers and sons, Wilson would not challenge the father's place. Merging with the bleeding body of the nation, he would atone for the untold battlefield dead. Violence sanctified the new order when a leader of sufficient greatness sacrificed himself. If the living Wilson could not take America into "pastures of quietness and peace," he would lead there in death: "We desired to offer ourselves as a sacrifice to humanity. And that is what we shall do."[54]

Wilson had evoked American pastures before, in the campaign of 1912, as he envisioned Columbus coming on the New World. "The hemisphere lay waiting to be touched with life," he imagined. "Life cleansed of defilement . . . so as to be fit for the virgin purity of a new bride." Immigrants coming to our shores, Wilson continued, also dreamed of an "earthly paradise," a land where they would be "rid of kings" and of "all those bonds which had kept men depressed and helpless."[55]

Columbus's dream, the immigrant's, Lincoln's, suited an agrarian, individualistic America. In the complex, corporate, industrial age, Wilson continued, life was not so simple. "Freedom has become a somewhat different matter."

> I have long had an image in my mind of what constitutes liberty. Suppose that I were building a great piece of powerful machinery. . . . Liberty for the several parts would consist in the best possible assembling and adjustment of them all, would it not? If you want the piston of the engine to run with absolute freedom, give it absolutely perfect alignment and adjustment with the other parts of the machine, so that it is free, not because it is alone or isolated, but because it has been associated most skillfully and carefully with the other parts of the great structure.[56]

Government was not a dead machine, Wilson had said, and here he brought the machine to life. The pastoral promise at America's birth would be redeemed in technological utopia. The dynamo and the "virgin . . . bride" were one. Wilson's body politic absorbed lonely, competing individuals into an organicized machine. The president was not "alone or isolated" if he embodied the people; a piston was not alone or isolated if it was part of the engine. "The locomotive runs free," Wilson explained, only when adjusted "to the forces she must obey and cannot defy." The New Freedom was the freedom to rise with corporate, mechanical power.[57]

Now, near the end of his life, Wilson's "locomotive" failed to transport him into "pastures of quietness and peace." The son who had lost his mother, Wilson was not returned to the virgin bride. In contrast to Lincoln, he offered Nixon the model of failed sacrifice. Wilson's body royal died in 1919, unable to carry out the duties of office. But his human body lived on four more years, dreaming the people would turn to him again, "living witness," in Lincoln's phrase about the revolutionary fathers, to the failure of presidential self-sacrifice to give birth to the league and "emancipate the world."

Responding to a query about his health the month before he died, Wilson repeated the words of another aging ex-president: "John Quincy Adams is all right, but the home he lives in is dilapidated, and it looks as if he would soon have to move out." Driven from his "Body politic," the White House, the ex-president retained the "natural Defects and Imbecilities" of his "Body mortal." Wilson died in a replica of Lincoln's bed. His last words were, "I am a broken piece of machinery. When the machinery is broken—I am ready."[58]

IV

Young Richard Nixon's "earliest ambition" was to be a "railroad engineer." "At night I would lie in bed and hear the whistle of that train and think of all the places that it went." That "child" who "hears the train go by at night and dreams of faraway places," Nixon told the 1968 Republican convention, "tonight . . . stands before you—nominated for President of the United States. You can see why I believe so deeply in the American Dream. For most of us the American Revolution has been won, the American Dream has come true."[59]

"I was born in a house that my father built" is the first sentence of Nixon's memoirs. But for Nixon, as for Lincoln, the journey from home to White House signified our revolutionary "birthright." Son of a streetcar conductor and, like Lincoln, descendant of wanderers, Nixon lacked defining loyalties to a particular, local place. Like Wilson's ideal American, he was "at home nowhere." (It was appropriate, as Anthony Lukas has pointed out, that the major Watergate encounters that did not take place inside the White House occurred not in homes but in places of transit—motels, hotels, restaurants, and airport lounges.)[60]

The "spirit" that is at home nowhere, said Wilson of Lincoln, is "very lonely." It cannot "reveal itself completely to anyone." Vice President Nixon, in words echoing Wilson's, once remarked, "A major public figure is a lonely man—the President very much more so, of course. You can't enjoy the luxury of intimate personal friendships. You can't confide absolutely in anyone."[61] Nixon spoke, like Wilson, to more than the president's office; he spoke to his own character. But while Lincoln, losing his body mortal, shared his *corpus mysticum* with the nation; and while Wilson tried to rise above the body natural in spiritual apotheosis;

Nixon trapped himself inside his exposed human corpus and so was expelled from the king's royal body.

Like Wilson, Nixon saw foreign policy as the path to presidential greatness. "I have always thought this country could run itself domestically without a President," he said in 1971. "You need a President for foreign policy." Wilsonian internationalism generated a Red scare after World War I, and Nixon owed his political career to the post–World War II Red scare. "Today the issue is still slavery," he explained in a 1950 Lincoln's birthday speech; only now slavery posed a threat not just to America but to the entire free world. As late as 1969, Nixon defended America's role in Vietnam on the Wilsonian grounds of self-determination; we were guaranteeing, he explained, "the free choice of the South Vietnamese people themselves."[62]

But Nixon did not accept Wilson as his model uncritically. Wilson's "eloquent tongue" transformed unsharable, private secrets into public oratory. He demanded open covenants, openly arrived at. Wilson's desire for open diplomacy, Nixon told Garry Wills in 1968, was his one mistake. He did not understand the need for secrecy.[63] Thanks both to the exhaustion of convincing public purposes for the war in Vietnam and to his own personal character, Nixon did.

Lincoln made public the human injustice of slavery and the human devastation of war. Perhaps because the wish to be free still spoke to authentic possibilities in a society of small property holders, his rhetoric embedded the American dream in homely, lived reference. Lincoln retained a connection to the personal and the social body. Condemned by press and politicians, he greeted White House throngs daily; he claimed these "public opinion baths" connected him to the popular will.[64] Wilson, soaring above the industrial capitalist age, retained a transcendent vision. His vision embodied only spirit, however. It separated state from society, political language from personal and social life. Wilson took "communion" with the people, not low-church, full-immersion, baptismal "baths." As if to compensate for the thinness of his dream of freedom, Wilson universalized it to the world.

Vision, used and embodied by Lincoln, attenuated and failed for Wilson, was exploited and absent in Nixon. Nixon completed the separation between public rhetoric and personal and social reality. Sleepless after the Kent and Jackson State killings, Nixon was drawn first to the Lincoln sitting room and then to the Lincoln Memorial. Once at the memorial, however, he spoke to the students there of football. Nixon's aides planned, as Greil Marcus discovered, to build his second inaugural address around readings from Lincoln's. They had to abandon that plan when they read Lincoln's actual words. Lincoln's language had awakened the tangible senses—touch, sight, even taste and smell. Wilson retained only the voice. Nixon embodied "the great Silent Majority of my fellow Americans."[65]

Nixon represented the silent partly because he presided over a war requiring political silence. There was a chasm throughout the 1960s between America's stated goals and practice in Vietnam and the actual policies it pursued. By the time Nixon assumed office, the war could not be justified in public terms at all; it had to continue as a secret. Secretly bombing Laos and Cambodia while claiming he had a secret plan to end the war, Nixon planned to replace American troops with American technology and devastate Southeast Asia forever.

Secrets are vulnerable to exposure. Daniel Ellsberg's release of the Pentagon papers, like the discoveries of the Cambodian bombings and the secret war in Laos, revealed the actual policies hidden behind the facade. Exposure brought home the human realities of the war. It revealed, in Ellsberg's words, the "real men and women" who made up the "killing machine." It also revealed the real casualties of battle. Instead of fighting Lincoln's war of punishment and redemption to free slaves from their time on the cross, the country that took its identity from "the bleeding heart of Christ" was, in Norman Mailer's words, "killing Christ in Vietnam."[66]

To protect his foreign policy secrets from exposure, Nixon brought the war home. Defending "national security" against leaks, he accelerated the domestic spying and disruption begun by his predecessors. To win reelection while continuing an unpopular war, he initiated what Attorney General John Mitchell was to call "the White House horrors." The "second American revolution" Nixon promised in 1971 would emancipate the boy for whom "the American revolution has been won" from the need to justify his policies. As Assistant Attorney General (now Supreme Court Chief Justice) William Rehnquist argued, the president could claim executive privilege, or gather information by any means, in any area of his constitutional responsibility; he need explain his purpose to no one.[67] The president was constructing a hidden government within the executive branch. Nixon's revolution, reversing that of the Declaration, would end the need for authority to justify itself. Unlike Lincoln and Wilson, Nixon embarked on a founding in secret.

This secret founding radically differentiated politics and personality in the Nixon White House from its models. Larger purpose no longer sanctified executive expansion. Language provided Nixon with no mediation between private nightmare and legitimate public vision. The techniques of manufacturing celebrities that had propelled the southern Californian to the top, moreover, widened the chasm between presidential image and ordinary mortal capacities. Exposure of "real men and women" was not merely politically dangerous, it endangered the president personally as well. Nixon's body royal and his body mortal were fatally at odds. That division forces us to examine a private language that, unlike Wilson's, contains images of the natural body but, unlike Lincoln's, contains them in forcefully unsublimated forms.

Wilson relied on the transcendent power of rhetoric. Nixon ferreted out the private conversations of others and secretly recorded his own. Wilson orated his important words in public; Nixon spoke his in private and recorded them on the White House tapes. The conviction that the language of bodies public concealed the secrets of bodies natural placed electronic surveillance at the center of the Nixon presidency.

"We have," wrote Edmund Wilson, "accepted the epic that Lincoln directed and lived and wrote."[68] Lincoln, in this poetic overstatement, imposed the private meaning of his political life on America. As impeachment resolved itself into a battle for possession of the tapes, Nixon, in spite of himself, imposed his. Without the tapes, Nixon would have remained president. If the tapes cost him the presidency, however, they did so on his own terms. The model of Lincoln was much on Nixon's mind as he rose and fell. But there was a major difference between Lincoln's epic and Nixon's epic. While Lincoln found legitimate public form for his interior life, Nixon had to keep his interior secret from the prying eyes of the world. The president who could not "really let my hair down with anyone . . . not even with my family" was forced progressively, as he put it, to "undress" in front of everyone.[69] Recording and losing the White House tapes, Nixon visited his private hell on the nation.

It might be a tape recording, right? [says Norman Mailer's D. J., in *Why Are We in Vietnam?*]. Did you ever know the seat of electricity? It's the asshole. . . . I mean, just think of the good Lord, Amen, and all the while we're sleeping and talking and eating and walking and pissing and fucking . . . why there's that Lord, slipping right into us, making an *operation* in the bowels of Creation so there's a tiny little transistorized tape recorder . . . and it takes it all down, it makes all the mountainous files of the FBI look like paper cuttings in a cat shit box, and so there is the good Lord . . . there *He* is getting a total tape record of each last one of us . . . and now face your consequence, the Lord hears . . . the total of all of you, good and bad . . . and . . . one of his angels passes you on. To here or to there.[70]

The bug is seated in the anus, as D. J.'s mother's psychiatrist might explain, because it records shameful secrets. It collects one's contaminated inner body contents and exposes them to authority. Mailer borrowed his excremental vision of the last judgment from late medieval images; Flemish painters like Bosch and the van Eycks show the devil defecating sinners into hell (Fig. 3.8). "The whole world is possessed by Satan," said Martin Luther. "I am the ripe shard and the world is the gaping anus." The tape recorder is the modern, mechanical descendant of Satan's body.[71]

"What was Watergate?" Nixon asked in one recorded conversation. "A little bugging." The bugger—the word's two meanings are iconologically identical—invades one's private, physical space. Violating the most intimate, physical privacy, he inserts his device into office, home, symbolic body. The language of the White House tapes, over and over again, connected bugging and exposure to filthy inner body contents. Nixon and his official family concerned themselves obsessively with leaks, plumbers, dirty tricks, laundered money, with what Nixon called "espionage, sabotage, shit." Exposure meant, according to Nixon, "Sloan starts pissing on Magruder and then Magruder starts pissing on who, even Haldeman." "Once the toothpaste is out of the tube," in H. R. Haldeman's version, "it's hard to get it back in." Nixon called "the upper intellectual types . . . ass-holes, you know, the soft heads, soft." As the cover-up unraveled, everyone tried, as John Dean put it, to "cover his own ass." Fear meant inability to control the bowels: when Alexander Haig revealed to the White House staff a tape dangerous to Nixon, he could "hear the assholes tightening all over the room." Clark McGregor, remarked Dean Burch, "broke out into assholes and shit himself to death." In White House iconology, weak men—medium-grade assholes, D. J. called them—lost control of their bodies, exposed themselves, and invited invasion and domination.[72]

Bugging others gave the president power over their dirty secrets. In Nixon's view of the world, however, "Everybody bugs everybody else." If Nixon bugged Dean, then perhaps Dean had bugged him. Where on his body could Dean have carried a concealed recording device, the president wanted to know. If CREEP (Committee to Reelect the President) bugged Democratic National Headquarters, then "obviously I was concerned about whether the other side was . . . bugging us." The public discovery of the tapes brought the nightmare of exposure home to the White House and turned Nixon's weapon against himself. As if echoing Mailer's D. J. and Tex Hyde (best friends and doubles in *Why Are We in Vietnam?*), Arthur Burns said when he read the tapes, "Here is a Doctor Jekyll. A split personality. What does it all mean? Does Nixon lead a double life?"[73] Arthur Burns had discovered Satan's body. In so doing, he alluded to another body, the one the tapes were meant to protect. That was the king's royal body into which, to cover his nakedness, Nixon had crawled.

Nixon longed to replace "the Body natural . . . subject to all infirmities" with "the Body politic . . . utterly devoid of natural Defects and Imbecilities." The White House provided for the spirit a home to replace the human body.

"This house for example," Nixon told his staff the morning after he resigned, "I was comparing it to some of the great houses of the world that I have been in. This isn't the biggest house. . . . This isn't the finest house. . . . But this is the best house. It is the best house because it has something far more important than numbers of people who serve, far more important than numbers of rooms or how big it is, far more important than numbers of magnificent pieces of art. This house has a great heart."[74] Like Wilson, Nixon gave up his home for the White House heart. The heart was the heart of the king's royal body.

The taping system aimed to gain Nixon secure possession of the king's royal body. Secret Service electronics specialists embedded five microphones in Wilson's oval office desk. They bugged Lincoln's sitting room. Control over the tapes would make Nixon into Mailer's "Lord," passing judgment on others. He could leak their secrets and protect his own. He could transform his "Body mortal" into a "Body that cannot be seen or handled." In control of his own "record," to paraphrase William Safire, he would not be vulnerable to the judgment of history.[75]

"The Lord hears" your tape "and passes you on," said D. J., "unless you can put false material into the tape recorder. Think of that." "Why can't we make a new Dictabelt?" the president asked one of his lawyers, to replace one recorded months before. Backdated like the deed Ralph Newman, the Lincoln scholar, had affixed to Nixon's vice presidential papers to qualify them for a tax deduction, the "false material" would pass a manufactured history off as a human one.[76]

Nixon not only proposed creating new tapes to protect his royal body but also destroying old ones that exposed his mortality. Suspecting that John Ehrlichman knew about the tapes, Nixon told H. R. Haldeman to claim "we only taped the national security, uh, information . . . all other information is scrapped, never transcribed." Nixon taped "national security"; it could not be said "the President . . . taped somebody."[77]

"Some sinister force," in Alexander Haig's words, did destroy part of one tape; it probably destroyed several others. It did not destroy them all. Instead, Nixon himself listened to tapes for days, deleting the material that most directly involved him in bribing the Watergate burglars and planning and covering up other illegal White House activities. The censored tapes, incriminating enough, fed the demand for more. Nixon buried himself in the Lincoln sitting room to listen to tapes the week before he resigned. There he and his two lawyers, Fred Buzhardt and James St. Clair, heard together the 23 June tape that sealed Nixon's doom. The release of that tape, on which Nixon ordered the CIA to obstruct the FBI's investigation of the Watergate break-in, finally forced the president to resign. Woodrow Wilson had rhetorically elevated himself above the body and approached the gates of paradise. As human body and royal body disastrously converged, Nixon flew fitfully from one house to another, from the White House to San Clemente and Key Biscayne. He had, notwithstanding, trapped himself inside his own exposed body mortal.[78] Created to replace the president's body with the body of the presidency, the tapes exposed Satan's body and brought Nixon down.

Had Nixon early destroyed the tapes, he would have remained in office. But he would have acknowledged also the failure of his project. Retaining the tapes, Nixon retained the sources and symbols of his body royal; destroying them would have reduced him to mortality. As Nixon discovered, however, he could not retain his body politic without exposing his body mortal. Indeed, there was probably an impulse to disclosure at work. Nixon had made a political career from exposures. The microfilmed Pumpkin papers that the young congressman held before news cameras revealed Alger Hiss's secret Communist past. Hiss's discomfiture, wrote Nixon in *Six Crises*, showed the Communist conspiracy in action, "twisting and turning and squirming . . . evading and avoiding." Nixon had first exposed the secrets of those in authority. Then he saved his career by turning the weapon against himself. His own secret fund revealed in 1952, the vice presidential candidate "bared his soul" to a mass television public and proved he was "clean." Exposing some secrets, he seems to have thought twenty years later, would save him from having to reveal all.[79]

In imitation of the Lincoln about whom he read, Nixon capitalized on his "anguish." He knew that Lincoln's ordeal finally silenced the many who questioned his motives, and Nixon had long made the display of his suffering a sign of his virtue. The redemptive value of self-punishment was a powerful theme in Nixon's presidential models and in the Protestant tradition he shared with them. Who could blame a sufferer for the violence he visited on others? But success so linked to masochism easily slid into failure. Nixon's self-punishing impulse broke free from its role as the servant of ambition to attack the prurient man at the top—now not Hiss but Nixon himself.

Nixon "destroyed" Hiss, he wrote in *Six Crises.* "I imagined myself in his place, and wondered how he would feel when his family and friends learned the true story." Nixon knew that he was twinned with Hiss from the beginning of his career. At its end, on the tapes, he compared himself to Hiss over and over again. "We got the Pumpkin papers," the president reminisced to John Dean. "Nixon ran the Hiss case the right way," he wanted Dean to tell Senator Sam Ervin. "We really just got the facts and tore him to pieces." Nixon wanted Dean to admonish the Senate Watergate committee to follow his own example and, the implication was, do to Nixon what Nixon had done to Hiss. The president called down on himself the judgment he had passed on Hiss. In the drama he imagined and secretly recorded, the tapes would become his Pumpkin papers. Was the man drawn to filthy secrets in others driven in self-loathing to expose his own?[80]

Nixon collaborated in the exposure and destruction of the mortal hidden in the king's royal body. His persecution of his "enemies," he acknowledged to David Frost, provoked their retaliation. Recognizing his complicity in his own downfall, Nixon called himself "paranoiac."[81] This self-analysis must be taken further. The man who located bad motives outside the self had a stake not only in creating enemies but also in losing to them. Defeat confirmed the victim's vision of the sinister, omnipotent forces arrayed against him; it proved their malevolence and his own innocence. From one point of view, innocence protected against self-loathing; but the two merged, finally, in their validation by punishment.

Nixon blamed himself not for self-loathing after his fall but for a form of (self) love. "I'm not a very lovable man," he admitted to Frost.[82]

But his guilt, as he understood it, lay not in hating his body natural but in loving the members of his body politic. Nixon, unlike Lincoln and Wilson, reduced that body politic to the White House staff.

Wilson's New Freedom offered the liberty of a well-functioning engine; Nixon had compared his mind to a "machine"; it was safe to take it "out of gear once in a while" to "recharge," but it should never be shut off. Nixon had, Garry Wills wrote, conducted a search-and-destroy mission against his interior. He had constructed a mechanical false self-system to protect Satan's body from disclosure. Nixon retreated from family and personal interrelations into self. But this project, which required replacing the human self with the mechanical body of the state, contained a contradiction at its core. Generated by the danger of emotional ties, it bound the president to his royal body; it invested the love of the White House "heart" with overpowering significance. Nixon had not made "mistakes . . . of the head," he told Frost. His mind was not faulty in itself, but it had failed to "rule his heart." As Nixon dramatized his fall, his remaining libidinal attachments made him vulnerable, deserving of punishment and forgiveness.[83]

The tapes, Nixon explained, revealed "mistakes of the heart." They were like "love letters," Pat Nixon said, and should have been destroyed. Nixon had remarked years before, "I can't really let my hair down with anyone . . . not even with my own family." Nixon let his hair down with his official family. The tapes, said presidential lawyer Charles Alan Wright, "showed what the president of the United States is like when he has his hair down." Nixon retained the tapes, one psychoanalyst surmises, because for once, on them, he expressed what he really felt. They were, in the Nixons' imagery, love letters to the White House heart. The tapes were evidence of Nixon's love affair with the king's royal body.[84]

Nixon tried to "contain" Watergate politically, he told Frost. Because his "motive" was not "criminal," he broke no law. How could political motives be "mistakes of the heart"? The heart that has political motives, Nixon explained, was the heart too emotionally tied to members of the White House staff. Eisenhower only cared if you were "clean," complained Nixon, remembering the general's humiliation of him over the secret fund exposure. Eisenhower was "cruel" to fire his old friend Sherman Adams and to send Nixon to do it. He didn't care that Adams was, like Nixon's own aides, "innocent in his heart." "But I don't look at it that way," the president told John Mitchell. "We're going to protect our people."[85]

Nixon could not protect Haldeman and Ehrlichman. Flanked by a

bust of Lincoln and a picture of his own family,[86] he publicly accepted
their resignations. After that, he told Frost, "there wasn't a happy time
in the White House except in a personal sense." Nixon distinguished
happy moments with his family—"in the personal sense"—from White
House happiness. He had forced himself to be a "good butcher" and
fire his two closest aides. "I cut off one arm, and then cut off the other
arm."[87] These were the limbs of the king's royal body.

Nixon insisted on the fusion of his own person with the presidential
office. His lawyers claimed that executive privilege covered everyone
working in the White House because "members of his staff . . . are ex-
tensions of the Presidency." This usage of "members" turned members
as individuals into members as limbs of a body politic. Alternatively,
Nixon made the limbs of his body natural into symbols of spiritual
power. "If you cut the legs off the President America is going to lose,"
he warned.[88]

Of course it was self-serving for Nixon to confuse his own survival
with the survival of the presidency and to claim as "mistakes of the
heart" actions he took to keep his official family under control. Of
course he gained concrete financial rewards from charging improvements on his Key Biscayne and San Clemente houses to the White House
and from ordering the General Services Administration to "perform
housekeeping duties at the Nixons' private home."[89] Nevertheless, Nixon's language betrayed deep identity confusions. Because he was unable
to acknowledge his self-interested purposes, they gained, as Wilson's
had, overwhelming power. Boundaries between self and environment
broke down. On one hand, absorbing office into self, threats to the man
were "so damn—so damn dangerous to the Presidency." On the other,
radically separating man from office, Nixon sacrificed "personal" feelings to the presidency. Although "sometimes . . . I'd like to resign," he
told Henry Petersen in 1973, "you have got to maintain the Presidency
out of this." Two years later "he put the interests of America" before
"every instinct in my body" and resigned.[90] Hypocritical though these
claims of self-denial are, they faithfully reflect Nixon's failure to join
redemptively the instincts of his body mortal to his body politic. Consider in this light how Nixon experienced his presidential death.

Nixon had at the end, one White House aide observed, "the look of
a man who knew he was going to die." His meeting with his remaining
congressional supporters the night he resigned, said a participant, "was
a kind of death tableau." Death was surely on Nixon's mind the next
morning. "My mother was a saint," he told his staff. "And I think of

her, two boys dying of tuberculosis, nursing four others . . . and seeing each of them die, and when they died, it was like one of her own." Nixon had taped one of his living brothers. But once he was no longer, in Lincoln's description of Richard III, "plotting the destruction of his brothers to make room for himself," he seems to have recalled his dead brothers in identification.[91]

Thomas Nast's immensely popular cartoon published after Lincoln's assassination showed Columbia weeping at Lincoln's bier (Fig. 3.9). The image symbolized the mother's role in the transfiguration of Lincoln's body into the mystic body of the Union. Wilson, sensitive to the same image as he neared his end, evoked mothers who had lost their sons. Nixon's mother had mourned his dead brothers and even four strange boys, but there would be no pietà for him.[92]

The president turned from his mother and brothers to a quote he "found as I was reading, my last night in the White House." He recited to his staff Theodore Roosevelt's expression of grief for the death of his wife: "As a flower she grew and as a fair young flower she died. . . . When she had just become a mother, and when her life seemed to be just begun and when the years seemed so bright before her, then by a strange and terrible fate death came to her. And when my heart's dearest died, the light went from my life forever."[93] The death of Nixon's "heart's dearest" was the death of his royal body. The "great heart" of the White House no longer beat for him.

Nixon, like Wilson, flirted with natural death. Wilson, who replenished his presidential body from communion with the people, traveled by train through the West; Nixon, who sustained his royal body in the company of other rulers, traveled by plane through the world. He traveled with phlebitis in one leg; "the President has a death wish," his doctor warned.[94] But the man who feared cutting the legs off the presidency did not lose his own. He died as king, not as Christ.

Christ's death united his human body (now to be present in communion) with his *corpus mysticum*. The crowned king, unlike the crowned Christ, retained two, separate bodies. Coronation, as the portrait of Richard II (Fig. 3.1) shows, merely added the realm to the human body. Stripped of its robe and crown, the king's royal body died; left with his natural body, the deposed king was "nothing." Conrad's cartoon *The King is Dead* shows only an overturned royal hat. The King Richard whom Nixon played at the end was not Richard III but Richard II. Had Nixon, like Shakespeare's King Richard, gained royal stature as he lost his crown, he might have found the language to say:

> Therefore, no no, for I resign to thee.
> Now mark me how I will undo myself:
> I give this heavy weight from off my head,
> And this unwieldy sceptre from my hand,
> The pride of kingly sway from out my heart;
> With mine own tears I wash away my balm,
> With mine own tongue deny my sacred state,
> With mine own breath release all duteous rites:
> All pomp and majesty I do foreswear.

Stripped of his royal adornments, Richard II stared unbelievingly at his reflection in the mirror and asked,

> Was this the face
> That like the sun did make beholders wink?
> . . . .
> Thus play I in one person many people,
> And none contented: sometimes am I king;
> Then treason makes me wish myself a beggar, . . .
> Then am I king'd again; and by and by
> Think that I am unking'd, by Bolingbroke,
> And straight am nothing.[95]

"No one can know how it feels to resign the Presidency of the United States," Richard Nixon said. "I felt that resignation meant that I would be in a position of not having anything to live for." In the lines Conrad put under his cartoon of Nixon as Richard II (Fig. 3.10):

> O . . . that I could forget what I have been!
> Or not remember what I must be now.

Stripped of his royal body, King Richard (Fig. 3.1) was nothing.[96]

Nixon dressed the White House police in royal uniforms. He surrounded the White House with the trappings of royalty; Lincoln did not. Yet Lincoln assumed his own robe of office immediately after his election. He grew a beard. The wrath of the Calvinist avenger marked Lincoln's naked, cadaverous face (Fig. 3.11). Deep-set eyes, skeletal cheekbones, tight lips, and a jutting, aggressive chin compose a physiognomy of judgment. Commenting on the early, bearded portraits (Fig. 3.12), Charles Hamilton and Lloyd Ostendorf write, "The heavy beard softens the lines in his face, and makes him less gaunt. His eyes are lifted, giving the features a benign, almost saintly expression. He is now the man whom tens of thousands of Union soldiers will shortly know as 'Father Abraham!'" Saintly Father Abraham "will shortly" send many times "tens of thousands of Union soldiers" to their death; the beard is a mask hiding Jehovah's retribution.[97]

Early in 1863, after signing the Emancipation Proclamation, Lincoln began to clip his beard. In the pictures taken a few days before his death, the beard is hardly there at all (Fig. 3.13). As Hamilton and Ostendorf say, "The mask hiding Lincoln's intense emotions has fallen away and revealed a man at peace with himself."[98] We falsely remember Lincoln with full beard because he has absorbed its softness into the lines on his face. Taking the suffering of the Isaacs on himself, Father Abraham looks ready for his sacrifice.

Nixon could not strip off the robe of office or, to use his own metaphor, let his hair down. "It's something like wearing clothing—if you let down your hair, you feel too naked." Lincoln, his face marked by experience, seems in his last photos to accept responsibility peacefully for his tragically inevitable fate. Secluded in San Clemente as the end neared, Nixon read *Abraham Lincoln: Theologian of American Anguish*; it was too late to learn the part. Like a bad actor too preoccupied with his audience, Nixon imitated only the external signs of the character he had chosen to play. He could not play the role from within. That is why Nixon seemed self-consciously to manipulate his appearances before others and at the same time to be driven by irrational forces ("the heart") beyond his control.[99]

Lincoln may have dreamed of death, courted assassination, and provided the script to interpret its meaning; yet, because he embodied his passion, there seems nothing willful in his sacrifice. "I have impeached myself," Nixon told Frost. "I brought myself down. I gave 'em the sword. And they stuck it in, and they twisted it with relish."[100] Conrad shows Nixon busily nailing himself to the cross (Fig. 3.14).

Nixon's mother was a devout Quaker. At his father's Sunday school classes, young Richard learned about "the blood of the lamb." The children were directed to look for the political significance of Christ's sacrifice, Nixon's cousin, Jessamyn West, has recalled, in hopes "that the blood had not been shed in vain."[101] (Her words echo the Gettysburg Address echoing the New Testament.) Republican Congressman Edward Biester worried as Nixon's impeachment drew near. He feared that America was killing another king "to bring about a reunification and rebirth of the people." It was, Biester thought, a bloody, never-ending process. Pagan tribes sacrificed their kings, said Biester. But Christ was the last king to be killed, and his sacrifice signified that men could stop the cycle of killing kings and reenact it symbolically in the mass. Biester had a picture of Lincoln in his office. He hoped America would be guided by Lincoln's "forgiving humility" and spare Nixon.[102]

Biester associated Christ with Lincoln's forgiveness, kingship with human sacrifice. In the American political imagination, however, Lincoln's teaching is inseparable from his sacrifice. The Revolution's symbolic killing of the king did give birth to the new nation.[103] But America achieved "reunification and rebirth" in Lincoln's blood sacrifice. His sins washed white in the blood of the lamb, Lincoln rose to political immortality.

Biester finally supported impeachment. American presidents, he realized, were not kings, and impeachment showed they were not "above the law."[104] As Biester implied, Nixon's demise renewed American faith in a battered constitutional system. It did so because Nixon had placed himself above the law and cast himself as king in American revolutionary symbolism.

Yet Biester's original suspicion of the sacrifice of kings should give us pause. Lincoln achieved a martyr's death; Nixon fell as tyrant. Nixon's rise and fall parodied Lincoln's, to be sure, but the victim of black comedy also has his social function. Nixon imagined he was protecting America from knowledge of the means he and his predecessors required to prosecute foreign war and preserve order at home. The constitutional system, in turn, loaded its sins upon Nixon to isolate him from normal politics and restore confidence in a government of laws. Nixon sank under a burden the nation did not wish to share. Lincoln's sacrifice gained the country's love; he became its lamb of God. Nixon drew upon himself the country's hate; he was its scapegoat. The separation of man from office did not merely expose the body mortal; it reaffirmed the office as well.

Nevertheless, Saint Nixon, his halo a tape recorder spool in one of Conrad's cartoons (Fig. 3.15), achieved his own crucifixion and apotheosis. As the president entered the helicopter bearing him from the White House for the last time, he turned and raised his arms in the familiar V sign. Eisenhower had his arms raised high above his head when Nixon first saw him, and Nixon adopted the gesture as his own. This time, so it seemed, Nixon could not lift his limbs much above his body. Arms outstretched, propeller halo overhead, he looks crucified to the helicopter (cf. Figs. 3.2 and 3.16).[105]

Earlier, at the height of Nixon's power, Dwight Chapin saw the pope "clearly blessing" Nixon's helicopter as it lifted from Saint Peter's Square. Now the helicopter, symbol of the Vietnam War and of the mechanical new freedom Nixon had failed to attain, raised him above the White House (cf. Figs. 3.4 and 3.16). This "dynamo" was not a "virgin bride" reclaiming her sacrificed son. Transferred to *Air Force One* and alone in his private compartment, Nixon flew to his "pastures of quietness and peace," the estate he had renamed "Casa Pacifica" (House of Peace) in San Clemente. The House of Peace was no paradise for Nixon. He had called "pitiful" "those who have nothing to do . . . just lying around at Palm Beach." Now he was one of them. Others might envy a life in the sun. For Nixon it signified perpetual motion, no exit, and no place to go. It was hell. There were only "the very nice house," "golf," "nice parties . . . good clothes and shoes, et cetera, et cetera, et cetera. Or [said the boy who heard the train go by at night] travel if you want to."[106]

3.1. The king's two bodies: coronation portrait of Richard II

3.2. Christ's body: Matthias Grünewald, *Crucifixion*

3.3. *When Washington Was the Sole Standard*, Vanity Fair, 7 July 1860

3.4. Washington and Lincoln (*Apotheosis*), 1865

3.5. Washington and Lincoln (*Apotheosis*), 1865

3.6. Olaf Gülbransson, *Jetzt ist Amerika schön in der Tinte! Simplicissimus,*
11 May 1914

3.7. Stanislav Rembski, *Woodrow Wilson*

3.8. Satan's body: Hubert and Jan van Eyck, *Crucifixion and Last Judgment*

3.9. Thomas Nast, *Columbia Grieving at Lincoln's Bier, Harper's Weekly,* 29 April 1865

3.10. Conrad, Richard Nixon as Richard II

3.11. Abraham Lincoln, 26 August 1858

3.12. Abraham Lincoln, 24 February
1861

3.13. Abraham Lincoln, 10 April 1865

3.14. Conrad, Richard Nixon as Christ

"Blessed are those who have not heard, but still believe me!"

3.15. Conrad, *Blessed Are Those* . . .

3.16. Richard Nixon leaves the White House for the last time

CHAPTER IV

Nonpartisanship and the Group Interest

I

"Name the political scientist who has made the most important contributions to the discipline since World War II," members of the American Political Science Association were asked in 1962. David Truman was among the six men most often mentioned.[1] Truman's classic work of "group theory," *The Governmental Process*,[2] had legitimized both a politics of group conflict and a process-oriented approach to the political world. Obscured by the frenetic activity Truman presented, however, were the masses of largely inactive group constituents. How were these masses connected to the political process? How could one assert that the active minority represented the inactive majority? Truman's great achievement, without which his theory of democratic politics could hardly have had its impact, was to provide reassurance on those questions.

The original focus on organized groups had not been reassuring at all. Robert Michels, the first modern writer seriously to consider the internal life of private associations, concluded that leaders failed to represent members.[3] Large formal organizations, wrote Michels, were inevitably run by leaders insulated from rank-and-file control. Oligarchs not only ruled the organizations, they also developed interests of their own, which they sought to realize at the expense of membership interests. Leaders desired to maintain themselves in office. They formed friendships with other group leaders and with prestigious individuals in the wider society. Their desire to protect the organization led to activities divorced from membership goals. In short, for Michels leadership positions carried with them perceptions and interests opposed to those of the rank and file.

After Michels discovered his "iron law of oligarchy," writers attempted to disprove it. But their efforts largely missed the point. For Michels's assertion that group leaders monopolized power was not his most significant contribution. Here he was impressionistic, inconsistent, and often unpersuasive. Michels's major insight was not empirical but theoretical. He focused attention on possible conflicts of interest among leaders and members. His work ought to have made it difficult to assume that leaders' actions automatically represented members' interests. It ought to have led to studies of the role leadership interests play in the genesis and content of voluntary association policies.

But this was not the direction taken in *The Governmental Process*. Michels's insight opened a Pandora's box for democratic philosophy that Truman had no desire to face. He did not ask whether group leaders "represented" their constituencies. Perhaps the question seemed too theoretical and normative for empirical political science. Perhaps it would have provided a standard to judge the actual operations of the group process. Instead, Truman buried the problem of representation within a reified group, in which leader and member interests were made identical by definition. Truman located the interests of each group in its ruling elite.

Truman, I will argue, turned interest groups into what his theoretical forebear Arthur F. Bentley called "spooks."[4] He created "soul stuff" that distorted the real interest group and its operations. This accusation may seem perverse, since Truman, after all, is preeminently concerned with power and interests. A self-proclaimed realist, he is impatient with abstractions that disguise the presence of conflict. Consider, for example, his analysis of the public-interest spook. Many people, he writes,

> assume explicitly or implicitly that there is an interest of the nation as a whole, universally and invariably held and standing apart from and superior to those of the various groups included within it . . . such an assertion flies in the face of all that we know of the behavior of men in a complex society. . . . The differing experiences and perceptions of men not only encourage individuality but also . . . inevitably result in differing attitudes and conflicting group affiliations. "There are," says Bentley in his discussion of this error of the social whole, "always some parts of the nation to be found arrayed against other parts."[5]

But Truman himself falls victim to the error of the group whole. For the abstraction of the public he substitutes the abstraction of the interest group. Having refused to speak of a public interest, he speaks continuously of group interests. In the real world, however, groups do not "claim," "wish," or have "interests," as Truman's language suggests; only individuals do.[6] To paraphrase Bentley, the group itself is nothing other than the complex of individuals who compose it.[7] "When we personify the choosing capacity of a society [read group], we are putting a spook behind the scenes."[8] Truman understands that persons have interests and abstractions do not, but he treats groups as persons rather than as abstractions. He is thus a group fetishist; he treats the group spook as if it had real and concrete existence. This is less the epistemology of a realist than of a Realist.[9]

According to one definition of interest that Truman ignores, however, it might be legitimate to speak of group interests. For political thinkers of an earlier day, to say that the interest of x was y meant that y was good for x. By this token, an individual's interest was what benefited the individual, a group interest was what benefited the group—and the public interest was what benefited the nation. In rejecting a public interest, however, Truman joins other social scientists in discarding this definition of interest. What benefits an actor is, after all, inevitably subjective and value-laden; it may permit us to understand what an interest is in theory but leaves us with the enormous problem of determining what does in fact benefit the individual, group, or nation. Therefore, Truman defines interest as what someone wants, not what is to his benefit; interest becomes synonymous with desire. Thus the interests of a group are the attitudes "shared" among its members "toward what is needed or wanted in a given situation."[10] But if there is no public interest, because all citizens never want the same thing, surely all members of a group are equally unlikely to share a desire unanimously.

Truman knows that group members have conflicting points of view. Leaders of voluntary associations often present a picture of unanimously supported group decisions arrived at through mass participation.[11] But groups, as Truman sees them, are no freer from conflict than is the nation as a whole, and group decisions are not the outcome of mass democratic discussion. Truman does not assume internal group unity, as many group leaders do. The primary task of the group is to *achieve* unity. If a group is not cohesive, argues Truman, it cannot be effective.[12] But how can Truman speak so repeatedly of group cohesion and effectiveness without raising the very questions he himself would ask about concerted public action, namely, cohesion on whose terms and effectiveness for whose interests?

Here group leaders enter the picture, not to undermine the concept of group interest, as Michels argues, but to rescue it. The social affiliations of ordinary people, Truman asserts, provide them with special interests. But leaders develop from their leadership positions no social affiliations or special interests, only an interest in achieving "group" goals. In a complex modern society, Truman explains, "no individual is wholly absorbed in any group to which he belongs." Each individual is a member of many groups and has many interests. These overlapping group memberships constantly threaten the cohesiveness of a group and therefore its effectiveness. Having discussed various intraorganizational conflicts stemming from these overlapping memberships, Truman continues:

> It is at this point that the skills and strengths of the group leadership . . . become relevant and crucial. Leaders can scarcely control the multiple group memberships of the rank and file, but within limits they can isolate or minimize the effects. The maximization of cohesion in such circumstances, whether to perpetuate the tenure of leaders or to achieve group goals, is the continuing and primary task of leadership in the internal politics of interest groups.[13]

For Truman, group members bring different and conflicting interests to the group; conflicting interests do not arise out of organizational positions within the group. The organized group is subject to conflicting interests, but it does not create them. Like a billiard ball, Truman's reified group is hit from the outside but does not generate its own activity from the inside. There is no room for conflict generated from intragroup roles. Conflicts of interests occur only among members, as in a union whose members are Catholic and Protestant, Democratic and Republican. Leaders as leaders (and members as members) do not have interests.

Leaders may desire to maintain themselves in office. But this, Truman informs us, will help promote group cohesion, "the continuing and primary task of the leadership." Threats to the group come from internal conflicts of interest, not from the self-perpetuation of leaders. Conflicts of interest are dangerous because in threatening group cohesion they threaten group effectiveness. Leaders desire cohesion; they therefore have the function of reconciling various interests.[14] Thus, since leaders will normally want increased cohesion, Truman can in effect identify their goals with the goals of the group as a whole. In the real world, however, leader-created cohesiveness will not necessarily increase group effectiveness in achieving *members'* goals. Since Truman equates cohesiveness with effectiveness, he cannot consider this problem.[15]

"The problem of internal politics," concludes Truman, is to achieve "maximum cohesion." A "secondary" and "incidental" problem is the "matter of continuing the existing leadership of the group in the privileges that its status provides." This problem is secondary, we are assured, "not for moral reasons, but because the make-up of a particular leadership element depends primarily upon the group's situation and only secondarily upon the leaders' skills."[16]

The meaning of Truman's sentences is not immediately clear. One should not be misled into thinking that he presents the "matter of continuing the existing leadership of the group in the privileges that its status provides" as a threat to the membership. From the phrase quoted one might have expected a discussion of the stake existing leaders have in their privileges, and the consequences for membership interests. Instead, we are told that in the achievement of group goals the perpetuation of the existing leadership is of secondary importance. Not only can the existing leaders achieve group goals but other individuals in leadership statuses probably could as well. Far from worrying about existing leaders, Truman is reassuring us about potential ones.

Again the problem is "instability," and the solution is cohesion. "Leadership skills" can help promote cohesion, but in providing these skills no particular individuals are indispensable. If the only significance of particular leaders in organizations lies in their differential skills, no wonder that maintaining existing leaders in their positions is a secondary problem. For the conflict of leadership and membership statuses has been made into no problem at all.

By identifying leader with member interests, Truman has avoided inquiring into whether or not, under what circumstances, and by what standards group leaders "represent" their members. Without such an inquiry, empirical information about how much power leaders and members actually have is beside the point. The problem with the Truman volume is not that it attributes too much power to members, just as Michels's significance did not lie in attributing so little.

Truman has sidestepped the difficult problem of representation by allegedly restricting the use of the term "interest" to cases where all group members agree. The absence of unanimity is sufficient to refute the idea of a public interest, and its presence (under the heading of "shared attitudes") defines the group interest. But the goal of unanimity is a utopian one; more than that, Truman recognizes that there will indeed be conflicts of interest among group members. He is thus driven to the expedient of other theorists of unanimity, from Lenin to Samuel Gompers. He must take refuge in a leader assumed by definition to represent the group. The leader's interests (defined as desires) implicitly stand for what is in the interest of the members (interests now equated with benefits). By sleight of hand, Truman has located the interests of the group in its ruling elite.[17]

The major work of group theory ironically avoids the major problems organized groups present—conflicts of interest between leaders and members, the extent of democracy in a group-dominated society, and the possible genesis of group goals in special leadership preoccupations. Such monumental blindness suggests a hidden purpose. Again Truman's own discussion of the public interest points the way. How does Truman explain the use of "public interest" terminology, given its scientific absurdity? He writes, "There is a political significance in assertions of a totally inclusive interest within a nation. . . . Such claims are a tremendously useful promotional device by means of which a particularly extensive group or league of groups tries to reduce or eliminate opposing interests."[18]

Alleging a totally inclusive group interest clearly serves political functions for group leaders. It permits them to claim to represent members when in fact they may not.[19] The group-interest spook also performs an important function for Truman. In spite of his protestations, Truman does believe in a public interest—the survival of the American political system. He has come to believe that one must rely on leaders to protect that system and favors more centralized elite control to meet recurrent crises. Thus Truman's confidence in leaders is more than a matter of definition; it reflects personal, normative political choices.[20] These, however, are hidden in an allegedly scientific analysis. By burying the question of representation, Truman need not defend his preference for leaders against charges of elitism. Instead, he can assume that conflict among interest group leaders achieves the goals of the constituents of a constitutional society.

Reifying the group permits Truman implicitly to transpose the classical market model of individual competition among equals to the organizational-political sphere. Many writers have noted that concerted group activity is the only way in which individuals can achieve their political goals in a large and complex society. But it is possible that groups, although necessary to achieve the representation of individual interests, also frustrate that representation. Whether they do so, and to what extent, are empirical questions. They are among the most important empirical questions raised by the existence of groups. But to raise those questions is to permit doubts about the extent to which modern constitutional societies like the United States have solved the classical democratic problems of representation and power. One who can assume that groups represent their members is an essential step closer to asserting that the conflict between organized groups realizes the popular will.

II

Truman's normative evasion has serious empirical consequences. Clearly, it is difficult to understand the internal processes of voluntary associations if one ignores leader-member conflicts of interest. More important for our purposes, the group-interest spook distorts understanding of interest group demands and tactics. Having identified leaders' interests with group interests, one accepts as accurate leaders' statements about their goals and behavior. A theory of groups ought to examine the impact of organizational structures and leadership behavior on the constituency allegedly represented. Truman's group theory was an elaborate effort to avoid such questions. I want now, analyzing the political approach of the American Federation of Labor, to address them.

Large, craft-based international unions dominated the American Federation of Labor in the years before the New Deal. Within these internationals craft-union officialdom was preeminent.[21] Yet no study of AFL political tactics has taken off from these facts. Instead, AFL tactics[22] have been presumed to flow directly from the position of American workers,[23] an assumption that has distorted the substance of the strategies, the reasons for them, and the consequences for the working class.

Long before group theory became prominent, federation leaders and labor historians had described labor's political approach as "nonpartisan." That their description remains widely accepted, however, owes much to group theory.[24] Samuel Gompers's admonition that the AFL would "reward its friends and punish its enemies" has become the classic epigram of nonpartisan politics. Scholars view the approach of the pre–New Deal AFL as a prototype for the political methodology of interest groups in general. In the words of one historian, AFL leaders "proposed to attempt to keep labor's vote 'independent,' and thus induce the two parties and their candidates to vie with each other for 'labor's vote.'"[25] Another explains the general tactic at greater length:

> Nonpartisan political action turns largely on the use of pressure techniques and the lobby, and it rests on the possibility of exchanging labor votes for governmental behavior favorable to labor. . . .
> . . . To the extent that it aims to win support on issues significant to labor from all political parties—in practice from the two major parties—and not at causing the parties to divide over these issues, it may be accurately described as bipartisan. Up to the present, this has been the dominant pattern in organized Labor's political behavior. . . .
> . . . [Nonpartisanship] is, of course, also the characteristic mode of behavior of employer, business, farmer, and other more specialized interest groups.[26]

This picture of AFL political tactics bears little relation to reality. The description is probably no closer to the activities of other groups. Nonpartisanship served to disguise political strategies, not to describe them. Let us examine the nonpartisan ideology, the actual political approach it rationalized, and the interests it served.

□ □ □

National leaders of the American Federation of Labor never expressed enthusiasm for politics. As they saw it, previous attempts to organize workers had foundered on the rocks of political controversy. Politics diverted attention from and created disagreement about the immediate economic issues that most concerned workers. "When it is so difficult," said Henry White at the 1903 AFL convention, "to get the working men to agree upon the simple everyday issues, how can you expect to get them to agree upon the complex propositions that political action implies."[27]

But labor's stated coolness toward politics manifested itself in very different ways. In the forty years following its birth in 1886, the AFL adopted three distinct political strategies, all covered by the nonpartisan label. For the first twenty years of its existence, the federation combined an antagonism for party politics with a long and socialist-sounding set of political demands (including compulsory education; an eight-hour day for government employees; municipal ownership of streetcars, waterworks, and gas and electric plants; and nationalization of the telegraph, telephone, railroads, and mines).[28] Federation spokesmen emphasized the corruption of bourgeois politics and stressed the antagonism of the bourgeois state to the interests of workers. Although this attitude was suspicious of bourgeois party politics, it was not inherently antipolitical. In its earliest years the federation had greeted independent political action on a local level "with pleasure."[29] But as these local attempts met with universal failure, the federation became discouraged. AFL leaders still held out union political power as an ultimate goal but did not want to jeopardize the young and growing unions by premature political experiments. Gompers explained, "Before we can hope as a general organization to take the field by nominating candidates for office, the workers must be more thoroughly organized and better results achieved by experiments locally."[30]

For the present, however, the federation would not involve itself in reform politics, which had decimated unions in the past. In practice the AFL ignored its own political demands. Gompers refused to endorse Bryan in 1896, explaining that there was a difference between political action in the interests of labor (which he was for) and party political action.[31] In 1900 Gompers asked AFL treasurer John B. Lennon not to stump for Bryan; again the federation based its refusal to endorse a presidential candidate on nonpartisan principles.[32]

By 1906, however, it was clear that this antipolitical stance was hampering union growth and activity. Employer hostility to unions had increased, and cooperative judges were using the labor injunction promiscuously. Judge-made law challenged labor's traditional economic weapons—the strike, the boycott, and the picket line. For violating injunctions union officials were fined and imprisoned. Moreover, with the formation of the Industrial Workers of the World (IWW) in 1905, there was increased competition from left-wing groups. Politics could no longer be relegated to the future, attacked, or ignored. If political activity introduced divisions into trade unions, these would have to be faced.[33]

In the period before 1906, AFL leaders had accepted the party preferences of workers as givens and therefore sought to steer clear of issues that would divide workers along partisan lines. Now the goal must be to emancipate workers from political party allegiances, so that they could exert their united strength at the polls: "The American Federation of Labor has often declared and often emphasized that, as our efforts are centered against all forms of industrial slavery and economic wrong, we must also direct our utmost energies to remove all forms of political servitude and party slavery, to the end that the working people may act as a unit at the polls of every election."[34]

The meaning of nonpartisanship changed drastically. Before 1906 no

one spoke of rewarding friends and punishing enemies. The only political activity countenanced by nonpartisanship was an occasional "local
experiment" in independent political action. According to Gompers,
support for partisan political candidates violated nonpartisan principles. Now nonpartisanship was revised to include, even to insist upon,
rewarding friends and punishing enemies within the major parties. As
Gompers explained, "If an endorsement of our contention by a political
party is to compel us to abandon these contentions, then it needs but
such endorsement of our very existence to compel us to disband. . . .
Partisanship is exhibited by adherence to a party which refuses its endorsement, and nonpartisanship consists in continued work for our
principles regardless of what any political party may do."[35]

One should not conclude, however, that the AFL's nonpartisan principles required it to shuttle between the major parties. From our knowledge of the strength of traditional party loyalties, the low issue-
consciousness of American voters, and the relatively minimal electoral
impact of pressure groups, we should be suspicious of any organization
that claims to propel voters between the major parties on the basis of
the issues. Moreover, the federation and its affiliates engaged in virtually
no grass-roots political activity. Between 1906 and 1922 the AFL simply allied itself with the national Democratic party. The *Federationist*
and most leaders of the AFL endorsed the Democratic presidential candidate every four years and supported most northern Democratic congressional candidates.[36]

After 1914, although the AFL–Democratic party alliance continued,
the AFL attitude toward politics shifted once again. The organization
had entered politics not in the service of broad social reforms but to
emancipate itself from the labor injunctions and the antitrust laws; with
the passage of the Clayton Act, labor leaders mistakenly believed this
goal had been accomplished. Progressives in the unions had seized on
increased labor political interest to push for unemployment insurance,
wage and hour laws, and other social legislation. But Gompers and
other federation leaders, wanting unions to be the only source of welfare
benefits, opposed such laws.[37]

Federation leaders therefore returned to the antipolitical attitudes of
the turn of the century. There was, however, a significant difference between the two periods. Union antipathy for politics was no longer characterized in radical, syndicalist terms. Politics was a corrupt and coercive arena, not because it was controlled by business but because of its
inherent nature. For many years federation leaders, parroting social

Darwinist doctrine, argued that all politics was coercive. The economic sphere, dominated by voluntary associations, permitted free, uncoerced activity. By the 1920s labor-management cooperation became the alternative to working-class political action. In his autobiography Gompers wrote, "I have often allowed myself to dream of the possibilities of production if all were to work unretarded by the existing restraints. . . . Foremost in my mind is to tell the politicians to keep their hands off and thus to preserve voluntary institutions and opportunity . . . to deal with problems as the experience and facts of industry shall indicate."[38]

World War I hastened the incorporation of the AFL into business-dominated America. The war inspired federation leaders to heights of patriotic nationalism. In addition, it brought them into friendly contact with businessmen serving in Washington. As a result many trade-union officials overcame their suspicions of business and saw little need for politically engendered conflict. They looked forward to a postwar period in which all problems would be worked out in a spirit of patriotic cooperation, as they had been during the war.

Nevertheless, federation leaders were temporarily and reluctantly drawn into reform politics after World War I. Hundreds of thousands of workers, organized because of government muscle behind war-born "cooperation" (and soon to become unorganized when that muscle was taken away) were receptive to political action. The flurry of postwar radicalism and the open-shop campaign that followed further pressured AFL officials. In 1920 the federation convention adopted a resolution favoring government ownership of the railroads, over the opposition of Gompers and the old guard. Four years later progressive pressure and major-party rebuffs forced the AFL to endorse La Follette for president,[39] although in fact the federation did little for La Follette beyond the formal endorsement.

After the 1924 presidential campaign, national political activity played an insignificant role in AFL operations. Although the AFL lost members and strength during the 1920s, its antipolitical attitude lasted well into the Great Depression.

□ □ □

Throughout the history of the American Federation of Labor, its leaders justified almost every conceivable political tactic with the nonpartisan label. Nonpartisanship justified refusal to endorse major-party candidates; it required their endorsement. Nonpartisanship was an alternative to third-party political action; it permitted the endorsement of a third-party candidate. It justified labor's flight from politics but held out the hope of ultimate labor political power. It required the AFL to shuttle between the major parties but obscured a national alliance with one of those parties. Nevertheless, one consistency does appear to underlie this welter of inconsistencies: nonpartisanship permitted a great variety of political tactics. That was perhaps a virtue. It always explicitly excluded any permeation of union affairs by politics and any close and continuing tie to a single political party machine. But for the first forty years of its existence, local union alliances with political machines dominated the affairs of the urban craft unions.

Labor historians and group theorists alike are fond of pointing out the disadvantages that attach to labor's exclusive dependence on a single political party. The AFL survived, it is often said, because it knew how to resist the lure of politics.[40] However, in local politics, the most important political arena for the craft unions that dominated the AFL, nothing could be further from the truth.

Whatever the abstract virtues of labor's coolness toward politics, there were concrete reasons that thrust local craft unions into political alliances. First, these unions needed favorable legislation—safety and sanitation laws, licensing and apprenticeship statutes, building and other codes. Proper enforcement of these laws was essential to protect union interests; labor must have friendly appointments to building inspectors' jobs, for example. City contracts—an immense source of jobs—must be awarded to union labor; the police must be friendly or at least neutral during strikes; and the local administration could perform a variety of other political favors for the unions. There were also the leaders to consider; business agents and local officers wanted patronage plums and often their share of political graft.[41]

The common theme was jobs—for members and leaders. National and reform politics did not help craft unions supply and protect jobs. Local politics did.[42]

Given labor's need for local political involvement, AFL unions could not be nonpartisan. Most large cities were under the control of the political machine of a single party. In city after city, unions obtained political access through a close and continuing friendship with the political machine of the dominant party. Despite nonpartisan principles, local Gompers supporters made no attempt to "remove all forms of political servitude and party slavery," to steer clear of partisan entanglements, or to choose between the parties on specific issues.

In New York, for example, craft-union officialdom maintained a continuing alliance with Tammany Hall. Every power in the New York building trades in the first three decades of the twentieth century had Tammany backing; many held Tammany offices.[43] Tammany provided many services for craft-union officials. While John Hylan was mayor, political influence was exerted so that public works would be built of natural stone instead of terra-cotta.[44] This move protected the Stone Cutters Union, whose international president, James Duncan, was one of the staunchest verbal opponents of labor political involvement.[45]

Tammany also aided New York officials in crushing rank-and-file revolts. These sometimes occurred in New York and other cities because unionists tied to urban machines had sacrificed bread-and-butter union goals for their personal aggrandizement. Some revolts also had a political thrust. Machine-union ties thwarted worker involvement in national and local political reform movements.

In the folklore of labor history, unions opposed labor parties in order to steer clear of political involvements. Often the close ties between local leaders and political bosses provided more persuasive reasons. The central labor bodies of Brooklyn and Manhattan, under the influence of Jewish socialist and other progressive trade unionists, endorsed a local labor party following World War I; Gompers and Tammany Hall quickly intervened. State AFL leaders with Tammany connections packed one meeting of the Manhattan body with ostentatiously armed "delegates." These men physically prevented a walkout by the regular representatives and voted to support Gompers's "nonpartisan" policies. After the central bodies were reorganized, Gompers personally taking a hand, many union officials who had opposed the labor party received Tammany appointments.[46]

Four years later Tammany became anxious to promote the Al Smith presidential boom. A New York city statute, long ignored, required that day laborers for the city be paid the prevailing wage. Now the law was generally enforced. "The only exceptions were in those trades whose loyalty to Tammany had not been the order of the day."[47] After the Democratic party refused to nominate Smith, powerful craft unions like the Carpenters, with local political ties, bitterly fought the AFL endorsement of La Follette. Although the federation did endorse the Wisconsin senator, the national office of the AFL immediately began hearing from local officials who saw their carefully constructed arrangements with urban machines endangered. As a result of this local pressure, the AFL gave little to La Follette beyond the formal endorsement. In New York the Central Trades and Labor Council urged the election of the Democratic party nominee, John W. Davis.[48]

Gompers's nonpartisan policies received their most important New York support from local craft-union officials integrated into the political machine. Craft-union connections with the dominant Republican machines in Wayne County (Detroit) and Philadelphia paralleled the ties with Tammany in New York. In Chicago and San Francisco, labor-machine connections were also intimate.[49]

Union alliances with political machines violated nonpartisan principles, and their existence was not publicized. Instead, nonpartisanship disguised and protected the alliances. First, the main enemies of the machine unionists were socialists and progressives friendly to independent labor political action. Support for labor parties could always be attacked on nonpartisan grounds. Second, nonpartisan principles prevented an explicit national alliance with one of the major parties; such an alliance might harm local political arrangements. Nonpartisanship permitted local unions to be Democratic in Democratic cities and Republican in Republican cities. Third, nonpartisanship promoted emphasis on narrow issues of immediate significance to union organizations; it allowed labor endorsement of machine politicians indifferent or opposed to broader working-class demands.[50] Most of the unionists opposed to a labor alliance with machine politicians were not supporters of Gompers's nonpartisan policies. Unlike Gompers, they supported progressive social legislation and were sympathetic to various local labor-party ventures.[51] In theory the nonpartisan attack on general programs of political reform permitted unions to steer clear of politics; in practice it protected their local political ties.

Others besides machine-oriented trade unionists supported nonpartisanship for antiradical rather than antipolitical reasons. Urban craft-union officials were largely Irish Catholics. During the first decades of the twentieth century, the church took an increasing interest in labor affairs. Although many priests favored social legislation, all were anxious to halt the spread of socialism among organized workers. Catholics utilized nonpartisan rhetoric, not because they were antipolitical but rather because they sought to undermine the political emphasis of the socialists.[52] Like the craft-union politicians, Catholics found nonpartisanship a convenient ideological mask for their activities.

Finally, nonpartisanship de-emphasized national politics and political reforms. It thus protected the trade union against such potential competitors for working-class loyalty as the state, the labor political-action committee, and the political party. Opposing unemployment insurance, one powerful craft-union official explained, "If you feed lions cooked meat, they are not going to roar. . . . The only way to get wage-earners interested in the trade union movement and make it a driving force is to convince them that . . . it is only through the strength, the fighting strength of that economic organization that you are going to get higher wages and shorter hours."[53]

III

Nonpartisanship did not describe the actual political tactics of the American Federation of Labor. It obscured some and contradicted others; that was its function. Nonpartisanship provided an unanalyzed abstraction around which a number of union factions with their own political interests could unite. It promoted the cohesion of the AFL.

Cohesion is a word we have encountered before; it is the centerpiece of Truman's analysis of the internal process in groups. Moreover, in stressing the lack of concrete content in nonpartisanship, we have argued that the ideology restricted the AFL to no specific political strategy. Truman also stresses the need for flexibility in the choice of effective political tactics. Nonpartisanship was meant to be a pragmatic weapon, not a consistent theory; perhaps the variety of tactics it could sanction simply indicated its viability.

To function as a unifying ideology, however, nonpartisanship had to disguise actual federation policies, deny that these were generated by special leadership interests, and insist that they benefited all members equally. Truman, anxious to bolster the myth of neutral leaders, has treated nonpartisanship at face value,[54] as if no organization intervened between working-class experience and nonpartisanship politics. There is limited validity to this. Nonpartisanship did grow out of the experience of craft workers as well as union officials. It reflected craft-worker concern for immediate wages, hours, and working conditions and the failure of the broadly based, reform-oriented Knights of Labor. Certainly, the broad attitudes of American workers and the structures of a business-dominated society limited the alternatives open to the AFL. The development of a powerful, independent labor party was extremely unlikely.[55] But to argue that the multitude of specific decisions made in the name of nonpartisanship in the first forty years of the federation's existence were equally inevitable—that the leaders had no choices if

they were to preserve their unions—is to subscribe to a remarkable degree of historical determinism. Certainly there were limits beyond which
union leaders could not consistently go without provoking serious rank-
and-file dissension. But from what we know of the internal structure of
the international unions and the political awareness and sophistication
of the mass of the population, the bounds within which leaders could
act freely were very wide.[56] Moreover, except perhaps for the time of
original organization, unions did not utilize participatory structures
that could form and activate mass consciousness of interests.[57]

Leadership independence, then, was a fact in the AFL. What did it
mean for the representation of members' interests? Most social scientists
argue that legitimate functions attach to leadership. Leaders are better
informed than members. They can better see long-term consequences;
they are more skilled in organizational tactics. Leaders are better able
to achieve members' demands, it is argued, than members themselves.

This justification of leadership may be a good starting point, but its
implications are not always understood. If leaders are permitted to act
independently of the specific desires of members, then how is one to
judge leadership actions? No longer are the members' desires alone sufficient. The ultimate or long-range desires of the members remain crucial. But in the vast intermediate range in which most political decisions
are made, the members (this line of argument implies) are not the best
judges of their own interests. The interests of the members are implicitly
no longer equated with their desires, but rather with what is to their
benefit.

Given their special interests and the extent of their power, however,
group leaders are not the only legitimate judges of what policies will
benefit the membership. Truman equates leadership desires with membership benefits, having denied the appropriateness of an inquiry into
benefits in the first place. This approach is both internally inconsistent
and unreasonable. If the actions of groups leaders are to be judged by
whether they benefit the group constituency, then the outside observer
as well as the group leader must investigate that question.[58]

This conclusion can lead to a thicket of normative disagreements
about what was best for American workers in the pre–New Deal period.
But while the question of representation forces us to acknowledge value
disagreements, it also requires us to examine the organizational sources
and constituency consequences of group policies. These matters are at
least in principle empirical, and my interpretation of nonpartisanship
focuses on them.[59]

Nonpartisanship met many leadership interests—desire to maintain friendly relations with local political machines, fear of competitors for working-class loyalty, anxiety to discredit socialist unionists, among others. These interests derived from intraorganizational and wider social concerns. First, union leaders became committed to their organizations and to their own tenure in office, often divorcing these commitments from the original, substantive union goals. Since their prestige, power, and personal identities depended on the stability of their organizations, craft-union officials exaggerated the dangers from dual unionism, internal factionalism, and other competitors for working-class loyalty. They tended to be cautious in adopting new tactics, preferring to safeguard gains rather than to risk them.

Second, the more established their organizations and the longer they remained in office, the friendlier the AFL officials became toward business leaders and others powerful in the outer world. They developed continuing relations with these men, which often turned to admiration. They often used their organizational positions to obtain wealth and status outside the labor movement. Many writers now praise this process of bourgeoisification, arguing that it creates moderate leaders more willing to compromise.[60] Yet the bourgeoisified AFL leadership of the 1920s was more extreme in its antipathy to politics, its suppression of internal disagreement, and its superpatriotic rhetoric than at any other time in its history. Surely much depends on what leaders become bourgeoisified into. AFL leaders in the 1920s resembled the nationalistic, social Darwinist businessmen against whom their unions had originally been organized.[61]

The security sought by union leaders colored federation political action. AFL unions had organized around narrow constituencies, as homogenous as possible. To use Gompers's words, nonpartisanship also followed the line of least resistance, vis-à-vis both the external environment and the different factions within the AFL. It sought to find a least common denominator around which different factions with different interests could unite. It sought to protect union organizations in a hostile environment and promote their cohesion. Invoking independence, nonpartisanship obscured the federation's dependent, junior position vis-à-vis the national Democratic party and local urban machines. In the process of denying its own weakness and adapting to hostile forces, the AFL helped defuse potential working-class opposition to capitalist America.

Nonpartisanship helped incorporate the organized working class into the dominant values and institutions of American society. Locally, unions reinforced the power of political machines. Nationally, the federation avoided large-scale reform political action that would have challenged the centers of power and used politics to restructure society. Instead of a divisive, conflict-oriented politics, the AFL offered a two-pronged consensus approach. Narrow demands for political favors benefited job-hungry leaders and entrenched craft unions, without challenging upper-class holders of wealth and power. Nonpartisanship also expressed broad Americanist rhetoric that could unify workers because it was shared throughout the society. At best such rhetoric was so vague it required no action; at worst it was racist and superpatriotic.[62] In either form it sought, like the nonpartisanship offered by conservative municipal reformers in the same period, to obscure and avoid conflict. Nonpartisanship was a means of adapting—more and more as the AFL matured—to the dominant values and powers of America.

There are analogies here to ethnic assimilation. AFL politics helped promote cultural assimilation far more than structural assimilation.[63] Culturally, it reinforced the emphasis on narrow, business values; the federation even adopted business's opposition to social legislation. Nonpartisanship also supported working-class superpatriotism analogous to ethnic superpatriotism. Instead of trying to organize the unskilled, AFL leaders used racist arguments to support immigration restriction and Oriental exclusion. During the war and the 1920s superpatriotism and antiradical hysteria dominated the rhetoric of the organization. Nonpartisanship opposed, on the other hand, structural assimilation or at least an effort to redistribute power and wealth through political action. Such politics would have benefited unskilled workers, weaker unions, and the unorganized.

Perhaps AFL leaders did reflect the normal preferences of the bulk of craft-union members. But two points are crucial here. First, the leaders and the organizational structures surely helped form and reinforce the attitudes of trade-union activists, and probably the attitudes of workers as well. A labor party, unlikely as it was to be formed, would have promoted a different set of values. Second, no theory of social change posits a permanent crisis mentality among the potential radical agents. In normal times the organizational bureaucracy may well reflect the attitudes of its constituency. When objective conditions radicalize sections of the masses, however, the bureaucratic leadership becomes a brake both on the development of radical consciousness and on the creation of new organizational structures. As we have seen in the case of the labor-machine alliance, the intervention against radical action was often open and brutal. If other obstacles to radicalization are strong, the role of the conservative bureaucracy may be crucial.[64] Socialists remained strong in the labor movement until the 1920s; orthodox AFL leaders, both through their ideological impact on the rank and file and through their coercive intrusions in times of crisis, helped keep them from triumphing. The failure of American radicalism was surely overdetermined. Nonpartisanship, as practiced and defended by leaders of the AFL, played its own humble part.

Group conflict over narrow goals is the politics of *The Governmental Process* and the AFL alike. For Truman in theory and for the AFL in practice, this politics is conservative, accepting and working within the dominant social structures. But when Truman makes such a politics natural, he obscures its enforcement by group leaders and its consequences for the mass of the population. Obliterating any critical consciousness outside the process, the American science of politics fails to comprehend the society it mirrors.

CHAPTER V

Liberal Society and the Indian Question

Our conduct toward these people is deeply interesting to our national character.

*Andrew Jackson, First Annual
Message to Congress, 1829*

I

Underneath the "ambitious expansionism" of modern western societies, writes Henri Baudet in *Paradise on Earth*, "with their economic savoir faire, their social ideology, and their organizational talents," lies "a psychological disposition out of all political reality. It exists independently of objective facts, which seem to have become irrelevant. It is a disposition that leads [its adherent] 'to die' rather than 'to do,' and forces him to repent of his wickedness, covetousness, pride, and complacency."[1] The worldly orientation, Baudet argues, points to history and practical consequences, the inner disposition to a primitiveness beyond history. The first is expansive, the second regressive. This regressive, inner disposition, Baudet believes, has fastened on images of the noble savage, the garden of Eden, and paradise on earth.

In America, however, "ambitious expansionism" encountered the "regressive impulse" as a "political reality." This conflict between expansion and regression, I will suggest, is the precise cultural meaning

I am grateful to Paul Roazen for directing my early reading in psychoanalytic sources, to Leslie and Margaret Fiedler, and to the political theorists once together in Berkeley—Norman Jacobson, Hanna Pitkin, John H. Schaar, and Sheldon Wolin—for providing, with our students, the intellectual setting in which this essay was written.

Portions of a draft of this paper were presented at the University of North Carolina Symposium "Laws, Rights, and Authority," Chapel Hill, 20–22 February 1970, and at the Annual Meeting of the Western Political Science Association, Sacramento, 3 April 1970.

Americans gave to their destruction of the Indians. Their language teaches us some intolerable truths about regression, maturity, and death in liberal America.

In calling America a liberal society, I mean to evoke the unchallenged primacy of propertied individualism across the political spectrum. At the outset the contrast between expansionist, liberal America's self-conception and its image of the Indians seems clear enough. Liberalism insisted on the independence of men, each from the other and from cultural, traditional, and communal attachments. Indians were perceived as connected to their past, their superstitions, and their land. Liberalism insisted upon work, instinctual repression, and acquisitive behavior; men had to conquer and separate themselves from nature. Indians were seen as playful, violent, improvident, wild, and in harmony with nature. Private property underlay liberal society; Indians held land in common. Liberal relations were based contractually on keeping promises and on personal responsibility. Indians, in the liberal view, were anarchic and irresponsible. Americans believed that peaceful competitiveness kept them in touch with one another and provided social cement. They thought that Indians, lacking social order, were devoted to war.

Disastrously for the liberal self-conception, however, its distance from primitive man was not secure. At the heart of ambitious expansionism lay the regressive impulse itself. Indians were in harmony with nature; lonely, independent, liberal men were separated from it, and their culture lacked the richness, diversity, and traditional attachments to sustain their independence. The consequence was forbidden nostalgia, for the nurturing, blissful, and primitively violent connection to nature that white Americans had had to leave behind. At the core of liberalism lay the belief that such human connections to each other and to the land were dreams only, subjects of nostalgia or sentimentalization but impossible in the existing adult world. By suggesting the reality of the dream, Indian societies posed a severe threat to liberal identity. The only safe Indians were dead, sanitized, or totally dependent upon white benevolence. Liberal action enforced the only world possible in liberal theory.

The intimate historical encounter with the Indians still further undermined liberal identity. "In the beginning," John Locke had written, "all the world was America."[2] Then men relinquished the state of nature, freely contracted together, and entered civil society. But that was not the way it happened—in America. True, settlers had come to escape the corruption and traditional restraints of Europe, to begin again, to return to the state of nature and contract together. They aimed, as Hamilton put it in the *Federalist Papers*, to build a state based on "reflection and choice" rather than on "accident and force."[3] But while the origins of European countries were shrouded in the mists of obscure history, America had clearly begun not with primal innocence and consent but with acts of force and fraud. Stripping away history did not permit beginning without sin; it simply exposed the sin at the beginning of it all.

In the popular culture of films, Westerns, and children's games, seizing America from the Indians is the central, mythical, formative experience. Its dynamic figures prominently in the Vietnam War, providing symbols for soldiers, names for combat missions, and the framework for Pentagon strategic plans.[4] But historians have ignored the elimination of the Indians and minimized its significance for American development. This was the one outcome American statesmen in the two centuries before the Civil War could not imagine. For the dispossession of the Indians did not simply happen once and for all in the beginning. America was continually beginning again, and as it expanded across the continent, it killed, removed, and drove into extinction one tribe after another. I will focus here on the first half of the nineteenth century and particularly on the "Indian removal" program of Jacksonian democracy.[5]

Expansion across the continent was the central fact of American politics from Jefferson's presidency through the Mexican War. Indians inhabited almost all the territory west of the Appalachians in 1800; they had to be removed. The story is bloody and corrupt beyond imagining, and few American political figures escape from it without dishonor. From 1820 to 1844 one hundred thousand Indians were removed from their homes and transported west of the Mississippi. One-quarter to one-third of these died or were killed in the process.[6] Indian removal was Andrew Jackson's major concrete political aim in the years before he became president; Van Buren later listed it as one of the four major achievements of Jackson's administration, along with the bank war, the internal improvements veto, and the nullification fight.[7] Six of the eleven major candidates for president in the years from 1820 to 1852 had either won reputations as generals in Indian wars or served as secretaries of war, whose major responsibility in this period was relations with the Indians.[8]

How to reconcile the elimination of the Indians with the liberal self-image? This problem preoccupied the statesmen of the period. "The great moral debt we owe to this unhappy race is universally felt and acknowledged," Secretary of War Lewis Cass reported in 1831.[9] In our relations to the Indians, wrote Van Buren, "we are as a nation responsible *in foro conscientiae*, to the opinions of the great family of nations, as it involves the course we have pursued and shall pursue towards a people comparatively weak, upon whom we were perhaps in the beginning unjustifiable aggressors, but of whom, in the progress of time and events, we have become the guardians, and, as we hope, the benefactors."[10]

Van Buren and the others felt the eyes of the world upon America. They needed a policy and rhetoric permitting them to believe that our encounter with the Indians, "the most difficult of all our relations, foreign and domestic, has at last been justified to the world in its near approach to a happy and certain consummation."[11] They needed to justify—the Puritan word means save for God—a society built upon Indian graves.

The theory and language American statesmen employed cemented the historical white-Indian tie with intimate symbolic meaning. America's expansion across the continent, everyone agreed, reproduced the historical evolution of mankind. "The first proprietors of this happy country"[12] were sometimes said to be the first people on earth. Early in time, they were also primitive in development. Human societies existed along a unilinear scale from savagery to civilization. The early, savage peoples could not coexist with advanced societies; civilization would inevitably displace savagery.[13]

So stated, the theory remained abstract; politicians and social commentators filled it with personal meaning. The evolution of societies was identical to the evolution of individual men. "Barbarism is to civilization what childhood is to maturity."[14] Indians were at the infant stage of social evolution. They were "part of the human family"[15] as children; their replacement by whites symbolized America's growing up from childhood to maturity. Winthrop Jordan writes, "The Indian became for Americans a symbol of their American experience; it was no mere luck of the toss that placed the profile of an American Indian rather than an American Negro on the famous old five-cent piece. Confronting the Indian in America was a testing experience, common to all the colonies. Conquering the Indian symbolized and personified the conquest of the American difficulties, the surmounting of the wilderness. To push back the Indian was to prove the worth of one's own mission, to make straight in the desert a highway for civilization."[16]

Not the Indians alive, then, but their destruction, symbolized the

American experience. The conquest of the Indians made the country uniquely American. Yet Jordan is right; America identified at once with the conquered and the conquering. The Indians—that "much-injured race," once "the uncontrolled possessors of these vast regions"[17]—became a symbol of something lost, lost inevitably in the process of growing up.[18]

If the Indians were children, whites thought of themselves as parents. These parents did not simply replace Indians; they took upon themselves, to use Van Buren's words again, the obligations of "benefactors" and "guardians." What meaning can be given to a policy of death and dispossession, centrally important to the development of America, over which considerable guilt is felt and which is justified by the paternal benevolence of a father for his children?

The myth of Indian disappearance, I will suggest, belongs to the pathology of family relations. The symbols of Indian policy expressed repressed anxiety at the premature separation from warm, maternal protection. In the white fantasy, Indians remain in the oral stage, sustained by and unseparated from mother nature. They are at once symbols of a lost childhood bliss and, as bad children, repositories of murderous negative projections. Adult independence wreaks vengeance upon its own nostalgia for infant dependence. The Indian's tie with nature must be broken, literally by uprooting him, figuratively by civilizing him, finally by killing him.

Men in the new American world had left behind the authority provided by history, tradition, family connection, and the other ties of old European existence. Political authority, as Locke demonstrated against Sir Robert Filmer, must derive not from paternal relations but from interactions among free men. In a world where inherited and ascribed qualities were meant to count for so little, political and paternal authority would be fragile and insecure. But Indians were not liberal men. The paternal authority repressed out of liberal politics found its arena in paternalism toward Indians.

For whites to indulge their paternal wishes, Indians had to remain helpless children. Liberal paternal authority required its objects to have no independence or life of their own; it envisioned no other alternative to manly independence. As Andrew Jackson advised his nephew, "Independence of mind and action is the noblest attribute of man. He that possesses it, and practices upon it, may be said to possess the real image of his creator. Without it, man becomes the real tool in the hands of others, and is wielded, like a mere automaton, sometimes, without knowing it, to the worst of purposes."[19] In their paternalism toward the Indians, men like Jackson indulged their secret longing to wield total power. Explicitly the father was to break the child's tie to nature, so the child could grow up. The actual language and practice substituted for the tie to nature a total, infantilized dependence upon the white father, and the fragmented workings of a liberal marketplace and a liberal bureaucracy.

Liberalism broke the Indian's tie to nature in the name of independence; but the destruction of actual Indian autonomy suggested a dynamic to American expansion that contradicted professed liberal goals. The separation anxiety underlying liberal society expressed itself in a longing to regain lost attachment to the earth by expanding, swallowing, and incorporating its contents. Liberalism sought to regain the "dual-unity" of the primal infant-mother connection from a position of strength instead of infant helplessness, by devouring and incorporating identities culturally out of its control. In relation to Indians, whites regressed to the most primitive form of object relation, namely the annihilation of the object through oral introjection. America was pictured by defenders of Manifest Destiny as a "young and growing country," which expanded through "swallowing" territory, "just as an animal needs to eat to grow." Savagery would inevitably "be swallowed by" civilization. The "insatiable" "land hunger" of the whites struck alike critics of and apologists for Indian policy, and observers fell back upon oral metaphors to describe the traders and backwoodsmen "preying, like so many vultures, upon the vitals of those ill-fated tribes."[20] Indians were emancipated from the land only to be devoured by a white expansionism that could not tolerate their independent existence.

Child destruction was accomplished by a white father, whose maturity enabled him to accept Indian extinction with neither regret nor responsibility. Benevolence and greed, power and helplessness, were irrevocably split in this Jekyll-Hyde figure. The failure to achieve an integrated paternal figure who could accept responsibility for his actions recalls the failure to integrate childhood experience into the adult world. Just as these splits in the ego characterize schizoid personalities, so the inability to tolerate separation from the other, the longing to return to an egoless "dual-unity" stage, is a source of adult schizophrenia. But liberal society (and the men who carried out its Indian policy) neither disintegrated nor underwent a genuine maturing; liberalism had the power to remove the Indian menace instead.[21]

At the outset this interpretation of Indian destruction must seem bizarre. The myth about Indians was not the work of paranoids and social madmen but a consensus of almost all leading American political and intellectual figures. The sources of white expansion onto Indian land, moreover, seem straightforward. Surely land hunger and the building of a national empire provided the thrust; at most the cultural myth sought to come to terms with the experience after the fact.

But the centrality of Indian dispossession in pre–Civil War America raises disturbing questions about the American political core that are hardly met by viewing Indian removal as pragmatic and inevitable. Precisely such basic encounters, inevitable as their outcome may be once they reach a certain point, form the history and the culture of a country. Hannah Arendt, for example, has suggested that the prolonged meeting of "advanced" and primitive peoples forms an important factor in the origins of totalitarianism.[22] Consider the following as central to the American-Indian experience: the collapse of conceptions of human rights in the face of culturally distant peoples, with resulting civilized atrocities defended as responses to savage atrocities; easy talk about, and occasional practice of, tribal extermination; the perceived impossibility of cultural coexistence, and a growing acceptance of "inevitable" racial extinction; total war, with all-or-nothing conflicts over living space and minimal combatant-noncombatant distinctions; and the inability of the savage people to retire behind a stable frontier, provoking whites' confidence in their ability to conquer, subdue, and advance over obstacles in their environment. Noam Chomsky asks, "Is it an exaggeration to suggest that our history of extermination and racism is reaching its climax in Vietnam today? It is not a question that Americans can easily put aside."[23]

Admit that white symbolization of Indians had to cover a proto-totalitarian situation; does that make the symbols themselves significant causes of Indian policy rather than mere rationalizations for it? The issue of causality is complex, and I plan no extended defense of the importance of cultural myths to the ongoing cultural and political life of a nation. At the very least, attention to myth will tell us what whites made of their encounter with the Indians, what meaning it had for them. This meaning developed out of, and was enriched by, innumerable specific interactions and policy decisions before, during, and after the major events of Indian removal. Only a peculiarly split view of human existence holds that symbolizations of meaning operate in a closed universe of their own, divorced from the "real" facts of historical causation. Men make history; they develop complex inner worlds because (from infant frustrations through their experience as historical actors) they do not make it in circumstances of their own choosing. These inner worlds, projected outside, become part of the continuing history men do make.

The search for historical causes, moreover, may well be misleading. In the present case historical explanation ought to aim at the fullest significant description of the matrix of white-Indian relations. Any description that, in the name of pragmatism, behaviorism, or vulgar materialism, omitted the symbolic meaning actors gave to their actions would be radically incomplete.

Surely, however, if our concern is with actors' perceptions, Freudian categories and loose talk of madness are gratuitous intrusions upon the language actually employed. The problem is this. Americans uniformly employed familial language in speaking of the Indians; most historians and political scientists have been systematically deaf to it. Lacking a theory that sensitized them to such a vocabulary and helped them interpret it, perhaps they could not hear what was being said. Let us begin to take seriously the words of those who made our Indian policy.

II

In the antebellum white imagination the American family began with the mother and child. Indians were the "sons of the forest," "the children of nature."[24] Savages were children because of their unrestrained impulse life and because they remained unseparated from nature. The metaphors resemble, to their details, psychoanalytic descriptions of fantasies of the oral stage of infant bliss.

T. L. McKenney, chief administrator of Indian affairs from 1816 to 1830 offered the typical picture of the aboriginal tribes in pre-Columbian times. "Onward, and yet onward, moved the bands, clothed in winter in the skins of beasts, and in the summer free from all such encumbrances. The earth was their mother, and upon its lap they reposed. Rude wigwams sheltered them. Hunger and thirst satisfied, sleep followed—and within this circle was contained the happiness of the aboriginal man."[25]

Indians were perfectly at home in nature. They had a primitive, preconscious, precivilized innocence. They had not yet become separated from the earth but enjoyed "almost without restriction or control the blessings which flowed spontaneously from the bounty of nature."[26]

Savages lived in a world of plenty, protected and nurtured by mother nature. Their world was Eden, or paradise.[27]

The Indians' connectedness to nature in no way restricted their freedom, in the white view. Aborigines were free to wander from place to place without losing the tie to nature. Manly and independent, they "never submitted themselves to any laws, any coercive power, any shadow of government."[28] Although Indians spoke often to whites about the land and the bones of their father, the savages' connection to nature and freedom from paternal, governmental authority seemed most to excite white imaginations.

Francis Parkman reduced the metaphor to its psychological essence:

> The Indian is hewn out of rock. You can rarely change the form without destruction of the substance. Races of inferior energy have possessed a power of expansion and assimilation to which he is a stranger; and it is this fixed and rigid quality which has proved his ruin. He will not learn the arts of civilization, and he and forest must perish together. The stern, unchanging features of his mind excite our admiration from their very immutability; and we look with deep interest on the fate of this irreclaimable son of the wilderness, the child who will not be weaned from the breast of his rugged mother.[29]

Why the sense of doom in Parkman's passage? Why cannot the bliss of the infant at the mother's breast be sustained? Why must the Indian relinquish Eden or die, and why can he not give it up? The whites gave two related answers. First, the Indians would not work; they were improvident and lacked the "principles of restraint"[30] necessary to preserve themselves against adversity. Overlooking, for their own political and myth-making purposes, extensive Indian agriculture (which had kept the first white settlers from starving), they perceived the Indians simply as wandering hunters.[31] They could not be made to turn to agriculture; they would not "subdue and replenish" the earth, as the incessantly quoted biblical injunction ordered. They would not forsake the primitive, oral, accepting relation with nature and try to control and subdue her. They would not accumulate property, build lasting edifices, make contracts, and organize their lives around rules and restraints. They would not, so to speak, move from the oral to the anal stage.

The typical description of this unwillingness revealed the writer's own sense of loss, his own envy of the presumed Indian condition. Lewis Cass, the politician with the most dealings with northern Indians in the decades following the War of 1812, sympathized:

> It is easy, in contemplating the situation of such a people, to perceive the difficulties to be encountered in any effort to produce a radical change in

their condition. The *fulcrum* is wanting, upon which the lever must be placed. They are contented as they are; not contented merely, but clinging with a death-grasp to their own institutions. . . . To roam the forests at will, to pursue their game, to attack their enemies, to spend the rest of their lives in listless indolence, to eat inordinately when they have food, to suffer patiently when they have none, and to be ready at all times to die . . . how unwilling a savage would be to exchange such a life for the stationary and laborious duties of civilized societies.[32]

In McKenney's words:

Who are they of all the race of Adam, that would surrender all the freedom, and the abundance, that were enjoyed by the North American Indian, when his country was first invaded by our race, and place himself, voluntarily, under the restraints which civilization imposes? It is not in the nature of man to do this. It requires, before he can bring himself to endure the labor and toil that attend upon the civilized state, the operation of that stern law— necessity.[33]

As long as the Indians held property in common, they could not break their tie to nature; they would not work and save. "Separate property in land is the basis of civilized society." "The absence of it is the cause of want and consequently of decrease in numbers." Without private property there was no individual incentive to appropriate the fruits of one's labor. Moreover, the stage before private property was, in the liberal view, the stage prior to the development of active, individuated egos. "The absence of the *meum* and *teum*, in the general community of possession . . . is a perpetual operating cause of the *vis inertiae* of savage life. . . . [Private property] may not unjustly be considered the parent of all improvements." "At the foundation of the whole social system lies individuality of property. It is, perhaps, nine times out of ten, the stimulus that mankind first feels. With it come all the delights that the word home expresses."[34]

In Freudian theory the oral stage precedes the development of a separate, individuated ego. White Americans implicitly applied the same personality theory to the Indians. Indians, in the white view, lived in an undifferentiated relation to nature. Nature appropriated to oneself through work underlay ownership and control of the self.[35] Lacking private property, Indians lacked a self they could call their own. Since they remained in oral dependence on nature, Indians could not take care of themselves.

But he who does not work cannot eat. The primitive bounty of nature, Americans insisted, was not inexhaustible. As the whites invaded Indian land, killed the game, and destroyed the crops, Indians began to starve in large numbers. This was taken as a sign of their improvidence; their alleged failure to use government rations frugally was further evidence.[36] Horace Greeley, crusading antislavery editor and future presidential candidate, explained after a trip through the West in 1859:

> The Indians are children. Their arts, wars, treaties, alliances, habitations, crafts, properties, commerce, comforts, all belong to the very lowest and rudest ages of human existence. . . . Any band of schoolboys from ten to fifteen years of age, are quite as capable of ruling their appetites, devising and upholding a public policy, constituting and conducting a state or community as an average Indian tribe. . . . [The Indian is] a slave of appetite and sloth, never emancipated from the tyranny of one passion save by the ravenous demands of another. . . . As I passed over those magnificent bottoms of the Kansas . . . constituting the very best corn land on earth, and saw their men sitting round the doors of their lodges in the height of the planting season. . . . I could not help saying, "These people must die out—there is no help for them. God has given the earth to those who will subdue and cultivate it, and it is vain to struggle against His righteous decree."[37]

The self-righteous sadism in this passage has several sources. Childish irresponsibility will bring deserved death upon the Indians; one need no longer pity them or hesitate over expansion onto Indian lands. More deeply, such men as McKenney and Cass could not envy unambiguously the Indian world of childhood freedom and maternal protection. Such longing violated just the liberal independence and self-reliance that called it forth. Greeley's formulation directed rage at the need to forsake one's own private Eden against those who refused to forsake theirs. Having lost their own Eden, the whites could take Indian land as well.

The rage was not simply that of an anal society against its own fantasies of oral bliss. There was also an argument about another rage. The Indians, it was held, had given up their right to inhabit Eden by their own primitive violence.

In part those who emphasized Indian violence denied savage nobility. The mythology of violence turned Indians into "monsters in human shape." "Infuriated hell-hounds," they disturbed the "forest paradise" instead of inhabiting it.[38] The concept of the Indian was split into the noble savage and the "starved wolf." "The man who would scalp an infant in his cradle"[39] was a literary cliché.

There was a deeper intimacy, however, between innocence and violence. Many writers such as Francis Parkman and Lewis Cass stressed them both equally and found them inextricably related—as innocence and violent loss of self-control would be in children. Like children, Indians were not responsible for their violence; they lacked the intelligence and sense of responsibility of more advanced peoples.[40]

The common root of innocence and violence, in the liberal view of the Indian, once again recalls psychoanalytic descriptions of the oral stage. Melanie Klein has suggested that the infant at the breast has primitive rages as well as fantasies of bliss and plenty. He totally devours the breast in these "body destruction fantasies" and enters the mother and devours her imagined bodily contents. In part these fantasies of the "manic feast" are innocent in origin; in part they express the infant's primitive destructive impulses. Infant sadism is given added force from rage at the withdrawal of the breast. The infant wants to retaliate against the formerly protective mother who has withdrawn her nurture. These vengeful fantasies are themselves intolerable, as the infant both creates from his projections a persecutory mother who must be destroyed and blames himself and his devouring desires for the loss of the breast.

I am not sure what it means to speak of infant aggressive rages or to allege that separation anxiety engenders in the baby elaborated fantasies of oral bliss and rage. Such language may well impose adult categories meaningless to infant experience. But the oral stage engenders both the energy for adult fantasies and their content. Later childhood or adult longing to return to the imagined state of oral bliss is inseparable from vengeful rage against the mother, self-accusations, and persecutory fantasies.[41]

For our purposes two points must be stressed. First, oral bliss and primitive rage both aim to end the separation of the child from the mother; both involve "regression to the phase that precedes the evolution of the ego [and] . . . the testing of reality."[42] In fantasy the mother and the separate ego are destroyed. Since oral rage aims at total unity and destruction, Klein labels it "schizophrenic," or "insane."

Second, longing for union carries with it desire for vengeance. Those experiencing separation anxiety do not simply want union with the mother; they want to express primitive rage against her as well. But liberal men had no more right to primitive rage than primitive sustenance. Scapegoats, upon whom aggression was projected, would relieve the guilt engendered by these vengeful fantasies; they would embody violence and could be punished for it.

Indians well served this function. They were the bogeymen who frightened children at night in early America. Thomas McKenney makes the connection in a passage perfectly introducing our discussion of Indian oral violence:

> Which of us has not listened with sensations of horror to nursery stories that are told of the Indian and his cruelties? In our infant mind he stood for the Moloch of our country. We have been made to hear his yell; and to our eyes

have been presented his tall, gaunt form with the skins of beasts dangling around his limbs, and his eyes like fire, eager to find some new victim on which to fasten himself, and glut his appetite for blood. . . . We have been startled by the shriek of the dying mother; and hushed that we might hear the last sigh of the expiring infant.[43]

Melanie Klein comments about such childhood anxieties:

We get to look upon the child's fear of being devoured, or cut up, or torn to pieces, or its terror of being surrounded and pursued by menacing figures, as a regular component of its mental life; and we know that the man-eating wolf, the fire-spewing dragon, and all the evil monsters out of myth and fairy stories flourish and exert their unconscious influence in the phantasy of each individual child, and it feels itself persecuted and threatened by those evil shapes.[44]

White mythology pushed Indian violence back to the stage of primitive, oral rage in several ways. First, Indian violence was exterminatory; it threatened ego boundaries and the self. Second, the quality of the violence itself, as McKenney's images suggest, was oral. Third, women and infants were its targets. Finally, the violence was perceived as presexual.

Indians were most commonly attacked in the name of self-defense. If we personify America, as was common in the nineteenth century, then this resistance to the Indians acquires the personal significance of defense of the self. Indians attacked America before the secure emergence of the country. They exemplified fears that the independent nation could not survive, fears that had led many Americans to intrigue at its dismemberment.[45] Indians were the first enemies the young country had to conquer. Expressing his gratitude for Jackson's invasion of Florida in pursuit of the Seminoles, Mississippi senator George Poindexter proclaimed, "You have protected us in the time of our infancy against the inexorable Red Sticks and their allies; you have compelled them to relinquish possession of our land, and ere long we shall strengthen into full manhood under the smiles of a beneficent Providence."[46]

Indians attacked the young nation at its boundaries, keeping them confused and insecure. Whites' images indicate that concern over the country's boundaries aggravated, and was reinforced by, concern over the boundaries of their own egos. A securely individuated ego requires a stable sense of boundaries between self and environment, and whites insisted America, too, needed stable boundaries to mature. Mobility and expansion aborted stable environments in America, but whites located these qualities in Indian culture, not their own. Indians, one nineteenth-century authority explained, were peculiarly characterized by "the absence of private property," the "want of a home," the practice of "roaming from place to place," and "the habit of invading without scruple the land of others." Only private property, whose significance for liberalism I have already noted, saved mobile, expansionist Jacksonian America from fitting this description.[47]

Indians not only embodied the absence of boundaries; they also invaded white boundaries. Peace talks with the Indians "infesting our frontier," wrote the young Andrew Jackson in 1794, "are only opening an Easy door for the Indians to pass through to butcher our citizens."[48] As long as Indians remained on Georgia land, complained Governor G. M. Troup, Georgia's "political organization is incompetent; her civil polity is deranged; her military force cannot be reduced to systematic order and subordination; the extent of her actual resources cannot be counted; and all because Georgia is not in the possession of her vacant territory."[49]

The vision of Indian violence threatening the selfhood of young America reversed the actual situation. The expanding nation reiterated the claim of self-defense as it obliterated one tribe after another. Self-defense against the Indians excused expansion into Florida, Texas, and (less successfully) Canada.[50] "An Indian will claim everything and anything," complained Andrew Jackson, after including 10 million acres of Cherokee land in a treaty coerced from the Creeks.[51] Indians became the bad children upon whom was projected the whites' own aggressive expansionism.

Indians did threaten American identity, even if they could not destroy the country, since that identity required expanding over and obliterating savagery. In the name of attacking threats to the independent self, America could "swallow" one tribe after another.[52] Security was possible only once the Indian threat on the boundaries was finally stilled and whites need not coexist with independent realities unconnected to them and out of their control. Indian threats to the self-defense of expanding white America suggest that early time when a secure self has not emerged, when it is threatened with retaliatory extermination for its own aggressive rage.

White descriptions of Indian "atrocities" concretely expressed the terror of oral rage. Lewis Cass insisted that Indians were taught from infancy to take pleasure in war and cruelty, that they loved scalping, and that a "man-eating Society" that devoured prisoners flourished among some tribes.[53] A nineteenth-century history of the eastern frontier was more graphic: "The Indian kills indiscriminately. His object is the total extermination of his enemies. . . . Those barbarous sons of the forest exercised . . . the full indulgence of all their native thirst for human blood." Prisoners were saved "for the purpose of feasting the feelings of ferocious vengeance of himself and his comrades, by the torture of his captives."[54]

These passages and countless others like them pictured Indian violence as insane, exterminatory, and dismembering. Its method was oral; and it was protected by primitive magic. Melanie Klein and Géza Róheim describe the aggressive fantasies of adults experiencing separation anxiety in just these terms. The reality basis provided by methods of warfare among some tribes, isolated incidents, and acts by individual Indians or outlaw bands permitted these images to dominate the mythological Indian.[55]

Indians on the warpath were always "maddened," and their aim was the total extermination of the whites. Indians tortured and dismembered their enemies; scalping of corpses and other mutilations received prominent attention. Indian rage was oral; the aborigines were cannibalistic and had a "thirst for blood." One Indian claimed, it was said at the beginning of the Creek War, that he "had got fat eating white people's flesh."[56]

Indians were protected by primitive magic. Prophets convinced them they were omnipotent, beyond harm from bullets. War cries and terrifying war paint indicated to the whites that Indians sought victory through terror and awe, rather than practical, adult methods of warfare. White generals and Indian agents, sometimes whistling in the dark, insisted that their soldiers were not children and would not be frightened by Indian shrieks and costumes.[57]

Indians as monsters, then, carried out forbidden infantile violence. They at least partially embodied guilt felt over the child's own aggressive and destructive fantasies. Indian atrocities therefore not only justified wars against Indians; in response to Indian violence whites themselves engaged in fantasies and activities expressing primal rage. Punishing the criminal permitted them to participate in the forbidden criminal activity.[58]

Since Indian violence was exterminatory, whites could exterminate Indians. When a few Creek warriors killed some settlers at the outbreak of the 1812 War, the Tennessee legislature urged the governor to "carry a campaign into the heart of the Creek nation and exterminate them." The august *Niles Register*, commenting on the Second Seminole War, hoped that "the miserable creatures will be speedily swept from the face of the earth."[59] Andrew Jackson often called for the extermination of his Indian enemies.[60] In 1816, long after the end of the Creek War, he told a general serving under him to destroy every village refusing to turn over the alleged murderers of two whites. He had urged burning Creek villages well before the outbreak of that war and continued burning them well after the last battle.[61] A few years later he entered Florida, burned Seminole villages, and drove out the women and children, on the grounds that "the protection of our citizens will require that the wolf be struck in his den." In 1836 he urged that Seminole women and children be tracked down and "captured or destroyed" to end the Second Seminole War. He continued to apply the metaphor of wolves and dens.[62] Violations of Indian truce flags in that war and others were common, on the grounds one need not observe civilized rules of war with savages.[63]

Indian wars also permitted verbal participation in savage violence. Jackson wrote to the governor of Pensacola in 1814 that, if the Spanish forts were not surrendered, "I will not hold myself responsible for the conduct of my enraged soldiers and Indian warriors." "An eye for an eye, tooth for tooth, scalp for scalp."[64]

Indians directed their primal rage, in the white view, against "aged matrons and helpless infants." They "snatched the infant from the nipple of its mother, and bashed its brains out against a tree." Men could presumably defend themselves; their killing had little symbolic significance. But "helpless women have been butchered, and the cradle stained with the blood of innocence." "When we figure to ourselves our beloved wives and little, prattling infants, butchered, mangled, murdered, and torn to pieces by savage bloodhounds and wallowing in their gore, you can judge of our feelings." Jackson accused the governor of Pensacola of receiving a "matricidal band" after "the butchery of our women and children," "as the Father his prodigal Son."[65]

Indians thus became the bad "children of nature," whose exterminatory aggression totally destroyed the mother and the "innocent babe." Purified by his elimination of these monsters, the good child could grow safely to manhood.[66]

Indians not only murdered white women; they also treated their own women badly. Savages gained innocent bliss at the expense of their women. The Indian reposed in nature on the lap of his mother, McKenney explained, but "his squaw" paid the price. "Alas! then, as now, her shoulders were made to bear the weight, and her hands to perform the drudgery of the domestic labor." Indians had to be civilized so they would learn to respect their women.[67]

McKenney shared the view of women prevalent in Jacksonian America. The pure, honored, and respected white female personified civilized virtues. At the same time expanding America attacked and subdued mother nature and understood this victory in personal terms. Jacksonians' personifications of their enemies—whether effeminate aristocrats or the devouring, "monster-hydra" bank—exhibited fear of domination by women.[68] The culture resolved its ambivalence over women by splitting femaleness into passionate and uncontrolled demons, who had to be destroyed, and feminine enforcers of civilized values, who had to be protected. Because Indian men were not separated from savage, violent, rocklike nature, they brutalized Indian women. Once again Indians resolved white ambivalences in unacceptably self-indulgent ways and had to be punished for it. Liberal self-indulgence came only in the punishment.

The Indian threat to women was not perceived as sexual or oedipal. Indians did not kill men to possess women. Mothers, not fathers, were the targets of Indian violence. This violence, moreover, was not sexual. Sexual assaults played almost no role in stories of Indian atrocities, in striking contrast to the mythology of blacks. Winthrop Jordan writes,

> Negroes seemed more highly sexed to the colonists than did the American Indians. . . . Far from finding Indians lusty and lascivious, they discovered them to be notably deficient in ardor and virility. (Eventually and almost inevitably a European commentator announced that the Indian's penis was smaller than the European's.) And the colonists developed no image of the Indian as a potential rapist; their descriptions of Indian attacks did not include Indians "reserving the young women for themselves." In fact, the entire interracial complex did not pertain to the Indians.[69]

Jordan believes white mythology treated Indians more kindly than Negroes. Blacks were sexual threats who had to be repressed; Indians were the first Americans. Certainly there was greater sympathy and identification with Indians. But this did not make the Indian danger any less threatening. Blacks represented sexual threat and temptation; the relation had reached the stage of forbidden love. The Indian was a fragment of the self, that primitive, oral part that was dangerously pleasure seeking and aggressive and therefore, in the name of self-defense, had to be destroyed. Indians represented the pre-ego state of undifferentiated bliss and rage. As Leslie Fiedler puts it, if the blacks were about sex, the Indians were about madness.[70] The blacks were a sexual, oedipal threat to white men; the Indians were a pre-oedipal, aggressive threat to the mother-child relationship.

The Indians lacked authority; fathers had not yet entered the picture. It was the job of whites to introduce them. What kind of fathers would a culture that longed for the Indians' fatherless freedom offer them?

III

American policy makers insisted upon their paternal obligations to the Indian tribes; they sought to subject Indians to paternal, presidential authority. In legal relations, too, Indians were the "wards" of the state.[71] If one takes seriously the evidence of speeches and documents, whites could not imagine Indians outside the parent-child context.

"What then," asked Alabama governor John Murphy, "is to be done for this people, who had priority of us in the occupation of this favored land? . . . The United States should assume a parental guardianship over them" and extend the benefits of learning, religion, and the arts.[72] P. B. Porter, John Quincy Adams's secretary of state, explained, "In their present destitute and deplorable condition and which is constantly growing more helpless, it would seem to be not only the right but the duty of the government to take them under its paternal care, and to exercise over their persons and property the salutory rights and duties of guardianship."[73]

Such paternalism offered the Indians not simply help but a redefinition of their identity. It defined them as children, which in fact they were not. The paternal metaphor forced the tribes into childish dependence upon white society. This was particularly devastating in a liberal culture that had eliminated legitimate hierarchal authority and believed that "manly independence" offered the only proper basis for relations among men.[74] When such a society imported the family into politics, it was likely to impose an insecure and overbearing paternal domination. To insist that Indians be shown "their real state of dependence"[75] upon government was, I will argue, to infantilize them. Infantilization provides the major significance of the call for paternal authority.

The process of infantilization has been studied in many contexts: concentration camps; slave societies; total institutions such as insane asylums, old people's homes, and prisons; environments of isolation and sensory deprivation; schizophrenic families; housewives in suburban families; and efforts to manipulate mass publics for political purposes (such as to win support for the war in Vietnam). These environments, it is argued, break the social relations, cultural norms, and normal expectations of those subjected to them. "Ceremonies of degradation" destroy the victim's connection to his previously validated social self. Individuals lose social support for their own personal experience of reality. The infantilization process, calling into question one's basic security in and trust of the environment, undermines the independent ego. Elimination of ties to objects in the environment produces an extreme sense of object loss and a consequent regression to infantile longings for protection, connection, and loss of self. Infantilization creates acute separation anxiety and calls into question individuation beyond the oral stage.

The victim's blank and bare environment offers him only one remaining source of gratification, the authority who manipulates rewards and punishments. Thus the very oppressor becomes the source of values and sustenance. The infantilized victim, in the extreme case, identifies with his oppressor and seeks total dependence upon him.[76]

It could be argued that white rhetoric and policy did infantilize Indians, destroying tribal cultures and undermining, for large numbers, the simple will to live. The passive, affectless despair that decimated thousands of Indians after a certain stage of white engulfment struck many observers. Infantilization has often been studied from the child's perspective, but the infantilization imposed on victims may well serve needs for the self-appointed parent figures. My concern is with infantilization from the parent's point of view.

Whites perceived Indians, I suggested, as children in a sustaining, oral relationship to nature. Since that relationship was a projection of forbidden white longings, it could not be permitted to remain a cultural alternative. But the forbidden oral longings would not disappear. With the parental metaphor whites substituted paternal domination over infantilized Indians for the dependence on nature. Now the white father and his instruments became the only source of gratification. As parents, policy makers could participate in the dual-unity situation from the position of domination instead of dependence.

The model for the white father and his red children was not a family relation permitting growth but a family with schizophrenogenic elements. Of the parents in such families Searles writes, "In essence, the parent's need for security cannot allow him or her to feel the child as a separate identity, and the parent cannot give indication to the child that the child is capable of emotionally affecting the parent." The child must be "denied the experience of feeling himself to be an individual human entity, distinct from but capable of emotional contact with the parent."[77]

The theory of paternal assistance offered the Indians aid in growing up. But the very notion of growth was infantilizing. Indians were offered only the alternatives of civilization or death. The House Committee on Indian Affairs forecast in 1818, "In the present state of our country one of two things seem to be necessary, either that those sons of the forest should be moralized or exterminated."[78] Senator Thomas Hart Benton explained that the disappearance of the Indians should not be mourned. "Civilization or extinction has been the fate of all people who have found themselves in the track of advancing whites; civilization, always the preference of the advancing whites, has been pressed as an object, while extinction has followed as a consequence of its resistance."[79]

Such theories, it has often been noted, helped justify the white occupation of Indian land.[80] Since the "hunting tribes" did not "subdue and replenish" the earth, more advanced agricultural societies could take their land. The decline of the barbarous people was necessary to the progress of civilization.[81] But I want to focus on a somewhat different significance of the choice between death and civilization.

In the white scheme civilization, no less than death, meant the disappearance of the Indians.[82] They could not remain Indians and grow up; their only hope was to "become merged in the mass of our population."[83] "The ultimate point of rest and happiness for them is to let our settlements and theirs meet and blend together, to intermingle, and to become one people incorporating themselves with us as citizens of the United States."[84] Similar efforts to force indigenous peoples into a single "modernizing" pattern have continued to hypnotize American policy makers. "Merged" into liberal society, Indians would no longer offer subversive forms of experience, forcing whites to encounter identities not replicas of their own.

Requiring Indians to mature into whites or die irrevocably split childhood from adult experience. Savagery could maintain itself only by fleeing westward. Providence decreed that "the hunting tribes must retreat before the advance of civilization, or perish under the shade of the white man's settlements."[85] Alleged tribal willingness to leave their land for the West even indicated that, in white projections, if Indians did not wish to grow up themselves, their childhood would not stand in the way of the maturity of others.[86] Jackson and the other proponents of Indian removal promised the tribes that they could remain forever on their new land. But the spirit of the plan and the actual outcome were more accurately characterized by Cherokee agent R. J. Meigs. One educated Cherokee, he claimed, suggested that land given the Indians not be bounded on the west; the Indians could then continue to move west as the tide of civilization advanced from the east.[87]

But politicians who argued isolating the Indians would protect them also called for the march of civilization across the continent. The integrity of the savage experience could only ultimately maintain itself in death. Only dead or helpless Indians could safely be mourned. One historian, defending Jackson's Indian removal policy a generation later, explained that it permitted the inevitable Indian extinction to go on with less demoralization to the whites.[88]

Since civilization meant liberal uniformity, independent Indian growth could not safely be tolerated. Only embryonic liberals who had internalized adult values could be permitted freedom to grow. Indians were not liberal men; they required a greater exercise of paternal authority. The father's explicit task was first to break the Indian's tie to the land and then to help him grow up. The process is better understood, however, according to the theory of infantilization. Breaking the Indian's tie to his customary environment, the white father sought to substitute paternal domination.

The Jacksonian policy of Indian removal transported Indians from their land, which whites coveted, to land west of the Mississippi. Large-scale transfer of native populations, in the name of security and modernization, has continued to appeal to American statesmen. Indian removal bears resemblance to "forced draft urbanization" in Vietnam and urban renewal in our cities.[89] It sought to impose the American experience of uprooting and mobility upon the Indians. In Jackson's words,

> Doubtless it will be painful to leave the graves of their fathers, but what do they more than our ancestors did nor than our children are doing? To better their condition in an unknown land our forefathers left all that was dear in earthly objects. Our children by thousands yearly leave the land of their birth to seek new homes in distant regions. Does humanity weep at these painful separations from everything animate and inanimate, with which the young heart has become entwined? Far from it. It is rather a source of joy that our country affords scope where our young population may range unconstrained in body or mind, developing the power and faculties of man in their highest perfection. These removed hundreds and almost thousands of miles at their own expense, purchase the lands they occupy, and support themselves at

their new homes from the moment of their arrival. Can it be cruel in the Government, when, by events which it cannot control, the Indian is made discontent in his ancient home to purchase his lands, to give him a new and extensive territory, to pay the expense of his removal, and support him a year on his new abode. How many thousands of our own people would gladly embrace the opportunity of removing to the West on such condition?[90]

How, then, come to terms with the resistance of the natives and their ties to the land? Policy makers adopted strategies of both denial and rationalization. "Real Indians," the whites insisted, would offer no resistance to removal, since they led a wandering life anyway.[91] Denying Indian attachment to the land, whites called natural the wandering their policies imposed upon the Indians. Whites turned Indians into wanderers by killing their game, by destroying their crops and burning their villages, and by moving a tribe from one location after another as whites wanted the land.[92] Jackson innocently asked, "And is it to be supposed that the wandering savage has a stronger attachment to his home than the settled, civilized Christian? Is it more afflicting to him to leave the graves of his fathers than it is to our brothers and children?"[93]

From another perspective, however, breaking tribal ties to the land was urged and defended. As long as they were "clinging with a death-grasp"[94] to their land, Indians could not be civilized. In 1826 the Chickasaws refused to give up their land in Mississippi and move west, "fearing the consequence may be similar to transplanting an old tree, which would wither and die away." Commissioners Thomas Hinds and John Coffee replied, "The trees of the forest, and particularly the most useless trees, are most difficult of transplanting; but fruit-trees, which are more particularly designated by the Great Spirit for the nourishment and comfort to man, require not only to be transplanted, but to be nourished, cultivated, and even pruned, in order to bring forth good fruit."[95]

Breaking the Indian relation to the land had concrete as well as symbolic significance. To become civilized and grow up, Indians had to learn to work. They would remain "idle," as the whites saw it, as long as they could live purely by hunting and foraging. "The Indian must first find himself separated from his forests—and the game must be gone, or so difficult to find, as to expose him to want . . . before he will [begin] . . . earning his bread by the sweat of his brow."[96] "Necessity" was the "fulcrum" "upon which the lever must be placed" to civilize the Indians; they had to be situated so that they would starve if they did not work.[97]

The paternal interest of whites in Indian welfare thus required the government to take Indian land. Ohio politician and Cherokee agent R. J. Meigs explained, "I would lead them into civilization without injuring an individual, until they gradually and almost imperceptibly became blended with ourselves. And to effect this, they must circumscribe their immense limits; for while they can roam through extensive forests, they will not make use of their physical or mental faculties to raise themselves up. Poor human nature, alone, revolts at the thought of the labor required and the sacrifices to be made to arrive at a state of civilization."[98]

Work, to antebellum Americans, meant agriculture. "A father ought to give good advice to his children," President Madison told the Cherokees, urging them to plant crops.[99] Work also required private property. In Secretary of War Crawford's words, "Distinct ideas of separate property . . . must necessarily precede any considerable advance in the arts of civilization . . . because no one will exert himself to procure the comforts of life unless his right to enjoy them is exclusive."[100]

For a century beginning in the Jacksonian period, private property was the major weapon for teaching the Indians the value of civilization and, incidentally, dispossessing them of their land. Requiring Indians to take individual plots of land released enormous amounts of leftover Indian land for white settlement. In addition Indians could further "sell," be defrauded of, or lose for "debts" or nonpayment of taxes their individual plots. Private property in fact was more important to the disappearance than the civilization of the Indians.[101] But this only illustrates the underlying identity we have seen between civilization and Indian death.

Liberating Indians from their land, whites offered them paternal assistance in growing up. But the paternal relationship was insisted upon most persistently precisely at those moments when Indians by their behavior were denying its validity—expressing genuine independence, real power, or legitimate grievances. Indians were children; they could have no consciousness of grievances.[102] They fought because "of the predisposition of the Indian to war,"[103] not because whites were taking their land. Where wars, like the Second Creek War, were obviously the result of white aggression, it was best not even to mention this possibility. But where the tribes that fought were more distant from white settlements, as in the 1812 War, it seemed safe to insist they could not have fought to protect their land: "It would disclose, not a mere trait of character, but a new feature of human nature, if these improvident beings with whom the past is forgotten and the future contemned, and whose whole existence is absorbed in the present, should encounter the United States in war, lest their country might be sold after the lapse of centuries."[104] Lewis Cass wrote those words in 1827, long after whites had settled the land taken from hostile (and friendly) Creeks during the 1812 War and during a period when he himself was arranging the transportation of formerly hostile northern tribes across the Mississippi.

Since the Indians were too immature to have grievances, any discontent must be the work of outside agitators or half-breeds who took advantage of the full-bloods. In particular, "the real Indians—the natives of the forest"—wanted to emigrate, but were restrained by "designing half-breeds and renegade white men."[105] In this metaphor white officials became the paternal protectors of the real Indians against the half-civilized or evil parents who exploited them. In fact, the aim was to make the Indians powerless and malleable. As Jackson wrote when his theft of Cherokee land met resistance, "If all influence but the native Indian was out of the way, we would have but little trouble."[106]

The most dangerous bad parents were the Spanish and British, who were to blame for every Indian war. Indians had to be "weaned" from the British and Spanish; "the savages must be made dependent on us."[107] Where foreign intervention could not be discovered, the Indians must have been "excited by some secrete [sic] influence."[108] Projecting evil designs onto bad parents justified America's aggressive expansionism. Men like Jackson directed paranoid rage against the foreign countries allegedly to blame for Indian wars; their influence was discovered everywhere. Illegally executing a Scottish trader and a British adventurer captured on his 1818 Florida invasion, Jackson explained that he could not have punished "the poor, ignorant savages, and spared the white men who set them on."[109]

There was more rage against the British and Spanish than against the "deluded" savages.[110] But sympathy for the Indians simply infantilized them and undercut their grievances. It did not save them from destruction. Major Thomas Butler explained, speaking for Jackson, that the British "only use them so long as they might be serviceable, and ultimately abandon them to the mercy of the government which has had too much cause to punish with vigour the innocent savage who has been schooled to the murder of his friends and thus made the instrument of his own destruction."[111]

Jackson and Cass insisted on their parental responsibilities with most vehemence just when the southern Indians were, in white terms, growing up. Prior to 1820 it had been possible to gain Indian land through

treaties, fraudulent or otherwise, and to rely on the spontaneous workings of society—speculators, intruders, traders, whisky, disease, and
bribery—to make the Indians consent to leave. But in the first quarter
of the nineteenth century, the southern Indians took increasingly to
commodity agriculture, developed government institutions to protect
themselves against whites, and refused to cede more land. In this context
Jackson, the man responsible for obtaining the bulk of southern Indian
land, developed the theory that treaties were not the proper way of
doing business with Indians. Indians were subjects of the United States,
not independent nations, and they had no right to refuse to cede their
land. Congress, as "the proper Guardian," "should extend to the Indians
its protection and fostering care." It should take Indian land as whites
needed it, at the same time providing for Indian needs.[112] Jackson could
not convince President Monroe to adopt this method, but he obtained
considerable Indian land by telling tribes, untruthfully, that Congress
planned to take their land if they did not cede it.[113]

As president, Jackson applied his interpretation to justify the extension of state law over the Indians, in violation of treaty rights. Mean-
while, Cass, soon to be Jackson's secretary of war, developed the paternal metaphor to defend Jackson's approach. Cass argued that, instead
of the system of treaties, in which the whites left the Indians to look
after themselves, the tribes would have been better off if from the beginning the United States has adopted the principle of "pupilage" in deciding which lands each party needed. The Jackson administration, Cass
believed, at last seemed to understand this. "If a paternal authority is
exercised over the aboriginal colonies . . . we may hope to see that improvement in their conditions for which we have so long and vainly
labored."[114]

Shortly thereafter Georgia governor William Schley applied the
Jackson-Cass argument to the Alabama Creeks. The Creeks had been
defrauded of their land during Jackson's Indian removal, which Cass's
paternalism had sought to justify. Settlers and speculators had illegally
occupied Creek land, seizing Indian farms and other property. A few
starving Creeks killed some settlers, leading Jackson and Cass to end
the fraud investigation and transport the entire tribe by force west of
the Mississippi. Governor Schley had urged this step: "These Indians
must no longer be permitted to remain where they now are, to murder
our people and destroy their property *ad libitum*. It is idle to talk of
treaties and national faith with such savages. The proper course to

adopt with them is to treat them as wards or children, and make them do that which is to their benefit and our safety."[115]

As helpless children, Indians had no independent identity. Bad Indians became "monsters," lost their humanity, and could be exterminated. Helpless Indians became things and could be manipulated and rearranged at will. Governor Wilson Lumkin of Georgia, urging the forcible removal of the Cherokees without the formality of a treaty, wrote Jackson, "Have not these Indians lost all claim to national character? Ought not these Indians to be considered and treated as the helpless wards of the federal Government?"[116]

White greed for Indian land dominated Indian-white relations. It was disorienting to the tribes and their genuine sympathizers to insist on the purely benevolent concern of the white father for his red children. The white father had no interests of his own but only a concern for Indian welfare. In his 1830 annual message Jackson explained, "Toward the aborigines of this country none can indulge a more friendly feeling than myself, or would go further in attempting to reclaim them from their wandering habits." He hoped that all true friends of the Indians would "unite in attempting to open the eyes of those children of the forest to their true condition," so they would remove west of the Mississippi.[117] As the House Committee on Indian Affairs asserted, "One common feeling, favorable and friendly towards the red children in question, pervades the bosom of every enlightened citizen in the Union."[118]

Such benevolence threatened to smother the Indians. It gave them no distance from the white father and denied them the anger that would preserve their connection with reality and their identity.[119] Nevertheless, it did not always work. Indians often responded with "ingratitude." Tribes were commonly accused of stubbornness and recalcitrance, failing to appreciate how much the president had done for them.[120] Unlike the benevolent whites, the Indians were creatures of emotion; they had desires, particularly greed for their land and unwillingness to part with it.

True, some whites were also acknowledged to be selfish and self-aggrandizing. But predatory whites were always split from Indian guardians and never contaminated them. Indeed, the benevolent father would protect the Indians against the greed and violence of less-enlightened pioneers. James Gadsden explained to the Florida Indians, "Like a kind father, the President says to you, there are lands enough for both his white and his red children. His white are strong, and might exterminate his red, but he will not permit them. He will preserve his red children." He would, that is, if the Indians ceded the bulk of their Florida lands.[121] In this treaty, as in countless others, the split between benevolent and predatory whites permitted the former to use the latter to club the Indians, without taking responsibility for the contemplated violence and extermination.[122]

Benevolent whites could also expiate America's guilt over its treatment of Indian tribes. For some this altruism had a clearly personal meaning. Thomas McKenney saw himself as a messiah befriending "those desolate and destitute children of the forest" against the injustices they had suffered.[123] The Indian commissioner's charged language and obsessional parental imagery suggest he identified Indians with a lost childhood of his own. Defending Indians against predatory whites, he could help them grow up without his own sense of longing and loss.

Like many others concerned with Indian affairs, McKenney put this parental benevolence into personal practice. He adopted a Cherokee boy the same age as his son. According to the commissioner, race consciousness prevented the boy from duplicating the happiness of the McKenney household in the outside world. The Cherokee became a frontier lawyer and killed himself when a white woman refused his offer of marriage. McKenney turned the story into a plea that Indians be permitted to become white.[124]

Andrew Jackson, fatherless at birth and orphaned at fourteen, adopted a Creek boy after his troops had killed the parents. "At the battle of Tohopeka," explained Jackson's close friend and future secretary of war, John Henry Eaton, "an infant was found, pressed to the bosom of its lifeless mother." Hearing that the Indian women planned to kill the baby, Jackson "became himself the protector and guardian of the child. Bestowing on the infant the name of Lincoier, he adopted it into his family, and has ever since manifested the liveliest zeal towards it, prompted by benevolence, and because, perhaps, its fate bore a strong resemblance to his own, who, in early life, and from the ravages of war, was left in the world, forlorn and wretched, without friends to assist, or near relations to direct him on his course."[125] Lincoier lived for some years in the Jackson household but died of tuberculosis before reaching manhood.

True benevolence required the white father to be strong as well as kind. The president, McKenney explained to the Committee on Indian Affairs, needed to employ military force to prevent Indian tribes from settling their disputes by war and "to enforce an observance of his fatherly councils. Our Indians stand pretty much in the relation to the Government as do our children to us. They are equally dependent, and need, not infrequently, the exercise of parental authority to detach them from those ways which might involve both their peace and their lives. It would not be considered just for our children to be let alone to settle their quarrels in their own way."[126]

After calling the Indians our "fostered children," Secretary of War Eaton stressed the need for military posts in Indian territory because "moral influence can be productive of little benefit to minds not cultivated."[127] General Edmund Gaines agreed. "The poisonous cap of barbarism cannot be taken from the lips of the savage by the mild voice of reason alone; the strong mandate of justice must be resorted to and enforced."[128]

Force was necessary not only to civilize the Indians but also to punish them for attacks on settlers. Here, too, the dominant metaphor was paternal. A strong father was necessary to "chastise" Indians when they went on the warpath. Occasionally, calls for extermination of the Indians were even brought within the family circle. Indian agent Joseph Street, seeking Sioux aid in Black Hawk's War, explained, "Our Great Father has foreborne to use force, until the Sacs and Foxes have dared to kill some of his white children. He will forbear no longer. He has tried to reclaim them, and they grow worse. He is resolved to sweep them from the face of the earth. They shall no longer trouble his children. If they cannot be made good they must be killed. . . . Your father has penned these Indians up, and he means to kill them all."[129]

For those who found the Indians essentially depraved, the need for strong, paternal discipline followed naturally. The only way to civilize the Indians, explained Georgia congressman John Forsyth (later Jackson's secretary of state), was to destroy the tribes and make the Indians subject to state law. "You might as reasonably expect that wild animals, incapable of being tamed in a park, would be domesticated by turning them loose in the forest. . . . Wild nature was never yet tamed but by coercive discipline."[130]

But the parental ideal of the more hopeful and philanthropic school was only slightly less fierce. Thomas McKenney, during a trip among the southern tribes, illustrated the proper method of helping the Indians to civilization. A warrior had attempted to stab his mother-in-law, who had hidden his goods so he could not trade them for whisky. McKenney asked Lewis Cass, then governor of Michigan Territory, what to do. The governor "answered promptly, 'Make a woman of him.'" McKenney placed the warrior in the center of a circle of a thousand Indians. He told him that henceforth he would be a woman, took his knife from his belt, thrust it into a flagstaff, and broke it at the hilt. He then stripped the Indian of his moccasins, decorated leggings, blanket, silver earrings, bracelets, and face-paint, describing the process later in loving, sadistic detail. Dressing the brave in a petticoat, McKenney explained that women were to be protected and valued by men, not murdered. Good treatment of women differentiated savagery from civilization. According to McKenney, the Indian women approved of the punishment, while the braves would never again admit the warrior among them. The humiliated Indian exclaimed, "I'd rather be dead. I am no longer a brave; I'm a woman." "Now this form of punishment," McKenney concluded, "was intended to produce moral results, and to elevate the condition of women, among the Indians. It was mild in its physical effects, but more terrible than death in its action and consequences upon the offender."[131]

This ceremony of degradation epitomizes the psychic war against the Indians. McKenney's altruism required helpless and dependent children. The commissioner understood the connection between death and destroyed identity. Paternal benevolence permitted symbolic castration and infantilization; the Indian no longer confronted the white world with independent power and subversive cultural alternatives. McKenney participated in the crime as well as the retribution (except that his domination was not over women but over a feminized man). The coldness, detachment, and tutelary quality of the punishment avoided intimacy and contamination. Relations with the Indians permitted that domination over men forbidden but longed for in liberal society. In a culture that undermined paternal authority, the father returned as a harsh and punishing figure in those areas where he was permitted to function at all.[132]

IV

Interaction among free, independent, and equal men had one crucial advantage over the theory of paternal authority. Liberal contractual relations diffused guilt; no one could be held responsible for the condition of anyone else. Since the Indians were offered only death or disappearance, it was particularly important to avoid the burden of guilt. The personal, paternal metaphor, therefore, was combined with another. The Indians were pictured as victims of mechanized and fragmented social processes for which no one was to blame and, at the same time, as autonomous beings who were free to choose their fate. This ultimate in the rhetoric of disorienting infantilization broke even the connection to a personified central authority and left individual Indians to contend with an irresponsible social pluralism, allegedly driven by inevitable historical laws. Indians were infantilized and destroyed, but white leaders were not to blame.

For two centuries treaties—fraudulent, coerced, or otherwise—imposed liberal contractualism upon the tribes. But by the 1820s treaties were foundering on Indian intransigence. The parental president had to interfere, but in such a way that he could not be accused of coercing the tribes. At times the language maintained a personal connection between the father and his children. T. L. McKenney, for example, announced that he would not force Indians to leave their land: "Seeing as I do the condition of these people, and that they are bordering on destruction, I would, were I empowered, take them *firmly* but *kindly* by the hand, and tell them they must go; and I would do this, on the same principle I would take my own children by the hand, firmly but kindly and lead them from a district of the country in which the plague was raging."[133]

This language implied coercion, however benevolent. More commonly, the only acknowledged coercion came from the tribal structure itself. Half-breed chiefs, it was alleged, prevented the full-bloods from emigrating. Indian commissioners commonly reported after the failure of treaty negotiations that a treaty would have been signed "had the authorities and the people been left to the free and unrestrained exercise of their own inclinations and judgements."[134] "I believe every native of this nation left to themselves," said Jackson, "would freely make this election [to remove], but they appear to be overawed by the council of some white men and half breeds, who have been and are fattening of the annuities, the labours, and folly of the native Indians." Eliminate these "self-aggrandizing," "bawling politicians," and the freed Indians would emigrate.[135]

It was unwise to attack the tribal structure directly. Jackson rejected a Florida Indian agent's contention that he had to "rebuke the Indian chiefs as if they were wrong-headed schoolboys" for opposing removal, by stripping them of their titles.[136] The same purposes were better served through bribery, which was legitimate—given the good aims of the government and the selfish "avarice" of the chiefs[137]—and through signing treaties with unrepresentative groups of Indians sympathetic to white blandishments.

Break apart the tribal structure, and Indians would be free to choose their own best interests. Destruction of communal restrictions on individual freedom by a strong central authority followed the tradition of early, European liberalism. Although Jackson frowned upon direct dethronement of chiefs, he intervened in other ways to destroy tribal authority. He took from the Cherokee leaders the annual annuity that supported tribal government. It was divided into equal amounts of forty-two cents and given to each Cherokee, or at least to those who bothered to make the long journey to agent headquarters.[138] The Creek, Choctaw, and Chickasaw removal treaties gave individual plots of land to thousands of Indians. Each was then free to sell his plot and cross the Mississippi or to remain under state law. Since the government had left each Indian free to make his own decision, it was not implicated in the extraordinary fraud, thievery, and violence that followed.[139]

The liberal principle behind such tactics was that coercion emanated only from the government and not from the economy or the society. If Indians were coerced by their situation to choose to sell their land but not forced to do so by the political authority, then they were not coerced at all. If each Indian could internalize his impossible situation, then he, not the president or the white society, would be responsible for the choices he made. Jefferson, for example, recommended establishing trading houses in Indian territory to increase Indian wants. Indians would then be forced into debt, and "we observe that when these debts get beyond what the individuals can pay, they become willing to lop them off by a cession of lands."[140] Jefferson's specific recommendations were followed in Chickasaw country, and tribal land there and elsewhere was later acquired through Indian indebtedness (often hugely inflated) to government and private traders. Here was an early example of what Margaret Mead would later call "democratic control," as opposed to totalitarian coercion and the Selective Service Board, "the American or indirect way of achieving what is done by direction in foreign countries where choice is not permitted." As a method of liberal planning, it found its way into government social policies from agriculture to draft deferments.[141] The principle was to structure the environment so that the dice were loaded strongly in favor of a single alternative and then to give the target of social planning the onus of the choice.

Liberal planning demonstrated its advantages over federal coercion when Georgia, Alabama, and Mississippi extended their laws over the tribes residing within state bounds. The Supreme Court correctly held that this action violated Indian treaties and federal law.[142] But Jackson refused to enforce the decision and acquiesced in the states' action. He and his friends favored the extension of state sovereignty, since it would eliminate Indians without attaching blame to the federal government.[143]

State laws deprived the chiefs of their titles and power. Indians could not testify in state courts, and the state would not prosecute intrusions and depredations on Indian land. Georgia divided up Cherokee territory for auction in a state lottery.[144] Extension of state sovereignty, as everyone understood, meant death to the Indians who remained on their land. As the secretary of war put it, "by refusing" to remove, "they must, necessarily, entail destruction on their race."[145]

At the same time Indians were reputedly free to stay or go. Jackson explained, "This emigration should be voluntary, for it would be as cruel as unjust to compel the aborigines to abandon the graves of their fathers and seek a home in a distant land. But they shall be directly informed that if they remain within the limits of the states they must be subject to their laws."[146] "God forbid," said future president James Buchanan in support of the Indian removal bill, "that I, or that any other gentlemen upon this floor, should entertain the purpose of using the power of this Government to drive that unfortunate race of men by violence across the Mississippi. Where they are let them remain, unless they should freely consent to depart. The State of Georgia, so far as we can judge from her public acts, entertains no other intention."[147]

What did this mean for the paternal metaphor? A Georgia senator explained that Jackson, "with a special regard for the welfare of the Indians," gave them a choice of land in the West or of remaining under Georgia law. "And this, sir, is [supposed to be] the language of a despot! . . . [It is only] a little friendly and parental advice from the President to the children of the forest."[148] The president was not a despotic father but one who helped the Indians make their own decisions.[149]

If the Indians, failing to take the president's advice, remained and were destroyed, the president was not to blame. In Jackson's words, "I feel conscious of having done my duty to my red children and if any failure of my good intention arises, it will be attributable to their want of duty to themselves, not to me." "I have exonerated the national character from all imputation, and now leave the poor deluded Creeks and Cherokees to their fate, and their annihilation, which their wicked advisers has [sic] induced."[150]

To free the government from responsibility for the Indian plight, however, was also to assert paternal helplessness. "Your great father has not the power to prevent" whites from moving onto Chickasaw land and Mississippi from extending its jurisdiction, Jackson told the tribe.[151]

The workings of society were not the responsibility of the government, and it was powerless to control them. The government took no responsibility for traders, squatters, and speculators, who defrauded Indians and were major forces in the social pressure for removal. Contractors who won with the lowest bid the right to transport and provision Indians removing west, who fed them rancid meat, led them through diseased areas, clothed them inadequately for the freezing southwestern winters, and crowded them on dangerous flatboats, were not, as independent businessmen, the responsibility of the government.[152] Paternal helplessness underlay the ideal of Indian freedom; the strong and benevolent father was not responsible for his acts.

The intractability of the Indian character contributed, it was alleged, to paternal helplessness. Countless efforts to civilize the Indians, explained Cass, had foundered on Indian improvidence. With Indian removal the government was trying yet again, and any "failure must be attributed to the inveterate habits of this people and not to the policy of the government."[153] In spite of efforts to civilize the Creeks and Cherokees, "the great body of the people are in a state of helpless and hopeless poverty. . . . The same improvidence and habitual indolence . . . mark the northern tribes." A few years ago, Cass illustrated, Congress even had to appropriate money to feed the starving Florida Indians.[154]

Such arguments only revealed the function of the assertion of paternal helplessness. The Seminoles were starving not because of the "inveterate habits" of the Indians but because the government had moved them once to land upon which little could be grown, was now planning to move them to the west, and had burned their crops and destroyed their cattle in a government-provoked war.[155] The demoralized Indians could hardly be expected to plant once again simply to leave crops behind or have them devastated. Assertions about the Indian character simply involved the refusal of the government to take responsibility for the consequences of its acts.

The worse the government policy toward Indians, the more insistent the attacks on Indian character. How else justify white crimes, particularly as the powerless Indians could not so easily be accused of provoking them. The remaining Indians were living reminders of white guilt; infantilization and dehumanization prevented the pain of experiencing their suffering. Cherokee leader John Ross wrote, "I knew that the perpetrator of a wrong never forgives his victims."[156]

Refusal to accept responsibility separated individuals from the consequences of their actions. This, as Tocqueville saw it, was the unique

feature of America's conquest of the Indians. Americans' "cold and im-
placable egotism" toward the Indians narrowed drastically their own
sense of responsibility. They could destroy nature and the Indians on an
enormous scale, "setting coldly about deeds that can only be explained
by the fire of passion." They did not intend that Indians starve and therefore were not to blame if their actions caused famines.[157] Apologists for
America's slaughter of Vietnamese peasants also explain that bombing
the countryside is not meant to kill civilians. Of this claim Mary
McCarthy writes, "Foreknowledge of the consequences of an act that is
then performed generally argues the will to do it; if this occurs repeatedly, and the doer continues to protest that he did not will the consequences, this suggests an extreme and dangerous disassociation of the
personality."[158]

America had begun with a radical assertion of the power of men to
control their fate. But the country progressed through the destruction of
another set of humans, and responsibility for that destruction could not
be faced. In Lewis Cass's words, white men were planted by providence
on the "skirts of a boundless forest." Subduing it by industry, they advanced and multiplied by providential decree. They had superiority in
arts, arms, and intelligence. How, then, could whites be blamed for the
Indian plight? "Their misfortunes have been the consequence of a state
of things which could not be controlled by them or us." Cass drew practical lessons from this theory of history. If the Creeks who chose to stay
in Alabama "finally melt away before our people and institutions, the
results must be attributed to causes, which we can neither stay nor
control."[159]

Cass still recognized that Indians might die in Alabama. In its most
extreme form the process of denial reached reality itself. The worse the
events, the less they could be admitted into consciousness. The roundup,
detainment in stockades, and military removal of the Cherokees killed
an estimated four thousand of the fifteen thousand members of the eastern branch of the tribe.[160] As the secretary of war described the process,
"The generous and enlightened policy . . . was ably and judiciously carried into effect by the General appointed. . . . Humanity no less than
good policy dictated this course toward these children of the forest."
The commissioner of Indian affairs amplified: "A retrospect of the last
eight months in reference to this numerous and more than enlightened
tribe cannot fail to be refreshing to well-constituted minds. . . . A large
mass of men have been conciliated; the hazard of an effusion of human
blood has been put by; good feeling has been preserved, and we have

quietly and gently transported eighteen thousand friends to the west bank of the Mississippi."[161]

Instead of facing actual deaths, Indian destruction became an abstracted and generalized process removed from human control and human reality. To face responsibility for specific killing might have led to efforts to stop it; to avoid individual deaths turned Indian removal into a theory of genocide. In Jackson's words:

> Humanity has often wept over the fate of the aborigines of this country, and Philanthropy has been busily engaged in devising means to avert it, but its progress has never for a moment been arrested, and one by one have many powerful tribes disappeared from the earth. To follow to the land the last of his race and to tread on the graves of extinct nations excites melancholy reflections. But true philanthropy reconciles the mind to these vicissitudes, as it does to the extinction of one generation to make room for another.[162]

Weeping over Indian deaths was immature. History rescued a man from melancholy; he could tread on Indian graves in peace. "Independence of mind and action," contrary to Jackson's advice to his nephew, could not be borne. Instead, a man like Jackson had to justify himself in "the image of his creator," as a "real tool in the hands of" a divine father, "wielded, like a mere automaton, sometimes, without knowing it, to the worst of purposes."[163] To be a man meant to participate, emotionally separated from the actual experience, in a genocide.[164]

CHAPTER VI

Nature as Politics and Nature as Romance in America

Since the Puritans of Massachusetts Bay, organized in covenants as a joint stock company, imagined themselves a mystic brotherhood reborn in the body of Christ, American history has progressed under the sway of two conflicting vocabularies. One, the language of exterior, marketplace relations, takes the contract as its master symbol. The other, the language of interior religious and psychological experience, centers around regeneration. The first vocabulary is economic, the second is familial.

At first both vocabularies defended the Puritan community against an alien wilderness. In time, however, American identity shifted from the Puritan God and his European interests to New World nature and her products. The search for visible signs of God's grace, combined with the material reality of nature, turned the Puritans toward economic acquisition and the American landscape. The original religious communities disintegrated in the process. What happened to the two vocabularies of American self-image, and what role does nature play in their development?

Political science is the child of the marketplace metaphor and finds the religious language of inner division and rebirth an alien one. I want

This paper was first prepared for delivery at the 1976 Annual Meeting of the American Political Science Association, The Palmer House, Chicago, Illinois, 2–5 September 1976. Two Berkeley colleagues, Richard Hutson and Norman Jacobson, helped suggest the perspective adopted in the essay. I am in their debt.

first to suggest that the contractual vocabulary came to define the American political self-image, while rebirth in nature came to define its identity in literature. But restrictive understandings of American politics are too narrow. The romance of nature, I will argue, plays a powerful role in the political tradition itself. I will introduce this idea via certain modern social scientists; then turn, via Ben Franklin, to the unifying significance of nature at the nation's founding; and then shift, via Marx, from the split in American culture between politics and literature to the one that divides nature itself, as the source of both bourgeois commodities and civic virtues. Finally, I will examine the two dominant images of natural virtue in the history of American politics—pastoral harmony and wilderness regeneration.

I

Contractual relations in society have formed the classics of American politics, rebirth in nature the classics of American literature. The political tradition that comes down to us from Benjamin Franklin and James Madison to such moderns as Daniel Boorstin and Robert Dahl pictures an America of individual and group conflicts, rational bargaining, and the struggle for concrete, material interests. This tradition ties the special destiny of America to politics, but politics of a peculiarly narrow sort. Derived from economic categories, it is characterized by economic and ethnic conflict and racial, sexual, and philosophic uniformity.

The literary tradition evolves from Charles Brockden Brown through Cooper, Hawthorne, Poe, Melville, and Twain to such moderns as William Faulkner and Norman Mailer. Here the major actions take place not in society but in nature, and racial division and emotional intensity replace social interdependence. Here the asocial innocent, searching for a lost pastoral idyll, encounters despair, nightmare, and wilderness apocalypse. Here America's special destiny is fulfilled in nature. Richard Hofstadter's *American Political Tradition* is the best description of the one America; D. H. Lawrence's *Studies in Classic American Literature* is the seminal exposure of the other.[1] The two books seem to describe entirely different countries.

Lawrence and Hofstadter both contrasted America with a feudally based, class-conscious Europe, but the comparison took them in opposite directions. Hofstadter and the social scientists who followed him distinguished ideological European politics from "the traditional problem-solving pragmatism of American politics."[2] Lawrence and the literary critics like Leslie Fiedler and Richard Chase who followed him, contrasted the European feel for social reality with the American predilection for psychological fantasy. Chase distinguished the European novel, where deeply rooted social relations, pervasive class distinctions, and powerful familial traditions formed and limited character, from the American romance, where the individual freed from society and alone in nature encountered his racial double and where "close involvement with real life" was abandoned for the melodramatic "underside of consciousness."[3]

Each tradition identifies different foundings, one in politics, the other in nature. Social scientists derive their America from 1776 and 1789. Actually to look back at the political foundings is to see their grounding in nature, in the natural rights of the Declaration of Independence and the scientific principles upon which the Constitution was built. "The United States of America have exhibited, perhaps, the first example of government erected on the simple principles of nature," wrote John Adams. "These governments were contrived merely by the use of reason and the senses, as Copley painted Chatham . . . , as Dwight, Barlow, Trumbull, and Humphreys composed their verse . . . ; as Godfrey invented his quadrant, and Rittenhause his planetarium; as Boylston practiced inoculation, and Franklin electricity."[4] There was good reason, nonetheless, why politics rather than the nature from which it was drawn became the stuff of the political tradition. Nature, like lightning, went into the American political transformer; politics, like electric power, came out. The natural right to acquire property and the natural distinctions among men, Madison argued in *Federalist* 10, required a diverse society of competing interests. A strong, balanced government prevented reversion to the state of nature and to the wicked schemes for "agrarian justice" (as Tom Paine called it) that flourished there.[5] "What situation can be pictured more awful than a total dissolution of government," asked Oliver Ellsworth in 1787, "a state of rude violence, in which every man's hand is against his neighbors?"[6]

"He will be a wild man; his hand will be against every man, and every man's hand against him" (Gen. 16:12). Ellsworth evoked the biblical wild man Ishmael to recall Americans to Abraham's covenant with God. Americans were, like Isaac, the children meant to live under law, not, like Ishmael, savage and slave children cast out by Abraham into the wilderness.

The founding memorialized in our literature, however, took place in the wilderness. Its heroes were not the fathers who founded America twice and for all time in Philadelphia but the Indian fighters, pioneers, and settlers continuously creating "the rebirth of American society" from the virgin land.[7] These wilderness literary heroes lack a secure paternal birthright; they are Ishmaels—in Cooper's *Prairie*, in Melville's *Redburn, Pierre*, and *Moby Dick*. (Where there is an Isaac, in Faulkner's *Go Down Moses*, he relinquishes his contaminated inheritance.) The classics of literature return to origins; going beneath the covenants, they uncover what Madison called the two "problem[s] most baffling to the policy of our country," which his interest politics failed to solve, "the case of the black race within our bosom . . . [and] the red on our borders."[8]

In a national survey conducted two decades ago, 85 percent of the American people named America's political institutions as a major source of their pride in the country.[9] From Cooper to the bicentennial, however, politics and its foundings have had little vitality in mythology and popular culture. There, westward expansion, natural idylls, wilderness struggles, and interracial encounters hold sway. Can we conclude, then, that the political tradition describes behavioral fact, the literary, romantic fantasy?

Daniel Bell's recent *The Cultural Contradictions of Capitalism* seems to support such a contention. The economy and the culture, Bell argues, form two separate and autonomous realms in modern society, one ruled by the imperatives of efficiency, the other by hedonistic norms of self-absorption and self-fulfillment.[10] Classic American literature, Bell might remind us, is fiction, in flight from the serious realities of American life. The great interpreters of "nature's nation"—Perry Miller, Henry Nash Smith, and most recently Richard Slotkin[11]—have been professors of English.

Frederick Jackson Turner's frontier thesis, product of a self-conscious scientific historian, might seem to undercut this distinction. But the Turner thesis, Hofstadter argued in an essay published the year after *The American Political Tradition*, had the appeal of myth; it had little to say about the actual forces that shaped American development.[12] The political tradition, from this Bell-Hofstadter perspective, would seem to be actual history, and its interpreters are modern social scientists.

Bell's actual position, however, is more complex. Culture and the economy, he argues, both make demands on politics, and he defends politics against a modern culture whose "idolatry of the self" is "subversive of contemporary society."[13] The classics of American literature may describe fantasies, but they are fantasies that become dangerously active in politics. Bell is, in *Cultural Contradictions*, reclaiming the territory he and Hofstadter staked out in the 1950s; he is defending the American political tradition against politicized cultural assault.

The American Political Tradition, published in 1948, was an interpretation of American politics, not an apology for it. In the 1950s Hofstadter's interpretation shifted its base from fact to a value, as he and other writers discovered an agrarian mystique opposed to the political tradition Hofstadter had identified a few years earlier.[14] "Boulders from the West," in Vachel Lindsay's populist poem, had threatened Plymouth Rock. The Isaacs were now defending it.[15]

The western farmers of *The American Political Tradition* were smallholding capitalists; agrarian dreams hardly appeared in the book. Like the former Marxist Bell, Hofstadter discovered agrarian myth only in the 1950s. The sentimental glorification of rural life, he wrote, generated intolerance of diversity, conspiracy theories of alien and secret power, and attacks on established political institutions. Bell feared moralistic or hedonistic assaults on a Madisonian politics of market decisions and interest conflict. The New Left of the 1960s was also said to care more about symbolic gratifications than achievable political ends; its disappearance into rural communes seemed to confirm the identification of politics with society, fantasy with the land.[16]

The Hofstadter-Bell analysis of the 1950s reconnected the American political tradition to its origins. It rediscovered the founders' fears of agrarian protest, of the state of nature upon which the political tradition had been imposed. Return to nature became not merely a problem of the literary imagination but of antipolitical politics as well.[17]

Whatever the virtues of the Hofstadter-Bell analysis, it had a noticeable Manichaean quality. Actual students of agrarian politics suggested, from within social science, a more organic connection between interest politics and agrarian fantasy. Hofstadter's discussion of agrarian fundamentalism in *The Age of Reform* was heavily indebted to the New Deal agricultural economist Paul Johnstone. There was, however, a crucial divergence. Hofstadter contrasted the myth of natural harmony among men living conflict-free on the land with the business methods and pressure group politics of farm interest groups. But Johnstone had shown that the professionalized agrarian leaders who brought scientific farming, social stratification, and corporate connections to the countryside continued to idealize the farm as a haven from worldly strife. Idealizing an innocent agrarian world in which success still rewarded personal virtue, they assimilated the business farm to the agrarian dream.[18]

In more theoretically developed analyses, Philip Selznick and Grant McConnell also showed that the rural idyll legitimized established organizations. They located the dream of natural harmony at the center of the farm interest group. A rhetoric of grass-roots democracy and local control, they argued, helped the American Farm Bureau Federation build an oligarchic organization from a narrow class base among wealthy farmers. Localist ideology stigmatized as alien invasions efforts to make agricultural policy serve the interests of competing social groups—urban consumers and poor rural whites and blacks.[19]

Moving beyond agricultural politics, McConnell and Theodore Lowi suggested that pastoral animosity to social conflict provided the underpinnings for American pluralism. Pluralism, these writers argued, stifled controversy instead of encouraging it. Large interest groups, wrote McConnell, claimed to inherit the virtues of local community. They pictured themselves as organic, homogeneous associations, protecting their members from external, political coercion. "The roots of this ideology," wrote McConnell, "reach into the nation's agrarian past. They have produced the association so frequently made between individual virtue and the simplicity of rural life."[20]

Madison was the father of the pluralist political tradition for Hofstadter; he was its chief critic for McConnell. Madison, wrote McConnell, rejected the agrarian dream that all citizens might have the same opinions, passions, and interests. Interest group spokesmen resurrected that dream inside their narrowed constituencies. The interest group, argued McConnell, derived from dreams of rural harmony, not from acceptance of political diversity; Jefferson and John Taylor of Caroline, not Madison, were its founders.[21] American pluralism, McConnell and Lowi argued, was characterized less by conflict than by fear of conflict; it divided government into bureaucratic complexes, each with hegemony in the relevant policy areas and each presenting itself as a natural community. Murray Edelman, in a complementary analysis, suggested that the mass public received symbolic gratifications from interest-dominated political language, while tangible benefits went to the group's clientele.[22] Offering itself as the alternative to political coercion and social conflict, Hofstadter's interest politics was, for all but its narrow constituencies, a romance.

Agrarian romance assaulted pragmatic, interest group politics according to Hofstadter and Bell; predatory interest group politics dressed itself in romantic clothes for McConnell. McConnell's analysis, although socially more acute than Hofstadter's, was not psychologically so complex. Both began with the idyll of rural innocence. McConnell exposed the ideological uses (in Mannheim's sense) of that idyll, which promoted passive acceptance of the power of organizational giants. Hofstadter showed how the pastoral dream became (to recall Mannheim again) dystopia. His history, like the classic literature, found innocence, betrayal, and violence joined together on the land. But Hofstadter found the psychology of an Eden betrayed only among radicals. The unhappy romance of nature, McConnell's analysis implies, did not merely generate peripheral attacks on the political center; it helped form the dominant political tradition itself.

How does the land figure, then, in the development of a distinctive set of American political images? Let us return to Ben Franklin, the man who took electricity from nature, as the founders made constitutions.

II

"The Internal State of America," Franklin's essay of 1786, begins with one of his stories. "There is a tradition," he writes,

> that in the Planting of New England, the first Settlers met with many difficulties and Hardships as is generally the Case when a civilized People attempt establishing themselves in a wilderness Country. Being piously disposed they sought Relief from Heaven, by laying their wants and Distresses before the Lord, in frequent set Days of Fasting and Prayer. Constant Meditation and Discourse on these Subjects kept their Minds gloomy and discontented; and like the Children of Israel, there were many disposed to return to that Egypt, which Persecution had induc'd them to abandon. At length, when it was proposed in the Assembly to proclaim another Fast, a Farmer of plain Sense arose, and remark'd that the Inconveniences . . . were not so great as they might have expected, . . . that the Earth began to reward their Labour and furnish liberally for their Subsistence; that the Seas and Rivers were full of Fish, the Air sweet, the Climate healthy . . . and that it would be more becoming the Gratitude they ow'd to the Divine Being, if, instead of a Fast, they should proclaim a Thanksgiving.[23]

What is the moral of this tale? Franklin wrote "The Internal State" in the troubled 1780s and the essay recalled his countrymen to their New World good fortune; its last words were, "Be quiet and thankful."[24] Those on the lookout for political ideology will hear in Franklin's soothing rhetoric an effort to quiet the agrarian unrest of the critical period. Franklin assuaged the "Complaints of *hard Times*" and, speaking the language he had given to Father Abraham in *Poor Richard's Almanac*, praised the "industrious, frugal Farmers."[25] Was Franklin directing his audience away from agrarian political agitation toward economic opportunity?

This interpretation gains support from Franklin's satire of the anti-Federalists, written during the ratification struggles two years later. Franklin compared the anti-Federalists who refused to surrender their liberty to the quarreling tribes of Israel. Those Israelites, he wrote, preferred Egyptian slavery (like the "Children of Israel" in "Internal State") to living under the Constitution God had handed down to Moses.[26] The Franklin of "Ancient Jews" and "Internal State" seems a confidence man from the pages of Lawrence and Melville,[27] making symbolic uses of Old Testament politics to promote the decline of agrarian democracy.

There is, however, a shift in "Internal State" more fundamental than the one from discontent to industry. A biblical, punishing God opens the essay; a pagan hymn to mother nature climaxes it. "We are the sons of the Earth and Seas," wrote Franklin, "and, like Antaeus, if, in wrestling with Hercules, we now and then receive a Fall, the Touch of our Parents will communicate to us fresh Strength and Ability to renew the contest."[28]

Countless eighteenth-century documents chronicle this shift from a God who stands against nature to one who resides within it.[29] For two and a half centuries, beginning with Columbus, Europeans found both earthly paradise and howling wilderness in America. The two images join together in a 1505 woodcut, the first pictorial representation of the New World's inhabitants: warriors in comradely embrace stand at one side of the print; at the other side a warrior's arm rests on the shoulder of a naked woman. Next to this arm there is another; this one, unattached to a body, is being eaten. Below, a mother suckles her infant; above a quarter of a human body hangs from a tree. The text reads, "The people are thus naked, handsome, brown, well-endowed in body. . . . No one . . . has anything, but all things are in common. And the men have as wives those who please them, be they mothers, sisters, or friends; . . . they also fight with each other; they also eat each other, even those who are slain, and hang the flesh of them in the smoke. They become a hundred and fifty years of age, and have no government."[30]

Such early symbolizations counterposed government to incest, murder, and cannibalism in the state of nature. Gradually the American Enlightenment imported order into nature and made it the foundation of American identity. Americans drew upon nature's authority to overthrow their European dependence. In economics as in politics, American nature reigned supreme. "The great Business of the Continent is

Agriculture," wrote Franklin; he contrasted feudal Europe, divided between "the few rich and haughty Landlords [and] the multitude of poor, abject, and rack'd Tenants," with American "happy Mediocrity," where "the Cultivator works for himself."[31] The self-controlled farmer in Franklin's utopia did not need to choose between Puritan fasting and Indian cannibalism.

But a fissure appeared in the American landscape to rent this eighteenth-century natural idyll. American nature was a source of both spiritual regeneration and economic wealth, and the dialectic of the two meanings explains much of the country's subsequent political development. The double American life with which we began cannot be conceived entirely as a split between politics and literature or between mainstream politics and agrarian political romance. There is a division at the center of American politics between a nature-become-commodities, which separates men in civil society, and a virgin land, which purifies and unites them. To understand nature's double identity, we must turn to the cultural contradictions of capitalism described not by Daniel Bell but by Karl Marx.

III

Under feudalism, Marx wrote in his essay "On the Jewish Question," there was no separation of politics from civil society. Organized segments of civil society—property, family, and work—were constituent elements of the state. Political revolution shattered civil society. "It retained the political spirit, which had been broken, fragmented, and lost, as it were, in the various cul-de-sacs of feudal society. It gathered up this scattered spirit, liberated it from its entanglement with civil life, and turned it into the sphere of the community." But the liberation of the political spirit from society also emancipated civil society from politics. The political doctrine of individual natural rights freed natural men to pursue their private economic interests. The idealism of the state complemented the materialism of civil society.[32]

Feudalism, Franklin had boasted, held least sway in America. Marx agreed, and he took almost all his illustrations of the split between the state and civil society from "the free states of North America." Political toleration, Marx argued, did not abolish religion in civil society. He contrasted American state constitutions that guaranteed religious toleration with Tocqueville and Beaumont's observation that America was "preeminently the land of religiosity." By the same token, although

American states abolished property qualifications for voting, they did not thereby overcome propertied distinctions among men. Politics, where all votes were equal, existed in an ideal realm that ratified inequality down below.[33]

Property belonged to man's private bourgeois existence. Identifying "the infinite splits of religion in North America," Marx wrote that religion, too, "has been tossed among numerous private interests" and made "a purely individual matter." Among "the pious and politically free inhabitants of New England," moreover, religion was thoroughly confused with property. "In North America," he explained, again relying on Beaumont, "the *very preaching of the Gospel* . . . has become an article of commerce." Anticipating part of Weber's analysis of Franklin in *The Protestant Ethic*, Marx described the interpenetration of religious and economic life.[34]

At the same time that sectarian, merchandizing religions flourished in civil society, the religious spirit infused the state: "Where the political state has achieved full development, man leads a double life, a heavenly and an earthly life, not only in thought or consciousness but in actuality. In the *political community* he regards himself as a *communal being*; but in civil society he is active as a *private individual*, treats other men as means, reduces himself to a means, and becomes the plaything of alien powers. The political state is as spiritual in relation to civil society as heaven is in relation to earth."[35]

Although "On the Jewish Question" was an antireligious tract, it retained the classic religious concerns. Marx rejected spiritual causality and heavenly solutions because they avoided earthly reality; but he shared the Christian perception that a material world of dead objects divided man within himself. The split Marx identified between state and civil society was reproduced within man; internally divided, he was the helpless prey of alien social forces. Protestant Americans diagnosed the same disease, and they thought they had found the cure.

Marx and Franklin both recognized that, since the Puritan decline, a theological state could no longer be shaped by specific doctrinal and organizational ties. Actual religious associations, wrote Marx, were "no longer the essence of community but the essence of division."[36] But Marx said nothing about the new spiritual content of American politics. In fact, as Perry Miller suggested, Americans turned in the eighteenth century from the squabbles among competing religious sects to "the enduring, the consoling, the uncontentious verities of nature."[37] Americans—and this connects Franklin's "Children of Israel" to Marx's "On the Jewish Question"—made nature their religion.

The material importance of American nature sustained its "heavenly" significance. Land was a medium of exchange and the predominant source of subsistence and commodity in early America. Land hunger fed state patronage and political factionalism; land speculation was the major way to wealth. Nevertheless, the "double life" of man as bourgeois and citizen undercut the consolations of nature.[38]

Marx, like Tocqueville, saw the role of nature only in civil society. Franklin's paean appealed to nature as commodity, too. Those who fear luxury are misguided, wrote Franklin, since "the Desire of adorning ourselves with fine cloaths, possessing fine Furniture, with good Houses, &c, is . . . strongly inciting to Labour and Industry." Such enthusiastic conversion of nature into objects embodies a process that prompted Marx to write, "The view of nature achieved under the rule of private property and money is an actual contempt for and practical degradation of nature," and prompted him to quote Thomas Münzer's complaint that "every creature should be turned into property, the fish in the water, and birds in the air, and plants of the earth." In Franklin's words, "He who draws a Fish out of our waters, draws up a Piece of Silver."[39]

Franklin converted fish into silver, but it would be mistaken simply to convert Antaeus into Poor Richard's Father Abraham showing the way to wealth. Although Franklin's consciousness was happily commercial, there was at the American political core an anxiety that mere acquisitive materialism would contaminate America's special destiny and generate factional strife. Ideal images of life on the land like Franklin's offered an Edenic alternative.

For Marx, men could only heal the division between egotistic bourgeois and abstract citizen by materializing the abstract community. Revolution would make community a lived experience, as humans took back into their sensuous selves, in shared, everyday activity, the alienated social power that pressed down upon them.[40] America offered a healing individual alternative to socialist community: the West. The importance of the West suggests a third reading of *Federalist* 10, neither Hofstadter's nor McConnell's, but William Appleman Williams's: Madison had tied the American future to empire and expansion rather than to communal control of wealth; he chose bourgeois political economy over a small republic of virtuous citizens.[41] But the West also offered images of virtue that mystified the social character of civil society. Each man gained strength from western nature by extracting personal use-values from her bounty. As articles of use turned into commodities, depleting nature and making man "the plaything of alien powers" (commodity production and exchange), new virgin land promised to restore to man his rightful powers. The myth of the West, a refuge from the significance of capitalist expansion, helped form the politics and culture of American capitalism.

About the time he described the internal state of America, Franklin also wrote a letter on individual internal states. "The Art of Procuring Pleasant Dreams" concerned nightmares. Franklin warned against the "stifled and poisoned . . . confined air" contained in closed rooms. He advised his correspondent to throw off her bedclothes, walk around, even change beds, in order to help her body heat escape. Sleeping unencumbered in the open air, he wrote, "is the order of nature to prevent animals from being infected by their own perspiration."[42] Perhaps the old fox was having one of his jokes; but perhaps he was offering, consciously or unconsciously, another political allegory. Jefferson shared this horror of closure. America would remain virtuous, he wrote Madison, "while there remain vacant lands in any part of America. When we get piled together upon one another in large cities, as in Europe, we shall . . . go to eating one another, as they do there."[43] Would Franklin's Thanksgiving feast, in the absence of available nature, metamorphosize into cannibalism after all?

Jefferson's anxiety over the end of the frontier has persisted throughout our history. "Personal liberty is incompatible with a crowded population," Representative Alexander Duncan insisted during the Oregon annexation debates.[44] Nightmares of closed space like Jefferson's and Duncan's contain two terrors—one of violence, the other of control by external forces. Wilderness combat and pastoral harmony, the positives developed from these negatives, constitute the political romance of nature.

IV

The two images of static pastoral idyll and violent wilderness regeneration have shaped the history of American politics. Both pastoral and what I will call gothic political heroes recall classic American literature. But political myths reject the outcast Ishmael identification so common in classic literature. Political heroes enter nature to sanctify their birthright as "the Children of Israel." The inheritors of Abraham's covenant derive their authority from the wilderness.

Both pastoral and wilderness ideals imagine men who are not "the plaything[s] of alien powers"; both heal the split between physical, productive bourgeois and ideal citizen. Both images of the land evoke the Puritan language of division and regeneration, but instead of substituting grace for nature, both promise second births through nature. Both ideals liberate the white male in agrarian space from social conflict in historical time. Both picture regression to a simple, presocial state. The West, in Frederick Jackson Turner's language, was "an opportunity for social development continually to begin over again, whenever society gave signs of breaking into classes. Here was a magic fountain of youth in which America continually bathed and was rejuvenated."[45]

Both pastoral and gothic heroes seek to recapture a lost childhood world. But while the pastoral mode evokes peaceful childhood dreams, the gothic calls up monsters of childhood nightmare. The archetypical pastoral hero is Franklin's "Farmer of plain Sense," the "industrious frugal Farmers . . . of whom the Body of our Nations consists."[46] The hero of wilderness regeneration is the hunter and Indian fighter, who in time becomes the cowboy.

Some versions of American pastoral imagine passive absorption into nature; thus Charles Wilson Webber pictured Daniel Boone moving ever further west "into the cool profound of the all-nourishing bosom of his primeval mother."[47] Other pastoral dreams evoke independence; thus Franklin and Jefferson portrayed self-sufficient yeomen learning self-control as they toiled. Some images recall a protective, paternal, rural world. "I should have thought myself the happiest man in the world, if I could have returned to my little hut and forty acres, which my father left me in Braintree," wrote John Adams in 1773.[48] Others picture a "self-made man" like George Bancroft's "orphan" George Washington, who, free of inherited identity, became father of himself in the West. (Bancroft's Washington owed his identity to the land, not to his parents. A wilderness surveyor in his teens, "the forests trained him, in meditative solitude, to freedom and largeness of mind, and nature revealed to him her obedience to serene and silent laws.")[49]

Pastoralism made nostalgia politically significant. It aimed to recreate in the West—and by social reform at home—a lost state of primitive innocence, independence, and simplicity. It identified a geographic and moral rural space, free from economic interest and political ambition, from which the great leaders of the country arose. One pastoral costume is the sheep's clothing in which farm organizations and other interest groups came to dress themselves. I can only touch briefly on some high-lights in the history of political pastoralism from Franklin to the Farm Bureau.

Southern soil nourished pastoralism at the birth of the republic, over-laying the image of virtuous yeoman independence with that of planta-tion hierarchy. Jefferson envisioned a natural planter aristocracy with a yeoman political base; but although he merged the two images politi-cally, their tensions persisted psychologically, embodied in his anxiety over the undermining of personal self-control by the interracial intimacy of plantation life. Jacksonian democracy buried planter-yeoman differ-ences in westward expansion. The differences emerged with a vengeance in the competing pastoralisms of the Civil War.

The Civil War was fought over whether free labor or slave labor would control the West. National geography, free western land, and the image of a garden nourished by machines sustained northern pastoral-ism.[50] Lincoln appealed against secession to an organic, geographic na-tionalism. "The great interior region," he told Congress, forms "the great body of the republic. . . . Our national strife springs not from our permanent part; not from the land we inhabit; not from our national homestead. There is no possible severing of this. . . . That portion of the earth's surface which is owned and inhabited by the people of the United States, is well adapted to be the home of one national family; it is not well adapted for two."[51]

Lincoln gave the West to the national family; the Republicans also promised free land to individual families. "The degraded vassal of the rich," George Julian promised in an early Homestead Act speech, "will find a home in the west; and stimulated by the favor of the Government, the desire for independence, and the ties of the family, the wilderness will be converted into smiling landscapes, and wealth poured into the nation's lap."[52]

Julian promised that the Homestead Act would "rescue thousands from the jaws of the land monopoly, and impart to them happiness and independence." Opponents of free land such as later anti-Populists and their academic descendants of the 1950s attacked radical "agrarianism." But Hofstadter knew in the 1940s that agrarianism was not the prob-lem. The Homestead Act, he pointed out, mystified westward develop-ment. Railroads given land grants and land companies disguised as homesteaders acquired the vast bulk of western land.[53]

The conflict between North and South pulled pastoralism apart, back

into southern, regressive, sensual repose and forward into mechanization. Southern pastoralism evoked a life lived close to the soil under
patriarchal planter authority. Claiming the entire pastoral inheritance,
southerners insisted that market competition and class conflict dominated northern society. Northern spokesmen attacked the degradation
of labor and the failure to master nature in southern, patriarchal agrarianism. Denying that industrial capitalism dominated northern society,
the North imagined a bustling rural landscape of small factories in the
fields.[54] By the end of the nineteenth century, industrial capitalist reality
had dwarfed that dream. The end of the frontier symbolized for the
country's political and cultural elite the disappearance of the virgin land
that had given the nation its identity. But the assimilation of the machine to the garden in the nineteenth-century imagination helped pro-
long the life of pastoralism in the twentieth century. The harmoniously
functioning machine would bring order to, or even replace, nature.

Pastoral nostalgia, as Hofstadter argued, dominated Progressive reform.[55] Progressives did not, however, imagine returning to actual pioneer conditions of individual independence. "We are in the presence of
a new order of society," Woodrow Wilson explained at the beginning
of *The New Freedom.* "Your individuality is swallowed up in the individuality and purpose of a great organization." But Wilson did not pro-
pose dismantling the "new order of society." Rather, he attacked "a
small number of men who control government" and who "make men
forget the ancient time when America lay in every hamlet, when America was to be seen in every fair valley, when America displaced her great
forces on the broad prairies, ran her fine fires of enterprise up over the
mountainsides and down into the bowels of the earth."[56]

Instead of overthrowing the "great organization," the Progressives
would purify it. Technological planning would create a new pastoral
harmony that was not restricted to self-sufficient homesteads but made
the entire country an organic unity. Reform would rely not on unregu-
lated frontier individualism but on social control from above.[57] The
great problem that faced America, said Theodore Roosevelt, was "the
problem of national efficiency, the patriotic duty of insuring the safety
and continuance of the nation."[58] The New Freedom, in Wilson's formulation, was the freedom to be part of the machine.[59]

Conservation policy, which bears most directly on the land, illustrates the Progressive approach. The end of the frontier, Theodore
Roosevelt told the Presidential Conference on Conservation, would not
end our dependence on nature. "Our part in the world has been attained

by the extent and thoroughness of the control we achieved over nature; but we are more, and not less, dependent upon what she furnishes than at any previous time of our history since the days of primitive man." In the past, Roosevelt continued, the frontier freed the generations from responsibility for one another. When the American settler "exhausted the soil of his farm, he felt that his son could go West and take up another." Now the sons were confined to their father's farms, and re-source planners would provide the benefits the sons had once taken di-rectly from nature. The essence of the Progressive conservation move-ment, Samuel Hays has shown, "was rational planning to promote efficient development and use of all natural resources." And scientific planning to restore agrarian ideals relied on government-corporate co-operation, not grass-roots enthusiasm.[60]

Social scientists interpret the New Deal as the definitive reorganiza-tion of American politics around urban ethnicity and class. Such a view, which exaggerates the break with pastoral tradition, is incomplete. Fas-cination with agrarian communities, Richard Pells demonstrates, char-acterized the popular and high culture of the 1930s. Sherwood Ander-son acknowledged "nostalgia for the land" among intellectuals of the 1930s who had been alienated from America. The exiles returned to the countryside symbolically and in actual journeys, not to urban class con-flict. In the popular imagination as well, industrial crisis had over-whelmed a simpler rural life of independence and joint action.[61]

The New Deal drew strength from this agrarian nostalgia. In his first inaugural address Roosevelt called upon "the American spirit of the pi-oneer" to solve the social crisis. The marketplace had created a "rough balance" of economic interests on the old frontier, Henry Wallace wrote in his *New Frontiers*. "The great challenge to the new frontiersman," argued Wallace, lay in recreating "the balanced operation of our eco-nomic machine." As the country reached "maturity," it had to create "social machinery" to "help restore the balance between the major producing groups and between the producing and consuming forces." Wallace connected farm support for government efforts to "balance the interests" to "the simpler and plainer environment wherein this democ-racy was born";[62] Franklin's "Farmer of Plain Sense" had grown to ma-turity as McConnell's and Lowi's interest group liberal. George Julian's homesteader, supposedly no longer "the degraded vassal of the rich," had given birth to Lowi's "new feudalism."[63]

American pastoralism, I have suggested, offered images of virtuous communion with nature as an alternative to marketplace competition.

But even though pastoralism buried economic competition, the market-place was supposed to harmonize relations among independent yeomen. Pastoral and marketplace images therefore reinforced each other; they merged in Roosevelt's technological efficiency, Wilson's perfectly func-tioning machine, and Wallace's balance of interests. Planned balance, like the nineteenth-century marketplace, promised to free men from personal dependence on each other but substituted for self-sufficiency a complex impersonal dependence. The new liberal harmony, Henry Wallace sensed near the end of *New Frontiers*, shut out the heroic, self-sacrificing, deeply personal encounters with nature that characterized the old frontier. In-creasingly evangelical, Wallace located "the new frontiersman of the fu-ture" in "the Kingdom of Heaven." He shifted back beyond Franklin's pastoral "Farmer of plain Sense" to his "Children of Israel."

"When those forty thousand undisciplined slaves, the Children of Is-rael, left Egypt," wrote Wallace, "they . . . thought of everything in terms of the fleshpots of Egypt. Before the promised land could be at-tained it was necessary for the younger generation, hardened by travels in the wilderness, to come to maturity." The old pioneers duplicated this experience. "The old frontier was real. There were Indians and fear of foreign conquest." Wallace found in wilderness struggle the sources of self-denying, nationally-unifying civic virtue. Identifying the new fron-tier as the "social wilderness," he explained, "The Indians, wild animals and disease of this new world are the forces of prejudice, fear, greed, and suspicion."[64] These twentieth-century enemies were unembodied and bloodless; the tradition upon which Wallace called was not.

V

A prominent western movie theme pits the farmer against the cowboy. Faithful to some actual conflicts in the Far West, this confrontation is false to the larger symbolic history of American politics. "The children of Israel," said Thomas Hart Benton, "entered the promised land with the implements of husbandry in one hand and the weapons of war in the other."[65] Monsters menace the American garden; the mild-mannered farmer takes off his homespun, puts on his buckskin, and slays them. These monsters may, like the demon rum, the popish plots, and the monster-hydra bank, derive from fears of European feudalism. They may also, like Indians, originate in nature.

Virginia governor Robert Dinwiddie, in Parson Weems's *Life of Washington*, refused to "give [Washington] the staff out of his own hand"; "the mother country" denied young George army command in the French and Indian War. Washington "retired to his plantation. . . . Here, Cincinnatus-like, he betook him to his favorite plough—but the season called for the sword." Indians ravaged the frontier "to drink the blood of their enemies." Washington himself came upon one cabin massacre. Weems has him say, "We saw a mournful sight indeed—a young woman lying on the bed floated with blood—her forehead cleaft with a hatchet—and on her breast two little children apparently twins, about nine months old, bathing her bosom with the crimson currents flowing from their deeply bashed heads."[66]

Such American gothic may seem to create Indian monsters as different as possible from their civilized foes, as useless to the formation of national character as the Indians of the 1505 woodcut I described earlier. In fact, Washington and his American hunters merged with the Indians. Led by their "young Buckskin" leader, in Weems's account, Washington's rangers embraced their Indian "brothers" in a death struggle. "Burning alike for vengeance, both parties throw aside the slow-murdering rifles, and grasp the swift-fated tomahawks. . . . Faces all inflamed with mortal hate, they level at each other their last decisive blows. . . . *Here* falls the brave Virginia Blue, under the stroke of his nimbler foe—and *there*, man on man, the Indians perish beneath the furious tomahawks, deep buried in the shattered brain."[67] General Braddock, the British commander, died; Washington survived his wilderness baptism of fire to lead the colonies to independence and become father of his country.

Weems's *Life*, although it fixed the popular image of Washington for the nineteenth century, is only one document. But Richard Slotkin and I have argued that westward expansion and Indian dispossession gave the new nation its national politics and culture. Intimate identification with the Indian double developed as America turned to nature. The hunter and Indian fighter, wrote Slotkin, returned to instinctual sources in nature, temporarily surrendered himself to them, and achieved domination in the kill. This figure became our culture hero. In the person of Andrew Jackson, the hunter formed our politics as well.[68]

Jacksonian democracy had two faces: the pastoral yeoman, which Marvin Meyers analyzed, revealed only one;[69] the Indian fighter showed the other. Jackson himself, as general, treaty negotiator, and president, was the single man most responsible for expropriating Indians in the antebellum decades of westward expansion. His Indian removal cleared the land for commodity capitalism; it prepared nature for the bourgeoisie. But it was powered by the language of virtue and the might of the state. In American culture Indians symbolized forbidden temptations to passive dependence and instinctual violence. Fantasies about the Indian's relation to nature and his murder of innocent mothers and babes reawakened infantile anxieties; mastery over Indians quieted them. "Like the Israelites of old in the wilderness," as Jackson put it, he "came to maturity" (Wallace) in Indian war. Conquering his Indian "brothers," he healed a self divided between chaotic, private violence and ungrounded legal and speculative acquisitiveness. In the Creek Indian war Jackson first acquired a legitimate "birthright" to the soil and gained authority over himself, his troop, and his Indian "children." Ultimately he became, in his own and the national symbolism, the second father of his country. The wilderness romance with Indians was a death struggle.[70]

Lincoln "had a good many bloody struggles with the mosquitoes" in Black Hawk's War, but he never saw any Indians.[71] The conflict between slave and free states shifted the national search for meaning from Indians to blacks—and brought civil war. Indians figured in the war, from the white point of view, only as meaningless victims; but meaningful black and white victims replaced them. Southern enemies, agents of the slave power conspiracy, were not the only victims of northern regeneration through violence. The country achieved a "new birth of freedom" in the national fraternal deaths of civil war. "If God wills that the War continue," said Lincoln in his second inaugural address, "until every drop of blood drawn with the lash, shall be paid by another drawn with the sword, as was said three thousand years ago, so still it must be said, 'the judgments of the Lord, are true and righteous altogether.'"[72]

America returned after the Civil War to the less self-flagellating saga of frontier violence, first against western Indians and then, with the close of the continental frontier, in overseas expansion. Social engineering, I suggested, met the threat to pastoralism posed by the end of the frontier. The threat to regeneration through violence was met overseas. The leaders of the struggle to impose national discipline on subject peoples abroad—Roosevelt, Wilson, Taft, Beveridge—became the leaders of Progressive social reform at home.

"This great pressure of a people moving always to new frontiers, in search of new lands, new power, the full freedom of a virgin world, has ruled our course and formed our policies like a fate," said Woodrow Wilson in a speech on the anniversary of a revolutionary war battle. It was these lessons he sought to apply to the Philippine War. Our "destiny" was expansionist, he wrote, and with the close of the continental frontier we had to step out in the world. Leaders formed in imperial idealism, like those who conquered nature in the nineteenth century, would create domestic national order and purpose.[73]

The technological "maturity" proclaimed in liberal reform reflected pastoral childhood dreams of control rather than human and political reciprocity; in the same way imperial patriarchy sustained the frontier violence of what Wilson called "our youth" as a nation. "The iron in the blood of our fathers," wrote Theodore Roosevelt, conquered the wilderness, won the Civil War, and placed "the American Republic . . . once more as a helmeted queen among nations." Like Wilson, Roosevelt worried that "the children" would fail to match the achievements of the fathers, and his worry evoked Franklin's old nightmare. We must not, wrote Roosevelt, "be content to rot by inches and ignoble ease within our borders . . . sunk in a scrambling commercialism."[74] The cowboy on his way to the White House took his frontier rhetoric more personally than the professor, both in the Spanish-American War itself and in wilderness hunts that tested him for political leadership.[75] Roosevelt's triumphant conquest of Panama, like subsequent Progressive interventions in Latin America, combined dollar diplomacy with heroic national idealism. Progressive expansion climaxed in World War I and in Wilson's self-crucifying effort to "lead us . . . into pastures of quietness and peace such as the world never dreamed of before."[76]

The history of the twentieth-century presidency is, in significant part, a development of world frontier expansion in the terms set by Roosevelt and Wilson. A few scholars, notably William Appleman Williams, had identified the frontier tradition in American foreign policy before the Vietnam War.[77] For those who fought and those who opposed the war, Vietnam brought Indians back to the center of American imagery. New Frontiersman John Kennedy shared Theodore Roosevelt's cult of adventure and identified himself with the wilderness heroics of the Green Berets. Lyndon Johnson, in the modes of Jackson and Franklin Roosevelt, evoked daytime pastoral promises of a T.V.A. for the Mekong Delta and guerilla "sneak attacks" that "strangled" "women and children" "in the night."[78]

The defeat in Vietnam may seem finally to have exhausted America's experience in nature as a source of political meaning. To invoke Karl Marx one last time, however, "the traditions of all the dead generations weigh like a nightmare on the brain of the living."[79] The three major presidential candidates in the bicentennial year came on stage dressed in the borrowed costumes of their ancestors. President Ford, balancing political interests, played the modern Madison. He stood within society, defending Washington against the double invasion from the country-side—the pastoral challenge of Jimmy Carter, rooted in the soil of the parity-supported and technologically streamlined peanut farm and the interest group that promoted it; and the gothic challenge of Ronald Reagan, the movie cowboy who blamed trees for pollution, said one redwood was just like another, and made a tax shelter from a cattle ranch. The farmer should not be confused with the cowboy. Yet the two together recall a rural image from that classic of American literary gothic, Davis Grubb's *Night of the Hunter*.[80] I have in mind the ingratiating, murderous backwoods preacher, brought to life in James Agee's screenplay and Robert Mitchum's movie portrayal, who had the letters *l-o-v-e* tattooed on the fingers of one hand, the letters *h-a-t-e* tattooed on the other.

CHAPTER VII

"The Sword Became a Flashing Vision"

D. W. Griffith's The Birth of a Nation

"He achieved what no other known man has ever achieved," wrote James Agee. "To watch his work is like being witness to the beginning of melody, or the first conscious use of the lever or the wheel; the emergence, coordination, and first eloquence of language; the birth of an art: and to realize that this is all the work of one man." The man was D. W. Griffith. The work climaxed in a single movie, *The Birth of a Nation*, "the first, the most stunning and durably audacious of all American film masterpieces," wrote Arlene Croce, "and the most wonderful movie ever made." *Birth* joined aesthetic invention to mass appeal. Nothing like it had ever been seen before, and it was seen by millions more people than had ever seen any other movie, more than would see any other movie for half a century. A *Variety* poll of two hundred film critics voted *The Birth of a Nation* the greatest motion picture in the first fifty years of the industry.[1]

Griffith's inspiration was *The Clansman*, a best-selling novel by Thomas Dixon and the second volume in a trilogy about the Recon-

I have borrowed insights from Ann Banfield, Kim Chernin, and Catherine Gallagher throughout this essay and benefited from their responses to an earlier version. Elizabeth Abel and Jim Breslin also supplied valuable readings, and I am grateful for the contributions of Joel Fineman, Kathleen Moran, Carolyn Porter, and Paul Thomas. Nancy Goldman of the Pacific Film Archive, University of California Art Museum, helped obtain films and arrange screenings. She and the archive provided indispensable support for this project. I want also to acknowledge the help of participants in the Christian Gauss seminar at Princeton, before whom this material was originally presented.

struction South. When his assistant Frank Woods brought him *The Clansman*, as Griffith told the story, he "skipped quickly through the book until I got to the part about the Klansmen, who according to no less than Woodrow Wilson, ran to the rescue of the downtrodden South after the Civil War. I could just see these Klansmen in a movie with their white robes flying. . . . We had had all sorts of runs-to-the-rescue in pictures and horse operas. . . . Now I could see a chance to do this ride-to-the-rescue on a grand scale. Instead of saving one little Nell of the Plains, this ride would be to save a nation."[2]

American movies were born, then, in a racist epic. "The film that started it all"[3] builds to its sustained climax from two attempted rapes of white women by black men. It depicts, after the triumph of death in the Civil War and in Lincoln's assassination, a nation reborn from the ride of the white-robed Knights of Christ against black political and sexual revolution.

Celebrants of *Birth*'s formal achievement, with few exceptions, either minimize the film's racialist content or separate its aesthetic power from its negrophobia. Against the evidence before their eyes, they split Griffith's "gift for making powerful emotional connections" from "Thomas Dixon's racial message." They imitate Griffith's split between good and evil, white and black, by blaming Dixon for the perversions in Griffith's movie. Griffith and his audience, in that view, did not share Dixon's propagandistic purposes; they were the victims of "unconscious racism."[4] That unconscious is visible on the screen in *Birth*, and it invites us not to avert our eyes from the movie's racism but to investigate its meaning. Instead of rescuing Griffith's form from his content, we will examine the relationship between the two by situating *Birth* at the juncture of three converging histories, the political history of postbellum America, the social history of movies, and the history of Griffith's early films. By placing the film in history before looking directly at it, we can grasp the multiple rescue operations performed by the ride of the Klan.

Birth brought together three southerners who moved north at the end of the nineteenth century, Griffith, Dixon, and Thomas Woodrow Wilson. Dixon and Griffith got to know each other as Johns Hopkins graduate students. After Dixon became a minister and Wilson a professor, Dixon nominated Wilson to receive an honorary degree at his own undergraduate alma mater, Wake Forest. "He is the type of man we need as President of the United States," Dixon wrote the board of trustees. Dixon resigned his pulpit to write novels and plays; Griffith, before he turned to movies, acted his first important role in one of Dixon's touring companies. Griffith used *The Clansman*, Wilson's *History of the American People*, and other materials provided by Dixon as sources for *Birth*, and he and Dixon worked together in making and promoting the movie. Dixon appealed to Wilson to see *Birth*. The president, who was not appearing in public because his wife had recently died, invited Dixon to show the film at the White House. This first movie screened at the White House swept Wilson off his feet. "It is like writing history with lightning," as Dixon reported the president's words, "and my only regret is that it is all so terribly true." When the new National Association for the Advancement of Colored People (NAACP) and humanitarian social reformers tried to have *Birth* banned, Dixon used Wilson's endorsement to promote the film for months, before political pressures finally forced the president publicly to separate himself from the movie. The three southerners did not hold identical views of the meaning either of *Birth* or of the history to which it called attention. But they shared a common project. They offered *The Birth of a Nation* as the screen memory, in both meanings of that term, through which Americans were to understand their collective past and enact their future.[5]

I

Asked why he called his movie *The Birth of a Nation*, Griffith replied, "Because it is. . . . The Civil War was fought fifty years ago. But the real nation has only existed in the last fifteen or twenty years. . . . The birth of a nation began . . . with the Ku Klux Klans, and we have shown that."[6]

Griffith appeared to be following Woodrow Wilson and Thomas Dixon and claiming that the Klan reunited America. But the Klan of Wilson's *History* and Griffith's movie flourished and died in the late 1860s. Griffith's "real nation," as he labeled it in 1915, "only existed in the last fifteen or twenty years." Dixon traced a line from the Klan to twentieth-century Progressivism, and Griffith may seem to be endorsing that view. But the floating "it" of Griffith's response made claims beyond those of Wilson and Dixon. "It" located the birth of the nation not in political events but in the movie. In Griffith's syntax the "it" that gave birth to the nation was *The Birth of a Nation* itself. Let us understand, in turn, each of these three linked attributions of national paternity, to the historic Klan, to Progressivism, and to the moving picture.

Among the freed Negroes of the postbellum South, wrote Woodrow Wilson, "some stayed very quietly by their old masters and gave no trouble; but most yielded, as was to have been expected, to the novel impulse and excitement of freedom. . . . The country was filled with vagrants looking for pleasure and gratuitous fortune. . . . The tasks of ordinary life stood untouched; the idlers grew insolent, dangerous; nights went anxiously by, for fear of riot and incendiary fire." There was, Wilson continued, a "veritable apotheosis of the negro" among northerners. They saw him "as the innocent victim of circumstances, a creature who needed only liberty to make him a man." Embracing Thaddeus Stevens's "policy of rule or ruin," the North determined to "put the white South under the heel of the black South."[7]

Stevens's policies, Wilson went on, caused "the veritable overthrow of civilization in the South." Forced "by the mere instinct of self-preservation" to take the law into their own hands, white southern men made "the delightful discovery of the thrill of awesome fear which their sheeted, hooded figures sent among their former slaves." "It threw the Negroes into a very ecstasy of panic to see these sheeted 'Ku Klux' move near them in the shrouded night," wrote Wilson, "until at last there had sprung into existence a great Ku Klux Klan, an Invisible Empire of the South."[8]

Griffith filmed *The Birth of a Nation* during Wilson's presidency. He used some of the words I have quoted for the subtitles that introduce Part Two of the film. He put on the screen the images—faithful blacks and rioting incendiaries, Negroes frightened by white sheets, northern illusions about black liberty contrasted with black dangers to white civilization—in Wilson's prose. But the very first shot after the intermission, the title "The agony which the South endured that a nation might be born," was taken not from Wilson's *History* but from Dixon's fiction. *Birth* followed Wilson in its sympathy for Lincoln's aborted dream of reunion; like Wilson, it justified the Klan as a response to Lincoln's assassination. But after Wilson's Klan suppressed black independence, a suppression necessary for the South to prosper, it grew lawless and was itself suppressed.[9] Wilson's Klan signified the continuing conflict between North and South. Dixon and Griffith's Klan gave birth to a united nation. Griffith was telescoping developments that came to fruition in the history not that Professor Wilson wrote but that President Wilson helped to make.

The plantation myth of postbellum America was as much a product of northern needs as southern ones. The rapid social transformation of the North after the Civil War, from predominantly rural and native-born to visibly immigrant and industrial, generated compensatory celebrations of the antebellum plantation South. At the same time, the massive influx of immigrants from southern and eastern Europe—"men out of whose ranks there was neither skill nor energy nor any initiative of quick intelligence," as Wilson described them, "as if the countries of the south of Europe were disburdening themselves of the more sordid and hapless elements of their population"—created northern sympathy for southern efforts to control an indispensable but racially inferior labor force. Imperialism reinforced this mixture of class and racial antagonism. The Spanish-American War and the suppression of the Philippine independence movement gave the nation its own colonial people of color, and the need for racial tutelage abroad merged with fears of racial uprisings at home.[10]

The Reverend Thomas Dixon (who had the largest Protestant congregation in New York City) resigned his pulpit after the Spanish-American War to lead a crusade against the "black peril." Dixon's evangelical sermons, which emphasized personal sin and social conduct, had been more concerned with immigrant mobs than with Negroes. The subjugation of the Philippines reconnected this transplanted southerner to his past. Wilson also defended the war against the Philippines. Imperialists like Wilson and Dixon tied the racial question at home to America's world mission abroad. Dixon subtitled *The Leopard's Spots*, the first volume in his Klan trilogy, *A Romance of the White Man's Burden*. "Our old men dreamed of local supremacy. We dream of the conquest of the globe," explains the novel's hero, and we must not be "chained to the body of a festering Black Death." The Spanish-American War "reunited the Anglo-Saxon race," wrote Dixon, "and confirmed the Anglo-Saxon in his title to the primacy of racial sway." As northern capital and xenophobia migrated south, replacing carpetbaggers and northern egalitarianism, only reluctance to embrace negrophobia, as Dixon saw it, stood in the way of the birth of the nation. "It was seen by thoughtful men that the Negro was an impossibility in the new-born unity of national life," Dixon wrote; he titled the chapter with those sentiments "Another Declaration of Independence." The original ending of *Birth*, "Lincoln's solution," showed masses of Negroes being loaded on ships; they are being sent back to Africa.[11]

Woodrow Wilson also endorsed the war on the Philippines for catapulting America to world power and providing a model for political leadership over immigrants and workers at home.[12] When the southern race problem became national, the national problem was displaced back onto the South in a way that made the South not a defeated part of the

American past but a prophecy of its future. Dixon, Wilson, and Griffith thereby reclaimed southern loyalties they had left behind in their personal quests for new, national identities.

The reunion between North and South climaxed during Wilson's presidency. The first southerner elected president since the Civil War, Wilson presided over the celebrations of national reconciliation that marked the war's fiftieth anniversary. Griffith began shooting *Birth* on 4 July 1914; he released the movie fifty years after Appomattox. Wilson was so impressed by *Birth* that he offered to cooperate with more of Griffith's historical projects. "I am deeply interested in what you intimate as to future motion pictures," he wrote the filmmaker, "and if it is possible for me to assist you with an opinion about them at any time, I shall certainly try to do so." Wilson was not the only Washington official who saw and blessed the film. Through his ties to North Carolina Progressive Josephus Daniels, Dixon obtained an interview with Edward White, Chief Justice of the Supreme Court. After the normally forbidding White confided that he had ridden with the Klan in his youth, he arranged a showing of *Birth* before an audience of Supreme Court justices, senators, and congressmen. Some of these men were later embarrassed by their participation in this event, once *Birth* came under widespread attack, but the Washington screenings had singled out *Birth* in an unprecedented way for the stamp of political approval. The North was ready for a film that, although it did not endorse the traditional southern view of the Civil War, sympathized with the antebellum South and nationalized the southern view of reconstruction.[13]

The similarities between immigrants and Negroes initiated the reunion between North and South. But as blacks became a sign of the negative American identity, Progressives took immigrants to the national bosom. Antebellum southerners had identified their oppression by a centralized state with the sufferings of the subject nationalities of the Hapsburg Empire. Dixon turned that decentralist tradition in a nationalist direction and based his Klan trilogy on the trilogy of a Polish patriot. Southern patriotism was beginning to mean not resistance to the northern state but loyalty to a united nation. "You are American by the accident of birth," the Polish hero of a later Dixon novel tells a native. "We are Americans because we willed to come. . . . We saw the figure of liberty shining here across the seas. . . . It is our country . . . as it can't be yours who do not realize its full meaning."[14]

Wilson also shifted his view of immigrants during the Progressive period. South Europeans were no longer a threat to America's historic,

Teutonic identity (the view in *History* and other early writings). Now, like Wilson himself, they had given up their inherited, local identities to embody American ideals. Wilson saw that regenerate national identity in Griffith's Klan. Its visionary brotherhood melded diverse individuals into a purposeful union. The fifty years that had elapsed between the Klan Wilson wrote about and the Klan Griffith filmed allowed Wilson to praise Griffith for transforming his *History* into prophecy.[15]

As Wilson embraced immigrants, he segregated government employees. Black officeholders—significant numbers worked in the Post Office and Treasury Department—were separated from their white co-workers. White women had been "forced unnecessarily to sit at desks with colored men," explained Wilson's son-in-law, Secretary of the Treasury William G. McAdoo, and this proximity created "friction." Beginning in the Wilson administration, blacks worked in separate rooms and used separate bathrooms. Black political appointees were fired, and those holding civil service positions were downgraded or dismissed as well. In appealing to immigrants at the expense of blacks, the Democratic party was returning to its antebellum roots. And it was seeking political support from the audience for motion pictures.[16]

The first movies were one-reel immigrant entertainment. They were shown in storefront nickelodeons in working-class neighborhoods for a nickel admission, which anyone could afford. The motion picture was "the first democratic art," said the *Nation*, and movies broke down class and gender divisions. Middle-class youths, wandering into the nickelodeons, were exposed to working-class temptations. "Girls drop in alone," complained Jane Addams, and "the darkness takes away the feeling of responsibility." When men offered girls "certain indignities," Addams warned, the girls found it hard to refuse. Movie houses in "undesirable localities" turned immigrant girls into prostitutes. Vice districts had once been places for men, but movies were threatening that gender distinction.[17]

The content of movies made them even more subversive. Over half the early motion pictures were made in Europe, and few presented such American motifs as the rags-to-riches story or the settlement of the West. They depicted instead, without moral judgment, poverty, premarital sex, adultery, and slapstick violence (often against people in authority). Making "a direct and universal appeal to the elementary emotions," movies appealed to "all nations, all ages, all classes, both sexes." Their stories were permeated, in the *Nation*'s words, "with the very ideas of the crowd in the streets."[18]

Addams and other reformers saw promise as well as danger in the movies. As the *Outlook* put it, "the very potency of the motion picture for degrading taste and morals is the measure of its power for enlightenment and education." Like political progressives, cultural reformers wanted not to exclude immigrants but to enlighten and Americanize them. Seeking to capitalize on the breakdown of class and cultural barriers, reformers sought a mass entertainment of cultural uplift, not one that exploited immigrant frustrations and pulled the middle class into the mores of the ghetto. Because we failed to organize leisure as we organized production, wrote Addams, city youth was exposed to violent temptations. The solution was to reform movies, not abolish them, so that the motion picture could operate like a "grand social worker." Reformers instituted movie censorship, but selective prohibition was not sufficient to turn movies to positive cultural use. Reformers needed an ally behind the camera. Griffith looked like the man.[19]

Griffith had begun making movies because he could not get work on the stage. He shared the reformers' discontent with the film of the present and their high hopes for its future. "Reform was sweeping the country," he later wrote. "Newspapers were laying down a barrage against gambling, rum, light ladies, particularly light ladies. There were complaints against everything, so I decided to reform the motion picture industry." He did so with a film which brought movies out of the nickelodeons and into the two-dollar theaters. *Birth* established film as a legitimate art, one whose appeal cut across class, ethnic, and sectional lines. The opposition between North and South in the film, as well as that between immigrant and native in the history outside it, had been replaced by the opposition between white and black.[20]

That opposition did not pit white bodies against black ones, however, for the same actors who rode under the Klan sheets also put on blackface. The contrasting disguises, which point to the common identity they aim to hide, expose the projective fantasized character of Griffith's blacks. The opposition that engaged Griffith, Wilson, and the mass audience was between represented black chaos on the one hand and a transformed and sanctified white host on the other. *Birth*'s visionary images completed Wilson's *History* by pointing to his future, to his world crusade to end all war. We will analyze those images and conclude with that crusade. To do so we must enter Griffith's world on the screen. The southern race war depicted in *Birth*, I have been suggesting, was not simply about itself; it was also a stand-in for sectional, ethnic, and class conflicts. It was a stand-in as well, we are about to see, for the conflicts between tradition and modernity and between men and women.

II

To understand Griffith, wrote Sergei Eisenstein, "one must visualize an America made up of more than visions of speeding automobiles, streamlined trains, racing ticker tape, inexorable conveyer belts. One is obliged to comprehend this second side of America as well—America, the traditional, the patriarchal, the provincial."[21]

D. W. Griffith, as Eisenstein implies, was a child of provincial America. He was born in 1875 on a Kentucky farm; when his father died seven years later, as Griffith told the story, Jake Griffith's faithful ex-slaves were at his bedside. But Griffith's father came to rest at home only in defeat and at the end of his life. He was a wanderer, drinker, gambler, and storyteller, wounded in mythic exploits during the Civil War. Instead of working the family farm, he took out three mortgages on it. After he died the family lost the farm and moved to Louisville. From there David Griffith wandered, alone or with touring acting companies—north to New York; west to Chicago, San Francisco, and points between; and back home to Louisville—before beginning to make movies in New York City.[22] Against stage authorities and theatrical "rules" and in the name of depicting "real life," Griffith invented the techniques of narrative cinema. He fathered the distinctively modern art form.[23]

Griffith's story of paternal failure and modern invention is one strand in the general crisis of patriarchy at the end of the nineteenth century. Traditional paternal authority, which had rigidified and become fragile, was assaulted in two modes, which Henry Adams's famous distinction between the dynamo and the virgin invoked—namely, that of scientific, industrial technology and that of the New Woman. Eisenstein pointed to one form of the crisis, in which mechanization took command. Griffith filmed speeding automobiles and streamlined trains, but he went beyond the motion shown in a scene to the motion that constituted it. Griffith found a formal vocabulary for the pace of modern life. Paralleling the other industrial arts, he broke up traditional sequences into their component parts and reassembled those parts to make something new. Life was "more fragmented and faster-moving than in previous periods," said the French painter Ferdinand Léger in 1913. As the cubists and futurists in different ways put movement on canvas, Griffith captured it on film. He invented few technical innovations, but he was the first to put the new film techniques to significant dramatic use.[24]

Griffith understood, like no filmmaker before him, that the unit of film was not the scene but the shot. He was "bitten by the lightning bug," complained the Reverend Dr. Stockton. Stockton counted sixty-eight shots in a single Griffith one-reeler; the average in non-Griffith films was eighteen to thirty. By cutting back and forth, Griffith juxtaposed events separated in time (the flashback) and space (the cutback) and collapsed the distinctions between images in the head and events in the world. By speeding up, reversing, and stopping time, he brought the past into the present (or rather, as Stephen Kern says, controlled what the past would become). By juxtaposing events widely separated in space, he overcame the barriers of distance (barriers overcome in the film plot by the ride to the rescue). Griffith created an art of simultaneities and juxtapositions rather than traditions and continuities.[25]

Griffith also used editing to dynamize action within single scenes. He broke up the homogeneity of physical space through camera angles and closeups. Cutting from medium to long shots and in to closeups and varying the lengths of the shots, he pulled the viewer into the action. He broke down the barriers not just of time and space and inside and outside but of audience and film. By establishing a camera-eye point of view, Griffith gave significance to objects, body parts, and faces. The symbolic meanings of these part-objects augmented or displaced traditional narrative conventions. Griffith made images the medium of film.

Griffith justified his movie method in the name of realism. "The motion picture," he said, "approaches more closely real life" than does the stage. "The motion picture is what technique really means, a faithful picture of life." "The Biograph camera doesn't lie," proclaimed advertisements for Griffith's one-reelers. Formal conventions, Griffith believed, separated the theater from reality. At the same time that paternal moral principles were giving way in politics (a subject of Adams's *Education*) and their intellectual formulas were being overthrown in the new social sciences, movie realism, too, was revolting against the formalism of the fathers.[26]

The realist movie required its own forms, however. Tom Gunning has recently argued that Griffith developed the narrative techniques of bourgeois realism in the Biograph one-reelers. Before Griffith, working-class audiences watched unmotivated characters engage in scenes of antisocial comedy and unmediated violence. These episodes were not made into stories. Griffith organized psychologically motivated social types into narratives of modern life. He wanted, like other middle-class progressives, to get closer to life without falling into chaos. Parallel editing, in which the director cut back and forth between two scenes or components of a single scene, responded to the demands of a complex narrative style.[27] But parallel editing did not simply contribute to storytelling; its juxtapositions, contrasts, dismemberments, and boundary breakdowns endangered narrative control and threatened to create chaos. The source of that chaos visible on screen was the female image.

Traditional patriarchal forms were under siege at the end of the nineteenth century not just from technology but from what was conceived of as nature, from regressive forces as well as progressive ones. The movement forward and outward in external time and space—railroads, clock-time, scientific exploration, and imperialism—entailed at the same time a movement backward and inward in psychological time and space. And women, whether out in the world or confined to the home, stood for that regressive, disorganizing power. Partly, they posed a threat to order in their own right because of their efforts at emancipation. Partly, they stood as a symbol and accessible scapegoat for more distant social and political disruptions. Instead of providing a refuge from modern disorder, the New Woman fueled it.[28]

The New Woman appears everywhere at the end of the nineteenth century, in the work force and reform movements, in literature, art, social thought, and psychology. Existing beneath and within the stereotypical Victorian roles of wife, mother, spinster, and fallen woman, a female presence emerged by the century's end (in the male imagination) as the prepatriarchal, originary source of male identity. As working girl, fashion-conscious wife, or lady of the night, the New Woman represented the modern city. But even where women stood for fecundity and reproduction, like Henry Adams's Diana of the Ephesians or Theodore Roosevelt's maternal ideal, they were a force larger than life. "She was the animated dynamo; she was reproduction," wrote Adams; he was describing a fertility goddess more than a domestic mother. Whatever her social form, the New Woman was imaged as monstrous and chameleonlike. Her permeable boundaries absorbed children and men.

The revolt of the sons against their fathers combined rebellion with sexual freedom, as young men imagined themselves on the side of women against patriarchal authority. But the alliance of youth and women that was intended to liberate the sons threatened to empower the female instead. We normally associate Griffith with victimized women, not powerful ones. But his films before *Birth* suggest that Griffith created women needing rescue in order to rescue himself from their female predecessors on his screen. Strong women in Griffith's early movies liberated him from patriarchy and tradition only to subject him to female power. *Birth* was the solution to that problem.

"*The Birth of a Nation* owes more to my father than it does to me," said Griffith,[29] and that movie may seem to retreat from modern realism to pastoralism and provincialism. In fact the film employs tradition to sanctify modern force. It returns neither to paternalism nor to history but replaces them. It celebrates not the restoration of southern patriarchy but the birth of a new nation. And it locates reality not in the world viewed, either pastoral or modern, but in the cinematic image and the camera eye. Instead of generating the powerful female images that threatened Griffith, *Birth* culminated the filmmaker's appropriation of a power experienced as female.

III

Between 1907 and 1913 Griffith made hundreds of one-reel motion pictures for the Biograph Company. The social exploration and psychological interiorization in these movies, the film cut and the intrusive camera eye, opened a Pandora's box for the filmmaker as his techniques threatened to turn on their inventor. Four recurrent themes in these movies make up the prehistory of *Birth*: the presence of weak or repressive fathers, associated with provincialism and tradition; the emergence of female sexuality, imaged in the phallic woman, associated with modernity, and represented by the actress Blanche Sweet; the presentation of domestic, interior space as claustrophobic, imprisoning, and vulnerable to invasion; and the use of rides to the rescue. These rescues are meant to reassert the contrast between good and evil, the domestic refuge and the menacing invader, male strength and female weakness, but they leave behind traces of a dangerous boundary breakdown. The collapse of gender and social difference that emerged in these films led Griffith to generate a new and deeper system of differences in *Birth*.[30]

There is not space here to trace *Birth*'s genealogy through the Biograph one-reelers. But the troubles taking over Griffith's screen climaxed in the two most important longer films he made between the one-reelers and *Birth*—*Judith of Bethulia* (1913) and *The Avenging Conscience* (1914).

Judith of Bethulia (Blanche Sweet) is a widow dressed in black at the beginning of Griffith's version of the biblical story. Her Jewish town is menaced by the Assyrian general Holofernes. Judith puts on makeup, adorns her head with spiky peacock feathers (Fig. 7.1), and veils her face. By masquerading as a painted lady, a courtesan, Sweet transforms herself from a helpless victim in need of rescue (her role in the one-reeler *The Painted Lady*) to the rescuer of Bethulia. Her depersonalized erotic flowering points to Holofernes's death.

Holofernes (Henry Walthall) is a bearded patriarch. He commands a bacchanal from his couch-throne and seems to have the women around him at his service. But languishing on his couch as he observes his dancing girls, Holofernes is a curiously passive figure (Fig. 7.2). The women move in *Judith*; Holofernes, like the movie audience, is a voyeur. His soldiers worship Holofernes's sword, but it is Judith who will seize it. The scene between Judith and Holofernes, orchestrated for a sexual climax, climaxes when she cuts off his head.

Judith caresses Holofernes as he lies on the couch; she gives him wine, they drink, he passes out. Cut to his head and shoulders, then to her raised arm. Her hand is off camera. Judith stands behind Holofernes; cut to the sword in her hand. Judith holds up the sword (Fig. 7.3); in shape and in location above her head, it has replaced the peacock feathers she no longer wears. Judith in close-up raises the sword. Cut to Holofernes's head rolling from the couch and bouncing on the step below. Cut to his headless body, one arm limply outstretched. The shot, of one arm instead of two, at once calls attention to the single, phallic member and (by way of the missing arm and head) to its metaphoric absence.[31]

In cutting up Judith before she dismembers Holofernes, the camera fetishizes the female body, for it substitutes eroticized body parts for the whole. Such fetishized part objects, argued Freud, assuaged the male viewer's fear of castration. Since the boy child imagines the female as a castrated male, the fetish restores her missing male member. But the fetishized body part or object—foot, hand, hat, sword—also stands in for the intact female body. Were that body whole, moreover, it would call attention to the absent phallus. Film cuts that dismember the woman on screen thus doubly disempower her, it is argued, by substituting a (male) fetish for her bodily integrity. At the same time, man looks and woman is looked at. The male gaze inherits the father's phallic power, on this line of thought, as it looks at a passive woman on display. The eye establishes sexual difference by observing what the female lacks.[32]

The erotics of voyeurism and the fetishization of women lie at the origins of cinematic form, and Griffith's films as a whole connect the founding moment in American cinema to a particular political, sexual, and racial content. But *Judith of Bethulia* read by itself assigns power not to the male gaze but to the filmmaker who directs it. Griffith may have cut up Judith to control her, since he was making a woman his parricide. The camera-fetishized Judith turns on the male viewer nonetheless, for she decapitates Holofernes. He is the headless body; she is the woman with the penis. When Holofernes's soldiers see his headless body, they become a disorganized mass. The Jews, who have placed his head on a pole, rout the Assyrians in battle.

Judith of Bethulia was Griffith's first spectacular. He broke Biograph's rules about time and money in making the movie, and the excitement of taking power animated the entire set. Decapitating the patriarch, Griffith freed himself from Biograph's restrictive production rules. Decapitation also freed his camera. Cutting back and forth between opposed forces in the familiar ride to the rescue did not engage Griffith's talents in this film. Instead he invented what Eisenstein (denying Griffith had done it) would call dynamic montage, the creation of a wholly new set of images from the dismembered parts of the quotidian world.

Griffith's commitment to patriarchy and provincialism, Eisenstein argued, blocked his formal progress, allowing him to juxtapose contrasting images but not to constitute fundamentally new ones. In Eisenstein's view the dualism of Griffith's social vision (which Eisenstein attributed to Griffith's inability to transcend class rather than racial and sexual divisions) generated parallel montage; it prevented Griffith from discovering dynamic montage.[33]

Eisenstein grasped the relation between form and content but overlooked Griffith's breakthrough. For the first time on film, in the Assyrian siege of Bethulia, Griffith juxtaposed separate shots to create a single, complete, new mental image. The camera shifts from the beleaguered people behind the walls to the defenders atop them, to the attackers outside, to Judith in her chamber, to Holofernes in his camp. Like a cubist painter, Griffith liberated the eye to roam everywhere. The siege of Bethulia is the first example of dynamic montage on film; Holofernes's beheading is the second.[34]

Griffith freed himself from Biograph by making *Judith*; when Biograph took away his artistic control over future productions because of the length and cost of this film, he left that company and formed one of his own. Its most important production before *Birth* was *The Avenging Conscience*.

Beginning in 1910 and with increasing frequency over the next three

years, critics had complained that Griffith's films were becoming mor-
bid. The psychological, expressionist melodramas that troubled the critics featured suicide, neurosis, family estrangement, forbidden temptation, and failed rides to the rescue. *Conscience* is the culmination of
these gothic one-reelers. One critic calls it his most important film before *Birth*, a judgment that is justified not cinematically but psychologically. Based on several Edgar Allan Poe stories and intercut with lines
from "Annabelle Lee," *The Avenging Conscience* took Griffith further
inside the parricidal psyche than he wanted to go. *Birth* took him out
again.[35]

Blanche Sweet as Annabel has no sword in *Conscience*, and she is
not an active subject like Judith. The primitive, pre-oedipal source of
life and death seems to have been replaced by a passive sexual target of
oedipal rivalry (Fig. 7.4). But as the subject, object, and eliciter of desire,
Sweet as Annabel disempowers both herself and the two male protagonists. Their collective disturbance generates madness and parricide.

Henry Walthall plays an orphan who has been raised by his uncle.
This withered old man wears an eye patch, and his dessication contrasts
to Sweet's ripeness. She caresses her furry little dog with her foot and
lifts the fence for it to crawl under. Cut to her meeting with the nephew.
Griffith juxtaposes their erotic encounter to the embittered, isolated uncle. The cut from her sexuality to his single eye, by contrasting her
puppy to his missing organ, underscores the uncle's emasculation.[36]
"Embittered by youthful happiness" as he sees another young couple
besides the one played by Sweet and Walthall in love, the uncle forces
his nephew to send Annabel away.

The nephew watches a spider devour an ant and determines to murder his uncle. Griffith borrowed Poe's hieroglyphic method, wrote
Vachel Lindsay, to replace narrative by symbol.[37] Visual emblems like
the fly and the spider pull viewers "into the plan of a fevered brain." As
the nephew raises a gun to shoot his sleeping uncle, Griffith cuts to an
"Italian" laborer (George Siegmann) with his arm around a girl. The
Italian relinquishes the girl; the nephew lowers his gun. After this double
anticlimax the Walthall character imitates the spider instead of the masculine laborer and strangles his uncle. He walls the body up in the fireplace and joins Annabel.

A flower that wilted when the uncle separated the lovers comes alive
again after the murder. But the detective (Ralph Lewis) plucks another
flower for his buttonhole as he comes in the nephew's door. It is a sign
that the nephew will not enjoy the fruits of his crime. The Walthall

character is also at the mercy of the Italian, who has witnessed the murder and blackmails the murderer. But psychological bond overcomes narrative logic and turns Siegmann into Walthall's assistant. Siegmann serves Walthall, since the Italian stands for the access to women that provoked the nephew's crime. The detective, investigating the crime, represents the uncle's prohibition. Although he finds no evidence of foul play, the detective awakens the nephew's avenging conscience. The uncle's ghost materializes behind the lovers; it appears to the Walthall character as he sleeps. Questioned again by the detective, the nephew stares at the pencil that the detective taps on the table; it mimics the beat of his uncle's heart. The detective has repossessed the pencil-penis as well as the flower. Griffith uses an iris-in (in which an image in the shape of an eye opens up until the whole screen is filled) on one of the detective's eyes to invoke the one-eyed uncle. But the detective's eye, like the camera eye and unlike the uncle's eye patch, can see into the murderer.

"They are neither man nor woman; they are neither brute nor human; they are ghouls, ghouls, ghouls," announces a title; we watch, with the nephew, as human bodies with animal heads dance in the fireplace. The Walthall character's nightmares drive him to an isolated cabin, on which the opposing forces, one led by the detective and the other by the Italian, converge. Trapped in the cabin (the detective had earlier nailed shut its trap door), the nephew prepares to hang himself. Cut to Annabel leaping into the sea. At that moment the Walthall character awakens; his uncle is alive, the flower is wilted, and we realize we have been inside his dream. The uncle blesses the lovers, and the film ends with Walthall and Sweet on a hillside overlooking the water. But that happy ending fails to erase the film. The successful slaying of the patriarch in *Judith* required giving the woman the sword. Taking it from her and making her the object of desire was even more disturbing, for it entombed the young man in parricidal, self-destructive guilt. Nonetheless, by intensifying Griffith's nightmare of desire, *Conscience* allowed him to engage in an inspired act of inversion and free himself from the demons that were taking over his screen.

IV

Turned inside out, the characters and images of *Avenging Conscience* gave birth to *The Birth of a Nation*. The figures from Walthall's fevered brain step out of *Conscience*'s claustrophobic private interior. Walthall awakens from his nightmare into history; more accurately, he enters epic history in the form of Griffith's dream. *The Birth of a Nation* is the dream wish that rescues Walthall from his avenging conscience. The film is divided into two parts. After an initial meeting between the northern Stoneman boys and their southern Cameron cousins, Part One is devoted to a display of the Civil War. Part Two chronicles the Cameron-Stoneman romances that were promised in Part One and interrupted by the Civil War. The Ku Klux Klan saves the white South from northern Reconstruction and black sexual assault.

Ralph Lewis, as the northern Reconstruction leader Austin Stoneman, orchestrates the white South's punishment out of his passion for a female mulatto. The little colonel, played by Henry Walthall, loves Stoneman's daughter, Elsie, and he leads the Klan to rescue her from the blacks whom her father has unleashed. Sexual desire generates violence, in *Birth* as in *Conscience*, but that desire belongs to Lewis as Austin Stoneman, not to Walthall as the little colonel. Siegmann, the Italian representative of Walthall's libido in *Conscience*, plays Silas Lynch, the mulatto protégé and extension of Lewis's desire in *Birth*. Spottiswoode Aitken, who played Walthall's uncle in *Conscience*, plays his father in *Birth*. He is still emasculated, but now his helplessness is permission giving for the young man, not life denying. Instead of having to relinquish what Aitken is denied or kill him, the little colonel rescues his father. In *Birth*'s climax as in *Conscience*'s, two forces—one good and the other evil—converge on an isolated cabin. But his innocent family has replaced the guilty Walthall inside the cabin, and Walthall leads the ride to their rescue. The psychological pursuit of detective Lewis after criminal Walthall turns into the physical chase of Walthall's Klan after Lewis's Negroes.[38] Griffith has projected Walthall's internal turmoil onto blacks and Klansmen. Blacks save Walthall by appropriating his desire; the Klan acquires his conscience. Since that conscience is now directed at the other rather than the self, Walthall can ride at its head.

The Klansmen "look like a company of avenging spectral crusaders," remarked the *New York Times*. A writer described them in one scene as "vanishing like ghouls." "Moving," in Dixon's words, "like figures in a dream," the Klansmen have emerged from Griffith's dream. Making their "spectral dash through the night," they save Walthall from his nightmare (Fig. 7.5).[39]

The mounted Klansmen invert, repeat, and dematerialize Walthall's ghouls. They are the ghouls turned upside down, since instead of animal heads atop human bodies, human heads ride animal bodies. The Klansmen (called cyclopes) are horned, like Walthall's ghouls. But those ghouls, like the uncle's personal ghost, remain grotesquely physical. The white robes that cover horns, riders, and horses transfigure human bodies into an impersonal, anonymous "spectral army," as one reviewer saw it, "a vast grim host in white."[40]

Blanche Sweet's leap to her death in *Conscience* pays for Walthall's murderous desire. Sweet's leap anticipates the little sister's leap to her death to escape a black rapist's murderous desire in *Birth*. Walthall and his lover look down over the water in the happy endings of both movies.[41] Blanche Sweet is not that lover in *Birth*, however, for Griffith excised her from the second film. That single failure of repetition is the key to *Birth*'s inversion of *Conscience*. When Sweet left *Birth*, she took with her the female sexuality that had provoked first the hero's desire and then his avenging conscience. Mae Marsh, who played the little sister in *Birth*, replaced Sweet in the leap to the death; Lillian Gish replaced Sweet as the object of Walthall-Siegmann's desire.

Griffith had planned to cast Sweet as Elsie Stoneman. When she was temporarily unavailable to rehearse the scene in which Siegmann (as Silas Lynch) seizes and forcibly embraces her, Griffith asked Gish to stand in (Fig. 7.6). Gish recalls, "I was very blonde and fragile-looking. The contrast with the dark man evidently pleased Mr. Griffith, for he said in front of everyone, 'Maybe she would be more effective than the mature figure I had in mind.'" The Walthall-Sweet couple was destroying itself in the films before *Birth*: Walthall commits suicide in *Death's Marathon*; Sweet beheads him in *Judith*; she kills herself in the dream that constitutes *The Avenging Conscience*. *Birth* marked Sweet's disappearance from Griffith's screen.

When Griffith replaced Sweet with Gish he was shifting sexuality from the white woman to the black man. The regression to the presexual virgin and the invention of the black demon went hand in hand. White supremacists invented the black rapist to keep white women in their place. That strategy, counterposing the black man to the white woman, hid a deep fear of union. Griffith wanted what one viewer called the "contrast between black villainy and blond innocence" to undo the association of his unconscious, which had merged women and blacks (see Fig. 7.6). Critics who excuse Griffith's "unconscious racism" and separate it from his sexism overlook the link in Griffith's unconscious (as Faulkner's Joe Christmas would run it together): "womenshenegro."[42]

Griffith had romances with his leading actresses. The "mature figure" Sweet developed as she reached adulthood led him to shift his affections first to Marsh and then to Gish. Inverting the oedipal triangle of one woman and two men (depicted, for example, in *Conscience*), Griffith was squiring both Marsh and Gish when he made *Birth*. If Gish emerged from her dressing room after rehearsals dressed for the evening, Marsh would know Griffith was taking the other actress out, and she would make other plans. If Gish left in street clothes, Marsh dressed up.[43] The two women assaulted by blacks on camera were the objects of Griffith's attention offscreen.

Griffith's cinematic mirroring of his offscreen relations to his heroines was duplicated in his use of his villain. As the mulatto Silas Lynch, George Siegmann carried out Austin Stoneman's orders. As the director's chief assistant, he carried out Griffith's orders. Just as Lynch sees to the details of Stoneman's plan to "put the white South under the heel of the black South," so Siegmann passed Griffith's orders on to the cast and oversaw the logistical details of the production. Karl Brown, assistant cameraman on *Birth*, described Siegmann as a "gentle-hearted, soft-spoken human elephant, sensitive to Griffith's every whim, yet powerful enough to bend everyone else to his will."[44] Stoneman bends Lynch to his will only to discover that Lynch's will is for his daughter. Tracing Lynch's actions back to their source—to Griffith behind the camera and Stoneman in front of it—breaks down the divisions Griffith set up between male and female, white and black, the production of the film and its story.

Thomas Jefferson fathered the normal American racial fantasy that freed the fathers from desire. Inverting the social psychology of the slave South, Jefferson located desire in the black man and made the white woman its object.[45] The rapist Gus and Silas Lynch (whose name turns the black victims of lynching into aggressors) are Jefferson's children. Read as the successor to the Blanche Sweet films, *Birth* shifted sexuality from white women to blacks. Stoneman's liaison with his mulatto mistress, moreover, allowed Griffith to retain the sexual woman by making her black; Lydia's arm-waving gestures recall Judith's simulation of passion.

At the same time *Birth* registered, in however distorted a way, the origin of desire that Jefferson denied. Stoneman's liaison called attention to the mulatto (Lynch as well as Lydia), and the mulatto in American history signified the white man's desire for the black woman. Tracing that desire back to its paternal origin, Griffith made Stoneman's passion for Lydia the source of the South's oppression. Griffith wanted to demonize blacks and keep them under control at the same time. It was already provocative to depict black revolutionaries on-screen; no one had done it before and no one would do it again for half a century.[46] To give the black man a will of his own, in addition, violated the constraints of the political unconscious. Depriving these id figures of their reason kept them politically dependent and retained them as projections of white desire. If blacks were not to have minds of their own, however, the film required a bad white father.

Griffith employed two reversals to distinguish Stoneman from the actual patriarchs who controlled black slaves. He made Stoneman subservient to Lydia, and he moved the interracial union from the South to the North. Stoneman, as audiences were intended to know, was modeled on Thaddeus Stevens. Stevens had a mulatto housekeeper, and she was probably his mistress.[47] Fidelity to historical detail allowed historical distortion, since this interracial constellation typified the antebellum South, not the North.

Griffith borrowed the details of his Stevens caricature—massive brown wig, clubfoot—from hostile southern descriptions of the Pennsylvania congressman. Stevens was a "horrible old man," as one biographer of Andrew Johnson put it, "craftily preparing to strangle the bleeding, broken body of the South." He wanted to watch "the white men, especially the white women of the south, writhing under Negro domination." Both Dixon and Griffith focused on Stoneman's clubfoot—"the left leg ended in a mere bunch of flesh"—as a distended, sexualized, aggressive weapon. But in two seemingly contradictory ways, Griffith departed from the southern caricature. Stevens was an ascetic-looking, cadaverous, "pale, emaciated, death-like" old man during the Civil War and Reconstruction. Griffith's wife described Griffith, too, as a "cadaverous-looking young man," and Dixon was also "weirdly gaunt" and "almost cadaverous." But unlike Stevens and Dixon, Griffith has a sensual face; he gave that sensuality to Stoneman. Stoneman is the most negroid looking of all the major characters in *Birth*, blacks as well as whites (Fig. 7.7). By making Stoneman northern and negroid, Griffith wanted to distance him from the southern white man, who was actually the male bearer of historically significant interracial sexuality. That splitting allowed Griffith to depict monstrous paternal desire.[48]

At the same time, Griffith gave Stoneman children, although Stevens had none, and made him a loving father. The conscious intention was to make Stoneman's love for his daughter a counterweight to his love of blacks. The unconscious intention was to confuse the two desires, for

Stoneman's sensuality first emerges in seductive contact not with his mulatto mistress but with his daughter.

After beginning with the slave trade, which sowed "the seeds of disunion," *Birth* shows the divided Stoneman family. Elsie fondles her father and adjusts his wig. The scene shifts to Stoneman and Lydia in a house from which his children are excluded. Lydia's embrace of Stoneman parallels Elsie's. That juxtaposition of white family and black will break down after the Civil War. In Part Two of the movie, scenes 508–50, Lynch appears for the first time.[49] Stoneman is shown with his mulatto mistress and mulatto protégé, as if they constituted a family. He tells Lynch not to scrape, that he is the equal of any white man. Elsie replaces Lydia in the next scene. Lynch stares at her and, after he leaves, she caresses her father. The sequence establishes a circuit of desire initiated by Lydia that runs from Lynch to Elsie to Stoneman. The camera also sets up the formula that Stoneman is to Lydia as Lynch wishes to be to Elsie. Drop out the two middle (shadow) terms, and Stoneman's wish is for his daughter. The blacks have been invented as a defense against what their invention allows to return, father-daughter incest.

Stoneman, like the father in Freud's primal horde, monopolizes his women and directs the mob of (black) men. There is no Stoneman mother, and her absence suggests a family triangle too explosive to be more explicit. Were Elsie's mother present, she would either separate Elsie from Lydia or else be the mulatto herself. The one alternative is insufficiently charged, the other forbidden. Having moved southern racial and sexual entanglements north, Griffith can give the southern family a mother. Whatever the ages and genders of the antebellum southern blacks, they are all asexual children.

The missing Stoneman mother at the film's opening establishes the racial division within the Stoneman family as the central division in the movie. The film's second opposition, between North and South, supersedes the racial contrast in Part One in order to give way to it in Part Two. The visit of the Stoneman boys to the Cameron plantation, home of Ben Cameron, the little colonel, promises to override the sectional division, and the Civil War does not frustrate that promise but realizes it.

Griffith's battle scenes twin North and South in two ways, one private and sentimental, the other epic and impersonal. Two sets of Camerons and Stonemans meeting in battle constitute the first mode. One younger brother is about to stab the other when, at the moment of recognition, he is fatally shot. The two die embracing. The older Cameron, Ben, leads a charge against Phil Stoneman's lines, is wounded (Fig. 7.8) but survives. Like the family interactions earlier in the movie, these scenes are emotionally overwrought. On the other hand, the panoramic battle scenes are distant, beautiful, and otherworldly; they are a cinematic triumph.

An iris-in opens up from a woman and her children onto the first panorama, Sherman's march to the sea. The camera takes the woman's position, and we look down on a slow, curved, marching line. Griffith cuts back and forth from the still observers to tiny soldiers silhouetted against a red flame, as if "The torch of war against the breast of Atlanta" were the family's dream. The receptive camera displays an eerily pastoral landscape. Cut to a close-up of starved soldiers eating corn before Petersburg. The scenes of this battle compose an ecstasy of pain (Fig. 7.9). Panoramic shots of curved lines of battle alternate with close-ups of the charge. Tiny transparent soldiers move across the screen as hand-tinted red flames light up the sky; it is impossible to tell one side from the other. Union soldiers enter the screen from the right, Confederate from the left; otherwise the two sides are indistinguishable.[50] Clumps of trees on the battlefield and a hill in the background accentuate the roundness and passivity of the scene. "War's peace," a close-up of dead bodies, is reconstructed from a Mathew Brady photograph (Fig. 7.10). The camera's passivity has obliterated the differences between North and South.

Griffith censored out the greatest destruction at Petersburg, the one suffered by black troops sent into the crater opened up by northern mining under southern lines. He sentimentalized battle scenes like the little colonel's charge by personalizing them. But that charge is mock-heroic and fails. It does not spoil what Agee rightly labeled Griffith's unforgettable images of the war. The southern director left a record of war as the triumph of death.[51]

Southern extras who played both Union and Confederate soldiers objected to putting on northern uniforms. "My daddy rode with Jeb Stuart. I ain't no god damn Yankee," one protested.[52] Griffith's father rode with Joe Wheeler; the son shot, directed, and merged both sides. The South is the ultimate victim of Griffith's war, to be sure. But he used Lincoln to nationalize victimization. Stoneman and his blacks, not the North as a whole, torture the bleeding body of the South. A triptych of victimization linking North and South, which concludes Part One, justifies the reversal of Part Two.

Lincoln and Stoneman meet in the central scene of that triptych.

Stoneman, hobbling up to Lincoln, demands vengeance against the South; Lincoln refuses, and Stoneman hobbles away. This contrast, between the vengeful tyrant and the benevolent patriarch, actually feminizes Lincoln. A stooped, warm, androgynous figure, called "the great heart," Lincoln has responded to the pleas of Elsie and Ma Cameron at the end of the war and pardoned the little colonel. "I shall deal with them as if they'd never been away," he tells Stoneman of the Confederate states. The maternal image of Lincoln was a common one, promoted by Lincoln himself. It drained the president of war's ferocity and anticipated his martyrdom.

The assassination, the triptych's final scene, follows Lincoln's meeting with Stoneman. Lincoln draws his shawl around him in a feminine gesture that anticipates both his danger and his helplessness. The president's martyrdom twins him with the defeated South. Booth limps from the stage onto which he has jumped after the shooting; the limp twins him with Stoneman. Lydia's embrace of Stoneman when they learn of the assassination brings Part One to an end.

Ben Cameron's return home, the first panel of the triptych, sets the tone for the two Lincoln scenes. After a title, "The homecoming," we see the Cameron street and front yard; everything is in need of repair. Ben enters the picture and limps slowly toward home. The defeated, limping colonel climbs the stairs of his porch in the longest single shot in all of Part One (fifty-seven feet) and is greeted by his little sister. (Only two single shots in Part Two are longer: Ben shows little sister his Klan costume in one; in the other he holds her as she dies.) Female arms reach out from the door and draw Ben in (Fig. 7.11).[53]

Cameron's limp foreshadows Stoneman's and Booth's in the next two scenes. The intent of the repetition is to contrast the devastation that makes cripples to the devastation wrought by them. The limping Stoneman walks away from Lincoln, who has promised to bring the South home; the limping Ben is welcomed home by a woman. But Stoneman's "weakness which will blight a nation" (a conflation of his passion for the mulatto with his clubfoot) shades into the little colonel's weakness. Lydia's arm around Stoneman repeats the arms around Ben. The contrast collapses between mulatto and the white female, sex and family, for both villain and hero are placed intolerably under the power of a woman.

Eisenstein contrasted Griffith's invocations of patriarchal calmness to his displays of modern speed. Part One ends in stillness, not motion; that stillness, however, a landscape after battle, registers not the triumph of patriarchy and tradition but their defeat. The father-daughter incest that, in the Stoneman family, is displaced onto the mulatto returns to its maternal source in Ben's homecoming. Fathers were once sons, and the father's desire for the daughter, the homecoming suggests, defends against being drawn back into the power of the mother. The bifurcation between mulatto and mother, a second defense besides father-daughter incest against the mother-son bond, breaks down at the end of Part One. Mother and mulatto threaten to unite, not to dismember the father by using the sword as Judith had but rather to emasculate the son by confining him in the home. Griffith takes the sword from Judith in Part Two, runs it through black aggression, and puts it into the hands of the Klan. The blacks who take over Piedmont's streets and invade the Cameron home, by intensifying the little colonel's claustrophobic familial confinement, give him the opportunity to bring it to an end. The Klan's ride to the rescue that saves a nation from black rule saved Griffith from (and thereby allowed him to make) *The Birth of a Nation*, Part One. Griffith could register war's devastation and southern defeat because he was also filming the triumph of the Klan. Critics who want to rescue *Birth*'s greatness by excising Part Two of the film fail to see the dependence of each part on the other.[54] Overriding the binary oppositions in the film between North and South, black and white, male and female, is the opposition between Parts One and Two.

V

Griffith displaces sexuality from white men to women to blacks in order, by the subjugation and dismemberment of blacks, to reempower white men. The project of disempowering women that culminates in Part Two of *Birth* emerges from the pre-*Birth* history of Griffith's movies. It also emerges from his source. The Elsie of Thomas Dixon's *Clansman* is a New Woman, a believer in female equality. "I deny your heaven-born male kingship," she tells Ben. "I don't care to be absorbed by a mere man. . . . My ideal is an intellectual companion." Ben, by contrast, is a southern cavalier indifferent to politics. The black threat politicizes Ben, and Elsie adopts his point of view. Repudiating her previous identity as "a vain, self-willed, pert little thing," she tells him, "in what I have lived through you I have grown into an impassioned, serious, self-disciplined woman."[55]

Charles Gaston, the hero of *The Leopard's Spots*, Part Two, also wins his bride by leading a negrophobic crusade. "You will share with me all the honors and responsibilities of public life," he tells Sallie Worth. She responds, in the novel's last words, "No, my love, I do not desire any part in public life except through you. You are my world." Gaston's triumph marks the defeat of Sallie's father. General Worth opposed their marriage; he is "beaten," he tells Gaston, by the force of the hero's negrophobia.[56]

Stoneman is also beaten at the end of *Birth*. These defeats may seem to represent the transfer of women from fathers to husbands, the reinscription and transmission of patriarchy. Gaston does promise "to eliminate the negro from our life and reestablish for all time the government of our fathers." But Gaston repudiates the paternalist stance that made the negro "the ward of the republic." He wants blacks subject to the law not of paternalist planters but "of the survival of the fittest."[57] *Birth*, Part Two, also restores male dominance, but the instrument of that restoration is not the traditional father but the warrior brothers. Unlike such nostalgic pastorals as *True Heart Susie* (1919) and *Way Down East* (1920), Part Two invokes traditional values in the service of modern force.

"*The Birth of a Nation*," Griffith wrote in his autobiography, "owes more to my father than it does to me." Yet Griffith shot the war in which his father was shot, the war that registered his father's defeat. The movie dwells on defeated fathers. Dr. Cameron, the sympathetic paternal figure, is thrown to the ground and paraded in chains before his former slaves. Helpless to resist the raiders who invade his home during the war, he cannot keep black troops out of it after the war is over. Griffith's father, to be sure, is the model for the little colonel, not the doctor. Griffith remembered hearing stories of his father's exploits in the war and of his mother staying up nights sewing Klan robes. He made *Birth*, he said, from those stories. "Underneath the robes and costumes of the actors playing the soldiers and night riders, rode my father." But Griffith's father never rode in the Klan. He drank, told stories, did no work, and lived in the past in the years before he died. When Griffith recalled thread in connection with his father, it was not the thread that sewed Klan robes but the thread that sewed up his father's war-torn stomach. That thread was rotten, Griffith claimed, because the northern blockade prevented good surgical thread from reaching the South. The rotten thread broke, as Griffith told the story, his father's stomach burst, and he died. Griffith did not mention that his father was swilling bourbon and eating pickles when he got his fatal attack. Griffith's father was a cavalry officer, but the horse charges that dominate *Birth* are those of the Klan. In the memories transmuted into film, Griffith's mother sewed the sheeted shroud from which his father's failed body was reborn. Roaring Jake Griffith rode through—in Wilson's words—"the shrouded night," a member of a "spectral army, . . . a vast grim host in white." "The ghostlike shadowy columns," as Dixon called the Klan, were led by the father's shade. Haunted by Griffith's father, *Birth* celebrates not his living body but his ghost.[58]

Patriarchal weakness raised the specters of black and female power in the movie Griffith made to honor his father. These specters are not laid to rest by the restoration of traditional patriarchy in the form of either the gentlemanly Dr. Cameron or the primal Austin Stoneman. Defeated as a black mob, the primal horde is reborn as a white mass. Split in two, it slays the father. Griffith put on the screen Rev. 19:14–15: "And the armies *which were* in heaven followed him upon white horses, clothed in fine linen, white and clean. And out of his mouth goeth a sharp sword, that with it he should smite the nations."

"About the first thing I remember was my father's sword," Griffith told an interviewer after *Birth* was released. That sword inspired *Birth*. Griffith explained, "As I started the book [*The Clansman*], stronger and stronger came to my mind the traditions I had learned as a child, all that my father had told me. The sword I told you about became a flashing vision. Gradually came back to my memory the stories a cousin, one Thurston Griffith, had told me of the Ku Klux Klan." "The sword remains the first memory I have of existence," Griffith repeated in 1930. In the trailer to the sound version of *Birth*, released that year, Walter Huston presents Griffith with a cavalry sword like the one his father carried in the war.[59]

Griffith first used that sword in *His Trust* and *His Trust Fulfilled* (1910) to symbolize a dead master's power. Consciously or unconsciously, in *His Trust* he filmed the opening scene of *The Leopard's Spots*. The widow of a soldier killed in the war, wrote Dixon, "took the sword of her dead lover husband in her lap, and looked long and tenderly at it. On the hilt she pressed her lips in a lingering kiss." Then she hung the sword on the wall.[60] In the film as in the book, a slave has brought the sword home. He refuses to leave his mistress after emancipation and devotes himself to his dead master's child (Charles Gaston, who will grow up to be the hero of *The Leopard's Spots*, Part Two). Griffith's black hangs the sword in his own cabin after the big house burns down. For him and for the widow, it signifies devotion to the dead master. The associations of sword, child, Negro devotion, and the dead father's power that Griffith found in *The Leopard's Spots* awakened a childhood memory.

> About the first thing I remember was my father's sword; he would put it on to amuse me. The first time I saw that sword was when my father played a joke on an old Negro, once his slave but who with the heads of four other families refused to leave the plantation; those four families were four important factors in keeping the Griffith family poor.
>
> Down South the men usually wore their hair rather long; this Negro, who in our better days had been the plantation barber, had been taken to Louisville, . . . and had seen Northern men with their close-cropped hair; when he came back he got hold of my brother and cut his hair close, Northern-style.
>
> When father saw this he pretended to be enraged; he went into the house, donned his old uniform, buckled on this sword. . . .
>
> Then, drawing his sword, he went through the technical cuts and thrusts and slashes, threatening the darkey all the time with being cut up into mincemeat.
>
> The old Uncle was scared pale, and I took it seriously myself until a wink and a smile from father enlightened me.[61]

Griffith had been unconsciously preparing to make *Birth* since age five, he said, which would have been his age in this scene. He recalled the barber story at the height of his powers, just after he filmed *Birth*. Fifteen years later, when he was no longer able to make movies, the darker side of the sword memory took over. "The only person I ever really loved was my father," Griffith confessed, but he doubted that his father loved him, and as his first memory he replaced the story of the sword and the Negro with a tale of a dog and a gun.[62]

His favorite sheepdog, as Griffith remembered it, fell in helpless, forbidden love with the sheep. In its passion, the dog bit them to death. Griffith's father tied the dog to a tree to shoot it and young David fled the scene, "but I couldn't run fast enough to get away from the report of the gun." The boy identified in both memories with victims of his father's violence. He was saved from the terror of sharing the black's fate by the discovery that his father was playacting, but he could not escape participating in the fate of the dog. In the sword memory, the boy shifted, by way of theatricality, to the side of his father; in the gun memory, as a violently hungry self, he remained his father's victim. It was a black, Griffith remembered, who told him to go on the stage, and an actor called Gloomy Gus (Griffith gave the name Gus to *Birth*'s rapist) who told him to try Biograph. Both the sword and the gun were screen memories, but only one led Griffith to the screen. The other returned only after the screen was lost.[63]

One child who worshiped his father's sword (in *The Leopard's Spots*) grew up to lead a negrophobic crusade. Another child who worshiped his father's sword grew up to film one. But the sword, so prominent in Griffith's accounts of the sources of *Birth*, is not prominent in the film we see. The little colonel, as he leads his failed charge, waves the Civil War sword of defeat (Fig. 7.12). "The sword [that] . . . became a flashing vision" originally formed *Birth*'s climax. But that sword, which castrated the black rapist, has been cut out of the film.

Birth realized progressive hopes for an uplifting cinema with mass appeal, a cinema with American themes. But the realization of those dreams, as Lary May has written, looked very different from what humanitarian reformers had imagined. Cultural guardians had always favored film censorship. Movies of the first black heavyweight champion, Jack Johnson, knocking out a white contender had been banned in the name of racial peace. Now white humanitarians like Jane Addams joined with black activists to support banning *Birth* as well.[64]

Birth showed white victory, not black, however, and the two were hardly reversible. The National Board of Review (set up by the industry to pass on motion pictures) applauded *Birth*, not on free-speech grounds but because of its historical accuracy and educational value. Most members of the cultural elite agreed, in Dorothea Dix's words, that the movie was "history vitalized." "Go see it," she urged her readers, "for it will make a better American of you."[65]

There were moments in the film, however, that the censors agreed to sacrifice. They cut out a quote from Lincoln opposing racial equality, although Lincoln had actually spoken the offending words. They censored "Lincoln's solution" at the end of the film, which showed blacks deported to Africa, although Lincoln favored emigration. They eliminated some graphic black sexual assaults on white women. And they cut out Gus's castration. Censors found truthful and educational the suggestions of black sexual violence (so long as they were implied rather than stated), but they wanted to bury the (more accurate) representations of white racist speech and action. The missing footage of castration, seen by Los Angeles audiences for weeks after *Birth*'s release and in the South for half a decade, takes us to the heart of Griffith's project.[66]

Viewers now watch Gus foam at the mouth as he lopes after little sister. In the original version he probably raped her, as he does in *The*

Clansman;[67] now she leaps to her death to escape him. Gus flees; he is captured and brought before a conclave of the Klan. As Gus lies passive and helpless, the little colonel takes off his hood. Walthall, who played a character exposed as a parricide in *Conscience*, now unmasks himself as the innocent avenging conscience. Gus is "Guilty" (a title announces) and about to be killed (Fig. 7.13).

The southern plantation novelist Thomas Nelson Page, who was the most popular novelist in early twentieth-century America and Woodrow Wilson's ambassador to Italy, blamed lynching on the preaching of racial equality by some whites and "the determination [of others] to put an end to the ravishing of their women by an inferior race." Page invoked "the ravishing and tearing to pieces of white women and children" to excuse the murder and dismemberment of black men. Early twentieth-century audiences knew southern blacks accused of sexual crimes were often lynched and castrated. The headline in a 1934 Alabama newspaper, for example, making history as well as reporting it, proclaimed, "Florida to Burn Negro at Stake: Sex Criminal Seized from Jail Will Be Mutilated, Set Afire, in Extra-Legal Vengeance for Deed." Reports of early viewings of Gus's punishment also referred to his "mutilation." That footage is now lost or unavailable, but Seymour Stern left a detailed record of it. (There is, regrettably for those who want to blame *Birth*'s racism on Dixon, no castration scene in *The Clansman*.)[68]

First a masked Klansman steps forward. (The picture of him towering over Gus was used in billboards and other advertisements for the film.) Then the little colonel performs a mystic ceremony with his sister's blood. (This ceremony now appears in the film after Gus's execution and will be described in a moment.) Cut to the Klansman. He raises his arm, with his back to the camera, and holds up a small sword. Against the background of the storm music from Beethoven's *Pastoral* Symphony, he plunges the sword down. He repeats this "ritualistic and totemic gesture," as Stern calls it, to the crash of Beethoven's storm. Cut to a closeup of Gus's face, his mouth flowing blood and his eyes rolling in agony. Griffith synchronizes his cutting to the cutting of the sword. "In flash-cuts, the Klansman's hand now plunges and rises, plunges and rises, again, again, and still again, on each down-beat of the timpani, all within a few frames of film. On the final thunder-crash of the series, there is a final flash of the castrated Negro's pain-racked face and body. Gus is dead."[69] The father's threat to make mincemeat of a black, which frightened the son, turned out to be play. The grown son, through his film cuts in a play, made that threat real. "My father's sword . . . became a flashing vision" to castrate Gus.

But the sword that castrates Gus has also been severed from the father's body. The father who wielded the sword in Griffith's memory, as Griffith went on to say, was "all shot to pieces," was mincemeat himself inside.[70] Griffith sensed the connection between violence and internal patriarchal weakness: a damaged body makes vindictive Walthall's uncle in *Conscience* and Stoneman in *Birth*. *Birth*'s aim, however, was to rescue the father, not expose him, to insulate the father from his violence, not to eliminate it entirely. To guarantee the sword's invulnerability, it had to be protected from the father's "shot to pieces" body (which ruptured soon after the sword memory) and from the threats that the father's weakness opened up. These dangers, which were at once displacements of the feared father and alternatives to him, were the threats of women and blacks. Griffith rescued the paternal sword by detaching it from the father's body and putting it into the hands of the father's specter. He not only gave the sword to the mystic body but also removed the hat (which was menacing on Judith since it prefigured her sword) from the woman's head to the massed horned Klansmen. Griffith paid homage to his father by turning the penis into a phallus. He sacrificed the member's vulnerable bodily connection and raised it to a weapon of vengeance.

The liberty blacks wanted, Dixon and Griffith insisted, was sexual. "Equality. Equal rights. Equal politics. Equal marriage" reads a placard in the black-dominated South Carolina legislature. Griffith and Dixon accused *Birth*'s opponents of promoting miscegenation. Dixon called the NAACP the Negro Intermarriage Society and claimed it "hates *The Birth of a Nation* for one reason only—it opposes the marriage of blacks to whites." One purpose of *Birth*, Griffith boasted, "was to create a feeling of abhorrence in white people, especially white women, against colored men." Griffith and Dixon imagined a monstrous America of the future, peopled by mulattoes. Stopping black men from penetrating white women gave birth to a redeemed nation. The nation was born in Gus's castration, from the wound that signified the white man's power to stop the black seed.[71]

Mixture of blood from "the surviving polygamous and lawless instincts of the white male," Dixon wrote in *The Leopard's Spots*, had "no social significance": the offspring of black mothers were black. But give Negro men access to white women, and they will destroy "the foundation of racial life and of civilization. The South must guard with flaming sword every avenue of approach to this holy of holies."[72] The sword guards the female genitalia not only to protect the white woman from the black phallus but also to keep her from acquiring a phallus of her own. The sword that passed from Griffith's father to Judith is put into the Klansman's hands; the sexuality displaced from the white male to the white female is cut off by that sword.

Castration protected white women, in the film's ideology. "The southern woman with her helpless little children in a solitary farm house no longer sleeps secure," warned the president of the University of North Carolina in 1901. "The black brute is lurking in the dark, a monstrous beast, crazed with lust. His ferocity is almost demonical." Beneath that public justification for dismembering the black beast lay an anxiety about the freedom not simply of blacks but of women. The scene at *Birth*'s final climax in which Lynch assaults Elsie (also not in Dixon's novel) is intended to repeat, invert, and justify Gus's castration. But the blacks whom Lynch orders to gag Elsie (Fig. 7.14) are doing the white man's work. When Stoneman's instruments break free from his control and assault and silence his daughter on screen, they reveal Griffith's desire behind the camera. "It may be no accident," writes Jacqueline Dowd Hall, "that the vision of the black man as a threatening beast flourished during the first phase of the southern woman's rights movement, a fantasy of aggression against boundary-transgressing women as well as a weapon of terror against blacks. Certainly the rebelliousness of that feminine generation was circumscribed by the feeling that women were hedged about by a 'nameless horror.'"[73]

Women and slaves resemble one another at the opening of *Birth*. Both move with short, jerky, childlike motions. The hidden danger is that women will mature; the filmed danger is that blacks will. The woman cannot have a penis, for that would be a sign of her power. But the woman without a penis is a sign of what can happen to the man. Having turned women into blacks to keep women childlike, Griffith castrates the black rapist to make him female. The passivity forced upon the defeated South is now enforced on Gus. It is not the white man who is in danger of becoming a woman, without a penis, says the castration, but the black. Blacks must either embrace the sword, as the loyal Negro does at the end of *His Trust Fulfilled* (miming his mistress's action at the opening of *His Trust*), or be castrated by it. Anticipating Joe Christmas's fantasy of "womanshenegro" when he created the black rapist,

Griffith anticipated Percy Grimm's fantasy when, just as Percy castrated Joe Christmas, Griffith castrated Gus.[74]

Judith climaxes as a severed head issues forth from the wound in Holofernes's trunk; the image merges castration and birth. *The Avenging Conscience* begins with a woman (Walthall's mother) dying in childbirth. The associations of castration, birth, and death, disturbing in those films, are redemptive in *Birth*. *Birth* entails, however, not just the sacrifice of the black male but of Ben's little sister as well. The camera that lingers on Ben and little sister in the three longest shots of the film, the overwrought scenes between the two siblings, and the confusion between Ben and Phil Stoneman (in the novel they look "as much alike as twins"), all locate fraternal desire in the incestuous subtext of the film. Just as Lynch is the dark side of Stoneman's desire for his daughter, so Gus mediates between the little colonel and his little sister. These forms of incest defend against the deeper, incestuous desire generated from the birth of the son. The homecoming to mother paralyzes Ben. Paternal and fraternal desire is displaced onto the blacks who are punished for it. The displacement and punishment of that desire gives birth to the new nation.[75]

The birth of a nation required Flora's blood as well as Gus's, and the original scene sequence, which joined the two rituals, came perilously close to mixing their blood together. In the present version we see four cyclopes dump Gus's body on Lynch's porch. After the title "The Klan prepares for action," audiences watch Ben Cameron soak a flag in a chalice. He speaks: "Brethren, this flag bears the red stain of the life of a Southern woman, a priceless sacrifice on the altar of an outraged civilization." Ben raises a small fiery cross and intones, "I quench its flames in the sweetest blood that ever stained the sands of Time." That bloody cross summons the Klan. The little colonel quenches the fiery cross in his sister's blood to bind the sheeted white males to hunt the black beast.[76]

The castration scene clarifies Griffith's intentions, which is why the censors took it out. But the cinematic transformation following that scene is manifest even in its absence. To the music of Klan clarion calls and the cheers of movie audiences, the Klansmen assemble. The ride of the Klan reenacts and reverses Civil War battles. Northern soldiers were indistinguishable from their southern brothers; the massed, white-robed men on horseback contrast to the chaotic black mob. Blue and gray intermingled in Civil War charges; the Klan stands out against and routs

the blacks. Hand-to-hand slaughter marked Civil War battles. Klansmen on horseback tower over black men on foot. Civil War close-ups
showed suffering; Klan close-ups show movement and power. Ben led
southern stragglers in his quixotic charge, and he alone reached northern lines. Now he stands before a massed, invincible Klan (cf. Figs. 7.8
and 7.15).

Klansmen ride with or into the camera; their power contrasts to the
futility of Civil War charges. A distant camera filmed passive, curved
Civil War battle lines. The Klan rides forcefully in close-ups and straight
lines. When the Klan is filmed in a curve, riding around a bend (Fig.
7.16), its power contrasts with the stillness of Sherman's curved march.
The confusions of night Civil War battles contrast to a breathtaking
single line of Klansmen silhouetted in a long shot at night. The tiny
transparent Civil War soldiers were shades; Klan shrouds incarnate
large forceful presences. Panoramic Civil War battle scenes, with remarkable depth of field, dwarfed the human participants. The Klan
fuses humans into an animal, mechanical, sacred power. The dead soldiers on the Civil War battlefields rise up, an "Invisible Empire," and
ride to regenerative victory (cf. Figs. 7.10 and 7.5).

Virtuoso parallel editing climaxes the movie, but the aesthetic force
of the climax is inseparable from its political message. Griffith moves
among Lynch's assault on Elsie ("Lynch, drunk with wine and power,
orders his henchmen to hurry preparations for a forced marriage" [Fig.
7.17]), the Negroes' assault on the Union veterans' cabin in which the
Camerons have taken refuge, and the Klan rides to the rescue. He cuts
in this montage from the Lincoln log cabin refuge ("The former enemies
of North and South reunited again in defense of their Aryan birthright")
to Elsie's fluttering, helpless motions (as Lynch seizes her and kisses her
white garment) to Klansmen moving forcefully through the water. The
Klan ride to rescue Elsie doubles the black assault on the cabin. Griffith's
parallel cross-cutting, his failure to transcend dualistic oppositions,
marks no victory of patriarchy and provincialism over modern speed.
The moving picture camera and the moving Klan, welding white individuals into a mystic union, embody Griffith's prophetic vision. Upon
the collapsed distinction between the mechanical North and the traditional South, he erected an apocalyptic division between black and
white.

The formal advances in Griffith's earlier films also juxtaposed oppo-
sites. But these contrasts—between what happened in one time or place
and what happened in another; between self and other, inside and out-

side, fantasy and reality; between public and private, rich and poor, good woman and bad—instead of reinforcing traditional distinctions threatened to break them down. In social terms modern technique seemed to augur the triumph of mass society, in psychological language it foretold a regression to dual unity with the primal mother. America would not be a democracy, said the young Woodrow Wilson in an unguarded moment, until there were a black woman in the White House.[77] *Birth* responded to that fear. It erected a system of differences—between male and female, white and black, good and evil—whose purpose was to withstand its own collapse and so defend against the breakdown of all difference.

The violent sacrifice of a monstrous double, in René Girard's terms, gives birth to a regenerate order. Ritual murder averts a sacrificial crisis of indiscriminate violence. It ushers in the distinction between culture and nature, a system of differences and a system without them. Griffith's system without differences is black, female, and democratic, the differentiated system is white, male, and hierarchic. But motion, speed, and the breakdown of difference constitute the new culture as well. In Girard's words about the "enemy brothers" who have slain the primal father, "We are left with a group of people all bearing the same name, all identically dressed. . . . Their resemblance is such that they do not possess identities of their own." The Klan not only brings about national unity; it also submerges human divisions in a merged, sacred brotherly horde.[78]

One image in this climax, however, unsettles the entire film. Two horsemen in blackface survey the Piedmont streets. Identified as "White spies disguised," they turn toward the room in which Elsie is imprisoned when they hear her cries for help. But the Negroes who bind and gag her when she screams for help (Fig. 7.14) are also whites in blackface. So is the "black spy" who sees a Cameron sister with that other disguise, the Klan robe. The "white spies" cannot be told from other Negroes in the film not because their paint covers their whiteness but because the other's paint does not. Masks transform some white bodies into a white host and other white bodies into a black mob. Whites in white sheets defeat whites in blackface. The climax of *Birth* does not pit whites against blacks, but some white actors against others.

Sometimes they were the same white actors. White extras switched back and forth from playing Klansmen to playing blacks, just as Griffith cut back and forth from one scene to another. Elmo Lincoln, first seen as the slave auctioneer at the opening of the film, played both a Klansman and the black owner of the gin mill in which Gus hid. Bobby Harron, killed as Elsie Stoneman's younger brother, was resurrected as a free Negro. Joseph Henaberry, assassinated as Lincoln, played thirteen bit parts in Part Two. He recalled, "In one sequence I played in a group of renegade colored people, being pursued by white people—and I was in both groups, chasing myself through the whole sequence." Griffith had split the fraternal primal horde into black desire and white punishment; blackface enabled whites to "impersonate" (Griffith's word for playing a role) both sides.[79]

Dixon and Griffith, one opponent of the film pointed out, "ought to realize that if the Negro was as bad as they paint him in these films he was what the South made him; he was the shadow of her own substance."[80] Historically and cinematically, that concessive "if" gives too much away. Griffith's Negroes were as bad as he painted them because he painted whites black. The obviousness of blackface, which fails to disguise, reveals that the Klansmen were chasing their own negative identities, their own shadow sides.

Griffith did use hundreds of black extras throughout the film. He gave several blacks small bits of business to do (an old black man dances the buck-and-wing early in the film), and one black woman has a small individuated role. Neither she nor any other black actors appear in the list of credits, however, and no blacks were given major parts. Griffith explained, "On careful weighing of every detail concerned, the decision was made to have no black blood among the principals."[81]

Blacks were barred from the theater stage; there were none in Griffith's company, and the scarcity of established black actors may have influenced Griffith's decision. But he preferred creating his own leading players to using established ones, and he wanted to invent his own blacks as well. He was following the tradition of blackface minstrelsy, the first form (before movies) of American mass culture, which appropriated black masks for white actors. Minstrels mimed blacks, but the referent was not allowed to possess his representation. A few black troupes did appear after the Civil War, however. When one played Louisville, where young Griffith was living, a local reporter commented, "The success of the troupe goes to disprove the saying that a negro cannot act the nigger."[82]

Griffith allowed a few blacks to act the nigger. But he did not want to let the representation of blackness go. On the one hand, Gus, Lynch, and Lydia were so menacing that only whites could safely play them. The contrast of "black villainy and blond innocence"[83] when Lynch seized Elsie (Fig. 7.6) had to remain metaphorical. The conventions of representation (that this was only a scene in a movie) broke down in the face of blackness, since no black could be allowed to manhandle Lillian Gish. On the other hand, whites in blackface allowed Griffith to inhabit the fantasies he imposed on blacks, to keep those fantasies his own. Griffith represented blackness without having it take him over. But his fear of giving blacks autonomy traces his blacks back to him.

Disguise is not only the method of *Birth* but (with the racial opposition that it seems to undermine) the movie's major theme. Austin Stoneman's wig, which Elsie adjusts at the film's opening, is a sign of his hidden bad motives. It marks him as a hypocrite. The first page of Griffith's pamphlet attacking film censorship shows a dark, devilish figure putting on the mask of reform (Fig. 7.18). Hiding under the disguise of virtue, "the malignant pygmy has matured into a caliban."[84] The contrast between a whiteness that protects the growth of blackness and a blackface that hides whiteness may appear unstable; blackface may seem to expose Griffith's resemblance to Stoneman, using "paint and powder" to deceive (as the later Griffith heroine, True Heart Susie, will refuse to do). The little colonel also employed disguise, however, masking his identity under Klan robes. On one level Griffith is contrasting masks of pretended with masks of genuine virtue, deception with regeneration, hypocrisy with grace. He is celebrating the role of costume and ceremony in personal transformation. (Griffith once attributed his virtues to the fact that as an actor he had "impersonated" Lincoln.) But to celebrate impersonation does not oppose the Klansman to the white in blackface. It joins them together, for the movie puts both disguises to regenerative use. White sheets and black masks establish a fixed opposition that real bodies resist. Sheets and masks enable rebirth without the mediation of female sexuality. Klan robes dress the warrior band in drag. They break down individual difference without obliterating the male self in merger with the female body. The deeper opposite of the white in blackface, indeed, of the system of represented binary oppositions itself, is the white with black blood, the mulatto.[85]

"Its purpose was to bring order out of chaos," Dixon wrote of the Klan in *The Leopard's Spots.* "Henceforth there could be but one issue—are you a White Man or a Negro?" If order depended on distinguishing white from black, however, Dixon's very next words threatened chaos. "There was but one question to be settled: 'Shall the future American be an Anglo-Saxon or a Mulatto?'" In shifting from black to mulatto Dixon acknowledged the mixture he was trying to prevent. He reestablished the boundary by making mulattoes into blacks: "One drop of Negro blood makes a Negro. It kinks the hair, flattens the nose, thickens the lip, puts out the light of intellect, and lights the fire of brutal passions. The beginning of Negro equality as a vital fact is the beginning of the end of this nation's life. There is enough negro blood here to make mulatto the whole Republic."[86]

The spread of blackness through interracial sex (Ike McCaslin's nightmare at the end of *Go Down Moses*) was one form of national rebirth; blackface was its alternative. Mulattoes with "black blood" were stuck in their blackness. Dressed in blackface (or watching others so dressed), whites played with blackness as part of their self-fashioning. Griffith took an interest in clothes as a young man, he later wrote, because he could not change his body.[87] Griffith discovered in *Birth* that changing clothes allowed him to leave the body behind.

Griffith wanted to assume negative identities if he could discard them, but he also required stable nurture and recognition from others. Self-abnegating blacks and women like the hero of *Trust* and the heroine of *True Heart Susie* supplied, in Erikson's terms, basic trust. The dependence on blacks and women, in Griffith's depiction, allowed white men to be free. But that dependence also rooted the mobile, self-making identity in its opposite. Boundary division was built on boundary breakdown, selfhood in one on its absence in the other. Griffith, who needed both dependence and autonomy, feared that the one wiped out the other; he sacrificed the autonomy of women and blacks. But the wish for basic trust that obliterates the autonomy of the other brings with it anxiety over vengeance. Given the primitive sources of the need for basic trust in infantile dependence and attachment, the women and blacks from whom support was demanded became repositories for the panic against which trust defends, of violence, loss, and mobile desire.

Blackface played with boundary breakdown, retaining control over it, and Griffith returned to blackface in the 1920s. He planned to star Al Jolson in a film called *Black and White*. Jolson would play a detective who puts on blackface to investigate a crime and saves a falsely accused man from being executed. Since both the suspect and the detective are innocent underneath their guilty appearances, *Black and White* took as its explicit theme the difference between blackface and blackness. When Jolson backed out of the movie, another actor and another director in Griffith's company made it. A few years later Jolson starred in the first talkie. Like *Black and White*, it moved blackface from method to subject. Blackface frees the character Jolson plays in *The Jazz Singer* from his inherited, Jewish immigrant identity. Jolson becomes a jazz singer over his father's objections; "Mammy," sung in blackface after he has become a star, expresses his gratitude to his mother. But self-consciousness about the method undercut blackface. *The Jazz Singer*'s homage to the technique that had founded American mass entertainment, first in minstrelsy and then (through *Birth*) in movies, brought blackface to an end.[88]

The Jazz Singer did not do away, however, with the principle for which blackface stands; it rather exhausted blackface as a way of standing for that principle. Blackface was a synechdoche for the freedom provided by representation. It pointed to Griffith's effort, thematized by white sheets in *Birth*'s plot and by blackface in its production, to replace history by image.

VI

The emphasis on impersonation may seem to contradict Griffith's belief in the historical accuracy of film. The director went to enormous trouble to reconstruct historical vignettes accurately in *Birth*, for he wanted to acquire the aura of history for film. The actors on stage at his Ford's Theater read the play that was performed the night Lincoln was shot; Griffith shot Booth shooting Lincoln at the same moment in the play. Critics praised the historical accuracy of *Birth*. The vice crusader Charles Parkhurst, who had tried to close the New York nickelodeons, insisted, "A boy can learn more pure history and get more atmosphere of the period by sitting down three hours before the films that Griffith has produced with such artistic skill than by weeks or months of study in the classroom."[89]

Griffith agreed. He imagined that in the public library of the future, instead of reading about history and "ending bewildered without a clear idea of exactly what did happen, and confused at every point by conflicting interpretations . . . you will merely . . . press the button and actually see what happened. There will be no opinions expressed. You will merely be present at the making of history."[90]

Accuracy, however, required impersonation. Joseph Henaberry was not Lincoln any more than he was black. Henaberry impersonated Lincoln by getting as close to the details of his beard, posture, and clothing as he could. Historical authenticity entailed disguise. Griffith and Dixon offered to pay ten thousand dollars to Moorfield Storey, president of the NAACP, if he found a single historical inaccuracy in *Birth*. The pretense may seem absurd; Thaddeus Stevens, for starters, had no children. But Ralph Lewis played Stoneman, not Stevens. He impersonated a historical type just as (in Vachel Lindsay's account of the gathering of the Klan) "the white leader, Colonel Ben Cameron (impersonated by Henry B. Walthall) enters not as an individual, but as representing the white Anglo-Saxon Niagara."[91]

When Storey asked Griffith what mulatto lieutenant governor had bound and gagged a young white woman to force marriage on her, Griffith avoided answering and tried to shake Storey's hand. Storey refused. By imitating the little colonel, who had refused (to Atlanta audience cheers) to shake Lynch's hand, Storey had gotten Griffith to play the lieutenant governor. But even if Griffith found himself on the wrong side of that reenactment, it testified to film's power. *Birth* used impersonation in the service of a vision that by tapping collective fantasies created a conviction of truth beyond history. Contingencies and conflicting interpretations constitute history. Griffith's aim was to abolish interpretation; that project made representation not an avenue to history but its replacement.[92]

Griffith claimed to be filming history in *Birth*, just as he said he was filming his father, but he also claimed to be bringing a new history into being. "We've gone beyond Babel, beyond words," he said in 1914. "We've found a universal language—a power that can make men brothers and end war forever."[93] That preverbal universal language did not simply create a historical eschatology, a move from the traditional to the sacred. It replaced history by film. Presented as a transparent representation of history (more transparent than language could ever be), movies actually aimed to emancipate the representation from its referent and draw the viewer out of history into film.

Movie images seen from afar allowed audiences to keep their distance, to be voyeurs instead of participants. But that protection, as in dreams, broke down defenses and opened a road to the unconscious. The size of the image and its reproducibility, the close-up and film cut, the magical transformations on-screen and film's documentary pretense—all these, Griffith sensed, dissolved the boundaries that separated audiences in darkened theaters from the screen. The silent-film epic, moreover, accentuated movies' visionary aura. "Words, after all, are a clumsy method of conveying thought. They close expression in so many ways," said Griffith. *Birth* used titles, to be sure, but it stood closer to music than to words. Not only were its filmic rhythms musical, but Griffith also used an orchestra to reinforce the beats and themes on screen. To watch and hear *Birth* as it was originally shown was to enter an immediate, prelogical universe of the primary processes.[94]

Griffith founded a preverbal art. It pulled viewers back to the condition, before language, of illusory unity with the originary source of being. Film, in Griffith's imagination, evoked and made itself the substitute for an ominous, preverbal, maternal power. *Birth* replaced birth.

"I have even heard it said that if it hadn't been for the transfusion of your blood into it the motion picture would have died," a reporter commented to Griffith after *Birth* opened. "I believe in the motion picture not only as a means of amusement, but as a moral and educational force," Griffith replied. "Man is a moving animal. It isn't so with woman. Their natures are different." Griffith was describing women as the victims of male mobility, victims whom the movie would rescue. "Do you know that there has been less drinking in the past five years, and that it is because of motion pictures?" asked Griffith. Men who once frequented the saloon went to the motion picture theater. Because they watched movement on the screen instead of moving themselves, Griffith concluded, "the domestic unities are preserved." Movies preserved traditional values by replacing modern life, by moving for modern men.[95]

The motion picture protected women from men, Griffith claimed. But in response to the reporter's metaphor, which broke down the boundary between body and film, he invoked the stereotypical gender division. Griffith's blood transfusion protected women by appropriating them. *Birth* transubstantiated Griffith's blood into celluloid so that he and his audiences could live inside film.

As film replaced the female body, it also ingested history. Plays, explained Griffith, were "the art of interpretation glorified." Movies were superior to plays because playgoers were aware of the artificial, representational effects. "Concealment [was] one of the rarest attributes of true art," wrote Griffith, and silent film concealed "the brain behind this art" as words could never do. Griffith's distinction went beyond the interpretation that points to itself and the one that, rendering itself invisible, "impersonates" reality. Silent film, like the "hand of God," lifted people from their "commonplace existence" into a "sphere of poetic simulations." It did not render reality. It was the Real. To be "present at the making of history" was to be present at the viewing of film.[96]

VII

The Birth of a Nation, by appropriating history, itself became a historical force. It not only showed millions of viewers how to see and enact domestic conflicts but also pointed toward the Great War. But Griffith's reentry into history through American entry into World War I initiated the process by which he fell out of film.

Birth, like *Wilson*, claimed to be against war. "Dare we dream of a day when bestial war shall rule no more?" asks the penultimate title, and a bestial war god (of the sort Africans worshipped) is succeeded on the screen by a white-robed Christ. But the white Knights of Christ who erased the Civil War were not pacifists. Like America in World War I, they were fighting a war to end war.

Karl Brown, the assistant cameraman on *Birth* and *Intolerance*, also connected Griffith's movies to American entry into World War I. He wrote, "Here was *his* story, the story he had used so effectively time and time again, played right before his eyes: his famous run to the rescue. Only this time it was not a handful of desperate people but a typical Griffith production on the most gigantic scale: all Europe under the iron heel of a monstrous enemy, with the rescue now coming from the massed might of America."[97]

That was Wilson's vision as well. Griffith put on the screen Wilson's "ghostly visitors," whose "invisible Empire" saved a nation. Now, as we saw in chapter 3, Wilson borrowed Griffith's images to celebrate the Americans who rescued Europe. "What we had to have," wrote George Creel, who headed Wilson's Committee on Public Information, "was no mere surface unity, but a passionate belief in the justice of the American cause that would weld the people of the United States into one white hot mass instinct with fraternity, devotion, courage, and deathless determination." "Those dear ghosts that still deploy upon the fields of France"—as Wilson evoked them after the Armistice—were the ghosts of Griffith's Klan.[98]

Dixon and Griffith also saw the connection between *The Birth of a Nation* and World War I. Dixon agitated in print and film for American entry into the war; he called his novel and movie *The Fall of a Nation*. "What we film tomorrow will strike the hearts of the world," Griffith had declared in 1914, "and end war forever." After *Intolerance* (1916), Griffith began *Hearts of the World* to bring America into the war to end war. Griffith began *Hearts* at Lloyd George's urging, to create sympathy for the Allied cause. He reported to Wilson during the production of the film and screened it at the White House.[99]

Hearts (1918) was the most popular war movie of its time, but the cross-purposes at work in the film fatally compromised it. On the one hand, *Hearts* was a remake of *Birth*. It contained, observed William

Everson, "the same family structure, the same separations and reunions, the same editing patterns." A romance is set against the background of war, in which Germany and France replace the North and the South. George Siegmann plays the German officer von Strohm instead of the mulatto lieutenant governor Silas Lynch; once again he chases, seizes, and mauls Lillian Gish. Scenes of German officers ravishing French girls, omitted from the film when it played after the Armistice, parallel the scenes of black sexual violence censored from *Birth*. Tramping Americans coming to rescue Europe fill the screen in the film's final image. They reincarnate the ride of the Klan. Griffith dedicated *Hearts* to President Wilson.[100]

Hearts could not simply repeat *Birth*, however, for the Germans had to stand simultaneously for the North of Part One and the blacks of Part Two. If American entry were to save Europe from World War I, then the American ride to the rescue would transform the Great War as American Civil War (*The Birth of a Nation*, Part One) into the Great War as Klan triumph (*Birth of a Nation*, Part Two). But had *Hearts* simply repeated Part One, it would have had to merge the Germans with the French. That would not justify an American ride to the rescue, so Griffith had to collapse Part One into Part Two. *Birth* made equivalent the two sides in the Civil War; *Hearts* distinguished the noble French from the bestial Germans. Neither of the two lovers in *Hearts* could be German, so their rescue could not reunite Europe. The French troops are sufficiently dirtied by the war, moreover, to fail to rise to the role of the Klan. Although they also ride to rescue Lillian Gish, they are too disorganized and battle-weary to replicate the Klan's transcendent order. Their ride to the rescue substitutes interminable length for visionary power.

Bobby Harron, who plays the Henry Walthall role, does not lead the ride to rescue Gish. Trapped together in the familiarly claustrophobic room (after she, not he, stabs a German soldier), Gish and Harron are both menaced by George Siegmann as von Strohm. They make a suicide pact in case the Germans break down the door. Griffith succumbed to more than propaganda exigencies when he merged Harron and Gish as victims. *Hearts* marks Griffith's fall into masochistic nostalgia.

Although that shift in Griffith's movies derived in part from his private history, his confidence, like that of Euro-American culture as a whole, was also shattered by World War I. In order to film a war that distinguished the French from the Germans, Griffith had to avoid the greater horrors of trench warfare, even in scenes where *Hearts* imitated

Birth's Civil War battles. Generally Griffith's battle scenes lacked the nonjudgmental implacability that marked his refusal to take sides in *Birth*. In personalizing the conflict and in showing troop breakthroughs, Griffith made meaning where no meaning resided. The war Griffith directed, said Richard Schickel, with its sweeping movements and decisive victories, was the war that generals on both sides were fantasizing. It was not the soldier's war.[101]

Griffith sensed the inadequacy of *Hearts* as a depiction of World War I. "Viewed as a drama," he said, "the war is in some ways disappointing. . . . I found myself saying . . . Why this is old stuff. I have put that stuff on myself so many times." Griffith's feeling that he had already staged World War I did not empower him, however. Instead it opened a gap between theatricality and the void underneath. "A modern war is neither romantic nor picturesque," Griffith continued. "Everyone is hidden away in ditches. As you look out across No Man's Land there is literally nothing that meets the eye but an aching desolation of nothingness. . . . It is too colossal to be dramatic. No one can describe it. You might as well describe the ocean or the milky way." Faced with world war, Griffith could not give dramatic form to the forces of history. Instead of appropriating reality, theater pointed to an emptiness it could not express. Europeans, Griffith explained, "become great actors. They talk and laugh and act much like the people over here, but it is acting, for the Great Fear is over everybody and everything." "After the war is over," as Griffith put it in another interview, "the farmer boy['s] . . . saber may flash as of old, but it will never be the same. Under the shining armor he will in imagination feel the crawling vermin of the trenches." Because Griffith sensed the failure of his filmed war to overcome the real one, *Hearts* lacks *Birth*'s conviction.[102]

Woodrow Wilson presided over a Red scare during and after World War I in which thousands of Americans were jailed or deported. As if he wanted to avert his eyes from the persecution his nationalism had unleashed, Wilson condemned *Hearts* for stirring up hatred by its depiction of German bestiality. *Birth* forged a bond between the president and the filmmaker; *Hearts* severed it.[103]

The League of Nations would have redeemed the horrors of war for Wilson and protected him from its actual character. But Wilson collapsed in the struggle for the league. His new wife ran the White House for months after the president was incapacitated, and although Wilson lived out his life for four more years, he was out of touch with postwar America. A culture of consumption at odds with Wilson's messianic dreams flourished in life and on film. But the Progressive vision that Wilson and Griffith shared also had its legacy—100 percent Americanism and a revived Ku Klux Klan. The new Klan, organized in 1915 in response to *Birth*'s popularity, screened the movie in the 1920s to help build a membership in the millions. But the new Klan's targets, immigrant Catholics and Jews rather than blacks, signaled the disintegration of the Progressives' melting-pot dream. Wilson's son-in-law, William G. McAdoo (he had presided over the segregation of the Treasury Department during Wilson's presidency and then become general counsel for Griffith's company, United Artists), received Klan support and a plurality of delegate votes for more than fifty ballots at the 1924 Democratic presidential nominating convention.[104]

Dixon attacked Bolshevism and the New Woman in his novels of the 1920s and 1930s; he also attacked the revived Klan, since it was anti-Catholic rather than anti-Negro. In Dixon's final novel, *The Flaming Sword* (1939), Negro Communists take over America. Dixon shared the fantasy of that danger with Martin Dies's House Un-American Activities Committee, with Mississippi's representatives Theodore Bilbo and John Rankin. But Dixon's obsessions had lost their national resonance. Although he saw *The Flaming Sword* as a sequel to *The Birth of a Nation*, it was a commercial failure.[105]

Griffith, like Wilson and Dixon, never recovered from World War I. "Are we not making the world safe for democracy, American Democracy, through motion pictures?" he asked.[106] But his own contribution to that project was coming to an end. Griffith continued to make significant movies after *Hearts*, but they lacked either the power of *Birth* and *Intolerance* or the freshness of the Biograph one-reelers. Retreating to an elegaic mode of pastoralism and tradition, Griffith embraced an aesthetic of victimization. His films did not celebrate patriarchy, but they were paralyzed by their failure to challenge it. In *Broken Blossoms* (1919) Lillian Gish plays a daughter whose father (Donald Crisp) beats her to death. In *True Heart Susie* (1919) Gish plays a virtuous country girl whose self-abnegation finally wins back her wayward childhood sweetheart. In *Way Down East* (1920) Gish is seduced and abandoned, loses her baby, and, cast out in a snowstorm, nearly drowns in an icy river. And in *Orphans of the Storm* (1924) Gish's head is beneath the guillotine for the prolonged climax of the movie. The guillotine is known as the black widow, recalling Judith; it is as if, in his last successful film, Griffith was finally taking back *Judith* by reversing the sexual politics of decapitation.

Audiences flocked to Griffith's movies for a few years after the war, until his financial difficulties cost him first his artistic independence and then his ability to make films. These troubles were not caused, Richard Schickel has recently shown, by production costs or box office failures. Griffith sabotaged himself with the enormous expense of building and operating his studio-estate in Mamaroneck, New York. There was no compelling artistic reason for that studio. But Griffith wanted a plantation, a patriarchal pastoral retreat. This flight from modernity, on-screen and off, could not sustain the filmmaker. Griffith had credited movies with reducing the consumption of liquor when he made *Birth*. As his movies declined in the 1920s, his drinking increased. His final film, *The Struggle* (1931), began as an attack on prohibition. But the fall of Griffith's alcoholic protagonist turned the movie into an exposé of drink. When audiences and reviewers laughed at the film's excesses, Griffith retired to his hotel room and drank for weeks. He never made another movie.[107]

Interviewed on film for the sound rerelease of *Birth* in 1930, Griffith recalled the stories of his father's heroic suffering during the Civil War and of his mother's sewing Klan robes afterward. When Walter Huston asked him whether the history recounted in *Birth* was true, Griffith replied, "You can't hear" such stories "and not feel it is true. . . . I think it's true, but as Pontius Pilate asked, 'What is Truth?'" Losing confidence in film's ability to transubstantiate childhood screen memories into reality, Griffith was sensing the violence of *Birth*'s project and identifying not with the white-robed Knights of Christ but with Christ's crucifier.[108]

Griffith lived sixteen more years after *The Struggle*; he was neither poverty-stricken nor friendless during most of that time. But two episodes, one at the beginning of his forced retirement and the other at the end, exhibit the consequences for Griffith of falling out of film. In 1932 an English producer invited him to direct a remake of *Broken Blossoms*. To convince the producer to replace the actress he had chosen for the Gish role with one Griffith preferred, as Gish had once replaced Blanche Sweet, Griffith himself played the scene in which Battling Burrows beats his daughter. He seemed to lose control and actually become Battling Burrows, and the terrified producer had to pull him off the girl. That night a drunken Griffith called Gish in New York and pleaded with her to come to England and rescue him.[109]

Fifteen years later a reporter who wanted to interview Griffith convinced a young woman (who had never heard of the once-legendary director) to call him on the phone. Griffith invited her to his hotel room, and although he tried to shut the door behind her, the reporter forced his way in. Griffith lunged for the girl a few times in front of the reporter, just as Siegmann ("drunk with wine and power") went after Gish in *Birth*'s forced marriage scene (Fig. 7.17). After she eluded him, Griffith refilled his glass and answered the reporter's questions.[110] No longer able to direct Donald Crisp and George Siegmann, Griffith was playing them. Six months later his body, weakened by drink like his father's, ruptured from within like his father's. Stripped of the shroud that had memorialized a mythic patriarch, Griffith had entered his father's dead body.

7.1. Judith (Blanche Sweet) in peacock feathers

7.2. Holofernes (Henry Walthall) observes Judith

7.3. Judith holds aloft the sword

7.4. Blanche Sweet as Annabel Lee in *The Avenging Conscience*

7.5. The ride of the Ku Klux Klan

7.6. George Siegmann (as Silas Lynch) embraces Lillian Gish (as Elsie Stoneman)

7.7. Ralph Lewis as Austin Stoneman

7.8. Phil Stoneman (Elmer Clifton) rescues Ben Cameron (Henry Walthall)

7.10. "War's Peace"

7.9. Civil War dead

7.11. The homecoming

7.12. The little colonel waves his sword

7.13. The Klan prepares to castrate Gus (Walter Long)

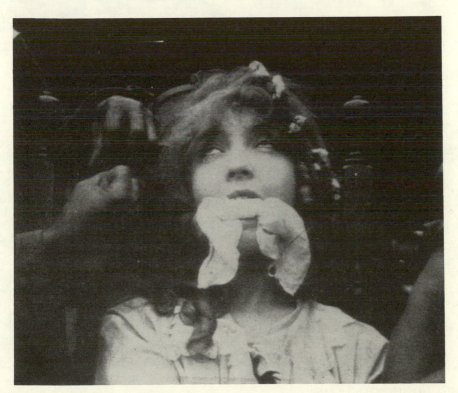

7.14. Lynch's blacks gag Elsie

7.15. Ben Cameron leads the Klan

7.16. The Klan rounds a bend

7.17. Lynch proposes marriage to Elsie

IN MEMORIAM
COLUMBUS
SOCRATES
THE CHRIST
ROBERT EMMET
JOAN OF ARC
GUTTENBERG
DANTE
ET AL

Intolerance resumes its time-honored mask.

7.18. The mask of censorship

CHAPTER VIII

Kiss Me Deadly

Communism, Motherhood, and Cold War Movies

I

The history of demonology in American politics comprises three major moments. The first is racial, pitting whites against peoples of color and placing race at the center of the most important divisions in American political life. Class and ethnic conflict define the second demonological moment. The targets of countersubversion moved from the reds and blacks of frontier, agrarian America to the working-class "savages" and alien "Reds" of urban, industrializing America. The defense of civilization against savagery still derived from repressive conditions of labor and internal, imperial expansion against autonomous communities. Class struggle did not displace racial combat, moreover, but rather rested on the older foundations; the most widely seen single cultural document of the industrial age was *The Birth of a Nation*. But that movie, I have argued, cannot be understood apart from its location in immigrant, modernizing America. And the dominant political and eco-

This paper interprets movies screened during the Pacific Film Archive series, "Hollywood and the Cold War," 29 September to 20 November 1982, at the University of California Art Museum. I am indebted to Linda Myles (former director of the archive) and Nancy Goldman for arranging the series and to Judy Bloch for her notes on the films (printed in the University Art Museum *Calendar*). I also benefited from conversations about these films with Linda Myles, Nancy Goldman, Judy Bloch, and Paul Thomas, from Jim Breslin's reading of an earlier version of the paper, and from comments by members of the editorial board of the journal *Representations*.

nomic struggles shifted in this period from racial conflict to ethnocentric class war.[1]

The cold war introduces the third moment in American demonology. The Soviet Union replaced the immigrant working class as the source of anxiety, and the combat between workers and capitalists, immigrants and natives, was replaced by one between Moscow's agents (intellectuals, government employees, students and middle-class activists) and a state national-security apparatus. The class and ethnic Red scare defined American politics from the 1870s to the New Deal. The third moment has had its vicissitudes, its surges and declines; we still live within it.[2]

Each red (or red and black) scare has revolved around a different core: first individual freedom, then class conflict, finally mass society and the state. At each moment the free man has both depended on and defined himself in opposition to his subversive twin. The discourse of expansion and slavery acknowledged that dependence, for proslavery apologists made black slavery a condition for white freedom, free labor ideology counterposed itself to slavery, and the free man created himself in western Indian combat. Capitalists depended on workers, just as free men needed Indians and slaves. But the persistence of a free labor ideology and the influx of immigrants buried that dependence, shifting a class opposition into an ethnic one that pitted Americans against aliens. When defenders of the national-security state invoked their Soviet counterpart, they returned to antebellum America's clarity about the source of doubleness, which had been muddied in the industrializing age. Now, however, countersubversive doubling justified not the free man but a centralized, secretive, inquisitorial state. Although liberals blamed McCarthyite attacks on responsible policymakers for the cold war Red scare, the rise of a security-oriented state bureaucracy was the most important new factor in the modern history of countersubversion.

American history in each countersubversive moment has constituted itself in binary opposition to the subversive force that threatened it. Demonology begins as a rigid insistence on difference. That insistence has strategic propaganda purposes, but it also derives from fears of and forbidden desires for identity with the excluded object. In countersubversive discourse, therefore, the opposition breaks down. Its cultural and political productions register the collapse of demonological polarization in a return of the politically and psychologically repressed.

The subversive in all three stages has threatened the family, property, and personal and national identity. But subversives melted into their surroundings as the racial and cultural differences that stigmatized them disappeared, and the imagined danger shifted from the body to the mind. Instead of representing only disorder and loss of restraint, the subversive signified control by a sophisticated, alien order. That danger was met in two new ways, each of which mirrored the enemy arrayed against it. One was the rise of the national-security state. The other was the production and surveillance of public opinion in the media of mass society.

This chapter examines the representations of American demonology in the films of the cold war. It analyzes movies made between 1943 and 1964, the years surrounding the cold war consensus. These movies helped produce that consensus. It fragmented after the Kennedy assassination, but by then it had done its work. The 1960s antiwar movement challenged cold war practices but did not do away with them. The 1980s president who moved from movies to politics in cold war Hollywood has revived the demonology that gave him political birth. Cold war cinema will give us access, at its founding, to the cold war discourse within which we continue to speak. As conscious anti-Communist propaganda and as an unintentional register of anxiety, these movies reflected, shaped, and expressed the buried dynamics of a repressive political consciousness. They display both the cumulative history of American demonology and the specific historical circumstances of the 1950s that placed the obsessions of that history under pressure.

Like other productions of American demonology, cold war movies sharply distinguished subversives from countersubversives. But the movies also made visible three developments that threatened to collapse that distinction. The first development was the rise of the national-security state, which counteracted Soviet influence by imitating Soviet surveillance. The second, which we will introduce in part 2 of this essay, arose from the simultaneous glorification and fear of maternal influence within the family. The third was the emergence of a mass society that seemed to homogenize all difference and make subversives difficult to spot.

Before America entered World War I, Woodrow Wilson had attacked "citizens of the United States . . . born under other flags . . . who have poured the poison of disloyalty into the very arteries of our national life." After the war those foreigners were blamed for the great strike wave of 1919 and the radical agitation surrounding it. Attorney General A. Mitchell Palmer and his young subordinate J. Edgar Hoover rounded up for deportation thousands of Americans born abroad. Palmer described the target of his raids as "alien filth," with "sly and crafty eyes

. . . lopsided faces, sloping brows, and misshapen features."³ "Communists," agreed Harry Truman's attorney general, J. Howard McGrath, thirty years later, "are everywhere—in factories, offices, butcher shops, on street corners, in private business, and each carries in himself the germs of death for society."⁴ McGrath was echoing Wilson and Palmer. But invisible, internal Soviet agents had replaced the alien working class as the target of cold war countersubversion. Even when aliens arrived from outer space in the science fiction movies of the cold war, they looked like everyone else.

The invisibility of Communist influence distinguished the Communist party from legitimate opposition groups. But just because Communists masqueraded as ordinary citizens, it was necessary to insist they were not. Truman and his liberal anti-Communist supporters contrasted mundane political conflicts with the struggle against Communism. The Communist party, they argued, was a secret, international conspiracy to overthrow American government; the party took orders from a foreign power, and its members committed espionage.

The distinction between political opponents and foreign spies was a legitimate one. But the government prosecution of alleged atomic spies, as I suggested in chapter 2, not only exaggerated the significance of espionage, it also blurred the line between political opposition and treason. The atomic spy trials of the late 1940s merged with the House Un-American Activities Committee investigation of Communist influence in Hollywood. Since HUAC exposed both Alger Hiss and the Hollywood Ten and since the accused spies, writers, and directors all went to jail, the distinction collapsed between microfilm and film. The celluloid medium of secret influence became the message. The Red scare joined together as one danger atomic spying, revelations of confidential government proceedings, Communist party membership, membership in "Communist front" organizations, manipulation of mass opinion, and subversive ideas. In that chain reaction of guilt by free association, ideas became the source of atomic contamination. As if to reverse the only actual use of nuclear weapons, the one by the United States, the Red scare made un-American ideas radioactive. The "germs" that spread the "poison of disloyalty" justified a state-initiated counterepidemic of anti-Communism.⁵

The free man's dependence on the state, which lies at the center of cold war ideology, goes back to the origins of America. American countersubversion has always defended the individual by mobilizing American nationalism. Both Indian conquest and slave labor were enforced not so much by heroic, individual achievements as by the armed might of the state. The free man and the military state are not two alternative poles in American ideology, nor are they merely a recent symbiosis. Their marriage goes back to the beginning. Nonetheless, the growing power of American public and private bureaucracies placed particular pressure on the free individual during the cold war. Those bureaucracies, whether corporate organizations or the national-security state, were presented as the free man's allies. They composed his free enterprise system and defended it against Communism. Still, if the free man was the polar opposite of the subversive in one structure of difference, the national-security state was in another. And the New Deal, the war, and the cold war had all given that state an unprecedented presence in American life. The boundary separating the free man's state from its subversive twin was always in danger of collapsing in an implosion that would annihilate the free man.

Cold war ideology established a double division, then, between the free man and the state on the one hand, and the free state and the slave state on the other. Cold war movies will show how the historical displacement of the first opposition by the second called into question an even more fundamental division and then offered a solution to the problem of that collapse. The division is the one between motherhood and Communism.

II

The unstable opposition that troubled public history also infected private life. Just as the free man was the polar opposite of the subversive in society, the subversive's opposite in the family was the mother. But just as the boundary between the free man and the state was a permeable one, so also the line dividing mothers from Communism proved to be no iron curtain.

Since appearing on the American scene, the subversive has made the home into his or her central target. Indians kidnapped and massacred mothers and children; blacks raped women; revolutionaries promoted free love; and the Communist state invaded the family's sanctity. In each image, the American mother was a passive victim whose violations demanded revenge. But while the free man is not so independent as the countersubversive pretends, the victimized mother turns out to be experienced as too powerful. Domestic ideology, which developed in the nineteenth century to give women social functions within the home, was double-edged in its impact on both family privacy and female power. Traditional methods of paternal coercion, as domestic ideologists saw it, failed to create self-disciplined children. They punished the body but did not reform the heart. Domesticity replaced physical force with loving, maternal influence. The domestic mother created moral character by giving and withholding love. She entered the self, formed it, understood its feelings, and thereby at once produced it and protected it from corruption.[6]

The mother in domestic ideology made the family a refuge and spread its influence throughout society. Domestic ideology justified women's confinement in the home by making mothers into the guardians of public morality. Mothers were called upon to shelter their families from marketplace stress and to replicate male personalities that could safely be loosed upon the world. That double demand unsettled the line between public and private. By wiping out the truly private, domestic ideology threatened the family it was supposed to support.

Women received moral power, in domestic ideology, in return for accepting their economic and political subordination. Confined to the home, they were promised substantial indirect power—the power to sacrifice their identities in service to others and live through the achievements of men. That solution did not free men from women, for the sons and husbands whose intimate needs women served felt dependent for their freedom on the women who attended to them. At the same time, the emphasis on female virtue generated female reform movements. Transferring domestic ideology from the home to society, such movements claimed direct political power. Opponents of female reform, in turn, invoked domestic ideology to return women to the home. They feared women who easily slid from nurturing influence to emasculating power.[7]

For a society anxious about maternal power, World War II created a crisis. As the depression deprived men of confident public lives, women came to play important nurturing roles. Then the men went off to war. Encouraged to replace their men on the job, women were promised significant work, independence, and even sexual autonomy. Resurgent postwar domestic ideology attacked mothers who abandoned their children to work; it also attacked female sexual aggression. Women were driven back to domestic subordination in response not only to their husbands' return from the war but also to their own newfound independence.[8]

The feminine mystique came to dominate American culture and so-

ciety at the same time that the cold war took over politics. Cold war
cinema emerged from that conjunction. I introduced the problem of the
free man and the state in the masculine mode, by making large, historical claims. Let me turn to mothers and Communism in a more intimate,
personal manner, by offering a synecdoche.

In 1942 Philip Wylie, an immensely successful writer for women's
magazines, published a book of social criticism. The book, *Generation
of Vipers*, was an immediate best-seller. The American Library Association selected it in 1950 as one of the major nonfiction books of the
first half of the twentieth century. The book made Wylie a celebrity
because of its attack on "momism." Mom, in Wylie's depiction, was a
self-righteous, hypocritical, sexually repressed, middle-aged woman.
Having lost the household functions of preindustrial women, according
to Wylie, mom got men to worship her and spend money on her instead. America, insisted Wylie, was "a matriarchy in fact if not in
declaration," in which "the women of America raped the men." Mom
dominated her husband and encouraged the dependence of her son. She
elicited his adulation to repress his sex and transferred the desire
that ought to go to another woman into sentimentality for herself. "I
give you mom. I give you the destroying mother," Wylie concluded.
"I give you Medusa."[9]

Momism is the demonic version of domestic ideology. It uncovers the
buried anxieties over boundary invasion, loss of autonomy, and maternal power generated by domesticity. Philip Wylie had been obsessed
with the dangerous attractions of women since the beginning of his career. He flirted with free love in his early fiction, but his men were as
vulnerable to sexually liberated women as to moms.[10] Although *Generation of Vipers* relinquishes free love, it still falls outside the boundaries of acceptable domestic attitudes. In making mothers his targets,
Wylie exposed anxieties that the mass public could not normally acknowledge. *Generation of Vipers* found an audience in the special circumstances of the war.

During the 1950s mothers were sanctified, not vilified. Although the
United States Army had endorsed Wylie's warnings that sons dependent
on moms would make poor soldiers, the Voice of America removed
Generation of Vipers from its overseas libraries. Nonetheless, the book's
attack on women was an instrument in the battle to return them to the
home. Wylie, like other 1950s domestic ideologists, opposed careers
for women and advocated companionate, sexually fulfilling marriages.
The American mother was to support her husband and let go of her

son; she was not, like mom, to dominate them.[11] Wylie was seeking the solution to momism in the domestic confinement that had generated the problem.

When Philip Wylie is still remembered, it is as the inventor of momism. Wylie had another obsession besides mothers, however—the menace of Communism. The author visited Russia with his half brother in the 1930s. He blamed the Russians for the cholera he contracted upon leaving the country and for his brother's fatal fall from a window. *Smoke Across the Moon*, serialized in the *Saturday Evening Post*, warned against Communism. An anti-Fascist as well as an anti-Communist, Wylie wrote a military manual in 1940 for soldiers entering the army. He advocated continued military preparedness after the war and warned that Americans (softened by moms) were not taking seriously the Communist threat. (He also blamed mom for McCarthyism.)[12]

The answer to Communism, Wylie believed, lay in nuclear armament and civil defense. Wylie visited the Nevada bomb test site in the late 1940s, prepared an imaginative list of nuclear weapons for the navy, and served as a special consultant to the federal Civil Defense Administration. He became an adviser to the Commission on Atomic Energy, a friend of its chairman, Senator Brien McMahon, and an advocate of building the hydrogen bomb.[13]

But as he supported atomic weapons, Wylie worried that the country was unprepared for nuclear war. He had collaborated in 1930 with the editor of *Redbook* on a science fiction novel, *When Worlds Collide*. This tale of the earth's destruction became a classic; Hollywood filmed it in 1951. (As cities are obliterated by earthquake and flood and a mob unsuccessfully storms a rocket ship, a picked group of skilled, white Americans escapes to the new, virgin planet whose sun has wiped out the earth.) Wylie himself had written screenplays for Hollywood. After the success of the movie version of *When Worlds Collide*, he began a screenplay on atomic war. He rewrote it as the novel *Tomorrow* and published it in 1954. Wylie dedicated *Tomorrow* "to the gallant men and women of the federal Civil Defense Administration." *Tomorrow* presents civil defense as a protection not only against Communism but also against momism and offers rearmament and nuclear war as the way to lay momism to rest.[14]

The atomic bomb dropped on Nagasaki was called "Little Boy." The plane that dropped the Hiroshima bomb was named "Enola Gay," after the commander's mother.[15] Mom fills her son with destructive power in

the nuclear naming ceremony. *Tomorrow* pays silent homage to that
hope by inverting it. Wylie's moms disempower their husbands and
sons. Mom is still the source of the bomb, as she was on the *Enola Gay*,
but only in Wylie's unconscious. In his consciousness mom is the target.

There are three moms in *Tomorrow*. Two dominate their weak husbands; the third, whose husband is dead, controls her son and runs the
whole town. All three moms oppose civil defense. They discount the
Soviet threat and resent the disruptions the drills cause in their shopping
rounds and social engagements. These moms are punished by nuclear
war. None takes shelter, and each suffers the consequence. The first
watches the blast of light from a window: "Her face, her breast, her
abdomen were sliced to red meat." The second is saved by her baby's
body, pressed up against her. The baby "received a pound of glass in her
back; she was torn almost apart." This mom's other children are all
gruesomely destroyed as well. The third mom, who has dominated
everyone around her and orchestrated an anti–civil defense campaign,
suffers a humiliating rescue. Crippled by the blast, her helpless fat body
is wheeled through the panic-filled streets in a wheelbarrow. *Tomorrow*
blames moms for, and punishes them with, body destruction.[16]

Philip Wylie was drawn to the apocalypse he claimed to be warning
against. *Tomorrow* presents civil defense as a method not of deterring
atomic war but of surviving it. The Russians follow their atomic bombs
with germ warfare and demand an American surrender. But the Americans have a secret weapon, an atomic submarine rigged as a cobalt
bomb. Some scientists think that if that bomb is set off in the Baltic Sea
it will destroy the world; others claim it will only destroy Russia. Ten
years later, in *Dr. Strangelove*, the submarine will have become a
doomsday machine. In 1954, however, the president believes the opti-
mists. He explodes the submarine without warning, and America wins
the war. Those "able to dream and put the dreams on paper" preside
over the rebuilding of a better world. The dreamer, Philip Wylie, has
built his own better world on paper, in the act of destroying moms.[17]

Liberated women represent the Communist threat in Wylie's earlier
fiction. The left-wing college student in *Smoke Across the Moon* believes that women should have careers. She rejects the role of supporting
a husband and mothering his children. This subversive, who favors sex
without commitments, seduces a minister. He hangs himself when she
refuses to marry him.[18] *Smoke Across the Moon* makes the familiar associations between independent women, sexual danger, and Communism. Female libertines are typically polarized against American moth-

ers. But Wylie's obsession with momism breaks down that binary opposition. In *The Disappearance* (1951) Wylie imagined that women vanished one day from the men's world and men from the women's. One consequence (in the male half of existence) is nuclear war.[19] Women are both essential and menacing in Wylie's world. He links both their absence and their presence to boundary invasion, body destruction, and apocalypse.

Merging Communism, mothers, and scientific catastrophe, Philip Wylie introduces the movies of the cold war. The motion picture industry refused to film *Tomorrow*,[20] perhaps because the script made connections gruesomely explicit that are present but buried in the movies. Cold war films depict the Communist threat as an invasive, invisible, deceptive, enslaving conspiracy. The films construct a Manichaean universe to protect American boundaries from invasion. But they register the breakdown of efforts to polarize not just free men against the state but mothers against Communism as well.

Cold war films present themselves as defending private life from Communism. Like domestic ideology, however, these movies promote the takeover of the private by the falsely private. They politicize privacy in the name of protecting it and thereby wipe it out. Domestic and cold war ideologies not only dissolve the private into the public; they also do the reverse. They depoliticize politics by blaming subversion on personal influence. That influence, in cold war cinema, is female. The films subordinate political consciousness to sexual unconsciousness. They inadvertently locate the need to make boundaries to protect identity in the fear of being swallowed not so much by Communism as by the mother.

In their simplest form the movies identify Communism with sexual seduction. But polarizing the mother against the seductress does not redeem mom, for the mother becomes the source of bad influence. Cold war cinema displays a progressive deepening of domestic anxiety, which is structured in three layers, family, state, and society; each is a response to the layer above. The first identifies Communism with secret, maternal influence. The second replaces mom's surveillance by that of the national-security state. Hollywood sacrifices the free man to the state to protect him from maternal invasion. But the symbiosis of state and family fails to defend against the deepest fear of maternity. Indifferent female reproductive power, in cold war science fiction, proliferates interchangeable identities. The aliens of cold war science fiction are deliberate stand-ins for Communists. The films suggest, however, that the menace of alien invasion lay not so much in the power of a foreign state as in the obliteration of paternal inheritance and the triumph of mass society.

III

The film that introduced cold war demonology into Hollywood was a hot war movie, *Mission to Moscow* (1943). It was made to create sympathy for Soviet Russia. *Mission to Moscow* employed the imagery of national defense and internal conspiracy to justify Stalin's purge trials. The film blamed a Trotskyist-Nazi alliance for weakening Russia against imminent German invasion. *Mission to Moscow* became a target of the House Un-American Activities Committee after the war, and its screenwriter, Howard Koch, was blacklisted.[21] The blacklist imitated the purges justified by the film. HUAC's appropriation of a pro-Soviet movie was emblematic of the larger historical relationship between the war against Nazism and the cold war. Although cold war filmmakers claimed to be protecting the American way of private life against Communism, they actually revived and inverted the politicized popular-front culture of the struggle against Fascism. Climaxing during World War II, the popular front subordinated private existence and internal political conflict to a sentimental American nationalism. World War II, moreover, provided the occasion for the emergence of the national-security apparatus; pro-Communists, who were to be the major targets of that apparatus, helped develop the countersubversive rationale. That is less a paradox than it seems, for countersubversive theory mirrors the enemy it is out to destroy.

Since twinning dominates the countersubversive imagination, I shall begin by treating cold war movies in oppositional pairs. That method elevates the double feature of the 1950s movie house to a structural principle of analysis. It will at once illuminate the boundaries these films try to maintain and chart their breakdown. (The boundaries break down, in the analysis presented here, when the mother of a Communist has a breakdown. Her collapse provides an entry for the state in the film, and the state and mass society in the narrative of this chapter, at which point the method of doubling films is abandoned.) The double of *Mission to Moscow* is *I Was a Communist for the FBI* (1951).

Mission to Moscow, derived from Ambassador Joseph E. Davies's book, presented itself as fact. Walter Huston played the ambassador, but Davies himself appeared at the beginning to introduce and sanction the film. The protagonist of *I Was a Communist*, Matt Cvetic, was also real, and Pittsburgh proclaimed Matt Cvetic Day for the premiere of *I Was a Communist*. Cvetic had named hundreds of Communists and Communist sympathizers in western Pennsylvania, costing many their jobs. He was later revealed, not in the film, to have had a history of mental illness.[22] The film, fictional both in Cvetic's fantasies and in the movie fictionalized from those fantasies, was nominated for an Academy Award as the best feature-length documentary of 1951.[23]

In *I Was a Communist* Warner Brothers reversed the ideology of its *Mission to Moscow*. Both films used a documentary voice-over to give fiction the sound of news; both showed factory sabotage; both glorified a secret, internal police; and both warned against imminent foreign invasion. A conspiratorial cabal in both films threatened the national defense, played upon divisive social discontents, and undermined the nation's will. The difference was that the threat was now from Russia, not to it.

Anti-Communist films like *I Was a Communist* warned against a political danger. But they depoliticized the appeals of Communism by using the conventions of the gangster movie and equating Communism with crime. Such films displayed the confusion institutionalized in the FBI between criminal activity and political dissent. But in equating Communism and crime, cold war films shifted sympathy away from the individual criminal of the gangster movie and toward the forces of law and order. Depression-era gangster movies had sympathy for the devil; their protagonists were outsiders and underdogs, self-made men who rose to the top. The racketeers and murderers Matt Cvetic exposes in the film are men in grey flannel suits who merely play upon sympathy for the underdog. The lonely heroism of the free man in *I Was a Communist* consists in the protagonist masquerading as one sort of organizational man when in fact he is another.

Both Davies and Cvetic entered Communist territory on the orders of their government. Davies enjoyed the luxury of supporting Soviet Russia as an American government official. Cvetic outdid him. He masqueraded as an actual party member and lost the protection of his patriotic identity. Davies was rewarded for his mission; Cvetic made himself into a pariah. Sacrificing his private life to patriotic work, Matt Cvetic introduces the anxious relationship of the personal to the political that pervades cold war cinema.

Communism not only threatened public stability in cold war films; it also turned family members against one another and endangered private life. The loving family represented America in cold war movies. Com-

munists subverted the family, sometimes in the person of a sexual seductress, sometimes as the representative of an intrusive state. The two figures entered cold war cinema together, dressed in innocent clothes, in
the pro-Russian World War II film *Song of Russia*.

Song of Russia (1943) elicited romance, then sacrificed it to patriotism and left its American hero bereft and alone. An American conductor on Russian tour falls in love with a young Russian woman, a pianist.
But she chooses her country over her husband after their marriage. She
leaves the conductor when the Nazis invade Russia and returns to fight
for her village.

One of *Song of Russia*'s screenwriters, Richard Collins, named the
other, Paul Jarrico, before HUAC; Jarrico was blacklisted. Robert Taylor was also called before the committee for starring as the American
conductor. Taylor played a victim of Russian patriotism on film. Later,
in his testimony before HUAC, he blamed the American Office of War
Information for pressuring him into that role. Taylor apologized for appearing in a Communist film and urged that the Hollywood figures he
named as suspected Communists be blacklisted. "The American people," Taylor reassured questioning Congressman Richard Nixon, "will
go along with anybody who prefers America and the American form of
government over any other subversive ideologies." Taylor's inadvertent
"other" made the American form of government as subversive as the
Russian. That slip, in the context of the actor's enthusiastic cooperation
with the committee, faintly echoes Nikolai Bukharin's deliberate sub-
version-by-overcooperation in his Moscow purge trial, where Bukharin's elaborate confession seemed to mock his accusers. Taylor may have
been recognizing unconsciously or even consciously that HUAC was
substituting one intrusive state for another and that such political intervention subverted his desire to be left alone. The actor rejected propaganda films in his testimony, in favor of entertainment. But committee
members objected that Hollywood had a patriotic duty as well as a
private, entertainment function. To make sure that Americans were protected from subversion, Taylor agreed with HUAC that "the motion
picture industry . . . should make anti-Communist pictures."[24]

The motion picture industry did. *Never Let Me Go* (1953) took back
Song of Russia. Clark Gable plays an American war correspondent who
marries a Russian ballerina during the war. But the Communists will
not let her out of Russia after the war is over. In *Song of Russia* Taylor's
wife dies fighting the Nazis and he returns to America alone. In *Never*

Let Me Go Gable secretly infiltrates Russia and brings his woman home.

Susan Peters, playing the pianist, chooses her country over her husband. Gene Tierney, playing the ballerina, chooses her husband. In *Kiss Me Deadly* (1955) the femme fatale masquerades as a Tierney, and even the hard-boiled Mike Hammer falls for her apparent helplessness. In fact she is more deadly than the atomic spies who also menace him. To turn Mickey Spillane's detective thriller into a cold war movie, Hollywood added atomic radiation. Hammer is on the trail of a stolen box containing radioactive material. The slightest opening of the box emits rays that burn and disfigure the body. The woman gains possession of the box in the film's climactic scene; she knows its value but is ignorant of its contents. Unable to restrain her curiosity, Pandora opens the box and a glowing fire leaps out. Since the woman is facing the camera from behind the box, the fire seems to leap out of her body. It consumes the woman and destroys the house to which she and the detective have come. *Kiss Me Deadly* locates Pandora's box as the seat of apocalyptic destruction; only Mike Hammer escapes.

Less seamy and violent anti-Communist films domesticated the subversive woman. In *I Was a Communist*, the party sends a seductive schoolteacher to spy on Cvetic, whose son is in her class. After Cvetic rejects the schoolteacher's advances in their first private encounter, she learns to mistrust the Communists and chooses the FBI agent over them. Because she leaves her sexuality behind when she leaves the party, she is no longer a threat to him; he now protects her from Communist efforts at murder.

Joseph von Sternberg's *Jet Pilot*, made in 1951 and released in 1957,[25] is a comic-strip variation on the same theme. (Its lack of seriousness may have convinced Howard Hughes not to release it at the height of the cold war.) A female Russian jet pilot, masquerading as a political refugee, seduces and betrays the American assigned to discover her secrets. This victory, of Janet Leigh over John Wayne, reproduces Marlene Dietrich's triumph in Sternberg's *Blue Angel*. In both movies a male sexual innocent is at first resistant to overt displays of female sexuality and then succumbs. Each hero discovers his woman's disloyalty after he marries her. But the American refuses to accept his humiliation. Like Gable in *Never Let Me Go*, Wayne enters Russia. He is now playing Leigh's role of a spy masquerading as a defector. Pretending he is still in Leigh's sexual power, Wayne outwits both her and the Russian state. His prowess is too much for the Russian Mata Hari. At the film's end she chooses Wayne over Russia, and the two jet pilots fly off to freedom together. Patriarchy and love in *Jet Pilot* prove stronger than Communism and sex.

"I woke up one morning and found I had a Party card," explains a contrite Communist in *Walk East on Beacon* (1952). It is like "finding yourself married to a woman you hate."[26] Anti-Communist films seem to pose the classic opposition between the free man, family, and love on the one hand, female sexuality, the state, and the invasion of the family on the other. They seem to stand with private life against threats that come from without. But the films actually suggest that such a polarization is too simple, for they also express anxiety about the internal vulnerability of the family. Both Cvetic's role and Taylor's testimony show that cold war cinema politicized privacy in the name of defending it. That paradox is not to be explained simply by the external threat of Communism. Cold war films imply that domestic ideology, far from protecting America against alien ideas, generated aliens from within its bosom. The 1950s movie which comes closest to blaming mom for Communism is *My Son John* (1952).

Two sons toss a football with their father in the opening scene of *My Son John*. The father drops the ball. "I was a tackle," he jokes. "They ran through you, dad," responds one of the sons. The camera pans up to a bedroom window. It reveals the mother, Helen Hayes, dressed only in her slip. The family is late for church, and the father cannot get her to come on time. He's never been able to, he says. When Hayes finally joins her family, she walks between and flirts with her sons. These sons are twins, and their interchangeability aggravates the disorientation of the opening of the film.

Leo McCarey, who directed *My Son John*, normally made Hollywood comedies. He had a comic intention in the opening scene of this movie. But the appearance of the absent son, John, transforms comedy into melodrama and casts a retrospective cold eye on the movie's beginning as well.

John's brothers are off to fight in Korea; they are their father's boys. The mother's bond is with John, the Washington intellectual, who stays away from their send-off. Like his brothers, John makes fun of his father, but his ridicule has an edge that theirs lacks. Robert Walker, who died while making this film, plays John. His distancing, derealizing persona calls the values of his family into question. Walker's irony is meant to expose John's contempt for wholesome American life. But his brilliant performance draws director and viewer in, so that the film presents the American family through John's detached and discredited eyes. *My Son John* may want to stand with the father, but it exposes his American Legion costume and his simple-minded patriotic slogans to ridicule.

John's father, speaking the message of the film, warns that Communists are no longer foreigners, but Americans. These internal enemies resemble patriots, the film tells us, whom they imitate in order to subvert. Communists were aliens in the first Red scare; they assaulted the American family. John's family has produced a subversive, and it is powerless against him.

John's father makes him swear on the family Bible that he is not a Communist. Then, provoked by John's mockery, he smashes the Bible over his head. The father's old-fashioned, coercive methods fail to discipline John, just as domestic ideology predicted they would not. John's father does not command respect; he is reduced to forcing the Bible on his son. John's mother insinuates it into him by interchanging it with food. "I'll make you cookies, pies, cake, and jam," she reminds John she used to tell him, "if you'll learn Matthew, Mark, Luke, and John." But the newer maternal methods of loving influence only make matters worse. John has become a Communist, the film implies, because of the liberal ideas and sexual availability of his mother. "You are part of me," John's mother tells him, and even as that line points to John's betrayal, it insists on the lack of boundaries between them. John has imbibed his mother's naive humanitarianism and, to distance himself from her, taken it in a sinister direction.

Helen Hayes plays a flaky, independent, sympathetic woman. The family doctor prescribes pills when her younger sons go off to war, and we applaud her refusal to take them. But Hayes's feistiness becomes a sign of her disturbance. Her intimacy with John gets her in trouble in the course of the film, and her eccentricities turn to madness.

My Son John capitalized on the Judith Coplon spy case. The film makes John not merely a Communist but a spy and thereby merges atomic and sexual secrets. John has betrayed his mother for a female spy, but he inadvertently leaves his key to the spy's apartment in a pair of torn pants that he gives his mother for charity. Mom turns him in to the FBI only after she flies to Washington, tries the key, and finds that it fits the other woman's lock. "Mothers . . . Our Only Hope," announced J. Edgar Hoover's article enlisting domestic ideology in the fight against crime. But in *My Son John* the special bond between mother and son engenders psychological and political bad influence.[27]

By psychologizing the appeals of Communism, *My Son John* located the problem in the very family that was supposed to provide the solution. Psychological explanations for Communism, like the reduction of Communism to crime, diverted attention from social injustice. But psychology pointed away from society not to the gangster but to the family. It located the threat to the free man less in the alien Communist state than in his loving mother.

The family constellation in *My Son John* consisted of an intrusive, sexually unsatisfied mother, a weak father, and a cold, isolated son. *The Manchurian Candidate* (1962) repeated that triangle and made it demonologically explicit. *The Manchurian Candidate* is a brilliant, self-knowing film. But far from mocking the mentality it displays, it aims to reawaken a lethargic nation to the Communist menace. Capitalizing on its improbabilities by mixing realism with science fiction, *The Manchurian Candidate* is the most sophisticated film of the cold war.

Laurence Harvey is the Manchurian candidate. The Communists capture his battalion in Korea, take the men across the Chinese border, and program Harvey to carry out political assassinations. During the brainwashing sessions, the American soldiers hallucinate that the Communists who give them orders are middle-aged club women. The playing card, the queen of diamonds, the residue of these moms, is Harvey's control card. He goes into a trance when he sees the queen of diamonds and obeys the orders of the next voice he hears.

Harvey's mother, played by Angela Lansbury, connects the fantasized Manchurian club women to the queen of diamonds. "She is a middle-aged puffin with an eye like a hawk," Philip Wylie wrote of mom;[28] he might have been describing Lansbury. Harvey hates his mother, but he is in her power. Her incestuous love for him, which repels Harvey but which he cannot escape, is the source of the party's hold on his unconscious. Helen Hayes is sympathetic, Lansbury is not. But both moms bring to the surface the entrapping, repressed, oedipal love that Wylie made the source of momism. As if to confirm Wylie's claim that moms will not let their sons go, Harvey is programmed to kill his own fiancée.

The Manchurian Candidate relinquishes the sympathy for the father figure that *My Son John* tried to retain. John's father, the simple-minded patriot, has become Harvey's stepfather, a drunken, ridiculous, malevolent, right-wing, anti-Communist senator, a character modeled on Joseph McCarthy. Although Lansbury masquerades as a superpatriot, she is secretly a Communist, and she controls her husband. After he is nominated for vice president, the Communist party orders Harvey to kill the man at the head of the ticket. If Harvey succeeds, his McCarthy step-father will be elected president and his Communist mother will run America.

But incest is stronger than Communism in this film, as it was in *My Son John*. Furious that the Soviets have made her son their sacrificial instrument, Lansbury vows to turn against them once her husband is president. She seals that pledge to herself with a long kiss on Harvey's lips. Kissing her son in close-up as she faces the camera, Harvey's mom is kissing the audience. We feel as sickened as he does by her inappropriate desire. But just as her incestuous love is stronger than Communism, so is his incestuous hate; it frees him from party control. Frank Sinatra, playing the army intelligence officer pursuing Harvey, does not reach him in time to prevent the assassination. But after climbing the stairs to the top of the convention hall and getting the presidential candidate in his sights, Harvey turns his rifle on his stepfather and his mother and kills them instead.

Domestic ideology promised that the American family would triumph over Communism. *The Manchurian Candidate*, by subordinating Communist to maternal influence, showed what that promise entailed. The family defeats Communism only by first generating Communism and then self-destructively replacing it. The incest fantasy that reduced Communism to momism is shown to be a wish. For the family nightmare defends against having actually to come to terms with politics. Freed from its roots in momism, Communism and anti-Communism would have to be seen as having lives of their own.

The Manchurian Candidate was a Kennedy administration film. Sinatra, a member of the Kennedy entourage, plays a ravaged, lonely Kennedy hero. He tries to rouse a credulous army bureaucracy to the danger posed by Harvey. The presidential candidate is asking Americans to sacrifice for their country when Harvey trains his sights on him. Like Kennedy, *The Manchurian Candidate* warned against both right-wing hysteria and bureaucratic complacency. Both the film and the administration aimed to breathe new life into the cold war.

The cold war needed reanimating in the early 1960s. Eisenhower seemed to turn pacific during his second term, the Korean War was over, and McCarthy had been reduced to impotence. As if in acknowledgment of the shift in the national mood, Hollywood had released no anti-Communist movies since 1957. Moreover, *Jet Pilot*, the last to be shown, had a comic ambience alien to vintage cold war cinema. *The Manchurian Candidate*, with a political and technical sophistication absent from its models, was supposed to initiate a political renewal. Instead it was the last cold war movie, for the assassination to which it pointed brought the cold war consensus to an end.

The Manchurian Candidate was released in 1962. The very next year a young man who had returned from behind the Iron Curtain carried a rifle with telescopic sights up several flights of stairs in a building. Like Harvey, he fired through a window on a target below. Unlike Harvey, he did not shift his aim. No doubt the assassination that imitated art was an eerie coincidence. But in 1981 another troubled young man acted out his identification with a movie assassin. *Taxi Driver* led John Hinckley to shoot at one president;[29] did Laurence Harvey stimulate Lee Harvey Oswald?

The coincidence in names, which unsettles the observer, may also have taken possession of Oswald. If the Russians did not program Lee Harvey Oswald, perhaps *The Manchurian Candidate* did. One has the additional fantasy that the film warned Oswald (or whoever programmed him) to avoid the mistake (merging motherhood and Communism) of those who programmed Harvey. No doubt Oswald was neither stimulated nor alerted by *The Manchurian Candidate*. His success nonetheless did have the consequence against which the film was warning. By killing his president where Harvey had failed, Oswald initiated the breakdown of cold war demonology. In the absence of a young hero who could reinfuse the cold war with meaning and in the presence of a violence that overwhelmed anti-Communist simplifications (or so it seemed), the cold war consensus temporarily disintegrated. *The Manchurian Candidate* was followed by *Dr. Strangelove* (1964), a movie entirely faithful to the film tradition it brought to an end.

Sterling Hayden, playing General Jack D. Ripper, who sets the holocaust in motion, was making reparation for his cooperation with HUAC.[30] *Dr. Strangelove* derived anti-Communism and nuclear holocaust from the free man's fear of female sexuality. Ripper protects his bodily fluids from women by withholding his seed. He uses the initials of "purity of essence" as the code that locks the bombers on their targets. George C. Scott, as the sexual cowboy General Buck Turgidson, is the mirror image of Ripper. Slim Pickens is the pilot who, waving his stetson, rides the bomb between his legs down to Russia. The bomb will set off a Russian doomsday machine that will wipe out not just momism and Communism (as it did in *Tomorrow*) but the entire world.

Strangelove makes gallows humor from the sexual politics of cold war cinema. It also brings to the surface the two other cinematic sub-texts to which we now turn. One is the free man's displacement by the technological state. Men are weak and fallible in *Strangelove*; technology takes over from them. Just as it parodied sexual politics, *Strangelove* here mocks another wish within cold war films. The second subtext is the buried fear of nuclear holocaust. That anxiety is doubly displaced in cold war cinema, moving from anti-Communism to science fiction and, within that genre, from real bombs to fantasy menaces—an alien invasion (at the site of a nuclear defense complex) in *Invaders from Mars*, radiation-caused mutations in *Them!* We shall first examine the technological state in cold war movies and conclude with science fiction.

The cold war cultural consensus produced political power in the 1950s. It helped build a national-security apparatus that survived the breakdown of the consensus and dominated the 1960s. By the time the cultural consensus stopped producing power, the powerful institutions were in place. We can see their genesis in our films. The national-security state, absent thus far from our reading of cold war cinema, is not absent from the movies themselves. Cold war films that exposed family weakness did not merely reveal troubles at the heart of American private life; they explored those troubles in order to promote their cure. Help for the insecure family lay in the national-security state. Two films directed by Edward Dmytryk introduce that state. He made the first, *Crossfire* (1947), before he was jailed as one of the Hollywood Ten. He made the second, *The Caine Mutiny* (1954), after he recanted, named names, and was allowed to work again.[31] *Crossfire*, set in the years of the emerging cold war, warned against the demonization of cultural and political difference. *The Caine Mutiny* returned to World War II in order to justify cold war America. Just as *I Was a Communist* was the mirror image of *Mission to Moscow* and *Never Let Me Go* took back *Song of Russia*, so *The Caine Mutiny* was Dmytryk's unwriting of *Crossfire*.

Crossfire was one of a handful of socially conscious films that got Hollywood in trouble. Its subject was anti-Semitism. Robert Ryan plays a character named Montgomery, who kills a Jew and tries to pin the crime on a confused young soldier. We see the Jew in flashback, explaining the feelings of purposelessness and violence that are emerging with the end of World War II. His talk soothes the young soldier; it enrages the ex-soldier Montgomery. But although Montgomery silences one voice of sympathetic understanding, there is no danger of a world out of human control in this film. Two strong men are in charge of the action. Once they start working together, the man caught in the crossfire is Montgomery rather than the accused innocent.

Robert Mitchum plays a tough sergeant, Kelley, the good counterpart to Montgomery. Robert Cummings plays Finlay, the more intellectual, soft-spoken policeman. Although both Kelley and Finlay work in law-and-order bureaucracies, the film ignores the institutions in favor of the individuals. In a film that claims to stand against authority, a policeman and a sergeant nonetheless become its heroes. *Crossfire* is populated by attractive, reliable, strong men.

There is a tough, authoritative officer in *The Caine Mutiny*. He is the captain of the minesweeper, the *Caine*, and he exits at the beginning of the movie. That captain is replaced by the dictatorial, pathetic, paranoid Captain Queeg. Fred MacMurray plays the tough-talking, cynical intellectual, Lieutenant Tom Keefer, who has no use for naval discipline. He plants in his fellow officers the idea that Queeg is insane. Keefer combines the figures of Montgomery and Kelley; he is Kelley in his apparent concern for the film's young protagonist and Montgomery in his alienation. In spite of *Crossfire*'s ideology, once the trap closes around Montgomery, sympathy shifts to him. Keefer inherits that sympathy for the rebel, in order, by the end of *Caine Mutiny*, to forfeit it entirely. Keefer instigates the mutiny but refuses to take responsibility for it. Instead he succeeds (as Montgomery does not) in making a young, innocent military man stand trial for a capital crime.

Van Johnson plays Lieutenant Steve Maryk, the neophyte officer of the deck who relieves Queeg of command during a storm. Maryk has a mom, one of Wylie's overstuffed, intrusive, middle-aged mothers. He emancipates himself from her influence during the movie and marries the young woman of whom she had disapproved. *Crossfire*'s soldier is also restored to his wife, but the authorities who take care of him are absent from *Caine Mutiny*. Maryk has no father. Queeg resembles John's father and Laurence Harvey's stepfather in his pathetic claims to power and in his embarrassing desires to be loved. He is hardly an adequate father-substitute. Maryk overthrows Queeg. But in the absence of a strong, male authority, that act does not free him from his mother; instead it threatens him with capital punishment. Maryk grows up through the intervention and support of the state.

The crucial figure in Maryk's rescue, as it is in the *Crossfire* soldier's entrapment, is a Jew. Both Jews explain a bewildering world to their neophytes, but while one is a kindly small-businessman victim,

the other is an angry lawyer in service to the navy. Jose Ferrer plays
the lawyer Barney Greenwald, who exposes Queeg's paranoia during
Maryk's court-martial. But outside the courtroom Greenwald stands with
Queeg, not against him. He turns to Keefer at the party celebrating
Maryk's acquittal and tells him, "The author of the Caine mutiny is
you." Greenwald is accusing not only Keefer, but also the Jew Herman
Wouk, who wrote *The Caine Mutiny*, and the ex-Communist Dmytryk,
who directed it. Greenwald is the Jew who has moved beyond a naive
and dangerous humanitarianism. Wouk and Dmytryk (through their
representative, MacMurray) must atone for their earlier rebelliousness.
Queeg is pathetic, Greenwald agrees; he is a victim of the ravages of
war. Just for that reason the crew and its natural leaders must rally
behind him. Keefer and Maryk should have responded to Queeg's appeals for help instead of treating him with contempt. In *Crossfire* there
is room for Kelley, the irreverent, cynical man of the world. In *Caine*
Kelley and Montgomery are no longer split into good and evil halves;
merged into Keefer they are expelled from the moral universe. Kelley
allies himself with *Crossfire*'s policeman to save the innocent soldier.
Keefer endangers both authority and the innocent. In fact, on the *Caine*
it is the innocent who should have rescued authority. When the captain
is weak, Greenwald implies, his crew must sacrifice their critical intelligence. They must bolster authority from below and cooperate with the
hierarchy above. When the fathers lack authority, says *The Caine Mutiny*, we must subordinate ourselves to the military state.

Explicitly anti-Communist films like *I Was a Communist* and *My
Son John* contain the same message. In such movies the state steps in to
restore not simply social order but sexual hierarchy as well. John's betrayal drives his mother to a breakdown, and his father is powerless to
help her. The FBI tracks John down and saves his parents; weakened
paternal authority requires the help of the state. Where the parents
themselves are guilty, as in the real-life Rosenberg case, they must con-
fess to the state or be killed. But here, too (and contrary to the evidence),
mom was seen as the person in charge. "Julius is the slave and his wife,
Ethel, the master," insisted Morris Ernst, co-counsel of the American
Civil Liberties Union. His theory formed the basis for a "psychological
study" that reached President Eisenhower's desk. Repeating the momism fantasy as he refused to grant clemency to the Rosenbergs, Eisenhower wrote that Ethel was "the more strong-minded and the apparent
leader of the two."[32]

Robert Warshow, the liberal anti-Communist film critic, thought *My*

Son John stood with the father, and he hated the movie for glorifying a
stupid anti-Communism. Unwilling to see his own statist politics reflected back at him in vulgar propaganda, Warshow was blind to the
fact that *My Son John* discredited the father to create a need for the
FBI. The only figure not undercut by the end of the movie is the FBI
agent, Stedman, played by Van Heflin. To use Catherine Gallagher's
terms, *The Caine Mutiny* and *My Son John* mark the victory of social
paternalism over domestic ideology.[33]

A patriarchal state does not replace the family, however. Men compose the state, to be sure; but they use the techniques of motherhood
and Communism—intrusion, surveillance, and secret domination. Moreover, they use these methods to save the family, not to destroy it. In a
militarist version of reformist and therapeutic practice, the family requires help from experts in order to maintain itself. The private feelings
that constitute the subject also constitute (in Foucault's pun) the means
for his subjection. The family is constructed in the name of privacy as a
field for social control. State and family interpenetrate in mutually supportive anxiety. The desire for privacy creates nervousness about the
intrusion of the state. But anxiety over intimate private relations generates state surveillance and protection. Better the interpenetration of
state and family than that of mother and son.[34]

Momism, presented as the source of Communism in a film such as
My Son John, may thus appear exposed as the source of anti-Communism. But because that simple reversal continued to assign power to
mom, even it participates in cold war distress. Fears of boundary invasion point to infantile anxieties over maternal power, to the state of dual
union with the mother.[35] In addition, by encouraging maternal surveillance, domestic ideology augmented anxieties over boundary breakdown, particularly insofar as actual mothers carried out its precepts at
home. Moreover, the specific version of domestic ideology current in the
1950s, the feminine mystique, played upon fears of the sinister power
of women in society to drive them back into the home. The feminine
mystique failed to assuage those fears, for it made the home at once the
arena of mom's influence and the confined space against which, in fantasies of female vengeance, she would rebel. The insistence on, at one
and the same time, rigid boundary divisions and maternal influence thus
created an unstable, contradictory masculine identity. Cold war movies
blamed Communists for that explosive mixture as a cover for blaming
mothers.

The resort to momism was, nonetheless, an escape from investigating invasive structures that, although they intruded on the family, were located outside the home. Filmmakers were under pressures that may have reawakened infantile anxieties, but those pressures came from Moscow, Washington, and Hollywood, not from mom. Soviet expansion on the one hand, American state invasion of the motion picture industry on the other, lay behind cold war cinema. Seeking Communist spies everywhere, cold war movies glorified the doubled agents of the American state. That filmic state was, to be sure, a wish as well as a reality. The movies presented a ubiquitous, intrusive American state apparatus, an ideal to which the actual national-security bureaucracy made an imperfect approximation. The American state ostensibly defended us from Soviet Russia; in the subtext of the films, the state defended us from mom. At a deeper level still, the state was itself the problem. The movies disguised that problem by shifting the locus of anxiety from the American state to the American family, on the one hand, and the Russian state, on the other.

By merging motherhood and Communism as the source of secret influence, moreover, the films deflected attention from themselves. Film, as HUAC investigators understood, was an intruder. It entered the unconscious of those who watched movies in darkened theaters throughout the land. The men controlling the hidden cameras were agents of Hollywood, not the FBI. But the Hollywood agents who controlled films were not the men who made them. Those in charge of movies were emissaries of larger political and economic structures, structures that pressed particularly hard upon filmmakers during the cold war. The intrusive state depicted on film may represent the filmmakers' anxiety about their own influence and their susceptibility to influence and, therefore, their Kafka-like rush into the arms of just those powerful forces—in Washington and the motion picture business—that they feared.

The Communists intend "to deliver America to Russia as a slave," Matt Cvetic warns. *I Was a Communist* ends with the "Battle Hymn of the Republic" on the sound track, as the camera closes in on a bust of Lincoln. Anti-Communist films attacked the police state, yet they glorified an FBI whose agents, cameras, and electronic listening devices, controlled from a central source, penetrate the deepest recesses of private life. Agent Stedman uses a car accident to insinuate himself into John's mother's home. He wins her confidence by his interest in her boys and elicits information without telling her his real identity. The FBI follows John's mother and films her humiliation at the other woman's apartment. Although the Communists kill John after the bureau converts him, we witness his redemption from beyond the grave. The stock Irish family priest, last shown sorting through old clothes given to charity, is supplanted by the technological state. A (spot) light shines down upon a tape recorder, which has replaced John's absent body. John's recorded voice addresses a college graduating class and delivers his confession. In Leo McCarey's technological version of modern Catholic anti-Communism, tape recorder equals mystic body and tape equals soul.

Walk East on Beacon (1952), another pseudo-documentary, also celebrated the technology of surveillance. The film was based on a book by J. Edgar Hoover and made with the FBI's "technical assistance." At its beginning a narrator extols the bureau for "protecting" us. We watch agents opening our mail. We see reassuring scenes of tape recorders whirring, agents listening, and cameras observing. Even in *I Was a Communist*, where there is a single hero, technology fills the supporting roles. Thus it is often difficult in such films to tell the faceless Communists from their counterparts in the FBI.[36]

Cold war families are endangered by anti-Communist public opinion as well as by the state. Matt Cvetic, the secret agent who plays Communist, is repudiated by his immigrant brothers. His son gets into fights and loses his friends because they think that his father is a Red. Unable to tell his son the truth, Cvetic loses him, too. In the name of showing Communism's threat to the family, *I Was a Communist* exposed the ravages suffered by families whose members were accused of subversion.

Anti-Communist films also violated the sanctity of the family from within. They justified the informer who betrayed subversive members of his or her own family. In the figure of the informer, anti-Communist films mobilized society in the service of the state. Both *My Son John* and *Walk East on Beacon* made informing on Communist family members into an act of moral heroism. *Storm Warning* (1951) and *On the Waterfront* (1954) moved the defense of informing into other walks of life, southern violence and labor racketeering. The effort to turn the informer into a culture hero had particular resonance in Hollywood, where naming names had become a condition of employment.

On the Waterfront was written by Budd Schulberg and directed by Elia Kazan; it starred Lee J. Cobb. All named names before HUAC, and the film has rightly been seen as a Hollywood parable.[37] *Storm Warning*, starring Ronald Reagan, has escaped similar analysis, perhaps because Reagan plays a southern district attorney who exposes the Ku Klux

Klan. The film even confused a recent Berkeley audience, for it presents Reagan as an opponent of the Klan. But the Klan is a stand-in for the Communist party in justifications of FBI surveillance. *Storm Warning* gives itself away by entirely avoiding race; although the real southern Klan was first and foremost anti-Negro, the targets of the movie Klan are not blacks. Like the party in *I Was a Communist*, *Storm Warning*'s Klan is merely a racket. The film wants to warn against a violent secret conspiracy without raising the specter of racial injustice. (Communists try to stir blacks to riot in *I Was a Communist*; a black crowd is menacing, and, echoing Hoover on the 1919 race riots, an FBI agent blames the Communist party for the Detroit race riots of 1943 in which blacks were actually the victims.)

As president of the Screen Actors Guild, Ronald Reagan led the fight to drive subversives out of Hollywood.[38] Reagan plays himself, as District Attorney Burt Rainer, in *Storm Warning* (Fig. 8.1). He is asked at the outset of the film if he plans to "name names" and expose the respected members of his community who secretly belong to the Klan. District Attorney Rainer responds that he stands for "law and order." (Reagan had starred the year before in a movie with that title.) Later a committee of prominent citizens asks him to leave the Klan alone and not encourage outsiders to divide the community. The actors speak the lines of the Hollywood Committee for the First Amendment, trying to protect the Hollywood Ten. *Storm Warning*'s committee members are fellow travelers of the Klan.

The committee wants a Klan murder to go unpunished; Rainer insists on prosecution. Marsha Mitchell, played by Ginger Rogers, has witnessed the murder in the film's opening scene. Rogers's mother had recently played a leading role before HUAC, protesting Communist influence in Hollywood and wishing she could name more names.[39] But the character played by Ginger Rogers refuses to name whom she has seen, in spite of Rainer's efforts, because her brother-in-law pulled the trigger. Although she finally decides to expose the murderer, her delay has placed her in danger. Had Marsha been forthcoming, Rainer could have protected her. She is brutalized by the Klan as a result of her family loyalty, and her pregnant sister is killed.

The sisters are punished for their sexuality as well as their secretiveness. The sister played by Rogers is a career woman. She rejects the advances of the salesman traveling with her at the beginning of the film. The movie wants to approve of her refusal, yet it marks her as sexually in charge of herself. The younger sister, played by Doris Day, represents

the contrasting danger contained within female sexuality, not independence but pleasure. She is turned on by, and in thrall to, the Klan thug
she marries. Just as *Storm Warning*'s justification of the informer prefigures *On the Waterfront*, its two sisters echo another Brando film, *A
Streetcar Named Desire*. The husband in both movies sexually assaults
an older sister. He wears a t-shirt, she wears a slip. The two attacks are
meant not simply to condemn the husband, but also to expose the victim. Combining sex with countersubversion, *Storm Warning* collapses
the two Brando movies into a reductionist whole.

The Ku Klux Klan kidnaps and publicly whips Marsha. That whipping indicts Klan sadism, to be sure. But it also punishes the woman
who thought she needed neither a man nor the state. And the Klan
bullet that kills the pregnant sister punishes her for her sexual bondage.
District Attorney Rainer (who is unmarried and lives with his mother)
is restoring law and order to the family as well as to the community.
His investigatory methods imitate and supplant mom's moral influence;
discovering Klan secrets justifies the force that ultimately destroys the
Klan.

Neither *Storm Warning* nor the explicitly anti-Communist films were
box office successes during the cold war, perhaps because they forced
together their twin themes of alien invasion and endangered private life
in too political a way. Movies popular during the 1950s either retreated
entirely to private life or posed the dangers to the American family in
science fiction terms. After he moved from president of the Screen Actors Guild to president of the United States, as we saw in chapter 1,
Reagan explained, "It is the motion picture that shows us not only
how we look and sound, but—more important—how we feel." Anti-
Communist films tell us how Hollywood opinion makers like Reagan
felt in responding to pressures from Washington and Moscow. They represent the feelings Hollywood wanted the rest of us to mirror as our
own. But such movies are not evidence for a mobilized, popular anti-
Communism. Cold war liberals like Richard Hofstadter, Seymour Martin Lipset, and Daniel Bell feared that a mass McCarthyite uprising endangered the liberal state. That view is supported neither by the content
of anti-Communist cinema nor by its reception. Cold war America suffered not from an active popular threat to political freedom but rather
from institutions that formed a public opinion fearful of unorthodox
political ideas and quiescent at their suppression. Hollywood, like
Washington, was an arena of institutional, not mass, power.[40]

When President Reagan insisted that movies show us how we feel, he collapsed the distinction between the producers and consumers of movies. That collapse had a social and psychological intention as well as a political one; it absorbed the world outside movies into film. We were to learn how we already felt by seeing our (ideal) selves reflected on the screen. If successful, that process would obliterate our subversive, hidden interiors and render the need for political surveillance obsolete. (Should movies fail in showing us how we felt, an emissary from Hollywood not altogether successful in them would have to enter politics and go to Washington.) But that very process, the loss of the self to its manufactured and controlled double, recurred as nightmare within one movie genre of the 1950s. Cold war science fiction generalized film as secret influence from the restricted homologies of family and state and depicted the spread of that secret influence throughout society.

If we use movie attendance figures to chart the intersection of popular feelings and Hollywood anxiety, then we must turn from explicitly anti-Communist films to science fiction. The American masses went to movies that raised anxieties not about politics but about mass society. Science fiction films presented an undifferentiated, homogeneous social world in which reality offered little resistance to the takeover by dream. Having examined the first two layers of American domestic anxiety—mom's identification with Communism and her replacement by the state—we look finally at the return of the repressed. Just as cold war movies made mom a condensation symbol and scapegoat for political and familial worries, science fiction films generated mass society not from movie but from female influence.

Aside from its anti-Communist films, Hollywood avoided political themes in the 1950s. Monogram Studios dropped plans for a movie on Hiawatha; it feared that his efforts for peace among the Iroquois nations would be seen as aiding Communist peace propaganda. Judy Holliday, called before HUAC for supporting Henry Wallace, insisted, "I don't say 'yes' to anything now except cancer, polio, and cerebral palsy, things like that." By listing diseases as the only safe evils to oppose, Holliday unwittingly suggested the logic of countersubversion that equated Communism with disease. She also inadvertently explained the popularity of those films whose alien invaders came not from political conspiracies but from outer space. Jack Warner attacked "ideological termites" before HUAC, "subversive germs hiding in dark corners." Gordon Douglas, who directed *I Was a Communist* in 1951, made the giant-ant movie *Them!* three years later. It was one of Warner Brothers' highest grossing movies of 1954. The "germs of death for society" that

Truman's attorney general said were carried by Communists spread from Hollywood through science fiction.[41]

Biology is out of control in such movies as *Them!*, *The Thing*, and *Invasion of the Body Snatchers*. Promiscuous, undifferentiated, vegetable reproduction threatens family bonds. Reproduction dispenses with the father in *Body Snatchers* and *The Thing*. The aliens multiply promiscuously, through detachable body parts in *The Thing* (1951) and through generative pods in *Body Snatchers* (1956). Like the opened box in *Kiss Me Deadly*, the ovarian pods spread destruction.

The monster was a sympathetic character in the classic monster movie. Embodying savage or aristocratic masculine desire, he stood against genteel, feminine culture. *The Thing* seems at first to carry on that tradition. Its monster, a lone, male descendant of King Kong, is menaced by the forces of civilization. But earlier monsters like Dracula and the werewolf were hungry males who fed off female bodies. The Thing reproduces himself; severed parts of his own body grow into new monsters. When we are shown the planter boxes in which these Things are multiplying, we lose all sympathy for the monster. We do not see simulacra of the male Thing, moreover, but plants with ovarian pods. The movie has transformed a single male monster into multiple, reproductive vegetables.[42]

The Thing is transitional between the classic movie monster and his 1950s female descendants. Male insects are present in *Them!* (1954); they fertilize the queen ants and die. A mutation from atomic testing has produced the giant ants, and a scientist working with the police destroys most of them. But a single queen, fertilized by the male members of her court, can give birth to enough ants to destroy all humanity. The danger of reproductive world destruction hangs over the movie.

Female ants undergo the transformation from "Cinderella" to mom that Philip Wylie depicted for women. Each female, a "princess" until she mates, then lays eggs for fifteen years. Never leaving her nest, she presides over an aggressive collectivist society. Ants are "chronic aggressors, [who] make slave laborers out of their captives," and a scientist shows movies to emphasize the "industry, social organization, and savagery" of the ants. "Unless the queens are destroyed," he warns, "man as the dominant species on this planet will probably be destroyed." The scientist is warning the audience within the film about ants; he is warning the audience outside the film about Communism. As in *My Son John* and *The Manchurian Candidate*, however, the sexual threat absorbs the political one.

Two surviving queen ants fly off with their "consorts" after the first giant-ant colony is destroyed. "They are gone on their wedding flight," explains the scientist. These ants are enacting the dark side of the John Wayne–Janet Leigh romance in *Jet Pilot*. The flying planes engaged in sexual foreplay, which first threatened the man but finally domesticated the woman. The male ants will die in the service of the mother. An observer who sees one of the airborne wedding parties describes "one big one [the queen] and two little ones [her consorts]." He is hospitalized for hallucinating, and his belt is removed so he cannot escape. The man who saw the queen ant clutches at his pants as he tells his story; he has become, like the male ants, her victim. We are shown the ants' world, which lies deep within the bowels of the earth early in the movie, deep within the Los Angeles storm drain system at its climax. That world is a matriarchy.

Traced to their cloacal sanctuary, the giant ants are finally destroyed. "Has the cold war gotten hot?" a reporter wants to know when the army is sent to Los Angeles. His words name the political allegory, antycommunism, but the action supplants it with the sexual allegory. Modern fire power is mobilized against the reproducing monsters as flamethrowing bazookas and other long guns invade the ants' inner space. The army penetrates to the "egg chamber," with its strong "brood odor," and destroys it in a holocaust of fire. Soldiers rescue two boys whom the ants have kidnapped and brought to the queen's chamber. The ants have killed the boys' father; they also kill the policeman (James Whitmore), the protagonist of the movie. But by restoring the boys to their mother, the army saves the (truncated) American family.

The ants are bad mothers who breed in storm drains instead of the home. But breeding itself is the problem in these films. The ants, the pods, and the Thing proliferate identities. The creatures they create are interchangeable parts, members of a mass society. Freed of the name of the father and of the mother's singular love, these creatures lack the stamp of individuality. They replace individual identities (identity as difference) with identities identical and out of control.

The mother in domestic ideology made her son feel loved by sacrificing her identity to his. *My Son John* exposed that special bond as the source of Communist influence. But if unique individual identity is suspect, its obverse is just as bad. Mothers in *Them!* claim direct power. The consequence (seen also in *Body Snatchers*) is the multiplication of identical selves. Deprived of maternal love, one identity is not different from another. The division of the products of labor has entered the reproductive labor process, mobilizing fears of procreation without love. The body snatchers replicate townspeople, who now function efficiently and interchangeably. Both *Them!* and *Body Snatchers* evoke the nightmare of uncontrolled female generativity. The two films join nature's revenge against man to the triumph of mass society.

Body Snatchers, unlike *Them!*, is a self-aware film; Don Siegel made it in protest against pressures for political and social conformity. Since socialization is triumphant both in McCarthyism and Communism (in the 1950s liberal view), "the malignant disease spreading through the country, cell for cell, atom for atom" can represent either danger. *Body Snatchers* could be a McCarthyite warning against Communism, like *Them!*; it could be a protest against what one writer has called the "unnatural, menacing, even alien . . . bloblike growth of the postwar," self-replicating suburbs. "I wanted to end the picture at the point where McCarthy is standing in the highway," Siegel has said. "He turns, points his finger at the audience and yells, 'You're next.'"[43] Siegel was referring to Kevin McCarthy, who starred in the movie; but the actor has the politician's name, as if to raise doubts about whether Joe McCarthy is the movie's hidden hero or villain. *Body Snatchers* may reflect awareness (unlike *Them!*) that fears of foreign, Communist influence displaced fears of mass domestic conformity. Nonetheless, its political consciousness, like that in cold war cinema generally, is subordinate to its sexual unconsciousness.[43]

Anti-Communist films demand eternal vigilance to protect self and country from invasion. Self-surveillance in *Body Snatchers* makes sleep itself impossible. Humans must stay awake forever, for they are replaced by pods when they sleep. The film deprives sleep of its function as social escape, for sleep makes the relaxed self vulnerable. Danger may come from without in *Body Snatchers*, but what needs to be defended against is the wish from within. The unconscious takes over from self-vigilance in sleep. And the dream wish of the 1950s was to escape from the anxiety of separate identity and to merge with society.

As if in support of Emile Durkheim's identification— "Society is the . . . nourishing mother"[44]—a woman is the unconscious's source of temptation in *Body Snatchers*. The film's heroine succumbs to sleep. Now a pod, she tries with a kiss to draw the hero into sleeping with her (Fig. 8.2). Her kiss is deadly, however, as he can tell from the dead feel of her lips. Totally alone, McCarthy must flee the sleep that would cost him his identity. Advertisements for *Body Snatchers* depicted the kiss as if it united the lovers. But alongside the copy, which presented them alone against the world, a menacing female reaches out to envelop her man (see Fig. 8.2). *Body Snatchers*, like *Manchurian Candidate*, united deceit with bodily invasion and located both in female influence.

Human beings are "hosts to an alien form of life" in *Body Snatchers*. Just as the Communists in *I Was a Communist* want "not just our bodies but our minds," so the body snatchers are "taking us over, cell by cell."[45] Matt Cvetic, pretending to be taken over by a Communist cell, represents Communism's threat to personal identity. That threat is deepened in *Body Snatchers* and *Invaders from Mars* (1953). Cvetic alienated his family by masquerading as a Communist. The pods in *Body Snatchers* and the people implanted with electronic control devices in *Invaders from Mars* alienate their families by pretending still to be themselves. Reds were visibly alien in earlier Red scares; they were the others. They moved inside our minds and bodies in the 1950s, and one could not tell them from anyone else. The vulnerability of the self to influence, upon which domestic ideology had hoped to capitalize, resulted in Communist influence instead. Surveillance and inquisition exposed domestic forces that had taken possession of the nation and the self. No longer part of a conflict between contrasting classes, 1950s Communists were the invisible members of (and thereby exposed anxieties about) American mass society.

Hollywood both responded to and encouraged the retreat to private life, the depoliticization of America encouraged by the Red scare. But in the Hollywood films of private life, the promised family sanctuary is problematic; it is threatened by invasion from without and seduction from within. Families under siege generated anxieties about who was to blame, anxieties that could take the form of anti-Communism. But anti-Communist films, in spite of their conscious intentions, exposed the connections between an endangered private life and a fear of political subversion.

Film critics Robert Warshow, Manny Farber, and Pauline Kael, writing in the early years of the cold war, contrasted the falsely felt, pious, middle-brow, liberal films of the 1940s and 1950s to more honest, violent, B movies. These critics located the former films in moralizing, popular-front, mass culture. The B movies, they thought, opened a window to the heart of America.[46] Cold war films reverse popular-front political values, but they inherit the aesthetic and political contamination. The only genuine work of art among the films that promote the cold war is a right-wing, anti-liberal B movie, Sam Fuller's *Pickup on South Street* (1953), which stands against the family and the state. Fascism aestheticized politics, in Walter Benjamin's famous epigram, and Communism responded by politicizing art.[47] Anti-Communism politicized art in the American 1950s. Anarchofascism, which was silent in political life but visible in *Pickup on South Street*, succeeded in making politics into aesthetics.

Pickup on South Street opens into a crowded subway. The camera follows a hand as it creeps into a woman's purse. Our eyes move back and forth, from the purse to the woman's face to the faces of two male onlookers. There is no talking at all. It is as if this tense, sexy lady, nervously licking her lips, were being aroused by the intrusion. Her unconsciousness of the hand intensifies the sense of sexual invasion and arousal. The two plainclothesmen watching the girl cannot figure out what is going on. Neither can the audience, which does not yet even know who the onlookers are. Later we shall learn that the purse contained stolen microfilm, and that the woman was nervous about its delivery. Still later she will learn, after the audience does, that the industrial crime in which she thought she was complicit was actually a theft of atomic secrets. The name of this film has a sexual and doubly criminal meaning. Candy (Jean Peters) looks like a pickup and plans to participate in one. But the pickpocket's hand thwarts the pickup on South Street. Without intending it, a petty criminal has acquired the secret of the atomic bomb.

Like *I Was a Communist*, *Pickup on South Street* derives from the gangster movie. But the former film makes Communists into gangsters and shifts its loyalty to the FBI. The latter makes Communists into bureaucrats and remains faithful to the outlaw. Instead of equating Communism with crime, Fuller makes crime the alternative to Communism. *Pickup on South Street* is, in its rhetoric, a virulently anti-Communist film. But by deliberately doubling the Communist and police bureaucracies, it makes explicit the unintended blurring of boundaries in orthodox cold war movies between the Communist party and the FBI. Fuller's hero is the pickpocket Skip McCoy, played by Richard Widmark, and he is as hunted by the police as Candy will be by the Communists. McCoy lives in a boat beneath the piers on the East River. He is a criminal outsider; and the film, which is photographed almost entirely at night,[48] stands with him against the police.

Instead of invoking the family, Fuller celebrates the sexual relationship that develops between Candy and McCoy. The film's opening scene prefigures that relation; it is based on male domination. McCoy slaps her around when she comes to retrieve the film and that turns her on.

Their combat ends with a kiss. (See Fig. 8.3. Where the man is in charge, the woman's elbow bends in, pressed to her body by his power. In the contrasting image on the *Body Snatchers'* poster [see Fig. 8.2], the woman's arm surrounds the man's neck and draws him down to her.)

McCoy's sexual violence saves Candy from her pansy Communist boyfriend. (It doesn't save her from being badly beaten by him for not telling him where to find McCoy.) Kisses are deadly in the other cold war films, where sex causes violence. Violence causes sex in *Pickup*. Both versions make women on top into targets. But while *Pickup* stimulates a sadistically charged eroticism, the other films wipe all eroticism out. (*Jet Pilot*, made by the director of *Blue Angel*, cannot help but be a partial exception. Nonetheless, eroticism ensnares Wayne; he establishes his domination, against Leigh's seduction, by physical force. Violence is an antidote to sex in *Jet Pilot*, not its generator.)

Other anti-Communist films stand for love, law, and order. *Pickup* closes with a promised happy ending, in which McCoy and Candy will marry and go straight. That surely would be the end of this film, for it stands with violent sex, outlawry, and disorder. *Pickup* celebrates an urban underworld, not some pastoral domestic retreat. It glorifies a brutal, unencumbered male individualism. *Pickup* and *Kiss Me Deadly* (the other anti-Communist B movie) are the most violent cold war films. The others also justify violence, but because they mask that commitment, their violence (in *Storm Warning*, for example) is not so much absent as prurient.

Other anti-Communist films claim to defend the American individual. But they marry him to supportive, entrapping institutions—motherhood, mass society, and the state. These institutions, which the filmmakers can neither believe in nor resist, spread a fog through cold war cinema. Fuller finds, by contrast, a place to stand with impious, violent, antibureaucratic Red-baiting. There is nothing at all attractive about such politics. *Pickup on South Street* harks back to a nineteenth-century, predatory individualism, moved from the frontier to the city and placed openly outside the law, in which property is acquired through theft. That individualism, always masked in political discourse by appeals to civilization, produced the very world from which Fuller was alienated. Making bureaucrats into enemies, Fuller brought fantasies of individualism back into film. His sexual politics, which were outside the cold war consensus, offered no political alternative. But by tapping an authentic core of American feeling buried by cold war pieties, Sam Fuller created a work of art. *Pickup* exploited, as in the film's opening scene, the viewer's guilty complicity with the intrusive camera eye. The voyeuristic moments in other cold war films fail to acknowledge that complicity. Fuller invented characters with rough edges and style, whose gestures and dialogue contrast to the mass-produced figures of other cold war movies. The most interesting of those characters is an individualized double of mom.

Mom's double is an informer named Moe, who sells her "boys" to the police for a price. (Figure 8.4 shows her ironing as she talks with McCoy, one of her boys. Moe looks up to the boy above her, like Mom in the scene with her son John [Fig. 8.5]. Both women are photographed in soft profile rather than hieratic, authoritarian full face.) John's mother also informs on her son, but while she informs as a sign of her dependence, Moe informs to serve her autonomy. John has a family mother who loses power to the state. Moe lives alone and, so long as she remains an informer, is in charge of her own life. She flourishes, like McCoy, in an amoral marketplace in which property is stolen and children are sold. Moe sells information about the gangsters and petty criminals of the street. The fiction with which the police are forced to cooperate is that she is really selling ties. Moe makes the police pretend to don the clothing of civilized virtue. Although she lives outside the home and makes money from selling her boys, Moe is an entirely sympathetic figure.

Unfortunately, Moe is also a patriot who, like John's mother, fails to recognize the interchangeability of the Communist party and the FBI. That faith in difference makes John's mother an informer. But it closes Moe's lips and thereby turns her into mom. No longer willing to let one of her boys take his chances in the marketplace, Moe decides to protect him. She refuses to sell McCoy's address to the Communists, and they kill her. Like John's mother, Moe is sacrificed to the cold war. Her death marks the defeat of a glorified underworld, however, not a demonized domesticity. Moe's death saves McCoy's life, only to serve him up to marriage and the state. Her murder, like John's, cements the alliance of the state and the family. But the ending that fulfills *My Son John* is slum clearance for South Street. *Pickup on South Street* protests against the world that the other cold war films were registering and helping to bring into being.

Pickup is the single anti-Communist film in which Communism seems detachable from the plot. A dubbed French version, made for audiences who would have laughed at the cold war politics, replaced the microfilm with heroin. That substitution was possible because, unlike its counterparts, *Pickup* is bound by no moralistic, anti-Communist straitjacket. But Fuller's film is not merely an old-fashioned gangster movie masquerading in anti-Communist clothes. Rather, Fuller takes cold war movies through the looking glass. The second half of a 1950s double feature, *Pickup on South Street* doubles and inverts pious, anti-Communist cinema.

8.1. Ronald Reagan unmasks the secret members of the Ku Klux Klan in *Storm Warning* (1951)

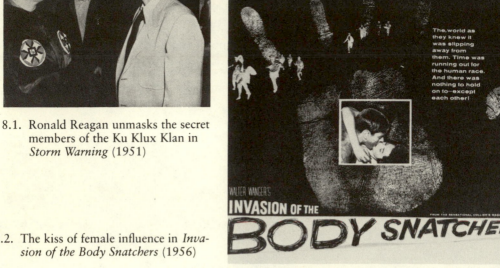

8.2. The kiss of female influence in *Invasion of the Body Snatchers* (1956)

8.3. The kiss of male domination in *Pickup on South Street* (1953)

8.4. Moe (Thelma Ritter) with one of her "boys" (Richard Widmark) in *Pickup on South Street* (1953)

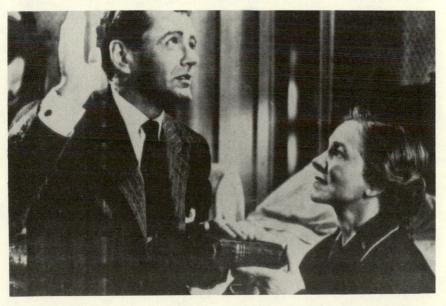

8.5. Mom (Helen Hayes) with her son (Robert Walker) in *My Son John* (1952)

CHAPTER IX

American Political Demonology

A Retrospective

I

The countersubversive imagination is not a new subject in American historiography. But efforts to comprehend the meaning of American political demonology suffer from a split that echoes the splitting mechanism in countersubversion itself, namely the bifurcation between the symbol and the real. There are two schools of thought about American political demonology. Realist scholars point to the rational purposes or descriptive accuracy of demonological images. They view such images as ways either of mobilizing support against political enemies or of focusing attention on the genuinely threatening character of the targeted group. American anti-Communism, for example, is reduced (from one political perspective) to a method of protecting dominant social interests and (from another) to a realistic depiction of the actual character of international Communism. Neither of these views is wholly false. But scholars in the realist tradition, having satisfied themselves that an image has a purpose or referent, avoid investigating its internal meaning and distorting power. By contrast, symbolists, as I shall call the second group of scholars, rightly see the fantastic character of the demons, but they avert their eyes from the material sources of political demonology in genuine social conflicts and deeply opposed world views. Both realists and symbolists distance themselves from the countersubversive imagination, the former by minimizing its symbolic power, the latter by sundering countersubversion from dominant American interests and values.[1]

The realist, instrumental approach is logically compatible with both radical and conservative politics. But for historical reasons it was originally employed by Progressive scholars like Charles Beard who were critical of dominant elites, scholars who uncovered buried special interests beneath claims to national virtue. The symbolist approach developed in reaction to interest-oriented exposés of the American political tradition. It shifted attention not only away from reason and interest and toward symbol and myth but also away from dominant American institutions and toward oppositional, fringe, and mass movements. This division in perspective split an American political tradition in two. Realists saw political repression when they examined countersubversion; symbolists saw paranoia.

Realists studied the suppression of political dissent and of movements for social change. Symbolists investigated the fear of conspiracy (to cite the title of a David Brion Davis volume) or the paranoid style in American politics (to name Richard Hofstadter's collection of essays). Political repression, as the realists examined it, ultimately served capitalism, the state, or other powerful institutions. The paranoid style, for the symbolists, was directed against such institutions. Political repression was carried out by ruling classes or elites; the paranoid style mobilized outsiders or extremists. Realists analyzed a repressive politics that moved out into the countryside from Washington, Wall Street, and the center's outposts in the hinterlands. Symbolists pointed to provincials from the hinterlands attacking cosmopolitan values and groups. Symbolists examined resentments against dominant forces in American life felt by politically marginal or culturally provincial populist groups or by once-dominant elites who faced dispossession.

Realists addressed interests and conscious political manipulation; symbolists addressed anxiety and unconscious grievances. Studies of political repression looked at economic and political power; studies of the paranoid style investigated symbols, subcultures, and status anxieties. The American political system narrows debate and excludes radical alternatives, for those studying repression. In the alternative view, an intolerance of diversity threatens the stability of a pluralist politics.

Consider the two classic volumes that seek to explain the prominence of alcohol in American political history. *Pressure Politics*, Peter Odegard's study of the Anti-Saloon League, exemplifies the realist position; Joseph Gusfield's book on the temperance movement, *Symbolic Cru-*

sade, shows the influence of attention to paranoid style. Odegard interprets Prohibition as the triumph of special interest politics and organizational tactics. Gusfield attributes the temperance crusade to declining, provincial Protestant elites who sought to maintain their status by stigmatizing and controlling immigrants. Analyses of cold war anti-Communism in the mode of political repression emphasize the recurrence of Red scares in American history and their manipulation by political and business elites. Paranoid-style interpretations, by contrast, ignore the historic fear of radical politics in America to root McCarthyism in radicalism itself, in nativist, provincial assaults on cosmopolitan centers of power. In the realist view, the Anti-Saloon League and the anti-Communists knew and got what they wanted. In the symbolist view, eliminating alcohol and domestic Communism could not assuage the grievances that fixed upon those targets.[2]

My aim is to break down the opposition between the two approaches to American political demonology. I take seriously the demonological worldview and its latent, unconscious meanings, as the instrumentalist, political repression position does not. But unlike the symbolists, I see a countersubversive tradition that exists at the core of American politics, not its periphery. I have focused on the major historical moments, political figures, and cultural documents that constitute a dominant American political tradition, and I have tended to ignore extremists, the normal subject of symbolist interpretations. The label countersubversion points to the fact that the important bearers of American political demonology have not been extremists or subversives, but their foes.

Symbolist interpretations of American politics, which came into prominence in the 1950s, at once participated in and sought to contain three intellectual currents that climaxed in cold war America. One was the burgeoning of American Studies and attention to the specific features of the American landscape that distinguished our politics from Europe. A second was the focus on the symbolic and irrational features of political life. And the third was attention to the personal sources of political behavior. By working through these three themes—American exceptionalism, ideology, and personal psychology—we will see how the symbolist position contained within it the sources of its own transformation. The 1950s was the decade of my own intellectual coming of age, and my first book was written against the symbolist approach to McCarthyism.[3] *The Intellectuals and McCarthy* was followed, however, by work that bore unacknowledged resemblances to the approach I had originally opposed. This conclusion places in historiographic perspec-

tive the preceding studies of political demonology by analyzing my subversive indebtedness to symbolist analysis. I begin with American
exceptionalism.

II

The doctrine of American exceptionalism developed within a wing of
American Communism in the 1930s to explain the failure of Marxian
socialism to take root in the United States. American exceptionalists
contrasted the limited and superficial conflicts in America to the more
tenacious European social and political divisions that had generated
revolution and dictatorship. American exceptionalism thus underlay the
consensus interpretation of American politics offered by such writers as
Richard Hofstadter and Louis Hartz, interpretations that dominated the
1950s. The United States, these scholars claimed, lacked the class loyalties, the fixed and deeply rooted statuses, and the powerful state structures of societies with feudal and absolutist pasts. Consensus historians
attributed American distinctiveness to such factors as material abundance, the pervasiveness of liberal individualism, social and geographic
mobility, ethnic conflict, and a pluralist political tradition. They argued
that this combination of factors created political fragmentation within
America instead of one or two large and explosive divisions.[4]

Countersubversives, in this view, failed to grasp the fundamental harmony of American political life. Importing European fears into America, they imagined enemies that did not exist. They transformed American pluralist realities into an imaginary, two-sided struggle between the
forces of good and an empire of evil. Paranoid fantasies generated conflict, to be sure, but that conflict had to be understood in distinctively
American terms. Instead of pitting classes against each other, American
politics was said to oscillate between interest and status conflicts. Interest politics was the struggle over achievable, material rewards. Status
politics called into question the identity and legitimacy of the competing
groups. By mobilizing anxieties about comparative worth, status politics engaged the symbols of politics rather than its substance. Groups in
the status arena contested not simply who was higher on the symbolic
ladder but who was more distinctively American.[5]

Men like Hofstadter, Seymour Martin Lipset, and Daniel Bell, who
pioneered the symbolist approach, came from an immigrant, urban mi-
lieu and had been socialists in their youth. They turned away from
Marxist categories in part by invoking the distinctive features of Amer-

ican life that had discouraged a class-based, ideological socialism and encouraged irrational, status-based movements instead. American history, as they saw it in the 1950s, was characterized not by the presence of revolutionary subversives but by (in McCarthyism) the irrational obsession with them. Deriving the paranoid style from ethnic and status-based conflicts in a nontraditional, mobile, affluent society, Hofstadter and his colleagues were shifting from a doomed search for what the United States shared with Europe to a discovery of what was distinctively American. Diversity made a cosmopolitan liberalism dominant in American life, they believed, particularly once the New Deal admitted the immigrant working class to a share of political and economic power. But the paranoid style was the price America paid on its margins for the complexity, tolerance, and interest-orientation at its center. Hofstadter's *American Political Tradition* (1948) had critically examined dominant political figures, mostly presidents, who exemplified the pervasive belief in propertied mobility. Hofstadter became more sympathetic to that interest-oriented tradition in the 1950s, as he discovered symbolic and status politics. But although he gave a large place in American history to anti-intellectuals, pseudo-conservatives, and anxious reformers, his essays on the paranoid style nonetheless concentrated on figures far from institutional centers of power.[6]

The twin emphases on consensus and conspiracy coexisted uneasily, to be sure, for the more one stressed the paranoid mind, the more America would have to be seen either as deeply divided or else as under countersubversive sway. Analysts gave differing importance to the paranoid style as they responded to different historical and contemporary events. But the dominant view, once the U.S. Senate censured Joe McCarthy, located the paranoid style more in the American provincial and nativist past than in its cosmopolitan future.

In classic American fashion, however, these historian children of immigrants were turning their own autobiographies into American history.[7] They were elevating the conflicts between immigrants and natives, the upwardly mobile and the downwardly mobile, into the central principle of non-interest-based American historical conflict. Protestants from the American hinterland—nativists, abolitionists, Populists, and Klansmen—were the alleged sources of the paranoid style. It was as if the children of immigrants were saying to their old-family targets, "You had the fantasy that our parents were dangerous to you; that fantasy made you dangerous to them. When America belonged to you, you tried to exclude us. Now with the New Deal, it belongs to us as well. But whereas you had only superstition and religion to delegitimize us, we can use modern, scientific methods to discredit you." Paranoid-style analysts were thus participating in the status politics they analyzed. American exceptionalism offered them a bridge from hopes for an American brand of socialism to the practice of American social science, from student radicalism in the 1930s to professional status in the post–World War II university.[8]

Symbolist interpretations of American history signal the coming of age in American intellectual life of the children of European immigrants. But in shifting from a class to an ethnic interpretation of America, these writers were still facing Europe. A genuine American exceptionalism would have to look not simply at European alternatives excluded by the American consensus but at American ones as well. It would have to recognize, to begin with, that the conflict between immigrants and natives for the possession of America began before the mid-nineteenth century, with the founding of America by the first immigrants and their children at the expense of peoples of color. Symbolists emphasized the fear of immigrant contamination by Americans who were already here; they avoided the expansionist history of the United States initiated in Indian conquest. Symbolists exposed the nativist hostility to European immigrants who, imitating the first settlers, brought themselves to America; they buried the significance of non-Europeans who were brought by force to the New World and enslaved.

The success of ethnic pluralism, as viewed from a post–New Deal perspective, marginalized nativism and gave credence to interpretations of American demonology that separated symbol from substance. Since immigrants fulfilled the American promise instead of destroying it, nativist anxieties seemed delusory. But racial conflict placed the paranoid style at the center and origin of American history, made it hard to argue for a happy, pluralist outcome, and broke down the easy distinction between interests and fantasies. The fantasies whites generated about peoples of color exposed and intensified actual conflicts of interest; interests and fantasies could neither be reduced to nor separated from one another.

Fully to contrast the histories of Europeans who came to the New World with the histories of those who stayed behind would have been to move beyond ethnicity to race. A genuine American exceptionalism would not separate America from Europe, moreover; it would place the United States in the European world order as a settler society. For actually to face what distinguished America at its foundation from Europe reconnected the two continents historically by locating America at the origins of the European capitalist world system. Then America could be seen not simply as a fragment of Europe with delusions about dangerous differences it did not contain but as a European fragment whose history was formed by the encounter between Europeans and peoples of color already present in or brought to the New World.[9]

The 1950s vocabulary of American exceptionalism was thus a way of avoiding America. To take that vocabulary seriously exposes the European face of the decade, in immigrant consciousness, totalitarian traumas, and cold war politics. But race was not the only subject elided by paranoid-style interpretations. In emphasizing mobility, interest conflict, immigrant-native rivalries, and status anxiety, 1950s social science avoided the major divisions that America shared with Europe—divisions of class, gender, and institutional power. Thus a massive history of right-wing extremism in America not only makes the anti-Catholic, anti-Jewish 1920s Ku Klux Klan into its emblem of countersubversion and ignores that Klan's anti-Negro predecessor; it also treats the abolitionists as extremists but avoids proslavery agitation; it attends to the late nineteenth-century anti-Catholic American Protective Association but is silent on antilabor and anti-Chinese violence in the same period; it expatiates on alleged Populist anti-Semitism while burying the Red scares that swept through the country between 1877 and World War I; it discusses McCarthyism but not the development of a countersubversive state security apparatus; and it has nothing at all to say about women and Indians. Claiming to cover right-wing extremism as a whole, the authors actually attack movements of which they disapprove that were neither right-wing nor extremist, and they cover up a countersubversive tradition that cannot be reduced to religious prejudice, ethnic conflict, and status anxiety.[10]

The historiography of the 1950s had a sociopolitical location—in ethnic mobility, New Deal success, European totalitarianism, and the cold war. The history writing of the 1960s and 1970s also had political origins. The civil rights movement and the war in Vietnam opened up the buried racial history of America. Racial questions provided entry in politics and in scholarship for issues of class, gender, and state power. The recovery of those divisions allows us to locate the paranoid style in the avoidance or demonization of fundamental differences within America rather than simply in the exaggeration of minor ones. Political demonology can now be seen as constituting an American political tradition that distorts some actual conflicts and generates others. Instead of making trouble for an America innocent of class war and totalitarian terror, countersubversion obscures and generates America's own forms of historical guilt.

It is possible, of course, to employ one style to analyze countersubversion and another to address fundamental divisions in American life. The distinction between status and class politics gestured in that direction. But since Hofstadter and Lipset meant interest when they used the word class, the class-status distinction diverted attention from deep cleavages and fundamental conflicts. Hofstadter, I suggested, shifted from interests to anxieties when he turned from the mainstream American political tradition to pseudo-conservatives, reformers, and anti-intellectuals. David Brion Davis moved in the opposite direction, from anxiety to interest and structure, as he addressed the American divisions between North and South, master and slave. When Davis shifted from the study of countersubversion to the subject of slavery, he abandoned the paranoid-style vocabulary for an emphasis on class and power. As a student of countersubversion, he examined mobility, ethnic conflict, and demonological images. As an analyst of slavery and antislavery, he emphasized class, racial, and institutional concerns. Even that contrast in subject matter broke down, however, since he treated the paranoid-style obsession with a slave power conspiracy in one book as he was addressing the problem of slavery in others.[11]

Davis's work is exemplary in both of its modes, but the two need to speak to each other. Surely it is mistaken to treat America as a mass society for some purposes and a racially and class-divided society for others. The problems of identity, anxiety, and mobility, the fears of identity loss and homogenization, do not exist in an environment hermetically sealed from class, race, gender, and institutional stratifications. The countersubversives examined here were rarely born to great wealth or power, but all achieved peak positions in political or cultural institutions. From one perspective they may look like Hofstadter's pseudo-conservatives, insisting on a rigid, traditional stability that contradicts their own history. Yet they are also real conservatives, defending privilege. The cultural power of mobility, far from undermining stratification, at once obscures social divisions and intensifies the need for them. To win, in the countersubversive tradition, is to be an English-speaking white man. To lose is to fall back among the undifferentiated mass of aliens, women, and peoples of color. Countersubversives desire the submergence of separate identities within an ideal America, but they also enforce divisions because they are threatened by boundary collapse.

That oscillation between a fear of the breakdown of all difference and a desire for merger lies at the core of American political demonology.

I aim, then, to join stratification to mass theory. One might, however, acknowledge the mixture of interest and anxiety that constitutes American countersubversion and still distinguish the pluralist politics at the center of American life from the treatment of racial and political outsiders. Such a distinction would turn the symbolist position upside down, for it would recognize that political outsiders have been more the victims than the perpetrators of the countersubversive tradition. It would acknowledge that the special targets of American political demonology have been peoples of color, women, aliens, radical workers, and Communists. But just as interests and anxieties reinforce each other, so there is no simple opposition between pluralism and countersubversion. The pluralist tradition itself derives from the distinction between legitimate and illegitimate conflict. Pluralists blame alleged extremists for intolerance, to read them out of legitimate political debate and thereby participate in the exclusionary impulse they attribute to their foes. Countersubversion can thus function as pluralism's negative underside, constricting the legitimate alternatives within the pluralist, interest group tradition.

In a period of political quiescence, those who insist on a pluralist consensus appear tolerant and expansive. When the center is under attack, however, then a choice must be made between tolerance or support of genuine alternatives and political repression; under those circumstances, pluralists can metamorphose into countersubversives. Thus some critics of the radical Right's paranoid style in the 1950s, responding to the pressures of New Left politics a decade later, have become allies of the 1980s New Right.[12]

Efforts to separate interest from anxiety and pluralism from demonology seek to preserve American exceptionalism by extruding countersubversion from the center of American politics to the margins. But just as the symbolists' insistence on American exceptionalism uncovered a country they did not want to see, their emphasis on ideology, symbol, and myth generated an unraveling of their position. The symbolists contrasted ideology—which they tied to extremism—to the interest-oriented, pluralist pragmatism they ascribed to mainstream politics. Minimizing the power of extremism in American life, they looked forward to the end of ideology in America. But their discourse also participated in the general turn in the 1950s from interests to values, the repudiation of Beardian and Marxian historiography, and the concern with the symbolic dimensions of social life. Symbolist political analysis coexisted with New Criticism in literature; an interpretive, cultural anthropology; and New York literary intellectuals' attention to the links between social complexity, political ideas, and cultural seriousness. Each of these tendencies concentrated on the meaning of what would come to be called cultural texts, whether the objects of study were canonical literary works of art, patterned social practices, or political beliefs.[13] Unless one characterized the American consensus in the crudest materialist terms, therefore, attention to cultural meaning would have to illuminate core American practices and not simply peripheral ones. Symbolists thus opened up the issue of ideology in American politics just at the moment they saw ideology coming to an end. They pointed, in spite of themselves, to the ideological presuppositions of the liberal center, the question to which we now turn.

III

It was widely realized by the 1950s that the vocabulary of interest-based, marketplace liberalism could not contain American politics. No sooner was the American consensus discovered than a variety of scholars questioned the unchallenged primacy in American political culture of liberal, propertied individualism. Some investigated symbolic politics. Others began to see the impact on political history of Protestant Christianity, classical republicanism, or local, communal loyalties. Acquisitive individualism coexisted, it was now argued, with a therapeutic politics that attended to child rearing, self-examination, and self-fulfillment.[14] Each of these emphases has spawned valuable works of historical interpretation in the past two decades. Although my work also stresses the importance of communal aspirations, it does so not by searching for corporate alternatives to liberal individualism but by examining communal and autarkic wishes within it. Instead, therefore, of seeking a place to stand inside America that is derived from the traditions of English Puritans, European republicans, or Scottish common-sense philosophers, my ground is the critical analysis of liberalism itself. And the European to whom I turn for this purpose is not John Calvin, James Harrington, or David Hume, but Karl Marx.

It may seem perverse to ground attention to ideas—as opposed to interests—in Marx. 1950s academics rightly insisted, against materialist reductions, on the autonomous power of culture. But by at once taking ideology seriously and insisting on its distorting power, Marx avoided the reciprocal shortcomings of 1950s cultural analysis. On the one hand, New Critics and interpretive social scientists claimed that they were not reading texts in ways that the authors or actors they studied would disallow. But that strategy lent itself either to accepting rationalizations within the cultural texts or to imposing the interpreter's meaning upon them covertly. Analysts of the paranoid style, on the other hand, judged and condemned their texts; in so doing, however, they not only distanced demonology from an unanalyzed American mainstream but also distanced themselves from deep investigation of the demonological worldview.[15]

The more one ascribes power to dominant political and cultural forms, the more one requires a place to stand outside them. Although Marx is sometimes seen as having minimized the power of ideology, by interpreting liberal theory as an inversion of bourgeois social relations he actually ascribed to ideas a large, distorting role. One need not share the traditional Marxist confidence in the distinction between the ideological and the real to look for the fissures hidden but present in cultural self-understandings.

Marx is commonly read as a theorist of historical conflict, but he also exposed the longing for community that exists under capitalism. He unmasked dominant social interests, elided in consensus theories of American politics. At the same time, he analyzed the liberal flight to community, seeing it as a wish to escape from the material divisions in bourgeois civil society. Liberal man, Marx argued, lives a "double life," in which communal aspirations are sundered from the actual property relations and social conflicts within civil society. Marx's bourgeois competes with self-interested individuals in the marketplace; his citizen glorifies the state.[16]

The desires Marx analyzed—to obscure, escape from, and reconcile oneself to social power—characterized the symbolists themselves. Ex-Marxist Jewish intellectuals found in post–New Deal America a happy combination of interest conflict and liberal consensus. Jews were accepted on university faculties and in civic life as a whole only after World War II, and their American legitimacy had particular significance in the wake of Nazi genocide. But the symbolists evaded Marx's argument in "The Jewish Question" that citizenship for Jews (and, by extension, other minorities) would not heal the split between citizen and bourgeois. Making Jews citizens, Marx argued, transformed neither the "Jewish" character of capitalist society (its grounding in material interest) nor the "Christian" ideal of a pure, disembodied state. Both the citizen ideal and bourgeois reality, Marx argued, atomized deeply rooted historic and communal ties. Seeing liberal harmony in postwar America, symbolists minimized the messianic demands for uniformity in the dominant citizen ideal, the corrosive character of bourgeois relations, and the consequent split between citizen and bourgeois.

That split is at the root of American countersubversion. American politics, as I suggested in chapter 6, is divided between a vocabulary of competition and self-interest and one of community and self. Interest politics, representing Marx's bourgeois, uses one vocabulary; nationalist politics (often represented by interest group leaders as well as political elites) uses another in an appeal against conflict and diversity and for Americanism. A succession of efforts to heal that split avoids its sources in society and the psyche and seeks unity by generating another split—between the countersubversive and his foe.

Marx, however, offers no more guidance than the symbolists to the historically configured content of the citizen ideal in America. Marx was responding to the French Revolution and to the statism that followed in France and Germany. America lacked such a statist tradition, since no strong central administration had developed to overthrow feudalism, to mediate among powerfully institutionalized social divisions, or to represent universal order in the face of political backwardness in civil society. State-worship replaced religion, in Marx's scheme. But America was formed by the shift from God not to the state but to the nation as the embodiment of God's chosen people. Some historians have found an American source for the citizen ideal in classical and Puritan republicanism. They have sought to give flesh in eighteenth-century and subsequent local political practice to what Marx saw as (except in revolutionary moments) fantasy. Republicanism has made a difference in America, particularly in sustaining oppositional political and social movements. Whatever the power of the classical tradition for eighteenth-century revolutionaries and constitution makers, however, republicanism has made a smaller contribution to the peculiarly American form of liberal nationalism than has the conjunction of Protestant Christianity with American westward expansion.

Sacvan Bercovitch has shown how Puritanism, identifying a chosen people with the European inhabitants of America, came to enforce a middle-class consensus that stigmatized those outside its fold. The original Puritan mission was subordinate to God. By the nineteenth century God was revealed in the settler society's march west. According to Bercovitch, "The Puritans had sought correlation between their environment and scripture; the Jacksonian romantics, expanding the outlook of the Revolutionary era, read the biblical promises in nature itself." By the nineteenth century American national identity had fused together God, the nation, the West, and the ego into what Quentin Anderson has called an imperial self.[17]

The imperial self is a distorted, ideal reflection of egoistic, bourgeois man, in the same way that Marx's citizen reflects bourgeois ideals of formal equality. And just as Marx's citizen ideal obscures bourgeois self-seeking, so the imperial self rises above and overwhelms merely material motives. By no means all manifestations of the citizen ideal, all appeals to an overriding American national interest, are countersubversive. The identification of America with nature or even with Protestant Christianity can take other forms. It did on the whole for such figures as Abraham Lincoln and Martin Luther King, Jr., insofar as they found redemptive value in American traditions, against dominant groups or social practices, without making devils of their foes. Demonological elements in a cultural document or political stance, moreover, do not necessarily define the whole. But when the nation itself is imagined as an imperial self we have entered countersubversive territory, for then the contradictions denied at the center of American life are located in the dark side of Americanism, the alien.

The alien comes to birth as the American's dark double, the imaginary twin who sustains his (or her) brother's identity. Taken inside, the subversive would obliterate the American; driven outside, the subversive becomes an alien who serves as repository for the disowned, negative American self. The alien preserves American identity against fears of boundary collapse and thereby allows the countersubversive, now split from the subversive, to mirror his foe. Countersubversive politics—in its Manichaean division of the world; its war on local and partial loyalties; its attachment to secret, hierarchical orders; its invasiveness and fear of boundary invasion; its fascination with violence; and its desire to subordinate political variety to a dominant authority—imitates the subversion it attacks.

Practices attributed to the subversive actually depict countersubversive aspirations; the more powerful the demonology, therefore, the more it speaks, against itself, truths about American politics. Accusations of terrorism, for example, allow American-supported "freedom fighters" to murder and terrorize the civilian population of Nicaragua. A president who accuses international Communism of seeking to overthrow independent governments can then voice the same intention himself. Al-

leged Russian belief in a winnable nuclear war justifies American preparations to win a nuclear war; a Russian civil defense program (allegedly lifted from an American report) proves the workability of an
American program. And Russia is accused of developing a first-strike
capability when it copies an American mobile missile supposedly designed to withstand a first strike. The budget deficit is blamed on a free-
spending, invasive state as if some other administration had created it.[18]
Such splitting and mirroring is no longer hidden in the deep structure
of American politics; it constitutes its surface normality. American exceptionalism thus raises the question of American national identity in a
more problematic fashion than the American exceptionalists had intended. A political tradition that splits off and demonizes the other convicts itself of psychological disturbance. I turn now to the connection
between national identity and personal identity.

IV

For the symbolists, the end of ideology meant a diminished force for
grand theories of politics. The symbolists began to shift from Marx to
Freud, replacing the interest-based theory of ideology by one that tied
conspiracy thinking to psychopathology.[19] But just as the American exceptionalism of these intellectuals stopped short of race and their attention to ideology elided class, gender, and institutional power, so their
analysis of the countersubversive mind avoided familial structures and
psychoanalytic interpretations. Like the symbolists, I want to connect
political worldviews to private troubles. But I want to do so in a way
that does justice to both internal worlds, that of countersubversive ideology and that of the countersubversive unconscious.

For Marx political factions represented social interests, interests derived from the economy. The essays here have occasionally linked political demonologies to economic interests or stages. But material and
symbolic bonds also create what Tocqueville called a body social, which
speaks in these essays mainly through the link between the personal and
the political.

Marx saw community as a false universal, a mental abstraction that
hid but also provided access to the social body. The American vocabulary of national identity, merging personal and national autobiography,
at once buries and reveals the historically constructed personal body.[20]

This book joins the public history of American politics to the familial
patterns and psychologically charged images of private life. It brings the

countersubversive mind down to earth by locating demonological moments in the details of political struggle and personal life. By placing persons in their smaller (private) and larger (public) histories, I seek to bring society and the psyche together. That effort to link the personal to the political raises three theoretical issues in relation to both the countersubversive tradition and my interpretation of it: the status of the personal in countersubversive discourse, the importance of the family, and the significance of the woman question for political demonology.

New Left and feminist writing made the personal political, either by insisting on the public significance of private relations or by addressing personal repression and liberation in structures outside the home. These essays share the radical impulse to break down the public-private distinction. The dominant culture also makes the political personal, in ways, however, that point to political accommodation rather than critique. American liberalism is normally seen as counterposing society to the individual, but such figures as Herbert Croly, John Dewey, and Jane Addams joined the two. European social theory and American class struggle in the late nineteenth century posed threats to the autonomy of the independent, middle-class ego, and American and European thinkers alike offered critiques of liberal individualism. But American celebrations of personal and communal possibility were liberal alternatives to European conservative and Marxist recognitions of social intractability. Addams, for example, imported the familial metaphor into the workplace to turn interest conflict into class reconciliation. Progressives turned to personality to save the self by finding it a social, institutional home.[21]

Progressive social theorists like Croly and Walter Lippmann made use of Freud, but they, like Americans after them, used him to transform deeply rooted conflicts into problems of personal adjustment. American misuses of Freud do not by themselves discredit efforts to connect the personal to the political.

Freud himself may have retained a false dichotomy between individual and society. That division enabled him, however, to recognize the resistance of instinct to culture, a resistance that American social-psychological and Freudian revisionist theory dissolved. Freud's discovery of repression and the unconscious provided his radical followers with a ground from which to criticize society. But Freudian approaches that avoid revisionist problems have also been challenged as depoliticizing and invasive, for Freud has been accused of postulating a psyche in opposition to society in order to promote the interpenetration of the two. Freud claimed he was uncovering a buried language of personal anxiety with unacknowledged consequences for politics. Michel Foucault has shown, however, that there was an open, pervasive discourse of sexuality well before Freud and that the scandals Freud claimed to excavate from the unconscious were part of the public language of the nineteenth century. For Marxists the attention to personal issues avoids social questions; for Foucault the obsession with personality places the analyzed self under institutional power.[22]

American political demonologists speak a sexually charged, familial political language; no Freud is required to uncover it. Recognizing the manipulation of personal symbols, however, ought to direct attention toward the socially constructed psyche, not away from it. The countersubversive tradition arouses personal anxiety for repressive, political purposes. Images of the black rapist and the Indian cannibal play upon fears about sexual desire and bodily integrity. As we have seen, the work on the self proposed by institutional reformers and domestic ideologists makes use of those fears as well. But it is mistaken to collapse all attention to the personal interior into efforts at social control. Political demonology expropriates personal experience, speaking for it and not to it. Countersubversives appeal to a false personal, analogous to Marx's false community. But Marx saw that the false promise of the citizen ideal generated social conflict, as some actors took citizenship seriously at the political level and others demanded equality not just in politics but in bourgeois society as well. The personal appeals in American political demonology invite the analyst to take an equally subversive step, to examine not simply the instrumental functions of the language of the self but its psychological meanings as well. If countersubversive images did not reach deeply into the self, they would lose their instrumental power. Countersubversive discourse promotes the interpenetration of society and the psyche, and so the personal nightmares in American demonology provide unintentional access to the unconscious conflicts that produced them.

Political demonology invokes the personal partly to deflect attention from economic interests, to be sure. *The Birth of a Nation* is one of our documents, and the film's sign of black rule in Reconstruction South Carolina is a placard demanding "Equality. Equal rights. Equal politics. Equal marriage." The missing "Equal property" points to the presence, not the absence, of fears of economic redistribution. But in directing attention away from economics and toward the family, the sign also points to the structure that forms personality, whose place in the countersubversive tradition must not be ignored.

V

Marx analyzed the contradiction in capitalism between bourgeois individualism and structures of hierarchical domination. He located that contradiction in the workplace, in the factory and the corporation. The contemporary Marxist Eric Hobsbawm, recognizing the role personal dependence played in the theory as well as the practice of nineteenth-century Europe, has pointed to the family. Hobsbawm wrote:

> The structure of the bourgeois family flatly contradicted that of bourgeois society. Within it, freedom, opportunity, the cash nexus and the pursuit of individual profit did not rule.
>
> It could be argued that this was because the individualist Hobbesian anarchism which formed the theoretical model of the bourgeois economy provided no basis for any form of social organization, including that of the family. And indeed, in one respect, it was a deliberate contrast to the outside world, an oasis of peace in a world of battle. . . .
>
> But it may also be that in the bourgeois family the essential inegalitarianism on which capitalism rested found a necessary expression. . . . Because its essential expression was money, which merely expresses the relationship of exchange, other forms of expression which demonstrated the domination of persons over persons had to supplement it.[23]

Describing Europe before the imperialist epoch, Hobsbawm fails to make the connections we have examined in American policy toward Indians between politics, familial dependence, and national expansion. He does not identify the paternalist components so central to plantation slavery and Indian relations. Focusing on Europe rather than America, Hobsbawm minimizes the implicitly antifamilial rhetoric of the self-made man. His picture of the family evokes order alone, without violence and the struggle to break free. The family in liberal society generates contradictory aspirations, of flight and independence as well as hierarchy and community, and we have found those double meanings at work in our subjects. But even if the meanings Hobsbawm assigns to family and economy require elaboration, he has nonetheless suggested the bearing on politics of the central, structural division in the bourgeois world.

The liberal public-private split normally refers to the separation of public values from private, material interests. Politics is then rooted, following "The Jewish Question," either in the satisfaction of material interests or in the realization of a transcendent national purpose. But Hobsbawm's analysis suggests that, once commodities are produced outside the home, the private itself is split into market and workplace on the one hand, family on the other. The one came in nineteenth-century ideology to be the domain of aggressive, self-seeking man, the other the preserve of domestic, self-effacing woman.

From one perspective that double division—of public and private, work and home—doubly insulated politics from family influence. Formal equality and instrumental relations characterize a liberal, public realm constructed in the image of the marketplace. Subordination and personal affection, in that view, find their place in the family. Those who recognize economic hierarchy beneath the rhetoric of liberty and equality still root politics in work and exchange. Marxists who see that Locke may have buried inequality still credit him with shifting political discourse decisively from patriarchy to contract.[24]

Locke was attacking Robert Filmer and the royal absolutists who derived political authority from patriarchy. But at the very moment that Locke set up, against Filmer, the division between politics and the family, he also required the family to penetrate politics. It was not simply that free contractual relations among liberal men were built upon what Locke called "the natural subjection of women." Locke and his successors also assigned to the family the task of forming the character of public, liberal men. The family, moreover, became (along with the Church) the legitimate communal source for public affective ties. Liberalism thus placed contradictory demands on the family, requiring it to be separate from, yet permeated by, the world outside the home. Family was a refuge that prepared men for the very society from which family offered escape. That contradiction placed a particular burden on women. Women were both the prepolitical, subjugated signs of nature and the agents who formed the character of civilized men. They were confined, assigned power, and made indispensable all at the same time. By denying to themselves the identities they created in their sons, women might be trusted to stay in their place. But that very absence of self threatened to make women at once glorified sources of altruistic authority and invasive threats to male independence.[25]

The struggle over feminism has exposed not only the exclusion of women from public life but also the dependence of liberal politics on domesticity. Moreover, by making the independent woman a central demonological symbol, neoconservatives and the New Right call attention to the sources of countersubversion in patriarchal politics. Women occupy a special place in the history of American demonology. Manifestly they have been made into victims whose persecution justifies revenge and into the guardians of civilized virtue who stand against aggression and anarchy. But women have also been cast, explicitly or implicitly, as the monsters. Countersubversion connects political to sexual anxiety by raising the specter of female power. Subversive women were central targets in the witchcraft persecutions, in antiabolitionist hysteria, in turn of the century racism, and in the Red scares. Family history, women's movements, the changing female presence in work and public leisure, and social anxieties that originate outside the home all mediate the association of women with chaos and violence. But the fear of being under female power derives from the special place assigned women in the home, a place located structurally in the conjugal family's contradictory relation to bourgeois society. That place has psychological significance; Melanie Klein, Norman O. Brown, and Dorothy Dinnerstein have rooted the splitting and demonization of women in the early childhood of female-reared males.[26] Analysis of the (immigrant, academic) fathers has opened up the American interior and brought us to an anterior world, that of the pre-oedipal mother.

VI

Efforts to connect political demonology to early childhood may seem doubly problematic, since they share the fixation on women that I attribute to countersubversion and employ a speculative theory of human development that many feminists oppose. Theories of early childhood cannot, to be sure, predict countersubversive targets, since these are generated by the larger history beyond the home. Maternally based anxieties cannot explain a countersubversive obsession at a given historical moment with blacks or Communists (or both). But attending to the origins of individual identity helps explain the structure of the countersubversive imagination, its sources in sexual anxiety, and the connections in political demonology between political and sexual chaos.

One may acknowledge a countersubversive need to keep women in their place without embracing psychoanalytic theory. Its persuasiveness is best judged in practice, in concrete historical narratives and the interpretation of political dreams. Nonetheless, my analysis includes a theory of early childhood, which I summarize here—not as scientific gospel but as a way of thinking about the deep sources of countersubversive fantasy.

A baby not yet separated from its mother experiences her as the source of all goodness and all harm. The baby's self is constituted in separation from her, but that separation entails overwhelming experiences of anger, pain, and loss. Longings to reinhabit the mother-child symbiosis and obliterate separateness, therefore, reawaken vengeful feelings as well as blissful ones. Since the small child cannot tolerate its hostility toward the nurturing source, it splits the mother into a benign nurturer and a demonic dismemberer. The bifurcation preserves the idealized early mother from contamination by her (fantasized) dark side and thereby sanctions the child's forbidden aggression. These good and bad mothers do not simply represent split images of women; since they become internalized fragments of the developing self, they constitute splits in the ego. This process, analyzed in the psychoanalytic theories of Melanie Klein, thus illuminates the association of women with boundary breakdown, loss of self, and violence. It helps to explain the subjection of women in a society where boys are under maternal power but men grow up to dominate mothers.

A temptation to forbidden merging as well as a target of forbidden violence, the mother poses a special threat to male identity. Masculine sexual identity, Nancy Chodorow has shown, requires a rigid definition of male boundaries to keep the son separate from the mother.[27] The male organ, for Freud, was a sign of the power of the father. Feminist psychoanalysis in one of its versions sees phallocentrism as a response to the power of the mother. Castration anxiety at the pre-oedipal stage signals the fear of being absorbed by the mother. At the oedipal stage it signals the desire to have her. In the one case danger comes from the mother, in the other case from the father. When the father's law ultimately establishes itself in the resolution of the oedipus complex, it does so against a (fantasized) prior maternal threat.

By signifying difference, the phallus may call attention to a maternal absence. But Freud was wrong to insist on the anatomical dimension of that absence (penis envy for the girl, castration anxiety for the boy as the fear of becoming a woman). Such an interpretation shares the fetishization of the phallus that it seeks to explain. Castration was central to Freud because he rightly saw the male organ as the conjoined locus of pleasure and power in his society. The sign of the entrance into patriarchal culture, the phallus acquires power as a replacement for the once-present but now absent maternal bond. By substituting for that bond, the phallus constitutes male identity in differentiation from, access to, and rule over the female.[28]

The early mother is powerful in the unconscious of us all. Ambivalence toward her is part of our humanness; the ability to integrate in one person the bad mother and the good is part of growing up. But certain political traditions, cultural configurations, historical moments, and traumatic events resolve early ambivalence by splitting the idealized mother from the monstrous one. Adults in the grip of political demonology return to fantasies deriving from dependence on and separation from the mother—fantasies that express splits in the ego, primitive divisions between bliss and rage, fears of incorporation and desires for omnipotence, exterminatory anger and Thanatos. The countersubversive tradition is dominated by splitting, by anxiety about boundary breakdown, and by invasive, devouring exterminatory enemies. To the psychoanalytic critic, such images call up the feared presence of the pre-oedipal mother. This is not to say that all adherents to a countersubversive worldview are deeply, personally disturbed, but rather that they share a disturbed ideology that functions as psychological protection.

Infant dependence, universal among humans, is the origin of our inner unconscious worlds. The special relation of women to small children has also extended throughout human cultures, although it is by no means biologically determined. A general theory of mothering like Klein's or Dinnerstein's cannot account, then, for the particular forms of misogyny in American history. Some theorists point to factors within the bourgeois family that give the Oedipus complex a historically specific form: the separation of home from workplace and the constriction of libido within the family; emotional ties to a very few parental figures (even where a nanny may be involved); and the creation of an internalized conscience to replace public, communal controls. These factors also give a special form to reawakened pre-oedipal anxieties. They help create a culture that radically opposes nurture to autonomy and assigns different structures and gender identities to the two roles, intensifying for men the attraction to and threat posed by the maternal orbit.[29]

The mother-centered, bourgeois family mediates between society and sexual anxiety. That family's relationship to society has not been a constant in American history,[30] but I have not attempted systematically to connect the psyche to changing social structures. Instead I have examined particular historical settings in which anxieties over female power recur, from Indian removal to cold war anti-Communism, from negrophobia to Ronald Reagan.[31]

VII

The early mother is one recurrent reference point in this volume; the political leader is the other. Certain of the essays and the book as a whole chart a movement from fear of maternal power to longing for political leadership. As analyzed in these pages, that longing belongs not so much to masses as to political leaders themselves. I do not directly engage the power of psychoanalysis as a theory of group bonds and mass psychology; any such claim, to begin with, would have to differentiate among and historicize the analyzed groups. The psychoanalysis employed here offers a theory not of group formation but of leaders' psychology. It illuminates aspirations to embody the nation entertained by figures from the political and cultural elite. Insofar as such appeals resonate widely, they may produce the sort of mass, popular responses that, for example, Andrew Jackson, *The Birth of a Nation*, and Ronald Reagan received. These essays analyze, however, not popular responses but the meaning of the appeals.

Fantasies about the early mother are a source of demonology; the political leader standing against hidden power and chaotic violence offers the solution. He signals the flight, in Hanna Pitkin's words, "from fantasized feminine engulfment into actual patriarchal domination."[32] The countersubversive political hero is not simply the binary opposite of the menacing early mother; he is also her ideal, mirrored substitute. He satisfies desires for merging, violence, and the loss of distinctive identity without entailing subjection to female, bodily power and often by taking revenge against it. These essays analyze the project of absorbing bodies and individuals into a person who claims to speak for them.

The derivation of political leadership from patriarchy was a commonplace of political theory in the sixteenth and seventeenth centuries. Hobbes and Locke may be thought to have shifted the sources of political authority from fatherhood to contract, requiring Freud to uncover unconscious connections beneath the modern separation of realms. Liberal men had continued, however, to exercise patriarchal power over those outside the liberal realm—women, children, peoples of color, and the inmates of total institutions. Weber's distinction between traditional patrimonial and modern bureaucratic authority notwithstanding, patriarchy also played a role in hierarchical organizations (factory, interest group, bureaucracy, army, state) whose members enjoyed, in their political life outside those institutions, the formal equality of the vote. It is no innovation to connect patriarchy to modern politics. I want to go further, however, and indicate prepatriarchal sources that join paternalism to political authority.

Freud, of course, linked patriarchy to politics. But just as Marx's historical analyses went further than his theoretical reductions, so Freud's personal investigations pointed beyond his own conclusions. Freud derived regicide from parricide and political submission from filial obedience. That simple equation fails to do justice to both historical and internal complexities. In *Group Psychology*, for example, Freud attributed the process of group formation to a regression from object choice to identification. Group members, he claimed, had given up the hope of possessing the leader and had internalized him as their ego ideal instead. They identified with one another because they shared the same internalized authority.[33] Freud thought he was showing how the group leader became a common father. In Freud's oedipal psychology, however, sons wanted to have the mother and not the father; they internalized the father only when the threat of castration made them relinquish the maternal object. The regression from object choice of a single figure to identification with that same figure reenacts relations not with the father but with the early mother.

Two factors prevented Freud from drawing that conclusion. One was his own repression of the early mother, his denial of ambivalent pre-oedipal ties. The other was the male sex of political leaders. But Freud's own analysis locates the formation of group bonds in subjection not to the punishing oedipal father but to the protective father as replacement for the pre-oedipal mother. Since Freud repressed that mother, moreover, he could not analyze patriarchy as a defense against her. The repressed returns in *Group Psychology*'s unacknowledged shift from mob chaos to organized authoritarian organizations. Freud's patriarchal army and church, in the subtext of his book, defend against the leaderless mobs with which he began. Although Freud seems to be exposing the group leader as father, the leader actually functions in his text to allay Freud's own anxieties about political chaos and mob psychology.[34]

I have used Freud's analysis to analyze its author, being concerned not so much with what his theory tells us about mobs and organizations as with what it says about *his* relation to them. Attention to individual leaders (in this case an author) runs through this book. My concern is not with what masses want from leaders but with what leaders want for themselves. The countersubversive leader speaks for a group or nation that is constituted by subjection to him. The group provides the leader with his identity, forming what R. D. Laing calls a false self system.[35] Merging separate identities to defend against chaos, the group becomes the individual writ large. A leader who claims that the nation speaks through him is making a claim beyond fatherhood to (spiritual) embodiment. He is not simply subordinating differences but obliterating them. The countersubversive leader disempowers the constituency in whose name he speaks; he substitutes for disputes between active citizens the monolithic struggle against an alien foe.

The desire to embody the group has a history in personal time, which Freud and his followers have analyzed. It also has a history in political time, which connects personal psychology to political theory. According to liberal political theory, the representative of a group is authorized by those he represents. But an examination of institutional ideology raises questions about the simple separation of the representative from the represented. A confusion between personal and corporate bodies aided in the transformation from a Christian to a statist worldview. The transubstantiation of Christ's body and blood into the *corpus mysticum* sanctified not simply the host but also the mystic community formed in Christ's name. That mystic community was assimilated in the early modern period to the king's body politic. Canon lawyers exploited the play on words contained in *mysterium* and *ministerium*, and the political leader thereby became, in Pierre Bourdieu's words, "an entirely real substitute for an entirely symbolic being." By a process of "political fetishism," wrote Bourdieu, "the representative makes the group he represents." The group spokesman is "personifying a fictitious person, a social fiction; he raises those whom he represents from the state of separate individuals, enabling them to act and speak, through him, as one man." Since the mandated representative receives from the group the power to create it, he "appears as the source of the power which he exerts on those who are its real source."[36]

Modern politics, it may be thought, is nominalist not Realist. It begins with individuals and clearly distinguishes the personal body from the body politic. But precisely because liberal individualism atomizes social bonds and discredits differentiated corporate statuses, it generates the opposite tendency. The collective representative who personifies the group holds disparate individuals together. In Anthony Giddens's words, "The religious symbolism of 'divine right' should actually be seen as a traditional accoutrement to something very new—*the development of 'government' in the modern sense, the figure of the ruler being the personalized expression of a secularized administrative entity.*"[37]

Giddens was describing not simply the shift from religious to secular politics but also the coexistence of sacred leadership cults and modern, bureaucratic states. I have argued that both languages of American politics, the religious and the economic, smuggle in a confusion between leader and group. The merger of public and private selves, sacred and secular bodies, has climaxed in the Hollywood production of Ronald Reagan.

VIII

The title, "*Ronald Reagan*: the Movie," calls attention to the creation of not an actual political leader but the image of one. The political hero represents one fulfillment of countersubversion in modern America; the motion picture of mass culture is another. Motion pictures do not normally have political subjects, and their links to politics are often obscure. But movies were founded as mass culture in the racial politics of *The Birth of a Nation*. Movies make political demonology visible in widely popular and influential forms. They not only have a power normally denied the word alone; they also show us what we are talking about. Movies provide more than additional evidence about demonology; they speak to the fundamental countersubversive impulse to ingest historical, physical, and personal reality. D. W. Griffith, I argued, aimed to appropriate history by image. That project continued in cold war movies and climaxed in the president who lives within them.

For nearly half a century, beginning with *The Birth of a Nation*, movies were the central medium of mass culture; they have been supplanted by another visual medium, television. A national-security state has arisen during the same period, with surveillance at the center of its operations. In one notable instance, the taping of Richard Nixon, surveillance turned against the surveillant. The contrast between the two presidents from southern California turns on how each made himself the object of the mass gaze. If by surveillance we mean the supervision of workers and other institutional occupants as well as subversives, then surveillance and the mass media become the distinctive and most important modern agents of social control within the borders of the nation-state.[38] These twin developments, for which Nixon's tapes and Reagan's films are synechdochal, place seeing and being seen at the center of modern political integration. What is the meaning of those visual processes?

The motion picture, President Reagan and film theorists agree, offers an ideal image. By being absorbed into film, the viewer disowns his or her bad self. At the same time, film magazines create a secret, intimate life for the star that fans voyeuristically share, a life separate from the sanitized screen persona but equally mediated through the mass media. (As politics becomes more and more a mass spectacle, it imitates the division between official self-presentation and behind-the-scenes gossip.)

The split between the star's life on- and offscreen is joined to another division within film itself. The moviegoer not only sees an ideal self; he or she also observes forbidden acts that can be enjoyed at a distance, protecting the ideal self from contamination. In that mode the motion picture viewer resembles the surveillant. Voyeurism protects the self from both participation and observation. The unobserved ego enters the spectacle without the awareness of self that would interrupt enjoyment. To be the target of surveillance, by contrast, is to turn from observer to object and, like Nixon, to have one's bad self exposed. But to become the object viewed is not necessarily to lose power, for the successful movie idol is aggrandized by audience attention.[39]

Seeing without being seen can signify either power (the surveillant) or impotence (the movie viewer). But the self is split in either mode. In psychoanalytic theories the split arises from the disjunction between the small child's bodily experience and his or her visual image. That disjunction is found both in Lacanian theories of a mirror phase, where the baby contrasts the helplessness it feels with the mirror image it sees, and in theories of narcissism, where the narcissist constructs an ideal image for others to approve, lives in that image, and hides the devalued inner core.[40]

The mirror phase, voyeurism, and the narcissist image are all forms of objectified seeing, forms on which surveillance and the media rely. The eye also offers other possibilities. Erik Erikson and D. W. Winnicott have described a reciprocal form of mirroring, in which the baby is mirrored not in the mirror (where it sees only an image of itself) but in the mother's gaze. A separate self precipitates out of originally permeable boundaries by seeing itself being seen, by basking in the mother's regard. In mutual mirroring, the baby sees and responds to the mother's response. Perhaps that is the substratum for Hannah Arendt's form of participatory politics, the shared seeing by actors of one another's deeds.[41]

Visual reciprocity is a standard for both personal development and political participation. If we were to restrict our vision to mutuality, we would be protected from surveillance and the media. But we would also be unable to look at paintings, photographs, movies, and plays (since none of these, in their traditional forms, look back). It is better to recognize that, because images come before language and reach deeply into the emotional and cognitive sources of being, they have extraordinary, immediate power. The political spectacle and the surveillance state place that power in the service of deception, hierarchical forms of mobilization, and terror. They do so partly by their radical separation of actor from observer and the powerful from the mass, and partly by the split between the images their photo opportunities offer and the power those images obscure.

The false intimacy of the modern, personified state has two faces. In one, subjects are encouraged to look at the sovereign as he relaxes at home or attends to the world's business. In the other, the sovereign's personal expressions of interest in ordinary citizens disguise his surveillance of them. This mixture of looking and being looked at parodies the mirroring Erikson and Winnicott describe; and indeed the infantilizing, empty reenactment is one source of modern state power.

Ways of seeing may seem far removed from the traditional subject matter of politics. But the visual points back to the first modern political theorist, Thomas Hobbes. Theatrical spectacle in the Tudor and Stuart court, Stephen Greenblatt and others have shown, elicited the obedience of the subjects of the Crown. Tudor jurists also relied on the doctrine of the king's two bodies to connect the person of the sovereign to the sovereign's realm. Hobbes, writing in exile from those who overturned the crown, resurrected the sovereign by instituting a modern conjunction between theatricality and the king's two bodies.[42]

A person, Hobbes explained, is he whose actions represent either himself or another, "the *disguise* or *outward appearance* of a man, counterfeited on the Stage . . . So that a *Person* is the same that an Actor is."[43] The sovereign, Hobbes continued, is an artificial person, that is, one whose acts represent others. But because the nonartificial person is already a disguise or outward appearance, he is no less representational than the artificial one. Both are actors, and so the subject's relation to his own person is not fundamentally different from his relationship to the sovereign representative. Since men have created the sovereign by consenting to have it represent them (just as they created their own persons to represent themselves), they are bound by his acts. Hobbes derived political authority from consent in order not to obligate the sovereign but to free him. By merging theatrical and political representation, Hobbes bound the original democracy that authorized the sovereign to the acts of the sovereign it had authorized.

9.1. *Leviathan*: detail of frontispiece

Personhood, in Hobbesian psychology, defended against violence, chaos, death—and against the natural mother. In the state of nature, wrote Hobbes, "the right of dominion over the child dependeth on her will."[44] The aim of artifice was to reverse the natural order and empower not the maker but the construct. To make citizens desire the state, Hobbes demonized a state he called natural. He made subjects complicit with the authority that at once overawed them and needed their support. In contrast, when Marx showed that people worshiped commodities as if they were not human creations, he intended to divest human-

made objects of their animistic power. Marx exposed the fetishism of
commodities to restore power to their creators. Hobbes's goal was to
empower the object.

Hobbes wanted subjects to feel they were part of the sovereign, to
identify with its actions as if those actions were their own. The theatrical metaphor by which he joined psychology to politics made spectacle
part of his project. Hobbes also offered a picture of Leviathan in which
the state took on human form. The image recalled medieval, corporate
metaphors in which the different feudal orders composed different limbs
and organs of the body politic. Hobbes' modern version, however, broke
down that organic body. The body of his artificial person, Leviathan, is
composed of tiny, complete homunculi. As Christopher Pye points out,
they gaze at the head of the mortal god, the author of *Leviathan*,
Thomas Hobbes.[45] (See Fig. 9.1.) The image absorbs viewers into the
body politic and keeps them passive observers at one and the same time.
It offers a preview and ideal type of the relationship between modern
mass society and the state.

Hobbes placed his own head on Leviathan's body, as if he were constructing a new body politic after Charles I's beheading destroyed the
old. Hobbes had argued, however, that the author of actions was represented by the actor, so that authors who originated the actor lost
power to him. If that were the fate of those who authorized Leviathan,
what about the author, Thomas Hobbes? Although Hobbes himself was
not one of them, there would be authors (especially Marx) who would
come to absorb the mass gaze in the modern age. But posters of Marx
in the so-called socialist countries remind us how the author can lose
power to actors who speak in his name. From that perspective, the visibility of the author's head is a sign that it is severed. Nonetheless, that
severed head still signifies power. It points not to the forces that prop it
up but to its own power to stand in for the body politic as a whole.
Contemporary American political theater has replaced the author's head
itself by the actor's, and it is upon him that the members of his body
gaze. The frontispiece of *Leviathan* uncannily presages the invocation
to President Ronald Reagan at the 1984 Republican convention (Fig.
1.17), in which Nancy Reagan, representing the television audience,
stares at the enormous head and shoulders of the chief of state.

Notes

PREFACE

1. Richard Hofstadter, *The Paranoid Style in American Politics* (New York, 1965).

2. Reagan's speech is reprinted in the *New York Times*, 17 March 1986, p. 8. For other references to Nicaragua as a cancer, see *New York Times*, 11 February 1986, p. 31; *San Francisco Chronicle*, 1 March 1986, p. 5; 18 March 1986, p. 12.

3. *San Francisco Examiner*, 16 March 1986, pp. A1, A13; *San Francisco Chronicle*, 18 March 1986, p. 12; "Talk of the Town," *The New Yorker*, 31 March 1986, pp. 19–20; *New York Times*, 10 November 1984, p. 4.

4. *San Francisco Chronicle*, 19 March 1986, p. 1; 15 April 1986, p. 11; Jack Citrin and Donald Philip Green, "Presidential Leadership and the Resurgence of Trust in Government," *British Journal of Political Science* (forthcoming).

CHAPTER I. *RONALD REAGAN*, THE MOVIE

1. *San Francisco Chronicle*, 28 September 1984, p. 24; 30 March 1985, p. 6; Robert Scheer, *With Enough Shovels: Reagan, Bush, and Nuclear War*, 2d ed. (New York, 1983), 283–86.

2. Neil Henry and Chip Brown, "John Hinckley Jr.'s Lonely Past," *San Francisco Chronicle*, 6 April 1981, pp. 7–8.

3. *New York Times*, 29 April 1981, p. 12; Mark Hertsgaard, "How Reagan Seduced Us," *Village Voice*, 18 September 1984, p. 9. Cf. Ernst Kantorowicz, *The King's Two Bodies* (Princeton, 1957).

4. Cf. George E. Reedy, *The Twilight of the Presidency* (New York, 1970), ix–xv, 17–23.

5. Kevin Brownlow, *The Parade's Gone By* (New York, 1968), 629–30. I owe this last point as well as other material used in this chapter to Harry Kreisler.

6. Michael Wood, *America in the Movies* (New York, 1975), 3–14; Martha Wolfenstein and Nathan Leites, *Movies: A Psychological Study* (Glencoe, Ill., 1950), 11–14.

7. Richard Schickel, *D. W. Griffith* (New York, 1984), 465.

8. Ronald Reagan with Richard G. Hubler, *Where's the Rest of Me?* (New York, 1965), 79. Subsequent citations will abbreviate this source as *WRM*. Cf. Carolyn Porter, *Seeing and Being* (Middletown, Conn., 1981).

9. Fredric Jameson, "Postmodernism and Consumer Society," and Jean Baudrillard, "The Ecstasy of Communication," in Hal Foster, ed., *The Anti-Aesthetic: Essays in Postmodern Culture* (Port Townsend, Wash., 1983), 111–34; Christopher Lasch, *The Minimal Self* (New York, 1984), 29–31.

10. Betty Glad, "Black-and-White Thinking: Ronald Reagan's Approach to Foreign Policy," *Political Psychology* 4 (1983): 52; Elizabeth Drew, "A Political Journal," *The New Yorker*, 29 October 1984, pp. 140–41; Martin Tolchin, "How Reagan Always Gets the Best Lines," *New York Times*, 9 September 1985, p. 9.

11. *San Francisco Chronicle*, 13 July 1985, p. 8; Elizabeth Drew, "A Reporter in Washington," *The New Yorker*, 8 April 1985, p. 100; 7 October 1985, p. 112; *New York Times*, 17 August 1981, p. 10; 9 September 1985, p. 9; *Public Papers of the Presidents*, 30 April 1981, pp. 85–86. The *Sixty Minutes* segment, "*Reagan*, the Movie," was broadcast 15 December 1985.

12. Robert G. Kaiser, "Your Host of Hosts," *New York Review of Books*, 28 June 1984, pp. 38–40; "Talk of the Town," *The New Yorker*, 26 March 1984, pp. 37–38.

13. Robert Dallek, *Ronald Reagan: The Politics of Symbolism* (Cambridge, Mass., 1984), 6–10; Lary May, *Screening out the Past* (New York, 1980), 196–97.

14. Dallek, *Reagan*, 6–10; Warren Susman, *Culture as History* (New York, 1984); Lasch, *Minimal Self*; Richard W. Fox and T. J. Jackson Lears, eds., *The Culture of Consumption* (New York, 1983); Leo Lowenthal, "Biography in Popular Magazines," in Paul Lazarsfeld and Frank N. Stanton, eds., *Radio Research, 1942–1943* (New York, 1944), 537; Scheer, 260.

15. Cf. Fredric Jameson, "Postmodernism, or the Cultural Logic of Late Capitalism," *New Left Review*, no. 146 (July 1984): 58–69.

16. Cf. Richard Slotkin and James K. Folsom, eds., *So Dreadful a Judgment: Puritan Responses to King Philip's War, 1676–1677* (Middletown, Conn., 1978).

17. Bill Boyarsky, *The Rise of Ronald Reagan* (New York, 1968), 260.

18. Ibid., 38; *WRM*, 8.

19. Joel Kovel, *White Racism: A Psychohistory* (New York, 1970), 32; *San Francisco Examiner*, 29 April 1984, p. 18; Lloyd De Mause, *Reagan's America* (New York, 1984), 161.

20. Lou Cannon, *Reagan* (New York, 1982), 49–50; Boyarsky, *Rise of Ronald Reagan*, 65; *WRM*, 57, 65–67.

21. Tony Thomas, *The Films of Ronald Reagan* (Secaucus, N.J., 1980), 19, 96; Cannon, *Reagan*, 59–61, 306. Thomas's book is a complete Reagan filmography; I have screened all the movies I discuss in any detail and seen many others as well.

22. William James, *The Varieties of Religious Experience* (1902; republished, New York, 1958).

23. Joseph Zsuffa, *Béla Balázs: The Man and the Artist* (Berkeley and Los Angeles, 1987), 787 (of MS).

24. *WRM*, 101–2.

25. Ibid., 49–50.

26. *WRM*, 49–50, 90–95.

27. *New York Times*, 18 May 1981, p. 12; *San Francisco Examiner*, 29 July 1984, p. C8; Elizabeth Drew, "A Political Journal," *The New Yorker*, 3 December 1984, pp. 156, 159.

28. Cannon, *Reagan*, 226.

29. Ibid., 228.

30. Cf. David Karnes, "The Glamorous Crowd: Hollywood Movie Premieres Between the Wars," *American Quarterly*, forthcoming, 18 (of MS).

31. *WRM*, 97–99.

32. Ibid., 3–5.

33. Ibid., 7–8, 52–54; Boyarsky, *Rise of Ronald Reagan*, 27.

34. Boyarsky, *Rise of Ronald Reagan*, 90; Larry Ceplair and Steven Englund, *The Inquisition in Hollywood* (Berkeley and Los Angeles, 1979), 209.

35. Wolfenstein and Leites, *Movies*, 101–2, 150–53. The novel is Harry Bellamann, *King's Row* (New York, 1940).

36. *WRM*, 6.

37. Wolfenstein and Leites, *Movies*, 140–45.

38. *WRM*, 4, 8, 10.

39. Ibid., 8.

40. Glad, "Black-and-White Thinking," 31, 54–56; Dallek, *Reagan*, 12–17, 53; *WRM*, 8, 53–54.

41. I owe this analysis—and the doodle—to De Mause, *Reagan's America*, 38–41.

42. *WRM*, 16, 289–90, 303, 310; Boyarsky, *Rise of Ronald Reagan*, 53–54.

43. Lawrence Leamer, *Make Believe: The Story of Nancy and Ronald Reagan* (New York, 1983), 19, 142, 147; *San Francisco Chronicle*, 14 January 1981, p. 35.

44. *WRM*, 117–20; Boyarsky, *Rise of Ronald Reagan*, 68–71.

45. *WRM*, 95.

46. *WRM*, 185–89; Thomas, *Films of Ronald Reagan*, 145–48, 160–62, 170–72, 193–97, 214–16. Reagan had wanted Todd's part in *The Hasty Heart*. Cf. Doug McLellan, *Hollywood on Ronald Reagan* (Winchester, Mass., 1983), 45.

47. Thomas, *Films of Ronald Reagan*, 149–81; *WRM*, 205. *She's Working*

Her Way Through College was based on the play *The Male Animal*, where the professor's ideas come under suspicion. Hollywood's replacement of politics by sex did no favor to Reagan.

48. Cannon, *Reagan*, 51; *WRM*, 192, 205, 212–13; Cannon, *Reagan*, 66.

49. Cannon, *Reagan*, 62, 87–89; *WRM*, 191–94, 213–14.

50. Leamer, *Make Believe*, 152. Wyman had her revenge in *Stage Fright* (1950), made while Reagan was on crutches. Richard Todd, Reagan's co-star in *The Hasty Heart*, played Wyman's boyfriend in the Hitchcock movie. Todd has been portrayed as above suspicion throughout the movie, an illusion the audience shares with the heroine. When he is exposed and tries to kill Wyman, a steel stage curtain falls like a guillotine and cuts him in two.

51. Ibid., 147; Cannon, *Reagan*, 62; Boyarsky, *Rise of Ronald Reagan*, 91; Ronnie Dugger, *On Reagan* (New York, 1983), 10.

52. *WRM*, 6–7.

53. Ibid., 6, 162.

54. Scheer, *With Enough Shovels*, 148.

55. See Victor Navasky, *Naming Names* (New York, 1980); Ceplair and Englund, *Inquisition*.

56. Ceplair and Englund, *Inquisition*, 68, 94, 109, 116, 125–27, 160, 229–38; Boyarsky, *Rise of Ronald Reagan*, 81–88; Dugger, *On Reagan*, 5–8.

57. Navasky, *Naming Names*, 79; Ceplair and Englund, *Inquisition*, 109, 116, 259, 279; Dorothy B. Jones, "Communism and the Movies: A Study of Film Content," in John Cogley, ed., *Report on Blacklisting*, vol. 1, *The Movies* (1956; republished, New York, 1972), 196–304.

58. Ceplair and Englund, *Inquisition*, 212–60.

59. David J. Saposs, *Communism in Labor Unions* (New York, 1959), 81; Ceplair and Englund, *Inquisition*, 209; Dan E. Moldea and Jeff Goldberg, "That's Entertainment: Ronald Reagan's Four Decades of Friendship with World Showbiz Colossus MCA," *City Paper* (Washington, D.C.), 5–11 October 1984, p. 10.

60. Dugger, *On Reagan*, 10–11.

61. Cannon, *Reagan*, 87.

62. *San Francisco Chronicle*, 19 April 1985, p. 23; *San Francisco Examiner*, 5 May 1985, p. A8. By blaming genocide on "one man," Reagan absolves such participants as the SS officers buried at Bitburg. The president's communication director, Patrick Buchanan, has attacked the deportation from America of Nazis who had murdered Jews. Buchanan's insistence that one accused man had been mistaken for a collaborator who was already dead was based on his confusion of the death of a character in the novel *Treblinka* with the fate of that Nazi's real-life counterpart. Cf. Lucette Lagrada, "Pat Buchanan and the 'Emigre' Nazis," *Nation*, 4 May 1985, pp. 525–26.

63. Cannon, *Reagan*, 13–14; Scheer, *With Enough Shovels*, 36–65, 241, 248; *San Francisco Chronicle*, 7 June 1984, p. 23; Dugger, *On Reagan*, 352; Francine du Plessix Gray, "The Progress of Klaus Barbie," *New York Review of Books*, 27 June 1985, pp. 12–17.

64. *WRM*, 194–95; Boyarsky, *Rise of Ronald Reagan*, 75.

65. *WRM*, 174; Boyarsky, *Rise of Ronald Reagan*, 75–76; Navasky, *Nam-*

ing Names, 78–195. Reagan quotes Hayden's testimony out of context to inflate his own importance. Cf. House Un-American Activities Committee, *Investigation . . .* , 82d Congress, 1st session, 161–62.

66. *WRM*, 133, 141; Dugger, *On Reagan*, 4.

67. Dugger, *On Reagan*, 435; *Oakland Tribune*, 11 July 1984, p. 12; Cannon, *Reagan*, 377–78.

68. Scheer, *With Enough Shovels*, 42; Cannon, *Reagan*, 368; Navasky, *Naming Names*, 89–90; Ceplair and Englund, *Inquisition*, 359. Reagan's role as an informant for the FBI is detailed in the *San Jose Mercury News*, 25 August 1985, p. 25A.

69. *WRM*, 235–41; "Nancy Reagan Tells Her Story," *San Francisco Chronicle*, 17 November 1980, p. 24; Moldea and Goldberg, "That's Entertainment," 9, 15.

Although Reagan invokes traditional family values, the actual family of our first divorced president comprises divorces in three generations (Nancy Davis's parents, Reagan himself, and Maureen Reagan); one daughter who has been married three times and another who lived out of wedlock with a member of a rock group; one son who starred in high school football and baseball while his father failed to see a single game and another who married a woman his parents had met but once (and who informed them of the wedding only after it was over); and a grandchild whose grandfather did not see him for the first two years of his life. The split between what *Ronald Reagan* represents and who he is, I believe, reassures Americans who are also confronted with difficulties in living out traditional familial values but who preserve them in the realm of the signifier. Reagan's rhetorical appeals to the traditional family coexist with actual family ties radically constricted in time and space to the current conjugal pair. Cf. Lawrence I. Barrett, *Gambling with History* (New York, 1984), 469–87.

70. *WRM*, 138–39, 301; Dugger, *On Reagan*, 11–12; J. Hoberman, "That Reagan Boy," *Village Voice*, 10–16 September 1980, p. 44; Cannon, *Reagan*, 90–94; Moldea and Goldberg, "That's Entertainment," 1, 6–15.

71. Boyarsky, *Rise of Ronald Reagan*, 104; William Leuchtenberg, "Ronald Reagan's Liberal Past," *New Republic*, 23 May 1983, pp. 18–25; Donald D. Hoff, "What He'd Be Like as President," *Fortune*, 19 May 1980, p. 77.

72. Cannon, *Reagan*, 31–32, 416; Leuchtenberg, "Reagan's Liberal Past," 25; *San Francisco Chronicle*, 24 March 1982, p. 1; Boyarsky, *Rise of Ronald Reagan*, 263; *WRM*, 8.

73. I am unable to recover the date of this incident. It was observed on television and commented on in newspapers.

74. De Mause, *Reagan's America*, 67.

75. Thurman Arnold, *The Symbols of Government* (New York, 1935); Christopher Lasch, *Haven in a Heartless World* (New York, 1977); Leuchtenberg, "Reagan's Liberal Past," 21.

76. *San Francisco Chronicle*, 26 March 1981, p. 10; 18 June 1981, p. 24; 25 September 1981, p. 24; 14 February 1982, p. 12; 10 September 1982, p. 11; De Mause, *Reagan's America*, 6–7, 119; William Greider, *The Education of David Stockman and Other Americans* (New York, 1982), 151; *San Francisco Chronicle*, 7 July 1985, p. 8; *New York Times*, 3 May 1985, p. 9; *Newsweek*, 26 November 1984, p. 40.

77. De Mause, *Reagan's America*, 119; Bertram Gross, "Failure of Nerve," *Nation*, 23 May 1981, p. 620; *Wall Street Journal*, 29 May 1981, p. 1.

78. Ron Wulf, "The High Road to Power," *San Francisco Chronicle*, 29 March 1981, "This World," pp. 8–12; Lionel Van Deerlin, "A Belief in Armageddon?" *Washington Times*, 22 August 1985, p. 3B.

79. *San Francisco Chronicle*, 19 December 1983, p. 16; Elizabeth Drew, "A Political Journal," 130–31; "Reagan and the Apocalypse," *New York Review of Books*, 19 January 1984, p. 26; *San Francisco Chronicle*, 17 October 1981, p. 7; De Mause, *Reagan's America*, 152.

80. Frances Fitzgerald, "A Reporter at Large (The Reverend Jerry Falwell)," *The New Yorker*, 18 May 1981, pp. 129–32; *London Observer*, 3 March 1985, p. 1.

81. *WRM*, 126, 254–55.

82. Thomas, *Films of Ronald Reagan*, 182–89, 198–213; above, pp. 260–62.

83. Ronald Reagan, *The Official Reagan Book*, 46, as cited in Alan S. Miller and Wendy L. Miller, *"I Hope You're All Republicans!" Controversial Quotations from Ronald W. Reagan* (Berkeley, Cal., 1981), 48; Barrett, *Gambling with History*, 212.

84. *WRM*, 247.

85. Cannon, *Reagan*, 70.

86. The *Challenger* tragedy echoes *Hellcats* when one considers the public relations function of the mission, Reagan's plan to speak to the astronauts from space during his State of the Union address, and possible White House pressure not to delay the launch. Now, however, the commander-in-chief is above the suspicion that he answered in the movie. Reagan perfectly fits the definition of chief of state offered by Harry McPherson, special assistant to President Lyndon Johnson. McPherson compared a chief of government like Johnson, "who loves to go down in the engine room . . . and bang around and work on things," to the "guys up on the bridge of the ship who saw the big picture and sailed ahead with their capes flowing in the wind" (see Fig. 1.16). Cf. Samuel Kernell and Samuel Popkin, eds., *Chief of Staff: Twenty-five Years of Managing the Presidency* (Berkeley and Los Angeles, 1987).

87. *WRM*, 290; *Life*, January 1985, pp. 10–11.

88. *San Francisco Chronicle*, 23 November 1985, pp. 1, 9; cf. 30 October 1981, p. 6.

89. "Talk of the Town," *The New Yorker*, 18 November 1985, pp. 39–40; *New York Times*, 14 November 1985, p. A15; 27 November 1985, p. B8.

CHAPTER II. POLITICAL REPRESSION
IN THE UNITED STATES

1. William Carlos Williams, *In the American Grain* (1925; republished, New York, 1956), 39; Karl Marx, *Capital*, 3 Vols. (Chicago, 1906–9), 1:823; Immanuel Wallerstein, *The Modern World System* (New York, 1974).

2. Howard Mumford Jones, *O Strange New World* (New York, 1964), plate 3 and p. 28n; Michael Paul Rogin, *Fathers and Children: Andrew Jackson and*

the Subjugation of the American Indian (New York, 1975), 3–11, 113–25; Robert F. Berkhofer, *The White Man's Indian: Images of the American Indian from Columbus to the Present* (New York, 1978); Elemira Zolla, *The Writer and the Shaman* (New York, 1973); Gary B. Nash, "The Image of the Indian in the Southern Colonial Mind," *William and Mary Quarterly* 24 (1972): 201–3.

3. George M. Fredrickson, *White Supremacy* (New York, 1981), 35; Virgil Vogel, ed., *This Country Was Ours: A Documentary History of the American Indian* (New York, 1972), 75–76.

4. Rogin, *Fathers and Children*, 165–247; and chapter 5.

5. Vogel, *This Country*, 193–94; William T. Hagan, *American Indians* (Chicago, 1961), 141–50; *San Francisco Chronicle*, 20 January 1983, p. 24.

6. Alan Trachtenberg, *The Incorporation of America* (New York, 1982), 29.

7. Terry P. Wilson, *The Underground Reservation: Osage Oil* (Lincoln, Neb., 1985), 82.

8. The quotes but not the interpretation of them come from Herman J. Viola, *Thomas L. McKenney, Architect of America's Early Indian Policy, 1816–1830* (Chicago, 1974), 37, 176; Berkhofer, *White Man's Indian*, 8, 173.

9. Cf. Richard Drinnon, *Keeper of Concentration Camps: Dillon S. Myer and American Racism* (Berkeley and Los Angeles, 1986).

10. Cf. Richard Slotkin, *Regeneration Through Violence* (Middletown, Conn., 1973).

11. Richard Drinnon, *Facing West: The Metaphysics of Indian-Hating and Empire-Building* (New York, 1980), 307–467; Eleanor Fuchs and Joyce Antler, *Year One of the Empire* (Boston, 1973); Thomas Sheehan, "El Salvador: The Forgotten War," *Threepenny Review*, no. 22 (Summer 1985): 3–4; *New York Times*, 2 March 1985, p. 8.

12. Richard Hofstadter, *The Paranoid Style in American Politics* (New York, 1965). Cf. Michael Zuckerman, "The Fabrication of Identity in Early America," *William and Mary Quarterly* 34 (1977): 183–214.

13. Fredrickson, *White Supremacy*, 54–93; Edmund P. Morgan, *American Slavery, American Freedom* (New York, 1975); Peter Wood, *Black Majority* (New York, 1974).

14. Rogin, *Fathers and Children*, 7, and *Subversive Genealogy: The Politics and Art of Herman Melville* (New York, 1983), 126–27.

15. Fredrickson, *White Supremacy*, 94–135.

16. Thomas Jefferson, *Notes on Virginia*, in Adrienne Koch and William Peden, eds., *The Life and Selected Writings of Thomas Jefferson* (New York, 1944), 262; Fredrickson, *White Supremacy*, 104; Winthrop D. Jordan, *White over Black* (Chapel Hill, N.C., 1968), 429–81; Eric J. Sundquist, *Faulkner: The House Divided* (Baltimore, 1983), 111.

17. Cf. Clement Eaton, *The Freedom-of-Thought Struggle in the Old South* (New York, 1964). On southern planter paternalism, compare Eugene D. Genovese, *The World the Slaveholders Made* (New York, 1969) and *Roll, Jordan, Roll* (New York, 1974), to James Oakes, *The Ruling Race* (New York, 1982).

18. Morgan, *American Slavery*.

19. Oakes, *Ruling Race*, 141; Pierre van den Bergh, *Race and Racism: A Comparative Perspective* (New York, 1967), 88; George M. Fredrickson, *The*

Black Image in the White Mind (New York, 1971), 58–70; Fredrickson, *White Supremacy*, 150–62.

20. Eaton, *Freedom-of-Thought*, 126–43, passim.

21. Leonard L. Richards, *Gentlemen of Property and Standing* (New York, 1970).

22. Cf. Lawrence Goodwyn, *Democratic Promise: The Populist Movement in America* (New York, 1976); V. O. Key, *Southern Politics* (New York, 1948).

23. Richard Hofstadter, *Social Darwinism in American Thought*, 2d ed. (Boston, 1955), 170–200; Thomas F. Gossett, *Race: The History of an Idea in America* (Dallas, 1963); Fredrickson, *White Supremacy*, 234–82.

24. Ronald T. Takaki, *Iron Cages: Race and Culture in Nineteenth-Century America* (New York, 1979), 14–15, passim; Alexander Saxton, *The Indispensable Enemy* (Berkeley and Los Angeles, 1971); Robert Justin Goldstein, *Political Repression in Modern America* (Cambridge, Mass., 1978), 267; Drinnon, *Keeper of Concentration Camps*.

25. The analysis in this and the following paragraphs is drawn mainly from Leonard W. Levy, *Legacy of Suppression* (Cambridge, Mass., 1960).

26. In addition to Levy, *Legacy of Suppression*, cf. Richard Hofstadter, *The Idea of a Party System* (Berkeley and Los Angeles, 1969).

27. Cf. David Brion Davis, "Some Themes of Countersubversion: An Analysis of Anti-Masonic, Anti-Catholic, and Anti-Mormon Literature," *Mississippi Valley Historical Review* 47 (September 1960): 205–24, "Some Ideological Functions of Prejudice in Ante-Bellum America," *American Quarterly* 15 (Summer 1963): 110, 125, and *The Fear of Conspiracy* (Ithaca, N.Y., 1971), 1–148; Rogin, *Fathers and Children*, 284–92, and *Subversive Genealogy*, 18–19, 120–51; Richard O. Curry and Thomas M. Brown, eds., *Conspiracy* (New York, 1972), 1–86.

28. Quotes are from Lyman Beecher, *A Plea for the West*, and Samuel F. B. Morse, *Foreign Conspiracy Against the Liberties of the United States*, excerpted in Davis, *Fear of Conspiracy*, 90, 97–99. Cf. also Seymour Martin Lipset and Earl Raab, *The Politics of Unreason: Right-Wing Extremism in America* (New York, 1971), 36; Ray Allen Billington, *The Protestant Crusade, 1800–1860* (New York, 1938); Richard Ellis, "Catholicism, Communism, and the Protestant Mind" (Unpublished seminar paper, University of California, Berkeley, 1983). Lipset and Raab (p. 95) call anti-Catholicism the anti-Semitism of the nineteenth century. Without minimizing anti-Semitism in American history and its consequences for Jews, anti-Catholicism played a far more central role in American politics as a whole than anti-Semitism. Following Ellis, I would suggest that anti-Catholicism (along with racialist phobias) was the anti-Communism of the nineteenth century. On anti-Semitism, cf. Lipset and Raab, 135–41, 160–71, 180–84, 351–54, and David Wise, *The Abandonment of the Jews* (New York, 1984).

The relative importance of race and religion in structuring antebellum politics is a complex and much-debated question. It is worth stressing, however, that efforts to organize the antebellum political system around nonracial targets, from the Anti-Mason Party at the beginning of the Jacksonian period to the

American party at its end, lost out to a racially based system—first in westward expansion and Indian removal, then in sectional conflict and Civil War.

29. Cf. Ernest Tuveson, *Redeemer Nation* (Chicago, 1968); Davis, "Themes of Countersubversion"; David Brion Davis, *The Slave Power Conspiracy and the Paranoid Style* (Baton Rouge, La., 1969); Karen Halttunen, *Confidence Men and Painted Women* (New Haven, 1982); Rogin, *Subversive Genealogy*, 236–56.

30. Billington, *Protestant Crusade*, 68–74.

31. Cf. Paul Johnson, *A Shopkeeper's Millennium* (New York, 1978).

32. Takaki, *Iron Cages*, 16–35; John K. Alexander, *Render Them Submissive* (Amherst, Mass., 1980), 6, 32.

33. Eleanor Flexner, *Century of Struggle*, 2d ed. (Cambridge, Mass., 1975), 151–69, 294–95.

34. Cf. Catharine Beecher, *A Treatise on Domestic Economy* (New York, 1841); Kathryn Kish Sklar, *Catharine Beecher: A Study in American Domesticity* (New Haven, 1973); Ann Douglas, *The Feminization of American Culture* (New York, 1977); Peter Walker, *Moral Choices: Memory, Desire, and Imagination in Nineteenth-Century Abolition* (Baton Rouge, La., 1978), 87–205; Barbara Berg, *The Remembered Gate: Origins of American Feminism* (New York, 1978); and Catherine Gallagher, *The Industrial Reformation of English Fiction, 1832–1867: Social Discourse and Narrative Form* (Chicago, 1985), 113–86.

35. Benjamin Rush, "Observations Intended to Favour a Supposition That the Black Color (As It Is Called) of the Negroes is Derived from Leprosy," *Transactions of the American Philosophical Society* 4 [1799]: 289–97, reprinted in Winthrop D. Jordan, ed., *The Negro Versus Equality, 1762–1826* (Chicago, 1969), 44–49.

36. Takaki, *Iron Cages*, 19–22; Alexander, *Render Them Submissive*, 157. Cf. for this and the succeeding two paragraphs, Michael Ignatieff, *A Just Measure of Pain* (New York, 1978), 69–70; Michael Meranze, "The Penitentiary Ideal of Late Eighteenth-Century Philadelphia," *Pennsylvania Magazine of History and Biography* 108 (October 1984): 419–50; Benjamin Rush, "Of the Mode of Education Proper in a Republic" and "The Effects of Ardent Spirits Upon Man," in Dagobert Runes, ed., *The Selected Writings of Benjamin Rush* (New York, 1947), 87–92, 334–41, and "An Address to the Ministers . . . Upon Subjects Interesting to Morals" and "An Enquiry into the Effects of Public Punishments . . . ," in *Essays, Literary, Moral, and Philosophical*, 2d ed. (Philadelphia, 1806), 114–24, 136–52. The classic studies of prison reform and the asylum remain David J. Rothman, *The Discovery of the Asylum* (Boston, 1971), and Michel Foucault, *Discipline and Punish* (New York, 1979). Cf. also Rogin, *Subversive Genealogy*, 187–92.

37. Ignatieff, *Just Measure*, 211–13; Alexis de Tocqueville, *Democracy in America*, 2 vols. (New York, 1969), 1:255.

38. David J. Rothman, *Conscience and Convenience—The Asylum and Its Alternatives in Progressive America* (New York, 1980); Christopher Lasch, *Haven in a Heartless World* (New York, 1977), 17.

39. Cf. Richard Slotkin, *The Fatal Environment: The Myth of the Frontier in the Age of Industrialization, 1800–1890* (New York, 1985). The quoted example is on p. 450.

40. Goldstein, *Political Repression*, offers a splendid history of its subject, and I have relied heavily on that book for examples and analysis in this and the following section. The quoted sentence and surrounding commentary in this paragraph are from pp. 24–28.

41. Trachtenberg, *Incorporation*, 71; Nick Salvatore, *Eugene V. Debs* (Urbana, Ill., 1982), 35.

42. Cf. Henry David, *The History of the Haymarket Affair*, 2d ed. (New York, 1958); Ray Ginger, *Altgeld's America* (New York, 1958), 35–88.

43. Ginger, *Altgeld's America*, 143–67.

44. On the IWW, cf. Melvin Dubofsky, *We Shall Be All* (Chicago, 1969).

45. Goldstein, *Political Repression*, 86–124.

46. This paragraph and the next summarize ibid., 113, 145–58, 167. See also William Preston, *Aliens and Dissenters* (Cambridge, Mass., 1963), and Robert K. Murray, *Red Scare* (Minneapolis, Minn., 1955).

47. This and the next paragraph are taken from Goldstein, *Political Repression*, 3–18, and Leon Wolff, *Lockout: The Story of the Homestead Strike of 1892* (New York, 1965), 69.

48. Quoted in Goldstein, *Political Repression*, 550.

49. For material in this and the next paragraph, cf. ibid., 148–49, 160; Frank J. Donner, *The Age of Surveillance* (New York, 1980), 34–37; David Williams, "The Bureau of Investigation and Its Critics, 1919–1921: The Origins of Federal Political Surveillance," *Journal of American History* 68 (December 1981): 561–79.

50. Donner, *Age of Surveillance*, 53–57.

51. Goldstein, *Political Repression*, 176, 249–53; Donner, *Age of Surveillance*, 241–42.

52. Goldstein, *Political Repression*, 252.

53. Ibid., 299–304. Other sources include David J. Caute, *The Great Fear: The Anti-Communist Purge Under Truman and Eisenhower* (New York, 1978), and Allan Barth, *Government by Investigation* (New York, 1955).

54. Goldstein, *Political Repression*, 374.

55. Ibid., 309.

56. Ibid., 328–32; Michael E. Parrish, "Cold War Justice: The Supreme Court and the Rosenbergs," *American Historical Review* 82 (October 1977): 840; Kim Chernin, *In My Mother's House* (New York, 1983), 234–60.

57. Donner, *Age of Surveillance*, 156–65; Goldstein, *Political Repression*, 394; Sigmund Diamond, "Kissinger and the FBI," *Nation*, 10 November 1979, pp. 449, 466–68.

58. Goldstein, *Political Repression*, 341, 394–95; Pat Watters and Stephen Gillers, eds., *Investigating the FBI* (Garden City, N.Y., 1973), xix.

59. Goldstein, *Political Repression*, 318; Parrish, "Cold War Justice," 811. The two most recent books on Hiss and the Rosenbergs, each of which has stimulated controversy, are Allan Weinstein, *Perjury: The Hiss-Chambers Case* (New

York, 1983), and Ronald Radosh and Joyce Milton, *The Rosenberg File* (New York, 1983).

60. Goldstein, *Political Repression*, 385–88; Athan Theoharis, *Seeds of Repression: Harry S. Truman and the Origins of McCarthyism* (Chicago, 1971).

61. Cf. Victor Navasky, *Naming Names* (New York, 1980).

62. Cf. Michael Paul Rogin, *The Intellectuals and McCarthy: The Radical Specter* (Cambridge, Mass., 1967), 216–60.

63. Stuart Ewen, *Captains of Consciousness* (New York, 1976), 36–37, 44–46, 63, 75–76.

64. T. J. Jackson Lears, "From Salvation to Self-Realization," in Richard W. Fox and T. J. Jackson Lears, eds., *The Culture of Consumption* (New York, 1983), 1–38.

65. Ewen, *Captains of Consciousness*, 91–92; Paul Lazarsfeld et al., *Voting* (New York, 1954); Todd Gitlin, "Media Sociology: The Dominant Paradigm," *Theory and Society* 68 (September 1978), 205–53.

66. Ewen, *Captains of Consciousness*, 191, 213.

67. Daniel Boorstin, "The New Barbarians," in *The Decline of Radicalism* (New York, 1979), 121–35.

68. Goldstein, *Political Repression*, 418–19.

69. Ibid., 419–22, 445–46; Donner, *Age of Surveillance*, 143–44, 204–6.

70. Cf. Goldstein, *Political Repression*, 430–37, 448; Donner, *Age of Surveillance*, 277–78.

71. Goldstein, *Political Repression*, 448–51; Donner, *Age of Surveillance*, 236–37; Watters and Gillers, *Investigating the FBI*, xx.

72. Goldstein, *Political Repression*, 487–94.

73. Ibid., 504–11.

74. On Watergate, cf. Goldstein, *Political Repression*, 461–83; Donner, *Age of Surveillance*, 243, 332–33; J. Anthony Lukas, *Nightmare: The Underside of the Nixon Years* (New York, 1976). See also chapter 3.

75. Thomas Powers, *The Man Who Kept the Secrets: Richard Helms and the CIA* (New York, 1979), 10, 302–4.

76. John Shattuck, "National Security a Decade After," *democracy*, Winter 1983, p. 64.

77. *San Francisco Chronicle*, 7 May 1986, p. 18.

78. John Shattuck, "Cutting Back on Freedom By Fiat," *Nation*, 11 June 1983, pp. 734–35; Lois P. Sheinfeld, "Washington vs. The Right to Know," *Nation*, 13 April 1985, pp. 426–28; Morton H. Halperin, "Never Question the President," *Nation*, 29 September 1984, p. 286.

79. *Nation*, 26 March 1983, p. 353; Shattuck, "National Security," 59–60; *San Francisco Examiner*, 26 May 1985, p. A2.

CHAPTER III. THE KING'S TWO BODIES: LINCOLN, WILSON, NIXON, AND PRESIDENTIAL SELF-SACRIFICE

1. Ernst H. Kantorowicz, *The King's Two Bodies* (Princeton, 1957), 7.

2. Joseph Galloway, "A Candid Examination of the Mutual Claims of Great

Britain and the Colonies," in Merrill Jensen, ed., *Tracts of the American Revolution, 1763–1776* (Indianapolis, 1967), 354; Tom Paine, "Common Sense," in Nelson F. Adkins, ed., *Common Sense and Other Political Writings* (Indianapolis, 1953), 32.

3. Richard Nixon, quoted in Thomas C. Blaisdell, Jr. et al., *The American Presidency in Political Cartoons: 1776–1976* (Salt Lake City, 1976), 252; Richard Nixon, interview with David Frost, *New York Times*, 20 May 1977, p. 16 (cited hereafter as Frost, *NYT*).

4. Paine, "Common Sense," 32; *San Francisco Chronicle*, 21 May 1977, p. 8.

5. Frost, *NYT*, 20 May 1977, p. 16. Lincoln actually wrote, "I felt that measures, otherwise unconstitutional, might become lawful, by becoming indispensable to the preservation of the constitution, through the preservation of the nation" (Abraham Lincoln to Albert G. Hodges, 4 April 1864, in Roy P. Basler, ed., *Abraham Lincoln, Collected Works*, 9 vols. [Springfield, Ill., 1953–55], 7:281).

6. See David Donald, *Lincoln Reconsidered* (New York, 1961), 188–91; Greil Marcus, "Lincoln and Nixon: Strange Bedfellows?" *Newsday*, 1 February 1973, pp. 20–21. Marcus and Garry Wills were the first to explore Nixon's effort to model himself on Lincoln. See Garry Wills, *Nixon Agonistes* (New York, 1971), 23–24, 42, 83, 105, 117–18, 140, 156–57.

7. Donald, *Lincoln Reconsidered*, 3–4, 61–63.

8. Wills, *Nixon Agonistes*, 82; Anthony Lukas, *Nightmare: The Underside of the Nixon Years* (New York, 1976), 635; Frost, *NYT*, 20 May 1977, p. 33; 26 May 1977, p. 40; Gerald Ford, 9 August 1974, in *Congressional Quarterly, Historic Documents of 1974* (Washington, D.C., 1975), 697–99.

9. Kantorowicz, *Two Bodies*, 15–17, 42–48, 61–78, 90–93, 194–206, 268; Erik H. Erikson, *Young Man Luther* (New York, 1958), 140–43; John Winthrop, "A Model of Christian Charity," in Edmund P. Morgan, ed., *Puritan Political Ideas* (Indianapolis, 1965), 84–92.

10. Wills, *Nixon Agonistes*, 83. Wills convincingly demonstrates Wilson's importance to Nixon. See pp. 30–31, 42, 386, 392–97, 419, 422–27, 429–33.

11. Abraham Lincoln, "Address before the Young Men's Lyceum of Springfield, Ill.," 27 January 1838, in Basler, *Abraham Lincoln* 1:108–15. Edmund Wilson was the first to suggest the importance of this speech for Lincoln's future career. See "Abraham Lincoln: The Union as Religious Mysticism," in *Eight Essays* (Garden City, N.Y., 1954). My sketch of Lincoln derives from this essay, from Norman Jacobson, "Lincoln's Abraham," *Helderberg Review* 1 (Spring 1971): 14–19; and, most important, from Dwight Anderson, "The Quest for Immortality: Abraham Lincoln and the Founding of Political Authority in America" (Ph.D. diss., University of California, Berkeley, 1972), now published as *Abraham Lincoln: The Quest for Immortality* (New York, 1982).

12. Abraham Lincoln, speech at Springfield, Ill., 16 June 1858, in Basler, *Abraham Lincoln* 2:461; Edmund Wilson, "Abraham Lincoln," 190–91.

13. Abraham Lincoln, speech at Kalamazoo, Mich., 27 August 1856; speech at Chicago, 10 July 1858; reply to N.Y. Workingmen's Democratic Republican Association, 21 March 1864; speech to the 166th Ohio Regiment, 22

August 1864; all in Basler, *Abraham Lincoln* 2:364, 499; 7:259–60, 512; Carl Sandburg, *Lincoln Collector* (New York, 1949), 162.

14. Abraham Lincoln, speech at Springfield, Ill., 26 June 1857; letter to Mrs. Lydia Bixby, 21 November 1864; in Basler, *Abraham Lincoln* 2:404, 8:117; see also George W. Wilson, "A Prophetic Dream Reported by Abraham Lincoln," *American Imago* 1 (June 1940): 48.

15. Donald, *Lincoln Reconsidered*, 5; Edmund Wilson, "Abraham Lincoln," 202; Jacobson, "Lincoln's Abraham," 18.

16. Sandburg, *Lincoln Collector*, 219; Edmund Wilson, "Abraham Lincoln," 201–2; Anderson, "Quest for Immortality," 211–16; Jacobson, "Lincoln's Abraham," 17–18; William Shakespeare, *Macbeth*, act 3, scene 2.

17. Abraham Lincoln, "Second Inaugural Address," 4 March 1865, in Basler, *Abraham Lincoln* 8:333.

18. Charles Hamilton and Lloyd Ostendorf, *Lincoln in Photographs* (Norman, Okla., 1963), 153. Elliot Gorn's important, unpublished seminar paper, "Glory, Glory Halleluiah" (University of California, Berkeley, 1974), discusses the genesis and meaning of the "Battle Hymn of the Republic" and its variants. On Father Abraham, see pp. 30–32. Stanton is quoted in Donald, *Lincoln Reconsidered*, 8. Lincoln had compared Negro slaves to the "children of Israel" held in "Egyptian bondage" (speech at Springfield, Ill., 26 June 1857), in Basler, *Abraham Lincoln* 2:409. On the Civil War as Calvinist retribution, see Edmund Wilson, *Patriotic Gore* (New York, 1962), 3–106.

19. Abraham Lincoln, speech at Peoria, Ill., 16 October 1854; "Emancipation Proclamation," 1 January 1863; "Gettysburg Address," 19 November 1863; in Basler, *Abraham Lincoln* 2:276, 6:30, 7:17–19. See Anderson, "Quest for Immortality," 185–220.

20. Basler, *Abraham Lincoln* 2:115.

21. Ibid. 8:333; Donald, *Lincoln Reconsidered*, 139, 148–49, 153; Herman Melville, "The Martyr," *Battle-Pieces and Aspects of the War* (1866; reprint, Amherst, 1962), 141–42.

22. Abraham Lincoln, address at Cooper Institute, New York City, 11 February 1861; speech in Independence Hall, Philadelphia, 22 February 1861; in Basler, *Abraham Lincoln* 3:522, 535–38; 4:190, 240. Also see Anderson, "Quest for Immortality," 132–35.

23. Henry Louis Stephens, in *Vanity Fair*, 7 July 1860, reprinted in Rufus Rockwell Wilson, *Lincoln in Caricature* (Elmira, N.Y., 1945), 13; Hamilton and Ostendorf, *Lincoln in Photographs*, 242.

24. Sir John Tenniel, in *Punch*, 3 December 1864, reprinted in Blaisdell, *American Presidency*, 101; Abraham Lincoln, annual message to Congress, 8 December 1863; "First Inaugural Address," 4 March 1861; annual message to Congress, 1 December 1862; in Basler, *Abraham Lincoln* 7:53, 4:271, 5:527–28; see also Edward Charles Wagenknecht, *The Films of D. W. Griffith* (New York, 1975), 59–61; Donald, *Lincoln Reconsidered*, 5; Edmund Wilson, "Abraham Lincoln," 197. Griffith's words quoted in the text are echoed in the book on Lincoln that Nixon read in his final days. See D. Elton Trueblood, *Abraham Lincoln: Theologian of American Anguish* (New York, 1973), 5–6.

25. Wagenknecht, *D. W. Griffith*, 60. Griffith uses Woodrow Wilson, *The*

History of the American People, 5 vols. (New York, 1908); and see chapter 7 and below, nn. 33 and 34.

26. Edmund Wilson, "Abraham Lincoln," 192, 197.

27. Marquis de Chambrun, *Impressions of Lincoln and the Civil War*, quoted in Edmund Wilson, "Abraham Lincoln," 186.

28. Wills, *Nixon Agonistes*, 395. Fawn Brodie told me that the desk Nixon thought was Woodrow Wilson's in fact belonged to Vice President Henry Wilson, the antislavery politician. Grant's vice president, Wilson, died in office in 1875.

29. Wills, *Nixon Agonistes*, 30–31, 386; Anderson, "Quest for Immortality," 227–30; Woodrow Wilson, speech at Boston, 24 February 1919; "Thanksgiving Proclamation," 7 November 1917, in *The Messages and Papers of Woodrow Wilson*, 2 vols. (New York, 1924), 1:433, 2:645.

30. Woodrow Wilson, "The Ideals of America," *Atlantic Monthly*, December 1902, pp. 721–23, 726; see Michael Rogin, "Max Weber and Woodrow Wilson: The Iron Cage in Germany and America," *Polity* 3 (Summer 1971): 566.

31. Woodrow Wilson, "The Ideals of America," 728–31; Rogin, "Max Weber," 567.

32. Woodrow Wilson, "The Ideals of America," 732–34; Woodrow Wilson, *Constitutional Government in the United States* (New York, 1908), 54, 59, 77. See also his *Congressional Government* (Boston, 1885).

33. Woodrow Wilson, *Constitutional Government*, 54–57, 60, 65, 68–69. A fuller account of Wilson's thought would have to address the relationship between his political economy and his infatuation with presidential leadership in an organic state. On the one hand, Wilson's economic New Freedom looked backward to a decentralized economic order. On the other hand, in distinguishing large corporations from trusts, Wilson showed a sympathy with technological organization that bridged the apparent gap between his nineteenth-century "man on the make" and the twentieth-century corporate giant. Wilson's commitment both to economic decentralization and to a state-directed, corporate economy pulled him in opposing directions. He rose above the contradictions in his political economy into political messianism.

34. Woodrow Wilson, *The New Freedom* (1913; reprint, Englewood Cliffs, N.J., 1961), 49–53.

35. Ibid., 30–31.

36. Ibid., 30–33; Alexander George and Juliette George, *Woodrow Wilson and Colonel House* (New York, 1959), 21.

37. Woodrow Wilson, address on Lincoln, 4 September 1916, *Messages and Papers* 1:320.

38. Ibid. 1:321–22.

39. Woodrow Wilson, *Constitutional Government*, 69; *Messages and Papers* 1:322.

40. Woodrow Wilson, address at Philadelphia, 10 May 1915; address at Saint Paul, Minn., 4 September 1919; in *Messages and Papers* 1:114–17; 2:846–47, 850, 853.

41. Woodrow Wilson, "The Ideals of America," 724, 728–30.

42. Woodrow Wilson, address at Sioux Falls, S.D., 8 September 1919; address at Saint Paul, Minn., 9 September 1919; response to King George V at Buckingham Palace, 27 December 1918; in *Messages and Papers* 2:823, 855, 581.

43. Woodrow Wilson, address at Philadelphia, 10 May 1915; address at Boston, 24 February 1919; address at Pueblo, Colo., 25 September 1919; address at Saint Paul, Minn., 9 September 1919; in *Messages and Papers* 1:114, 2:118, 638–39, 1113, 1124, 855–56. See George and George, *Woodrow Wilson and Colonel House*, 117–18, 320–22.

44. Woodrow Wilson, address on Lincoln, 4 September 1916, in *Messages and Papers* 1:322.

45. Woodrow Wilson, address at Gettysburg, 4 July 1913, in *Messages and Papers* 1:15–17.

46. Woodrow Wilson, address at Independence Hall, Philadelphia, 4 July 1914; address at Gettysburg, 4 July 1913; message to the National Army, 3 September 1917; in *Messages and Papers* 1:79, 14, 426; Wills, *Nixon Agonistes*, 430; Woodrow Wilson, address at Pueblo, Colo., 25 September 1919, in *Messages and Papers* 2:1127.

47. Woodrow Wilson, address at Pueblo, Colo., 25 September 1919; speech at Sioux Falls, S.D., 8 September 1919; in *Messages and Papers* 2:1127, 825; George and George, *Woodrow Wilson and Colonel House*, 292–93.

48. Woodrow Wilson, address at Pueblo, Colo., 25 September 1919; address at Boston, 24 February 1919; in *Messages and Papers* 2:1128, 642–43.

49. See Woodrow Wilson, *History* 5:58–64; Everett Carter, "Cultural History Written with Lightning: The Significance of *The Birth of a Nation*," *American Quarterly* 12 (Fall 1960): 347; and chapter 7.

50. Woodrow Wilson, *Division and Reunion* (New York, 1893), 294, and *Constitutional Government*, 49.

51. Wagenknecht, *D. W. Griffith*, 59; Carter, "Cultural History," 347; Woodrow Wilson, address at Saint Paul, Minn., 9 September 1919; address at Pueblo, Colo., 25 September 1919; in *Messages and Papers* 2:846, 1114; Woodrow Wilson, *History* 5:212–13. *Birth of a Nation* was based on *The Clansman*, a racist novel by Thomas Dixon (New York, 1905).

52. Carter, "Cultural History," 347; Paul O'Dell, *Griffith and the Rise of Hollywood* (New York, 1970), 35; Woodrow Wilson, address at Pueblo, Colo., 25 September 1919, in *Messages and Papers* 2:1130.

53. George and George, *Woodrow Wilson and Colonel House*, 21, 230, 292–94.

54. John Morton Blum, *Woodrow Wilson and the Politics of Morality* (Boston, 1956), 3–4; George and George, *Woodrow Wilson and Colonel House*, vi; Sigmund Freud and William C. Bullitt, *Thomas Woodrow Wilson* (Boston, 1967), 289.

55. Woodrow Wilson, *New Freedom*, 161–62.

56. Ibid., 162–63.

57. Ibid., 163–64.

58. George and George, *Woodrow Wilson and Colonel House*, 314–15; Blum, *Woodrow Wilson*, 3; Jacobson, "Lincoln's Abraham," 21.

59. Quoted in David Abrahamsen, *Nixon vs. Nixon* (New York, 1977), 78–79.

60. Richard Nixon, *RN: The Memoirs of Richard Nixon* (New York, 1978), 9; Lukas, *Nightmare*, 556.

61. Quoted in Abrahamsen, *Nixon*, 172.

62. Nixon quoted in ibid., 214; in Michael Rogin and John Lottier, "The Inner History of Richard Milhous Nixon," *Transaction* 9 (November–December 1971): 24; and in Wills, *Nixon Agonistes*, 393.

63. Wills, *Nixon Agonistes*, 30–31.

64. Donald, *Lincoln Reconsidered*, 64.

65. Abrahamsen, *Nixon*, 185–86; Marcus, "Lincoln and Nixon," 21.

66. Daniel Ellsberg, *Papers on the War* (New York, 1972), 41; Norman Mailer, *Armies of the Night* (New York, 1968), 210–12, 239.

67. Nixon promised a second American revolution in his 1971 State of the Union address. He is quoted in Blaisdell, *American Presidency*, 252. On Rehnquist, see Pat Watters and Stephen Gillers, eds., *Investigating the FBI* (Garden City, N.Y., 1973), 445.

68. Edmund Wilson, "Abraham Lincoln," 197.

69. Nixon quoted in Abrahamsen, *Nixon*, 173, and in Lukas, *Nightmare*, 630.

70. Norman Mailer, *Why Are We in Vietnam?* (New York, 1967), 23–25.

71. See the panels of hell in the Jan and Hubert van Eyck diptych, *Crucifixion and Last Judgment*, Metropolitan Museum, New York, (Fig. 3.8), and in the Hieronymus Bosch triptych, *Garden of Earthly Delights*, Prado, Madrid. The Luther quotes are from Norman O. Brown, *Life Against Death* (New York, 1959), 211, 226. Cf. 202–33. For a psychoanalytic interpretation of Nixon's personality in terms of secrecy and anality, written well before the Watergate exposures, see Rogin and Lottier, "Inner History."

72. See Alan B. Rothenberg, "Why Nixon Taped Himself," *Psychoanalytic Review* 62 (Summer 1975): 202–23. The phrases quoted in the text come, in order, from the tapes of 15 September 1972 (quoted in Lukas, *Nightmare*, 333); 17 March 1973 and 17 March 1973 (both quoted in Rothenberg, "Why Nixon Taped Himself," 205); 8 April 1973, 13 March 1973, and 19 March 1973 (all quoted in Lukas, *Nightmare*, 416, 394, 397); and from Bob Woodward and Carl Bernstein, *The Final Days* (New York, 1976), 369.

73. Richard Nixon to John Wilson and Frank Strickler, recorded conversation of 19 April 1973, quoted in Paul Conrad, *The King and Us* (Los Angeles, 1974), 190; Richard Nixon to H.R. Haldeman, recorded conversation of 25 April 1973, in Lukas, *Nightmare*, 515–16; Frost, *NYT*, 20 May 1977, p. 32; Woodward and Bernstein, *Final Days*, 168.

74. Richard Nixon, "Remarks to Members of the Cabinet and the White House Staff, in *Congressional Quarterly, Historic Documents* (Washington, D.C., 1974), 690. I am indebted to Nancy Shinabarger for calling my attention to this passage. See Richard Nixon to John Ehrlichman, recorded conversation of 14 April 1973, quoted in Conrad, *King and Us*, 86.

75. Lukas, *Nightmare*, 502, 507, 510.

76. Mailer, *Why Are We in Vietnam?* 25; Woodward and Bernstein, *Final Days*, 25–27; Lukas, *Nightmare*, 609, 486.

77. Lukas, *Nightmare*, 514.

78. Ibid., 624, 737–39; Woodward and Bernstein, *Final Days*, 124–32.

79. Richard Nixon, *Six Crises* (New York, 1962), 36–37, 70; Lillian Hellman, *Scoundrel Time* (New York, 1977), 80–81; Rogin and Lottier, "Inner History," 24–25; Wills, *Nixon Agonistes*, 93–114, 155–56.

80. Nixon, *Six Crises*, 35; Garry Wills, "The Hiss Connection Through Nixon's Life," *New York Times Magazine*, 25 August 1974, pp. 76–77, 87–89; "Nixon Relives the Hiss Case," *San Francisco Chronicle*, 3 May 1974, p. 5; Lukas, *Nightmare*, 391–92; Rothenberg, "Why Nixon Taped Himself," 219–20. See Conrad's cartoon, "The Pumpkin Tapes," *King and Us*, 61.

81. Frost, *NYT*, 20 May 1977, p. 16.

82. *San Francisco Examiner*, 4 September 1977, p. 11.

83. Rogin and Lottier, "Inner History," 21–22; Wills, *Nixon Agonistes*, 373–74; Frost, *NYT*, 5 May 1977, p. 33.

84. Frost, *NYT*, 5 May 1977, p. 33; Woodward and Bernstein, *Final Days*, 166; Abrahamsen, *Nixon*, 173, 220; Lukas, *Nightmare*, 581.

85. Frost, *NYT*, 5 May 1977, pp. 32, 33; Richard Nixon to John Mitchell, recorded conversation, 22 March 1973, quoted in Lukas, *Nightmare*, 408.

86. Lukas, *Nightmare*, 459. "Your parents have the strength of Lincoln," a Nixon speechwriter told Julie Nixon. See Woodward and Bernstein, *Final Days*, 304.

87. Frost, *NYT*, 5 May 1977, p. 33.

88. *New York Times*, 15 November 1973, p. 1; Lukas, *Nightmare*, 392; Rothenberg, "Why Nixon Taped Himself," 210; cf. Wills, *Nixon Agonistes*, 394–95.

89. Lukas, *Nightmare*, 474–84.

90. Ibid., 452; Richard Nixon to Henry Petersen, recorded conversation of 27 April 1973, *Submission of Recorded Presidential Conversations to the Committee on the Judiciary of the House of Representatives by President Richard Nixon, N.Y. Times*, ed. (New York, 1974), 783; President Nixon's resignation speech, 8 August 1974, *Congressional Quarterly, Historical Documents* (Washington, D.C., 1974), 685.

91. Lukas, *Nightmare*, 730; Abrahamsen, *Nixon*, 244–45; Nixon, "Remarks to Members of the Cabinet and the White House Staff," 691.

92. Blaisdell, *American Presidency*, 102; Hamilton and Ostendorf, *Lincoln in Photographs*, 279.

93. Nixon, "Remarks to Members of the Cabinet and the White House Staff," 691–92.

94. Woodward and Bernstein, *Final Days*, 214.

95. Conrad, *King and Us*, 215; William Shakespeare, *Richard II*, act 4, scene 1, act 5, scene 5. See also Kantorowicz, *Two Bodies*, 24–41.

96. Frost, *NYT*, 26 May 1977, p. 40; Conrad, *King and Us*, 75.

97. Abrahamsen, *Nixon*, 215; Hamilton and Ostendorf, *Lincoln in Photographs*, 70, 230.

98. Hamilton and Ostendorf, *Lincoln in Photographs*, 229–371.

99. Abrahamsen, *Nixon*, 172; Lukas, *Nightmare*, 634–35. For the understanding of Nixon as a bad actor, I am indebted to a good actor, Michael Lerner.

100. Frost, *NYT*, 5 May 1977, p. 33.

101. Abrahamsen, *Nixon*, 67.

102. Lukas, *Nightmare*, 752–53.

103. See Winthrop D. Jordan, "Familial Politics: Thomas Paine and the Killing of the King, 1776," *Journal of American History* 60 (September 1973): 294–308.

104. Lukas, *Nightmare*, 754.

105. Conrad, *King and Us*, 181; Nixon, *RN*, 80.

106. Wills, *Nixon Agonistes*, 28; Lukas, *Nightmare*, 206, 479, 481; Abrahamsen, *Nixon*, 245–48; Frost, *NYT*, 26 May 1977, p. 40.

CHAPTER IV. NONPARTISANSHIP AND THE GROUP INTEREST

1. Albert Somit and Joseph Tanenhaus, "Trends in American Political Science," *American Political Science Review* 67 (September 1963): 944.

2. David Truman, *The Governmental Process* (New York, 1951).

3. Robert Michels, *Political Parties* (New York, 1915).

4. Arthur F. Bentley, *The Process of Government* (Evanston, Ill., 1935), 222.

5. Truman, *Governmental Process*, 50.

6. Ibid., 31, 35, 37, 213, 227, passim. It is one thing to speak of acting groups as analytic categories, as Bentley did. It is quite another to refer to the actions of concrete collectivities like real interest groups. One may create an abstract model that contains "group" actors. In the real world only individuals act.

7. Bentley's real words were "Society itself is nothing other than the complex of groups that compose it" (Bentley, *Process of Government*, 222).

8. Ibid., 154.

9. Truman's group fetishism is analogous to the fetishism of commodities described by Marx. In both cases, "the productions of the human brain appear as independent beings endowed with life, and entering into relations both with one another and the human race" (Karl Marx, *Capital*, 3 vols. [New York, 1906], 1:83).

10. Truman, *Governmental Process*, 33–34.

11. Cf. Grant McConnell, *Private Power and American Democracy* (New York, 1966), 51–154; Michael Rogin, "Voluntarism: The Political Functions of an Anti-Political Doctrine," *Industrial and Labor Relations Review* 15 (July 1962): 525–30; Oliver Garceau, *The Political Life of the AMA* (Hamden, Conn., 1961), 83–103.

12. Truman, *Governmental Process*, 112.

13. Ibid., 156–59, 164.

14. Ibid., 193.

15. Only once does Truman recognize that "the well-situated minority [may] take action that does not conform to the decisions or preferences expressed by

the rank and file or by their elected representatives" (ibid., 111). But this does not lead to any discussion of bases for leadership-membership conflict of interest. Instead, when Truman returns to this problem (p. 194), he asks why followers sometimes tolerate "mediocre" leaders. The members' problem, as Truman writes of it, is never what leaders want, but leaders' incompetence in getting what members want.

16. Ibid., 210.

17. Some comments by Bentley are apropos. "Now this social will appears in many forms," he writes. "As a curious development of it we have a Novicow, who, needing an 'organ' to carry the will—for how absurd to have a function without an organ—places it in the élite. . . ." Then, addressing himself to proponents of a social will, he challenges "anybody who believes in its substantial participation in social life to locate it somewhere—not humourously, as in the élite, but seriously" (Bentley, *Process of Government*, 155, 158).

18. Truman, *Governmental Process*, 50.

19. Cf. McConnell, *Private Power*, 51–154; Rogin, "Voluntarism."

20. David B. Truman, "The Politics of New Collectivism" (Unpublished manuscript, Columbia University Library), 10–11, 13, 19, 21, as quoted by Shin'ya Ono, "The Limits of Bourgeois Pluralism," *Studies on the Left* 5 (Summer 1965): 64–66. See also Peter Bachrach, "Elite Consensus and Democracy," *Journal of Politics* 29 (1962): 439–52; Jack L. Walker, "A Critique of the Elitist Theory of Democracy," *American Political Science Review* 60 (June 1966): 286–87.

21. See, among other works, James O. Morris, *Conflict Within the AFL* (Ithaca, N.Y., 1958), 10–13, passim; Lewis Lorwin, *The American Federation of Labor* (Washington, D.C., 1933), 301–5, 417–52, passim; Philip Taft, *The A.F. of L. in the Time of Gompers* (New York, 1958); Robert Franklin Hoxie, *Trade Unionism in the United States* (New York, 1919), 177–87, 350–75; Sylvia Kopald, *Rebellion in Labor Unions* (New York, 1923); Rogin, "Voluntarism."

22. When I speak of the federation's political "tactics" or its demands, operations, etc., I do not mean to reify the group and ignore membership-leadership conflicts. The federation is personified solely in the interests of stylistic convenience.

23. See Truman, *Governmental Process*, 299–304; Avery Leiserson, "Organized Labor as a Pressure Group," *Annals of the American Academy of Political and Social Science* 274 (March 1951): 108–10, 114–16; Selig Perlman, *A Theory of the Labor Movement* (1928; republished, New York, 1949).

24. Truman, *Governmental Process*, 299–300; Leiserson, "Organized Labor as a Pressure Group."

25. Marc Karson, *American Labor Unions and Politics, 1900–1918* (Carbondale, Ill., 1958), 48. Karson argues, as I will, that this statement does not describe actual union political behavior.

26. Henry David, "One Hundred Years of Labor in Politics," in J. B. S. Hardman and Maurice F. Neufeld, eds., *The House of Labor* (New York, 1951), 91, 92.

27. AFL, *Proceedings* 1903:194.

28. AFL, *Proceedings* 1894:36–40.

29. AFL, *Proceedings* 1886:8.

30. AFL, *Proceedings* 1894:14.

31. AFL, *Proceedings* 1896:21–22.

32. Taft, *A.F. of L. in the Time of Gompers*, 292.

33. Karson, *American Labor Unions*, 29–41.

34. AFL, *Proceedings* 1906:32.

35. AFL, *Proceedings* 1908:223.

36. Karson, *American Labor Unions*, 54–62, 71–73, 81–89, 285.

37. For the AFL's opposition to social legislation, see Rogin, "Voluntarism," 530–34. The AFL had supported hours legislation in 1894 and 1899 before opposing it in 1914. This is a measure of the difference between the antipolitical stances of the two periods.

38. Samuel Gompers, *Seventy Years of Life and Labor*, 2 vols. (New York, 1925), 2:26.

39. Since 1906 nonpartisanship had been presented in practice as the alternative to support for third-party candidates. But Gompers explained that the AFL, in punishing the old parties and rewarding its friend La Follette, was not departing from nonpartisan tradition (Samuel Gompers, "We Are In To Win," *Federationist* 31 [September 1924]), 472.

40. Cf. Leiserson, "Organized Labor as a Pressure Group"; Truman, *Governmental Process*, 302–4; Perlman, *Theory of the Labor Movement*, 219.

41. In 1902, while Gompers was denying politics had any relevance to union goals, the AFL convention defeated a Socialist resolution forbidding union organizers from holding political jobs (AFL *Proceedings* 1902:154).

42. Cf. Philip Taft, "Labor's Changing Political Line," *Journal of Political Economy* 45 (October 1937): 635. At the 1895 AFL convention Jacob Weissman of the Bakery Workers Union, a staunch Gompers supporter, opposed sending a delegate to the International Conference of Social Work. "It embodied political action," he explained, "to which we were opposed." At the same convention Weissman introduced a resolution favoring the municipal regulation of bakeshops. Two years earlier he had favored laws requiring a day of rest for California bakers and preventing the construction of bakehouses in basements (AFL, *Proceedings* 1893:73, 1895:53, 64).

43. Harold Seidman, *Labor Czars* (New York, 1938), 11–17, 51, 81–85, 222–27.

44. Cf. Louis Stanley, "Prosperity, Politics, and Policy," in J. B. S. Hardman, ed., *American Labor Dynamics* (New York, 1928), 197–99.

45. Duncan was known throughout the federation as a philosophical anarchist, business-union variety. "Why wait for the slow process of law," he had once asked, "when we can exert a sure and certain economic power?" (AFL, *Proceedings* 1902:182).

46. This story is recounted in Lawrence Rogin, "Central Labor Bodies and Independent Political Action in New York City: 1918–1922" (Master's thesis, Columbia University, 1931), 16–34.

In Chicago labor-political ties also thwarted reform politics. There was a fight over municipal ownership of Chicago's street railways in the early 1900s. Fearing aggressive labor support of municipal ownership, Mayor Carter Harrison appointed many union officials to jobs on the city payroll, as building inspectors, bridge inspectors, and members of various bureaus. When, in 1903, the formation of the Union Labor party threatened Harrison's reelection, these men threw their weight against the new venture. See Ray Ginger, *Altgeld's America* (New York, 1958), 281.

47. Stanley, "Prosperity, Politics, and Policy," 199.

48. E. E. Cummins, "Political and Social Philosophy of the Carpenters Union," *Political Science Quarterly* 42 (September 1927): 410; Eric F. Goldman, *Rendezvous with Destiny* (New York, 1952), 228; Lawrence Rogin, "Central Labor Bodies," 29.

49. Cf. William Lederle, "Political Party Organization in Detroit: 1920–1934" (Master's thesis, University of Michigan, 1931), 63; Stephen V. Sarasohn and Vera H. Sarasohn, *Political Party Patterns in Michigan* (Detroit, 1957), 28, 31, 48; Robert Hunter, *Labor in Politics* (Chicago, 1915), 47–61; Henry John Gibbons, "The Labor Vote in Philadelphia's Political Upheaval," *Charities and the Commons* 15 (3 February 1906): 588–90; George P. West, "American Labor's Political Strategy—A Failure," *Nation*, 29 March 1922, p. 367; Seidman, *Labor Czars*, 30, 57–61; Ginger, *Altgeld's America*, 281, passim; Alvah Eugene Staley, "The History of the Illinois State Federation of Labor" (Ph.D. diss., University of Chicago, 1928), 224–28, 282–92; Walton Bean, *Boss Ruef's San Francisco* (Berkeley and Los Angeles, 1952); Alexander Saxton, "San Francisco Labor and the Populist and Progressive Insurgencies," *Pacific Historical Review* 34 (November 1965), 421–38.

50. For example, of the five Chicago congressmen mentioned as prolabor by Gompers in 1920, four had voted for the hated Esch-Cummins Railroad Transportation Act and the fifth was a tool of the anti-union Chicago meat-packers. See "No Time for Experimenting with Labor Party Theories," *Federationist* 28 (May 1920): 439; Harry Bird Sell, "The AFL and the Labor Party Movement of 1918–1920" (Master's thesis, University of Chicago, 1922), 79–80, 121–22.

51. In Saint Louis the city federation of local unions emancipated itself from machine politics only thanks to the influence of the powerful Socialist Brewery Workers (Edwin James Forsythe, "The St. Louis Central Trades and Labor Union: 1887–1945" (Ph.D. diss., University of Missouri, 1956), 41–47, 55–58.

52. Karson, *American Labor Unions*, 212–84; David J. Saposs, "The Catholic Church and the Labor Movement," *Modern Monthly* 7 (May 1933): 225–30, (June 1933): 294–98.

53. AFL, *Proceedings* 1932:342.

54. Truman, *Governmental Process*, 65–74, 300–304.

55. Hindsight, however, minimizes socialist strength during the progressive period. The Socialist candidate against Gompers obtained one-third of the vote in the 1912 AFL convention.

56. Angus Campbell et al., *The American Voter* (New York, 1960), 165–215; V. O. Key, Jr., *Public Opinion and American Democracy* (New York, 1961), 153–201.

57. Cf. Michael Walzer, "Civil Disobedience and Corporate Authority," in Philip Green and Sanford Levinson, eds., *Power and Community* (New York, 1970), 223–46.

58. This is also Hanna Fenichel Pitkin's conclusion in her authoritative *The Concept of Representation* (Berkeley and Los Angeles, 1967).

59. Sanford Levinson has pointed out, however, that the basic conflicts in contemporary political science go beyond values to conflicting interpretations of the facts. The standard American retreat from value conflict to agreement on the facts no longer seems to work. Levinson, "On 'Teaching' Political 'Science,'" in Green and Levinson, *Power and Community*, 59–84.

60. See Seymour Martin Lipset, "The Political Process in Trade Unions: A Theoretical Statement," in Walter Galenson and Seymour Martin Lipset, eds., *Labor and Trade Unionism* (New York, 1960), 238–39.

61. Support for the war in Vietnam by contemporary labor leaders is also best explained by leadership-organizational rather than working-class experience. Crucial to the AFL-CIO position were the internal fight with Communist and other left-wing unionists in the 1930s and 1940s and the incorporation of trade-union leadership into the Democratic party.

62. Alfred S. Cleveland, "NAM: Spokesman for Industry?" *Harvard Business Review* 26 (May 1948): 359–62; Karson, *American Labor Unions*, 136–41; Alexander Saxton, "The Indispensable Enemy: A Study of the Anti-Chinese Movement in California" (Ph.D. diss., University of California, Berkeley, 1967).

63. Cf. Michael Parenti, "Assimilation and Counter-Assimilation: From Civil Rights to Black Power," in Green and Levinson, *Power and Community*, 173–94.

64. Cf. Carl Schorske, *German Social Democracy, 1905–1917* (Cambridge, Mass., 1955).

CHAPTER V. LIBERAL SOCIETY AND THE INDIAN QUESTION

1. Henri Baudet, *Paradise on Earth* (New Haven, 1965), 8.

2. John Locke, *Of Civil Government* (London, 1924), *Second Treatise*, 140. For Hobbes and Rousseau, American Indian societies also demonstrated the historical existence of the state of nature. See Hoxie N. Fairchild, *The Noble Savage* (New York, 1961), 23–24.

3. *The Federalist Papers*, Roy P. Fairfield, ed. (New York, 1961), no. 1:33.

4. Cf. Noam Chomsky, "After Pinkville," *New York Review of Books*, 1 January 1970, p. 10, and *American Power and the New Mandarins* (New York, 1969), 279–80; Michael Rogin, "Truth is Stranger than Science Fiction," *The Listener*, 7 July 1968, pp. 117–18; Richard Drinnon, "Violence in the American Experience: Winning the West," *The Radical Teacher* (Chicago), 30 December 1969, pp. 36, 45–46.

Hippie and New Left youth identify themselves, and are identified by their enemies, with Indian resistance to American culture. It is fitting that the leading academic defender of American traditions has written an intemperate attack on the "new barbarians" of the New Left. This "rebellion of small groups" is "rude, wild, and uncivilized," "wild and disorganized," demands "infant-instantism," is wholly un-American, and "cannot last, if the nation is to survive" (Daniel Boorstin, "The New Barbarians," *Esquire*, October 1968, pp. 159–62, 260–62).

5. This essay interprets the prevailing cultural myth about Indians in antebellum America. It makes no effort to specify the social basis of that myth—class or mass, popular or elite, frontier or eastern, northern or southern, entrepreneurial or pastoral, speculator or backwoods. These themes are addressed in my *Fathers and Children: Andrew Jackson and the Subjugation of the American Indian* (New York, 1975). The discussion here will indicate that our leading politicians shared the myth and that it was particularly salient to those involved in Indian affairs. I believe that in some form the Indian myth reached deeply into all the social categories enumerated above. But it was sufficiently complex that different social types would stress different aspects. This sort of differentiation is not attempted here.

6. I am indebted to Mark Morris for this estimate. It is derived from Commissioner of Indian Affairs census records and other published sources. The figures in the text are conservative; removal during this period may have caused the deaths of forty thousand Indians.

7. Martin Van Buren, *Autobiography*, American Historical Association Annual Report (1918), 2:275. Cf. Mary E. Young, *Redskins, Ruffleshirts, and Rednecks* (Norman, Okla., 1961), 3–5, passim; Annie Heloise Abel, *The History of Events Resulting in Indian Consolidation West of the Mississippi*, American Historical Association Report of Proceedings (1906). Indians are simply not mentioned at all in perhaps the two major contenders for synthetic interpretations of the Jacksonian period. See Arthur Schlesinger, Jr., *The Age of Jackson* (Boston, 1945); Marvin Meyers, *The Jacksonian Persuasion* (New York, 1960). Thomas H. Benton's biographer largely ignores his important role in Indian affairs; Lewis Cass's biographer offers the most enormous, elementary, factual errors in his abbreviated account of the secretary of war and Indian removal. See William N. Chambers, *Old Bullion Benton* (Boston, 1956); Frank B. Woodford, *Lewis Cass* (New Brunswick, N.J., 1950), 180–83.

8. "Our Indian Affairs is . . . the most important branch of the war department," Andrew Jackson wrote, offering the secretaryship to Hugh Lawson White (*Correspondence of Andrew Jackson*, John Spencer Bassett, ed., 6 vols. [Washington, D.C., 1926–33], 4:271; hereafter cited as *JC*).

9. *American State Papers, Military Affairs* 4:714. Hereafter cited as *MA*.

10. Van Buren, *Autobiography*, 295.

11. Martin Van Buren, "Second Annual Message," 3 December 1838, in James D. Richardson, ed., *Messages and Papers of the Presidents*, 10 vols. (New York, 1917), 3:500.

12. Secretary of War James C. Calhoun, in *American State Papers, Indian Affairs* 2:190. Hereafter cited as *IA*.

13. Here and throughout I have relied heavily on Roy Harvey Pearce's seminal *The Savages of America* (Baltimore, 1965). See also Winthrop D. Jordon, *White over Black* (Baltimore, 1969), 89–91, 247–48, 477–81; George W. Stocking, Jr., *Race, Culture, and Evolution* (New York, 1968), 26–27, 75–100;

Arthur A. Ekirch, *The Idea of Progress in America, 1815–1860* (New York, 1944), 15–46.

14. Francis Parkman, *The Conspiracy of Pontiac*, 10th ed. (New York, 1962), 182–83.

15. General Edmund P. Gaines, in *MA*, 1:684.

16. Jordan, *White over Black*, 90–91.

17. Andrew Jackson, "First Annual Message," 8 December 1829, in Richardson, *Messages and Papers* 2:458. A few years later Jackson put on the headdress of the defeated Indian warrior Black Hawk shortly before receiving a delegation of petitioners for the United States Bank. "I don't think those fellows would like to meet me in this" (Marquis James, *Andrew Jackson*, 2 vols. (Indianapolis, 1933, 1937), 2:366; cf. *JC* 3:222.

18. Several interpretative works stress the American identification with nature or the Indians or both. See Henry Nash Smith, *Virgin Land* (New York, 1950); Leo Marx, *The Machine in the Garden* (New York, 1964); John William Ward, *Andrew Jackson, Symbol for an Age* (New York, 1955), 11–45. Perry Miller's breathtaking "Nature and the National Ego" demonstrates Jacksonian anxiety over the country's destruction of nature, the source of its identity (*Errand into the Wilderness* [New York, 1964], 204–16). Other discussions of nostalgia and regression in Jacksonian America include Meyers, *Jacksonian Persuasion*; Arthur K. Moore, *The Frontier Mind* (Lexington, Ky., 1957); Charles G. Sellers, Jr., *James K. Polk, Jacksonian, 1795–1843* (Princeton, 1957), 3, 92.

19. *JC* 2:441.

20. Sources for the quotations are Albert K. Weinberg, *Manifest Destiny* (Chicago, 1963), 195; T. H. Benton, in *IA* 2:512; James W. Silver, *Edmund Pendleton Gaines: Frontier General* (Baton Rouge, La., 1949), 106. Grover Cleveland, signing a bill that opened the way for the large-scale white appropriation of Indian land, remarked, "The hunger and thirst of the white man for the Indian's land is almost equal to his hunger and thirst after righteousness" (quoted in William T. Hagan, *American Indians* [Chicago, 1961], 141).

John Locke cited cannibalism by fathers of their children as the consequence of unrestrained paternal authority (*Of Civil Government, First Treatise*, 40).

21. The analysis summarized here seeks to join the psychoanalytic theories of Melanie Klein and Géza Róheim to a tradition of interpreting America as a liberal society. See Géza Róheim, *The Origins and Functions of Culture* (New York, 1943) and *Magic and Schizophrenia* (New York, 1955); Melanie Klein, *Contributions to Psychoanalysis* (London, 1948), and Melanie Klein et al., eds., *New Directions in Psychoanalysis* (London, 1955). The treatment of America as a liberal society derives from Alexis de Tocqueville, *Democracy in America*, 2 vols. (New York, 1959); and Louis Hartz, *The Liberal Tradition in America* (New York, 1955). Cf. Michael Paul Rogin, *The Intellectuals and McCarthy* (Cambridge, Mass., 1967), 32–44, and "Southern California: Right-Wing Behavior and Political Symbols," in Rogin and John L. Shover, *Political Change in California* (Westport, Conn., 1970), 178–201. Suggestive in bridging the gap between psychoanalytic theory and American society were Erik H. Erikson, *Childhood and Society*, 2d ed. (Middlesex, Eng., 1965); Kenneth Keniston, *The Uncommitted* (New York, 1965).

"Liberal" political movements, as Hartz makes clear, are not the sole repositories of the American liberal tradition. That tradition equally underlies American right-wing perspectives. The term "liberal" in this essay is not limited to a narrowly political referent.

22. Hannah Arendt, *The Origins of Totalitarianism*, 2d ed. (New York, 1958), 192–97. See also her discussion of imperialism, pp. 124–47.

23. Chomsky, "After Pinkville," 10. See also Drinnon, "Violence in the American Experience, 36–38, 44–46.

24. These phrases enter almost every discussion of the Indian question. On the identification of savages with children, see Fairchild, *Noble Savage*, 190, 230, 366–90.

25. Thomas L. McKenney, *Memoirs, Official and Personal*, 2 vols. (New York, 1846), 2:33. This sort of stock description of the noble savage endured in America after it died out in Europe; it was utilized precisely by the makers of Indian policy. See Fairchild, *Noble Savage*, 20, 79, 298–99, 363–64. For more of McKenney's comparisons of savages to children (for example, the infant King Alfred ruling his realm from a three-legged stool), see 1:78, 82.

26. William Robertson, quoted in Bernard W. Sheehan, "Paradise and the Noble Savage in Jeffersonian Thought," *William and Mary Quarterly*, 3d ser., 26 (July 1969): 337. Robertson was an eighteenth-century Scottish man of letters, whose writings on American Indians deeply influenced American perceptions. Lewis Cass, for example, cited Robertson as the foremost authority on the Indian and incorporated Robertson's views wholesale in his own essays and reports. See Drinnon, "Violence in the American Experience," 41.

27. In Sheehan's summary ("Paradise and the Noble Savage," 328), "The noble savage was . . . untouched by the hands of man. He was impulsive, unrestrained, unburdened by social conventions. . . . Rather than standing aside from his surroundings, as did the civilized man altering them to his own specifications, the noble savage blended into the surface paradise."

Indians themselves contributed to the dominant metaphor: "We love our land, it is our mother, and we do not think anyone would take it from us if we did not wish to part with it." "We have grown up as the herbs of the woods, and do not wish to be transplanted to another soil" (*IA* 2:230; Silver, *Edmund Pendleton Gaines*, 181n). See also Angie Debo, *The Road to Disappearance* (Norman, Okla., 1941), 42–44.

28. The language is Jefferson's; see Thomas Jefferson, *Notes on Virginia*, in Adrienne Koch and William Peden, eds., *The Life and Selected Writings of Thomas Jefferson* (New York, 1944), 210–13, 221. See also Pearce, *Savages of America*, 152–53; Sheehan, "Paradise and the Noble Savage," 352–55; Staughton Lynd, *Intellectual Origins of American Radicalism* (New York, 1969), 85.

29. Parkman, *Conspiracy of Pontiac*, 63. According to a 1794 school text, savage freedom kept the Indian "in a state of infancy, weakness, and the greatest imperfection" (quoted in Pearce, *Savages of America*, 161).

30. Lewis Cass, "Annual Report of the Secretary of War for 1831," *MA* 4:714.

31. Pearce, *Savages of America*, 68–70; Debo, *Road to Disappearance*, 19–21, 369; R. S. Cotterill, *The Southern Indians: The Story of the Civilized Tribes*

Before Removal (Norman, Okla., 1954), 9–11; Wilcomb E. Washburn, "The Moral and Legal Justification for Dispossessing the Indians," in James Morton Smith, ed., *Seventeenth-Century American Essays in Colonial History* (Chapel Hill, N.C., 1959), 19–23.

32. [Lewis Cass], "Removal of the Indians," *North American Review* 46 (January 1830): 75.

33. McKenney, *Memoirs* 1:123–24. A Cherokee version of the familiar metaphor appears in a letter to Secretary of War Calhoun (*IA* 2:474): "The happiness which the Indians once enjoyed, by a quiet and undisturbed ease, in their primitive situation, before the face of the white man was seen on this continent, was now poisoned by the bad fruits of the civilized tree which was planted around them."

34. U.S. Congress, *Register of Debates* 6 (1829–30): 1093; J. B. Kinney, *A Continent Lost, A Civilization Won* (Baltimore, 1937), 102, 109. Kinney is quoting from reports of the commissioners of Indian affairs for 1832 (E. H. Herring) and 1838 (T. H. Crawford). This book is an invaluable (albeit unconscious) sourcebook on white efforts to impose private property upon Indians.

35. C. B. McPherson, *The Political Theory of Possessive Individualism* (London, 1964), 53–70, 137–42, passim.

36. Among the many examples, see Captain Eugene F. Ware, "The Indian War of 1864," in Wilcomb E. Washburn, ed., *The Indian and the White Man* (New York, 1964), 284–88.

37. Quoted in James Parton, *Life of Andrew Jackson*, 3 vols. (Boston, 1863), 1:401n.

38. For some variations on the theme, see John K. Mahon, *History of the Second Seminole War, 1835–1842* (Gainesville, Fla., 1967), 265–70, 311; Malcolm J. Rohrbough, *The Land Office Business* (New York, 1968), 59; and Andrew Jackson, in Parton, *Life of Andrew Jackson* 2:451, and *MA* 1:705. Cotton Mather's "tawny serpents" is perhaps the most famous of these epithets. On Indians disturbing the forest paradise, see Parkman's "ungoverned children, fired with the instincts of devils" (*Conspiracy of Pontiac*, 463), and ibid., 323n, 436–37. Tennessee governor Joseph McMinn, urging removal of the Indians from the old Southwest, explained that then "each southern and western inhabitant will cultivate his own garden of Eden" (*IA* 1:856).

39. McKenney, *Memoirs* 1:112–13.

40. See Fairchild, *Noble Savage*, 90–91.

41. The psychoanalytic literature on the formation of a primitive, preoedipal superego is extensive and, in my view, convincing. See Melanie Klein, "The Early Development of Conscience in the Child," "A Contribution to the Psychogenesis of Manic-Depressive States," and "Mourning and Its Relation to Manic-Depressive States," all in *Contributions of Psychoanalysis*; Sandor Rado, "The Problem of Melancholia," *International Journal of Psychoanalysis* 9 (October 1928): 420–38; George Gero, "The Construction of Depression," *International Journal of Psychoanalysis* 17 (October 1936): 423–61; Annie Reich, "Early Identifications as Archaic Elements in the Superego," *Journal of the American Psychoanalytic Association* 2 (March 1954): 218–38.

42. Róheim, *Magic and Schizophrenia*, 224.

43. McKenney, *Memoirs* 1:230. Cf. Tennessee senator Felix Grundy (quoted in Parton, *Life of Andrew Jackson* 1:140): "If I am asked to trace my memory back, and name the first indelible impression it received, it would be the sight of my eldest brother bleeding and dying under the wounds inflicted by the tomahawk and scalping knife."

44. Klein, "Early Development of Conscience," 268.

45. For example, during the War of 1812, Jackson feared America would be "apportioned amongst the powers of Urope" and foresaw Russian intervention in the war (*JC* 2:32, 37). Before the adoption of the Constitution he had been sympathetic to a frontier intrigue to attach the Southwest to Spain, to insure navigation of the Mississippi and protection from the Indians (see James, *Andrew Jackson* 1:58–61). He also could never convince himself that Aaron Burr in 1806 aimed at anything more than gaining new territory for the United States (ibid. 1:110, 126–38).

46. Quoted in Parton, *Life of Andrew Jackson* 2:547.

47. James Hall, coauthor with McKenney of the most important antebellum volumes on the various tribes, quoted in Pearce, *Savages of America*, 120. Compare Tocqueville's description of America in "A Fortnight in the Wilds": "A nation of conquerors, . . . it is a wandering people" (Alexis de Tocqueville, *Journey to America*, J. P. Mayer, ed. [London, 1959], 339). Southern author William Gilmore Simms, criticizing the United States in 1843, wrote, "A wandering people is more or less a barbarous one," in Ekirch, *Idea of Progress*, 183.

48. *JC* 1:13.

49. *IA* 2:735.

50. Cf. George Dangerfield, *The Era of Good Feeling* (New York, 1952), 151; Abel, *History of Events*, 327–29; Parton, *Life of Andrew Jackson* 2:449–52, 498–99, 513–15; Silver, *Edmund Pendleton Gaines*, 192–215; *JC* 1:331, 396–97; 2:374–86, 395–98; 5:423–24; 6:278, 290; *MA* 6:1044–45; H. S. Halbert and T. H. Ball, *The Creek War of 1813 and 1814* (Chicago, 1895), 270–72.

51. *JC* 2:271–72. See ibid., p. 245 for an elaborate fantasy of Indian claims, which simply reverses the specific progress of white expansionism. The Creek name for settlers was "the-people-greedily-grasping-after-land." See Debo, *Road to Disappearance*, 54.

52. Thomas Hart Benton for the 1824 Senate Committee on Indian Affairs, *IA* 2:512.

53. [Lewis Cass], "Policy and Practice of the United States and Great Britain in Their Treatment of Indians," *North American Review* 55 (April 1827): 372–76.

54. Reverend Dr. Joseph Doddridge, "Notes on the Settlements and Indian Wars . . . ," in Washburn, *The Indian and the White Man*, 271–73.

55. Erikson and Róheim suggest that child-rearing practices among some primitive peoples encourage oral aggression; this would clearly bear on white fears, but my anthropological literacy is far too inadequate for this line of speculation. See Erikson on the Sioux, in *Childhood and Society*, 127–50; Géza Róheim, "The Evolution of Culture," in Bruce Mazlish, ed., *Psychoanalysis and History* (Englewood Cliffs, N.J., 1963), 72–76.

Some tribes, although generally not those in the Southwest, did engage in torture. But incidents were exaggerated and universalized to all "bad" Indians; in many cases tribes had only learned torture from Europeans who tortured them in the sixteenth and seventeenth centuries. See Nathanial Knowles, "The Torture of Captives by the Indians of Eastern North America," *Proceedings of the American Philosophical Society* 82 (1940): 151–225. The fascination with Indian "atrocities" out of all proportion to their importance served political and, I will argue, psychological functions.

56. For examples, see Parton, *Life of Andrew Jackson* 2:431; Washburn, *The Indian and the White Man*, 444 ("The ferocious creature had tasted blood and could not restrain himself til he could be surfeited"); *IA* 1:843; a host of letters reprinted in *IA* and *MA*, Congressional debates in the *Register of Debates*, etc.

57. *IA* 1:848; *JC* 1:337–38, 488; Parton, *Life of Andrew Jackson* 1:524. The terror and flight of the Illinois militia during Black Hawk's War are described in William Hagen, *The Sac and Fox Indians* (Norman, Okla., 1958), 158–61.

58. The classic statement is Sigmund Freud, *Totem and Taboo* (London, 1960), 72: "If one person succeeds in gratifying a repressed desire, the same desire is bound to be kindled in all the other members of the community. In order to keep the temptation down, the envied transgressor must be deprived of the fruit of his enterprise, and the punishment will not infrequently give those who carry it out an opportunity for committing the same outrage under cover of an act of expiation. This is indeed one of the foundations of the human penal system."

59. *JC* 1:416; Debo, *Road to Disappearance*, 78; Mahon, *Second Seminole War*, 122.

60. During the Creek War Jackson wrote, "I must destroy those deluded victims doomed to destruction by their own restless and savage conduct." He further insisted that all Creeks that did not fight with him against the hostiles should be treated as enemies (*JC* 1:422–23).

61. *JC* 2:238–39; 1:230, 500.

62. *IA* 2:162; *MA* 1:703; *JC* 5:468, 512.

63. Mahon, *Second Seminole War*, 198–300; Grant Foreman, *Indian Removal* (Norman, Okla., 1942), 342–63. During Black Hawk's War a boat commander, whose crew had fired upon an Indian party, killing women and children, explained, "As we neared them they raised a white flag and endeavored to decoy us, but we were a little too old for them" (Seymour Dunbar, *A History of Travel in America*, 3 vols. [Indianapolis, 1915], 2:464).

64. *JC* 2:42, 28–29, repeated 44.

65. The quotes in the text come, in order, from *JC* 2:386; U.S. Congress, *Register of Debates* 8 (1831–32): 791; *MA* 1:720; *JC* 1:231; *JC* 2:28–29. The second speaker is Missouri congressman A. H. Buckner; all the rest are Jackson. For still other Jackson variations, see *JC* 1:186, 225–26; *MA* 1:720; Parton, *Life of Andrew Jackson* 1:213, 426. For other contributions, see Mahon, *Second Seminole War*, 247–48; Doddridge, "Notes on the Settlements," 273; Par-

ton, *Life of Andrew Jackson* 1:546; *IA* 1:839, 843; Arthur W. Thompson, *Jacksonian Democracy on the Florida Frontier* (Gainesville, Fla., 1961), 33.

66. Nathaniel Hawthorne's work, preoccupied with oedipal guilt and the "sins of the fathers," contains an example of Indians as surrogate father killers. The hero of "Alice Doan's Confession" recalls a childhood scene in which he stands over the body of his dead father and imagines he has killed him. In fact he is innocent; the killing was done by Indians. See Frederick C. Crews, *The Sins of the Fathers* (New York, 1966), 44–45. On Indians and American women and children, see Leslie A. Fiedler, *The Return of the Vanishing American* (New York, 1968), 50–134.

67. McKenney, *Memoirs* 1:33–34; cf. Parton, *Life of Andrew Jackson* 1:401–2.

68. See Fiedler, *Return of the Vanishing American*; and Leslie A. Fiedler, *Love and Death in the American Novel* (New York, 1960). The bank "devoured the western cities in its jaws," officeholders only wanted "a tit to suck the treasury pap," etc. Cf. *JC* 4:14, 21, 5:52; Bray Hammond, *Banks and Politics in America from the Revolution to the Civil War* (Princeton, 1957), 259.

69. Jordan, *White over Black*, 162–63; cf. Mahon, *Second Seminole War*, 125.

70. Fiedler, *Return of the Vanishing American*, 178–79.

71. See *Worcester* v. *Georgia*, VI Peters (1832): 512–59; Kinney, *Continent Lost*, 9–10, passim.

72. *IA* 2:246.

73. *MA* 4:4. It would be greatly in error to think that the language of fathers and children was used only in communications to the Indians, not when whites addressed the problem among themselves. Indeed, Indians themselves often gave the rhetoric its peculiarly American significance. A Cherokee delegation, appealing to President Monroe, was "confident that his youngest children, as well as our elder brothers, will equally have a place in his mind, and that protection and measures for the amelioration of our conditions will be pursued until we can rise from our present state of minority to a state of more perfect manhood, and become citizens" (*IA* 2:147).

74. On the weakness of paternal authority in the American family, see Tocqueville, *Democracy in America* 2:202–6.

75. *JC* 2:387n.

76. Among the studies of infantilization, see Bruno Bettelheim, "Individual and Mass Behavior in Extreme Situations," *Journal of Abnormal Psychiatry* 38 (October 1943), and *The Informed Heart* (Glencoe, Ill., 1960), 107–263; Stanley Elkins, *Slavery* (Chicago, 1959), 81–139; Erving Goffman, *Asylums* (New York, 1961); Harold F. Searles, *Collected Papers on Schizophrenia and Related Subjects* (New York, 1965), 254–83, 717–51; R. D. Laing, *The Divided Self* (Middlesex, Eng., 1965), 172–205; R. D. Laing and A. Esterson, *Sanity, Madness, and the Family* (Middlesex, Eng., 1970); Jules Henry, *Culture Against Man* (New York, 1963), 322–474; Betty Friedan, *The Feminine Mystique* (New York, 1963), 276–98; Walter O. Weyrauch, "Law in Isolation, The Penthouse of Astronaughts," *Trans-Action* (June 1968): 13–16; Isidore Ziberstein, "Psy-

chological Habituation to War: A Socio-Psychological Case Study," *American Journal of Orthopsychiatry* 38 (April 1967): 467–68. For a magnificent early formulation, see Victor Tausk, "On the Origins of the Influencing Machine in Schizophrenia," in Robert Fliess, ed., *The Psychoanalytic Reader* (New York, 1948).

77. Searles, *Collected Papers*, 40–42. Tocqueville's observations about the pioneer are to the point: "Even his feelings for his family have become merged in a vast egotism and one cannot be sure whether he regards his wife and children as anything more than a detached part of himself" ("Fortnight in the Wilds," 339).

78. Quoted in Francis Paul Prucha, *American Indian Policy in the Formative Years* (Cambridge, Mass., 1962), 220.

79. Thomas Hart Benton, "Speech on the Oregon Question," in C. Merton Babcock, ed., *The American Frontier* (New York, 1965), 223.

80. See the discussion in part 1, above, and the references cited in n. 13. The bald argument that agricultural societies could take the land of hunters is stressed in the secondary literature somewhat out of proportion to its appearance in the sources; I may have, in retribution, slighted it here. A good, compact discussion is Mary E. Young, "Indian Removal and Land Allotment: The Civilized Tribes and Jacksonian Justice," *American Historical Review* 64 (October 1958): 37–38.

81. For example, Cass, "Removal of the Indians," 64, 77.

82. A southern congressman tellingly exploited the logic of the sentimental friends of the Indians. Taking direct control of Indian land, Congressman Richard Wilde began, "we should become their real benefactors; and we should perform the office of the great father." He concluded:

> But the race of Indians will perish! Yes sir! The Indians of this continent, like all other men, savage or civilized, must perish. . . . What is history but the obituary of nations? . . . Whose fate do we lament? The present generation of Indians? They will perish like the present generation of white men. . . .
>
> When gentlemen talk of preserving the Indians, what is it that they mean to preserve? Is it their mode of life? No. You intend to convert them from hunters to agriculturalists or herdsmen. Is it their barbarous laws and customs? No. You promise to furnish them with a code, and prevail upon them to adopt habits like your own. Their language? No. You intend to supersede their imperfect jargon by teaching them your own rich, copious, energetic tongue. Their religion? No. You intend to convert them from their miserable and horrible superstitions to the mild and cheering doctrines of Christianity.
>
> What is it, then, that constitutes Indian individuality—the identity of that race which gentlemen are so anxious to preserve? Is it the mere copper color of the skin, which marks them—according to your prejudices at least—an inferior—a conquered and degraded race?
>
> But alas! The Indians melt away before the white man, like snow before the sun! Well, sir! Would you keep the snow and lose the sun?

See *Register of Debates* 6 (1829–30): 1088, 1103.

83. Andrew Jackson, "First Annual Message," in Richardson, *Messages and Papers* 2:458.

84. Thomas Jefferson to Indian agent Benjamin Hawkins, quoted in Dangerfield, *Era of Good Feeling*, 27. Jefferson advocated that Indians turn to ag-

riculture, so they would need less land and could cede the excess to the advancing whites. In the sentence immediately preceding the one quoted in the text, he explained, "The wisdom of the animal which amputates and abandons to the hunter those parts for which he is pursued should be theirs, with this difference, that the former sacrifices what is useful, the latter what is not." "Castrated," to use Dangerfield's word, the Indians could safely merge with the whites.

85. From an 1834 pamphlet by Joel R. Poinsett, later Van Buren's secretary of war, quoted in Ekirch, *Idea of Progress*, 43–44.

86. It was said that Indians wanted to remain savage and therefore desired to separate themselves from whites. Henry Wadsworth Longfellow explicitly presented Hiawatha as part of America's childhood; his willingness to go west showed Indians would not resist progress. Cf. Young, *Redskins*, 47–51; Pearce, *Savages of America*, 173–74.

87. *IA* 2:115.

88. Parton, *Life of Andrew Jackson* 3:779.

89. Cf. Samuel Huntington, "The Bases of Accommodation," *Foreign Affairs* 46 (July 1968): 648–52; Chomsky, *American Power*, 11–13, 21, 53–56; Herbert Gans, *The Urban Villagers* (New York, 1962), 269–336; Marc Fried, "Grieving for a Lost Home: Psychological Costs of Relation," in James Q. Wilson, ed., *Urban Renewal* (Cambridge, Mass., 1966), 359–79.

90. "Second Annual Message to Congress," 6 December 1830, in Richardson, *Messages and Papers* 2:521. Cf. Lewis Cass's 1831 report as secretary of war, *MA* 4:714. The comparison with white emigration was used, unsuccessfully, to convince several tribes to move west. Cf. Jackson's 1830 talk to the Chickasaws, in Dunbar, *History of Travel* 2:575–77; Jackson and General Thomas Hinds to the Choctaws, 1820, *IA* 2:235: Indian Commissioners to Cherokees, 1823, *IA* 2:430; Commissioners to Chickasaws, 1826, *IA* 2:720.

91. Abel, *History of Events*, 244.

92. This was common; some tribes were moved several times in a single generation. See ibid., 267; Hagan, *American Indians*, 81–87.

93. "Second Annual Message to Congress," 6 December 1830, in Richardson, *Messages and Papers* 2:522. At other moments Jackson knew full well the problem lay in the peculiar Indian attachment to his land. Cf. Parton, *Life of Andrew Jackson* 1:433; and Florida governor Duval, quoted in Mahon, *Second Seminole War*, 53.

94. Cass, "Removal of the Indians," 75.

95. *IA* 2:720.

96. McKenney, *Memoirs* 1:124.

97. Cass, "Removal of the Indians," 75.

98. *IA* 2:114. This argument was tried on the Indians, with little success. Tennessee governor Joseph McMinn to the Cherokees, *IA* 2:487; Secretary of War John C. Calhoun to the Cherokees, *IA* 2:190.

99. Cass, "Policy and Practice," 382.

100. *IA* 2:26–27.

101. See Hagan, *American Indians*, 130–50; Kinney, *Continent Lost*, 81–311; Young, *Redskins*, 12–114.

102. When the Creek chiefs refused to meet privately with Georgia's com-

missioners during the investigation of a fraudulent treaty, the commissioners insisted federal officials must be behind the Indians' refusal, since "no savage" could have thought it up on his own (*IA* 2:833).

103. Lewis Cass on the origins of the Second Creek War, in *MA* 6:623. He gives the same explanation for Black Hawk's War in the Northwest in his 1832 report (*MA* 6:623).

104. Cass, "Policy and Practice," 417–20.

105. *JC* 2:243–44, 300–304.

106. *JC* 2:269.

107. Saint Louis superintendent of Indian affairs William Clark, quoted in Hagan, *Sac and Fox Indians*, 84–85; *JC* 1:368.

108. *JC* 1:209. Cf. ibid. 1:365–66.

109. Parton, *Life of Andrew Jackson* 2:485. Jackson invaded Florida on the pretext of an Indian war, to gain the territory for the United States. That story and the "trial" of Ambrister and Arbuthnot are reported in James, *Andrew Jackson* 1:300–330; Parton, *Life of Andrew Jackson* 2:463–85, 513–15; *JC* 2:365; *MA* 1:700.

110. Jackson in *MA* 1:697. Preparing to seize a Spanish fort on his earlier Florida invasion, Jackson had written to the Pensacola governor, calling him "the Head which countenanced and exalted the barbarity. He is the responsible person, and not the poor savage whom he makes his instrument of execution" (*JC* 2:28).

111. *JC* 2:154.

112. *JC* 2:278–80; also ibid. 3:31–32, 38; Prucha, *American Indian Policy*, 234–36; Abel, *History of Events*, 276–85.

113. "This plain language of truth," as he put it, "has brought them to their senses" (*JC* 2:387–88, on the Chickasaw treaty of 1818). Cf. the report of the 1820 Choctaw treaty proceedings in *IA* 2:237–41.

114. Cass, "Removal of the Indians," 80, 121. "We must frequently promote their interest against their inclination," Cass explained, "and no plan for the improvement of their condition will ever be practicable or efficacious, to the promotion of which their consent must first be obtained" (quoted in Woodford, *Lewis Cass*, 143).

115. *MA* 6:446.

116. *JC* 2:388; 3:351.

117. Richardson, *Messages and Papers* 2:517–20, 523.

118. *IA* 2:408.

119. Cf. Goffman, *Asylums*, 318–20.

120. For example, Generals Thomas Hinds and John Coffee to the Chickasaws, 1826, in *IA* 2:723.

121. *IA* 2:436.

122. Jackson's early relations with the Cherokees are a good example. He had included 10 million acres of Cherokee land in a treaty coerced from the Creeks in 1814. He had his friend John Coffee run the boundary line without authorization from Washington. Then he encouraged intruders to settle on the Cherokee land, while the secretary of war was ordering it returned to the tribe.

Jackson resisted orders to remove the intruders, encouraged them to stay, and aimed, ultimately successfully, to use their presence to force the Cherokees to sell. But his posture was one of kindness to the Indians. They must be made to see, if they do not sell their land, "what is really to be feared, that is, their own destruction by an irritated people" (*JC* 2:252–53; Abel, *History of Events,* 278–81).

123. McKenney, *Memoirs* 1:78. The passage continues,

> There were flowers and gems which needed only to be cultivated and polished, to ensure from the one, the emission of as sweet odors as ever regaled the circles of the civilized. . . . And yet they were, and are, neglected, trodden down, and treated as outcasts!
>
> At twelve o'clock on Monday, the signal gun for assembling of the council was fired—when were seen coming from all directions, the great multitude of the sons of the forest, to hear what their father had to say to them.

124. Ibid. 2:109–17.

125. John Henry Eaton, *The Life of Andrew Jackson* (Philadelphia, 1824), 436–37. Eaton himself subsequently adopted an Indian boy. See Peggy Eaton, *Autobiography* (New York, 1932), 162–68.

126. *IA* 2:264.

127. "Annual Report of the Secretary of War," 30 November 1829, in *MA* 4:154–55.

128. *IA* 2:161. Jackson stressed the benefits to the Indians of the "exertion of our military power," as opposed to "feeding their avarice" (*JC* 5:507).

129. Quoted in Dunbar, *History of Travel* 2:461. Jackson and General Hinds, in their 1820 talk to the Choctaws (*IA* 2:237), warned that if the tribe refused to remove across the Mississippi, it would inevitably disintegrate. Some would join America's enemies. "We would be under the necessity of raising the hatchet against our own friends and children. Your father, the President of the United States, wishes to avoid this unnatural state of things."

130. *Register of Debates* 6 (1829–30): 325.

131. McKenney, *Memoirs* 2:121. For similar humiliations of Indian chiefs, see Cotterill, *Southern Indians,* 129, and the description of Black Hawk's tour of the East in captivity, in Woodford, *Lewis Cass,* 176. Cf. the fictional description of a child's punishment in an 1835 best-seller analyzed in Bernard Wishy, *The Child and the Republic* (Philadelphia, 1968), 44–49.

132. Only one political figure of the period, to my knowledge, rejected the parent-child metaphor. Missionary Jeremiah Evarts's "William Penn" letters sparked the opposition to the Indian removal bill. In this pamphlet Evarts accused the whites of imposing the language of great white fathers and little red children on the Indians to avoid dealing with the tribes as autonomous, independent societies. The pamphlet ends with an equally unique appeal to the law. Evarts personifies the law not as a strong, forbidding, and punitive father enforcing uniformity and obedience but as a woman who can accept harmony and diversity in the world she rules. See "William Penn," *Present Crisis in the Condition of the American Indians* (Boston, 1829), 101. A similar, religious-based metaphorical contrast appears in Tocqueville's *Democracy in America* 2:386–87.

133. Quoted in Francis Paul Prucha, "Thomas L. McKenney and the New York Indian Board," *Mississippi Valley Historical Review* 48 (March 1962): 653. The author cites this passage to prove McKenney opposed coercing Indians.

134. Commissioner Duncan Campbell on the failure of a Creek treaty in 1824, *IA* 2:574.

135. Jackson, in *JC* 2:299, 300–304. This is Jackson's earliest use of the rhetoric of Jacksonian democracy, attacking leaders in the name of the people. Note the metaphors of independence vs. oral dependence. See also n. 68, above.

136. Quoted in Edwin C. McReynolds, *The Seminoles* (Norman, Okla., 1957), 195.

137. John H. Eaton, Jackson's first secretary of war, told the commissioners sent to the Cherokees to keep their identities secret at first.

> There is no doubt, however, but that the mass of people would be glad to emigrate; and there is no little doubt that they are kept from this exercise of their choice by their chiefs and other interested and influential men. . . . [It is necessary] to break the power that is warring with their best interests. . . . The best resort is believed to be that which is embraced in an appeal to the chiefs and influential men, not together, but apart, at their own houses, and by a proper exposition of their real condition, rouse them to think of that; whilst offers to them of extensive reservations in fee simple, and other rewards, would, it is hoped, result in obtaining their acquiescence.

The plan failed here, and ultimately the Cherokees—many in chains—were removed by military force. But similar efforts succeeded with other tribes. Eaton's letter is quoted by Senator Theodore Frelinghuysen in *Register of Debates* 6 (1829–30): 310.

138. Cf. Abel, *History of Events*, 387; Marion L. Starkey, *The Cherokee Nation* (New York, 1946), 150.

139. See Cass, in *MA* 6:590; and, for the whole monstrous story, Young, *Redskins*; Foreman, *Indian Removal*, 118–83; *MA* 6:575–780.

140. Quoted in Dangerfield, *Era of Good Feeling*, 27; another Jefferson letter with the same message is in Samuel C. Williams, *Beginnings of West Tennessee in the Land of the Chickasaws* (Johnson City, Tenn., 1930), 62. See also Cotterill, *Southern Indians*, 139–49; Hagan, *Sac and Fox Indians*, 9–14; Dunbar, *History of Travel* 2:419, 470–82.

141. Cf. Margaret Mead, *And Keep Your Powder Dry*, 2d ed. (London, 1967), 186–89; and the now-famous selective service pamphlet on "channelling," discussed in Richard Flacks, Florence Howe, and Paul Lauter, "On the Draft," *New York Review of Books*, 6 April 1967, pp. 3–6.

142. *Worcester v. Georgia*, VI Peters: 512–59. Jackson wrote to his friend General John Coffee, "The decision of the Supreme Court has fell still born" (quoted in James, *Andrew Jackson* 2:304–5).

143. Cf. Coffee to Jackson, quoted in Young, "Indian Removal," 36.

144. Congressman Edward Everett complained that Georgia law, "by reducing them to a state of minority . . . holds them to their infancy" (*Register of Debates* 7 [1830–31]: 696).

145. Eaton letter quoted by Senator Sprague in *Register of Debates* 6

(1829–30): 356. In Cass's words, "It is certainly better for them to meet the difficulties of removal, with the probability of an adequate and final reward, than, yielding to their constitutional apathy, to sit still and perish" ("Annual Report of the Secretary of War," 21 November 1831, in *MA* 4:714).

146. "First Annual Message," in Richardson, *Messages and Papers* 2:458.

147. *Register of Debates* 6 (1829–30): 594.

148. Ibid., 1034.

149. This meant, in practice, that Jackson coerced removal treaties from the Choctaws and Creeks by threatening otherwise to leave them to the mercy of the states. See Young, *Redskins*, 30–39, and the next paragraph in the text.

150. *JC* 4:169, 177. Commissioner of Indian Affairs Elbert Herring summarized Jackson's sentiments: "If it be consistent with their duty as chiefs to oppose removal, or to be passive on the subject, and to witness the consequent degradation and suffering of their people, they must take the responsibility and persist in their opposition" (*MA* 6:599–600). In the same fashion the American government blamed Hanoi for the death it rained on the South Vietnamese countryside. If the Communists did not resist the government relocation program, villagers would not be killed. See Chomsky, *American Power*, 131–32.

151. Quoted in Dunbar, *History of Travel* 2:575–76.

152. Cf. Foreman, *Indian Removal*, 56–69, 183–87, 258–63; McReynolds, *Seminoles*, 216–17, 238–42.

153. Lewis Cass, "Annual Report of the Secretary of War," 25 November 1832, *MA* 5:23.

154. Cass, "Annual Report of the Secretary of War," 1831, *MA* 4:714–15; Cass, "Removal of the Indians," 70.

155. Abel, *History of Events*, 327–31, 357–58; Mahon, *Second Seminole War*, 19–36; Foreman, *Indian Removal*, 342, 363.

156. Quoted in Starkey, *Cherokee Nation*, 283. Cass put it a little differently: "It is due to the character of the government and the feelings of the country, not less than to the moral and physical imbecility of this unhappy race, that a spirit of kindness and forbearance should mark the whole course of our intercommunication with them" (1831 report, *MA* 4:713).

157. Cf. Tocqueville, "Fortnight in the Wilds," 331, 339, and *Democracy in America* 1:364–69.

158. Mary McCarthy, "Report from Vietnam III: Intellectuals," *New York Review of Books*, 18 May 1967, p. 13.

159. Cass, "Removal of the Indians," 107, 120–21.

160. Foreman, *Indian Removal*, 312n.

161. Quoted in Dunbar, *History of Travel* 2:610.

162. "Second Annual Message," in Richardson, *Messages and Papers* 2:520–21.

163. Pp. 138–39, above.

164. American servicemen defending the Song My massacre against public outcry write, "Grow up Americans." "Why must Americans be so childish," they ask, so "politically immature?" (*San Francisco Chronicle*, 31 December 1969, p. 26).

CHAPTER VI. NATURE AS POLITICS AND
NATURE AS ROMANCE IN AMERICA

1. Richard Hofstadter, *The American Political Tradition* (New York, 1948); D. H. Lawrence, *Studies in Classic American Literature* (1923; republished, New York, 1964).

2. Daniel Bell, *The Cultural Contradictions of Capitalism* (New York, 1976), 80.

3. Richard Chase, *The American Novel and Its Tradition* (Garden City, N.Y., 1957), ix–xi, 1–22. For Fiedler the most important work is *Love and Death in the American Novel* (New York, 1960).

4. John Adams, *A Defense of the Constitutions of the Government of the United States of America*, excerpted in George A. Peek, *The Political Writings of John Adams* (Indianapolis, 1954), 117.

5. Alexander Hamilton, James Madison, John Jay, *The Federalist Papers*, no. 10; Thomas Paine, "Agrarian Justice," in Harry Hayden Clark, ed., *Thomas Paine, Representative Selections*, rev. ed. (New York, 1961), 336–53.

6. Quoted in Michael Lienesch, "The Concept of Time in American Political Thought, 1783–1800" (Ph.D. diss., University of California, Berkeley, 1977), 438.

7. Cf. Richard Slotkin, *Regeneration Through Violence* (Middletown, Conn., 1973); Henry Nash Smith, *Virgin Land* (New York, 1950). The quote is from Frederick Jackson Turner, "The Problem of the West," in *The Frontier in American History* (New York, 1965), 208. The essay was first published in 1896.

8. Quoted in Annie Heloise Abel, *The History of Events Resulting in Indian Consolidation West of the Mississippi*, American Historical Association Report of Proceedings (1906), 222.

9. Gabriel A. Almond and Sidney Verba, *The Civic Culture* (Princeton, 1963), 102. This was three times the percentage naming the economic system and six times the percentage naming anything else. Political institutions received majority praise in no other country sampled.

10. Bell is ambiguous about whether bourgeois, as opposed to postindustrial, society was characterized by this division. At one point he locates the beginnings of the division in the early nineteenth century. But when he addresses Marx's split between bourgeois and citizen and Van Wyck Brooks's between genteel culture and business life, he ignores the dialectical tensions created by these classic bourgeois splits and treats them as a coordinate part of a unified system. See Bell, *Cultural Contradictions*, xi–xii, 12–14, 20–21, 53–65, and below, n. 35.

11. The Smith and Slotkin references are in n. 7, above. For Miller, see the two collections of essays *Errand Into the Wilderness* (New York, 1964) and *Nature's Nation* (Cambridge, Mass., 1967).

12. Richard Hofstadter, "Turner and the Frontier Myth," *The American Scholar* 18 (Autumn 1949), reprinted in Ray Allen Billington, ed., *The Frontier Thesis* (New York, 1966), 100–106.

13. Bell, *Cultural Contradictions*, 19–20.

14. Cf. Richard Hofstadter, *The Age of Reform* (New York, 1955); Daniel Bell, ed., *The New American Right* (New York, 1955); and the discussion of these and other similar analyses in Michael Paul Rogin, *The Intellectuals and McCarthy: The Radical Specter* (Cambridge, Mass., 1967).

15. This poem, whose imagery the 1950s antiagrarians found significant, is quoted in Peter Viereck, *Unadjusted Man* (Boston, 1956), 193.

16. Among the many critiques of the New Left from this perspective, see Daniel Boorstin, "The New Barbarians," *Esquire*, October 1968, pp. 159–62, 260–62; cf. Quentin Anderson, *The Imperial Self* (New York, 1971), 201–40. For Daniel Bell's 1950s attack on antipolitical left radicalism, see his "The Background and Development of Marxian Socialism in the United States," in Donald Drew Egbert and Stow Persons, eds., *Socialism in American Life*, 2 vols. (Princeton, 1952), 1:213–405.

17. Anderson, *The Imperial Self*, blames the literary imagination for the antipolitical politics.

18. Paul H. Johnstone, "Old Ideals Versus New Ideas in Farm Life," in United States Department of Agriculture, *Farmers in a Changing World, Yearbook of Agriculture* (Washington, D.C., 1940), 116–31, 149–52, 165–66; see also his "Turnips and Romanticism," *Agricultural History* 12 (July 1938): 224–55.

19. Grant McConnell, *The Decline of Agrarian Democracy* (Berkeley and Los Angeles, 1953); Philip Selznick, *T.V.A. and the Grass Roots* (Berkeley and Los Angeles, 1949).

20. Grant McConnell, *Private Power and American Democracy* (New York, 1966), 91–101. The quote is on p. 93. See also Theodore Lowi, *The End of Liberalism* (New York, 1969).

21. McConnell, *Private Power*, 102–7. Cf. his "John Taylor and the Democratic Tradition," *Western Political Quarterly* 4 (March 1951): 17–31.

22. McConnell, *Private Power*; Lowi, *End of Liberalism*; Murray Edelman, *The Symbolic Uses of Politics* (Urbana, Ill., 1964).

23. Benjamin Franklin, "The Internal State of America," in *Writings*, Albert H. Smyth, ed., 10 vols. (New York, 1907), 10:116–17. I am indebted to Michael Lienesch for calling this essay to my attention.

24. Ibid., 122.

25. Ibid., 117, 121.

26. Benjamin Franklin, "A Comparison of the Conduct of the Ancient Jews and of the Anti-Federalists in the United States of America," *Writings* 9:698–703.

27. Lawrence, *Studies in Classic American Literature*, 9–21; Herman Melville, *Israel Potter* (1855; republished, New York, 1974), 58–79.

28. Franklin, "Internal State," 122.

29. The seminal essay is Miller, "Errand Into the Wilderness," in *Errand*, 1–15. See also Slotkin, *Regeneration*, 25–267.

30. Howard Mumford Jones, *O Strange New World* (New York, 1964), plate 3 and p. 28n; see also ibid., 1–70.

31. Franklin, "Internal State," 117, 120.

32. Karl Marx, "On the Jewish Question," in Loyd D. Easton and Kurt H.

Guddat, eds., *Writings of the Young Marx on Philosophy and Society* (Garden City, N.Y., 1967), 238–39.

33. Ibid., 222–26, 232.

34. Ibid., 227, 244.

35. Ibid., 225. For Bell's flattened-out reference to the bourgeois-citizen distinction, see above, n. 10.

36. Marx, "On the Jewish Question," 227.

37. Perry Miller, "The Location of American Religious Freedom," in *Nature's Nation*, 156.

38. See Michael Paul Rogin, *Fathers and Children: Andrew Jackson and the Subjugation of the American Indian* (New York, 1975), 7–9, 75–110.

39. Franklin, "Internal State," 122; Marx, "On the Jewish Question," 246.

40. Marx, "On the Jewish Question," 241, 248.

41. William Appleman Williams, *The Contours of American History* (Chicago, 1966), 145–46, 158–62.

42. Benjamin Franklin, "The Art of Procuring Pleasant Dreams," *Writings* 10:133–36.

43. Thomas Jefferson to James Madison, 20 December 1787, in Adrienne Koch and William Peden, eds., *The Life and Selected Writings of Thomas Jefferson* (New York, 1944), 440–41.

44. Quoted in Albert K. Weinberg, *Manifest Destiny* (Chicago, 1963), 117.

45. Quoted in Smith, *Virgin Land*, 297.

46. Franklin, "Internal State," 116, 121–22.

47. Quoted in Arthur K. Moore, *The Frontier Mind* (Lexington, Ky., 1957), 31.

48. Quoted in Jones, *O Strange New World*, 245–46.

49. Quoted in David Noble, *Historians Against History* (Minneapolis, 1965), 29.

50. See Eric Foner, *Free Soil, Free Labor, Free Men* (New York, 1970), 11–72; Leo Marx, *The Machine in the Garden* (New York, 1964).

51. Abraham Lincoln, "Annual Message to Congress," 1 December 1862, in *Selected Speeches, Messages, and Letters*, T. Harry Williams, ed. (New York, 1957), 198–200.

52. George W. Julian, speech on the Homestead Bill, 29 January 1851, in Louis H. Douglas, ed., *Agrarianism in American History* (Lexington, Mass., 1969), 47.

53. Ibid., 47; Hofstadter, "Turner and the Frontier Myth," 104–5. Cf. Smith, *Virgin Land*, 190–200.

54. For discussions of southern pastoralism, see William R. Taylor, *Cavalier and Yankee* (New York, 1961); Annette Kolodny, "'Stript, shrone, and made deformed': Images on the Southern Landscape," *South Atlantic Quarterly* 75 (Winter 1976): 62–68; Alexander Saxton, "Blackface Minstrelsy and Jacksonian Ideology," *American Quarterly* 27 (March 1975): 13–18. For the northern response, see Foner, *Free Soil*.

55. Hofstadter, *Age of Reform*, 130–36, 173–84, 213–18.

56. Woodrow Wilson, *The New Freedom* (1913; republished, Englewood Cliffs, N.J., 1961), 19–20, 26–27.

57. This argument is developed in Rogin, *Intellectuals and McCarthy*, 192–206; Samuel Haber, *Efficiency and Uplift* (Chicago, 1964); and David Noble, *The Paradox of Progressive Thought* (Minneapolis, 1958).

58. Theodore Roosevelt, "Opening Address by the President" to the Presidential Conference on Conservation, 13 May 1908, in Roderick B. Nash, ed., *The Call of the Wild (1902–1916)* (New York, 1970), 45.

59. Wilson, *New Freedom*, 163. Cf. Michael Rogin, "Max Weber and Woodrow Wilson: The Iron Cage in Germany and America," *Polity* 3 (Summer 1971): 562–75, and above, p. 99.

60. Roosevelt, "Opening Address," 39–40, 43–45; Samuel P. Hays, *Conservation and the Gospel of Efficiency* (Cambridge, Mass., 1959), 2, 265–72, passim.

61. Richard Pells, *Radical Visions and American Dreams* (New York, 1973), 96–100, 195–200, 214–18, 230, 337.

62. Franklin D. Roosevelt, "Inaugural Address," 4 March 1933, in *The Public Papers and Addresses of Franklin D. Roosevelt*, 13 vols. (New York, 1938–50), 2:14; Henry A. Wallace, *New Frontiers* (New York, 1934), 11–12, 46–47, 121–23, 127–28, 139, 145, 165, 199–200.

63. Lowi, *End of Liberalism*, 102–15.

64. Wallace, *New Frontiers*, 269–76, 282–83.

65. U.S. Congress, *The Congressional Globe* 8 (1839–40): Appendix, 71.

66. Mason L. Weems, *The Life of Washington* (1800 and 1808; republished, Cambridge, Mass., 1962), 37, 45, 48.

67. Ibid., 39, 40.

68. Cf. Slotkin, *Regeneration*, 16–24, 268–312; Rogin, *Fathers and Children*.

69. Marvin Meyers, *The Jacksonian Persuasion* (New York, 1960).

70. Cf. Rogin, *Fathers and Children*. The wilderness quote is from Jackson's letter to his wife Rachel, 20 April 1818, as quoted in Richard Drinnon, *Facing West: The Metaphysics of Indian-Hating and Empire-Building* (New York, 1980), 108.

71. Abraham Lincoln, "Speech in the House of Representatives," 27 July 1848, in Philip Van Doren Stern, ed., *The Life and Writings of Abraham Lincoln* (New York, 1940), 321.

72. Abraham Lincoln, "The Gettysburg Address" and "Second Inaugural Address," in Williams, *Selected Speeches*, 246–47, 282–83.

73. Woodrow Wilson, "The Ideals of America," *Atlantic Monthly*, December 1902, pp. 725–26, 728–34. Cf. Rogin, "Woodrow Wilson and Max Weber" and *Fathers and Children*.

74. Theodore Roosevelt, "The Strenuous Life," in Nash, *Call of the Wild*, 81–82.

75. Roosevelt's hunts played a central role in the 1970s movie *The Wind and the Lion*. Killing a grizzly, the president wants this animal to replace the eagle as America's totem. Roosevelt imitates the fighting position of the grizzly to show the taxidermist the shape the dead trophy of America should take. The movie connects Roosevelt's grizzly hunt to his hunt of a North Arab warrior bandit and women-and-children kidnapper. The movie Roosevelt identifies with

both his animal and his human prey against decadent European imperial powers and cautious, overcivilized Americans. This is the Roosevelt who, in the movie's celebratory romance, has the courage to seize Panama.

76. Woodrow Wilson, address at Pueblo, Colorado, 25 September 1919, in *The Messages and Papers of Woodrow Wilson*, 2 vols. (New York, 1924), 2:1130.

77. Cf. William Appleman Williams, "The Frontier Thesis and American Foreign Policy," *Pacific Historical Review* 24 (November 1955): 379–95, and *The Tragedy of American Diplomacy*, 2d ed. (New York, 1962).

78. Cf. Bruce Miroff, *Pragmatic Illusions: The Presidential Politics of John F. Kennedy* (New York, 1976), 18–19, 144–46; Slotkin, *Regeneration*, 562; Margaret Mead, *And Keep Your Powder Dry*, 2d ed. (London, 1967), 306–10. On the connections between Vietnam and Indian extermination, see Richard Drinnon, "Violence in the American Experience: Winning the West," *The Radical Teacher* (Chicago), 30 December 1969, pp. 36, 45–46; Richard Slotkin, "Dreams and Genocide: The American Myth of Regeneration Through Violence," *Journal of Popular Culture* 5 (Summer 1971): 38–59; and Michael Rogin, "Truth is Stranger than Science Fiction," *The Listener*, 7 July 1968, pp. 117–18, and Chapter 5, above.

79. Karl Marx, *The Eighteenth Brumaire of Louis Bonaparte, Selected Writings*, 2 vols. (Moscow, 1955), 1:247.

80. Davis Grubb, *The Night of the Hunter* (New York, 1953).

CHAPTER VII. "THE SWORD BECAME
A FLASHING VISION": D. W. GRIFFITH'S
THE BIRTH OF A NATION

1. James Agee, *Agee on Film* (Boston, 1958), 313; Arlene Croce, quoted in Martin Williams, *Griffith, First Artist of the Movies* (New York, 1980), 77; Roy E. Aitken, *The Birth of a Nation Story* (Middleburg, Va., 1965), 4.

2. James Hart, ed., *The Man Who Invented Hollywood: The Autobiography of D. W. Griffith* (Louisville, Ky., 1972), 28–29.

3. Herman G. Weinberg, quoted in Harry M. Geduld, ed., *Focus on D. W. Griffith* (Englewood Cliffs, N.J., 1971), 8.

4. Quotes are from Richard Schickel, *D. W. Griffith: An American Life* (New York, 1984), 299, 279. See also pp. 29, 213, 232–37. I have learned a lot from this detailed, sensitive biography, but Schickel minimizes and apologizes for Griffith's racism.

5. Cf. Raymond Allen Cook, *Fire from the Flint: The Amazing Career of Thomas Dixon* (Winston-Salem, N.C., 1968), 51–52, 72, 163–73; Edward D. C. Campbell, Jr., *The Celluloid South* (Knoxville, Tenn., 1981), 47; Seymour Stern, "Griffith: *The Birth of a Nation*, Part I," *Film Culture* 36 (Spring–Summer 1965): 34–36; Arthur S. Link, *Wilson: The New Freedom* (Princeton, 1956), 253; Thomas Cripps, *Slow Fade to Black* (New York, 1977), 62; Russell Merritt, "D. W. Griffith Directs the Great War: The Making of *Hearts of the World*," *Quarterly Review of Film Studies* 6 (Winter 1981), 47; John Hope

Franklin, "*Birth of a Nation*—Propaganda as History," *The Massachusetts Review* 20 (Autumn 1979): 417–33.

6. *New York American*, 28 February 1915, in Geduld, *Focus on D. W. Griffith*, 28.

7. Woodrow Wilson, *A History of the American People*, vol. 5, *Reunion and Nationalization* (New York, 1901), 19–20, 49–50.

8. Ibid., 49–50, 60.

9. Ibid., 62–64, 75–78.

10. Ibid., 212; see also Mary Odem, "Wilson and the Immigrants" (Unpublished seminar paper, University of California, Berkeley, 1984); George M. Frederickson, *White Supremacy* (New York, 1981), 188–91.

11. Maxwell Bloomfield, "*The Leopard's Spots*: A Study in Popular Racism," *American Quarterly* 16 (Fall 1964): 387–92; Cook, *Fire from the Flint*, 79–112; Woodrow Wilson, "The Ideals of America," *Atlantic Monthly*, December 1902, pp. 721–34; Thomas Dixon, *The Leopard's Spots: A Romance of the White Man's Burden* (1902; republished, Ridgewood, N.J., 1967), 334–35, 408, 439. See also Chapter 3, above.

Although critics blame "populism" for Dixon's and Griffith's racism, southern Populism poses the racial menace in *The Leopard's Spots*. Populism, as Dixon saw it, combined "the two great . . . questions that shadow the future of the American people, the conflict between Labour and Capital and the conflict between the African and the Anglo-Saxon race." Class relations could be humanized, Dixon believed, were it not for the threat of black power. But Populist demagoguery, by mobilizing the class resentments of blacks and poor whites, threatened racial amalgamation. Dixon's hero achieved political power and romantic success by uniting the white South against Populism. Walter Hines Page, the anti-Populist apostle of the new, industrial South, got Doubleday to publish *The Leopard's Spots*. Secretary of State John Hay read proof for and endorsed the second novel in Dixon's trilogy, *The Clansman*. Hay had been Lincoln's private secretary as a young man; he wrote the antilabor novel *The Breadwinners* and was the architect of America's imperial vision. Dixon's attack on Populism and the endorsement of his vision by Page and Hay further illuminate the intertwined racial, class, and imperial histories that lie behind *Birth*. Cf. Schickel, *Griffith*, 29, 76–78; Dixon, *Leopard's Spots*, 244–45; Fred A. Silva, *Focus on The Birth of a Nation* (Englewood Cliffs, N.J., 1971), 94.

12. Wilson, "Ideals of America," 721–34.

13. Cripps, *Slow Fade to Black*, 26–27; Schickel, *Griffith*, 224; Cook, *Fire from the Flint*, 171–72; Merritt, "Griffith Directs the Great War," 47.

14. Cook, *Fire from the Flint*, 71; F. Garvin Davenport, Jr., "Thomas Dixon's Mythology of Southern History," *Journal of Southern History* 36 (August 1970): 361.

15. Odem, "Wilson and the Immigrants," 1–16; Rogin, "The King's Two Bodies," above, pp. 94–99.

16. Link, *Wilson*, 467; Lawrence J. Friedman, *The White Savage* (Englewood Cliffs, N.J., 1970), 157–63.

17. Lary May, *Screening out the Past: The Birth of Mass Culture and the*

Motion Picture Industry (New York, 1965), 19–67; Russell Merritt, "Nickelodeon Theaters, 1905–1914: Building an Audience for the Movies," in Tino Balio, ed., *The American Film Industry* (Madison, Wis., 1976), 57–72; Jane Addams, *The Spirit of Youth and the City Streets* (New York, 1909), 75–103.

18. Merritt, "Griffith Directs the Great War," 63–65, 75–79; May, *Screening out the Past*, 36–37; Robert Sklar, *Movie-Made America* (New York, 1975), 105–6.

19. May, *Screening out the Past*, 52–53, 59; Addams, *Spirit of Youth*, 6, 75–100.

20. May, *Screening out the Past*, 71. The interpretation in these paragraphs draws heavily from May.

21. Sergei Eisenstein, *Film Form* (New York, 1949), 197.

22. I rely on Schickel for Griffith's biography unless another source is indicated.

23. Robert Welsh, "David Griffith Speaks," *New York Dramatic Mirror*, 14 January 1914, pp. 48–49, 54; Tom Gunning, "Weaving a Narrative: Style and Economic Background in Griffith's Biograph Films," *Quarterly Review of Film Studies* 6 (Winter 1981): 12–25.

24. Henry Adams, *The Education of Henry Adams* (Boston, 1973), 379–90, 428–35; Geduld, *Focus on D. W. Griffith*, 1; Stephen Kern, *The Culture of Time and Space, 1880–1920* (Cambridge, Mass., 1983), 11. For general discussions of Griffith's cinematic contributions, cf. Williams, *Griffith*, 34–44; Louis Jacobs, *The Rise of American Film* (New York, 1967), 98–110; Sklar, *Movie-Made America*, 48–54.

25. Jacobs, *Rise of American Film*, 98; George C. Pratt, "In the Nick of Time: D. W. Griffith and the 'Last-Minute Rescue,'" in Marshall Deutelbaum, ed., *"Image" on the Art and Evolution of the Film* (New York, 1979), 74–75; Kern, *Culture of Time and Space*, 29–30, 38–39; Welsh, "Griffith Speaks," 49, 54.

26. Jacobs, *Rise of American Film*, 14, 118–19; Welsh, "Griffith Speaks," 49, 54; May, *Screening out the Past*, 73; Morton White, *Social Thought in America: The Revolt Against Formalism* (Boston, 1957).

27. Gunning, "Weaving a Narrative," 12–25.

28. The interpretation of the patriarchal crisis and the male fear of women in this and the following paragraph derives from Nina Auerbach, *Woman and the Demon* (Cambridge, Mass., 1982); Rosalind Coward, *Patriarchal Precedents* (London, 1983); Carl Schorske, *Fin-de-Siècle Vienna, Politics and Culture* (New York, 1980), 208–80; Fred Weinstein and Gerald Platt, *The Wish to Be Free* (Berkeley and Los Angeles, 1969); Arthur Mitzman, *The Iron Cage* (New York, 1970); Michael Rogin, "Max Weber and Woodrow Wilson: The Iron Cage in Germany and America," *Polity* 3 (Summer 1971): 557–75, and "On the Jewish Question," *democracy*, Spring 1983, pp. 101–14; Martin Green, *The von Richtofen Sisters* (New York, 1974); David M. Kennedy, *Birth Control in America* (New Haven, 1970), 42–52; Adams, *Education of Henry Adams*, 379–90, 427–35, 441–47, 459–61; Debora L. Silverman, "Nature, Nobility, and Neurology: The Ideological Origins of 'Art Nouveau' in France, 1889–1900" (Ph.D. diss., Princeton University, 1983); Eugene W. Holland,

"Politics and Psychoanalysis," *Salmagundi*, no. 66 (Winter–Spring 1985): 155–70.

29. Hart, *Man Who Invented Hollywood*, 26.

30. On binary oppositions and their breakdown, filmic and social, in a Griffith one-reeler, see Rick Altman, "*The Lonely Villa* and Griffith's Paradigmatic Style," *Quarterly Review of Film Studies* 6 (Spring 1981): 123–34.

31. In "The Taboo of Virginity" Freud writes, "Beheading is well-known to us as a symbolic substitute for castration; Judith is accordingly the woman who castrates the man who has deflowered her." Judith links beheading to castration for Freud. But he only makes that connection by doubly disempowering the woman. Insisting that Judith is "using a patriotic motive to mask a sexual one," Freud sunders her act from the political significance of beheading a king. Moreover, by analyzing a German play in which Judith is a virgin and suggesting that the playwright had "divined the primordial theme that had been lost in the tendentious biblical story," Freud turns a widow's power into a virgin's revenge. There is nothing virginal about Griffith's Judith. See Sigmund Freud, "The Taboo of Virginity," in James Strachey, ed., *The Standard Edition of the Complete Psychological Works of Sigmund Freud*, 24 vols. (London, 1955), 11:205–8. I am indebted for this reference to N. Sine, "Cases of Mistaken Identity: Salome and Judith at the Turn of the Century" (Unpublished paper, 1985).

32. Cf. Sigmund Freud, "Fetishism," in *Standard Edition*, 21:152–57; Laura Mulvey, "Visual Pleasure and Narrative Cinema," in Karyn Kay and Gerald Peary, eds., *Women and the Cinema* (New York, 1977), 412–28; E. Ann Kaplan, *Women and Film* (New York, 1983), 31–52, 202; Stephen Heath, "Difference," *Screen* 19 (Autumn, 1978): 51–112.

33. Eisenstein, *Film Form*, 205, 223, 227–30, 234–37, 243–45, 253.

34. Cf. Sklar, *Movie-Made America*, 56.

35. Cf. Russell L. Merritt, "Mr. Griffith, *The Painted Lady*, and the Distractive Frame," in Deutelbaum, "*Image*," 47; Seymour Stern, "Griffith and Poe," *Films in Review* 2 (November 1951): 23.

36. Griffith had used puppies to signify female independence in *The Battle of Elderbush Gulch* (1913). The puppies figure in a mise-en-scène whose plot, actresses (Mae Marsh and Lillian Gish), and family name (the Camerons in both movies) presage *The Birth of a Nation*. Marsh's puppies run off at the beginning of the action, and Marsh recklessly follows them. In *Birth*'s parallel scene, Marsh kills herself to escape a black rapist; in *Elderbush Gulch* Indians kill a puppy instead and are killed in turn, precipitating an Indian attack. Gish's baby crawls into danger during the attack; by rescuing it Marsh atones for her earlier transgression. It is as if, in the repetition and undoing of the earlier scene, Griffith was illustrating Freud's belief that the mature woman replaces her wish for an active sexual organ with a baby.

37. Vachel Lindsay, *The Art of the Moving Picture*, rev. ed. (New York, 1970), 152–53.

38. Edward Wagenknecht, *The Movies in the Age of Innocence* (Norman, Okla., 1962), 98–99.

39. *New York Times*, 4 March 1915, p. 4; Stern, "*Birth of a Nation*, Part I," 123; Thomas Dixon, Jr., *The Clansman* (Lexington, Ky., 1970), 342; James

Shelley Hamilton, "Putting a New Move in the Movies," *Everybody's Magazine* 32 (June 1915): 680.

40. *Atlanta Constitution*, 7 December 1915, in Silva, *Focus on The Birth of a Nation*, 35.

41. Wagenknecht, *Movies in the Age of Innocence*, 98–99.

42. Lillian Gish, *The Movies, Mr. Griffith, and Me* (Englewood Cliffs, N.J., 1969), 133; Jacqueline Dowd Hall, "The Mind That Burns in Each Body: Women, Rape, and Racial Violence," in Ann Snitow et al., eds., *Powers of Desire* (New York, 1983), 331–33, 337; Milton Mackaye, "*The Birth of a Nation*," *Scribner's*, November 1937, 45–46; Schickel, *Griffith*, 233–34, 578; William Faulkner, *Light in August* (New York, 1968), 147. Cf. Frederickson, *White Supremacy*, 104.

43. Schickel, *Griffith*, 217–19.

44. Ibid., 220; Karl Brown, *Adventures with D. W. Griffith* (New York, 1973), 57.

45. Thomas Jefferson, *Notes on Virginia*, in Adrienne Koch and William Peden, eds., *The Life and Selected Writings of Thomas Jefferson* (New York, 1944), 256–62; Winthrop D. Jordan, *White over Black* (Baltimore, 1969), 429–81.

46. Donald Bogle, *Toms, Coons, Mulattoes, Mammies, and Bucks* (New York, 1973), 16.

47. Fawn M. Brodie, *Thaddeus Stevens, Scourge of the South* (New York, 1959), 86–91.

48. Ibid., 369–70, 386; Mrs. D. W. Griffith (Linda Arvidson), *When the Movies Were Young* (New York, 1925), 47; Cook, *Fire from the Flint*, 78; Dixon, *Clansman*, 39, 132, 143. Kim Barton has influenced my understanding of Stoneman.

49. Scene numbers are from Theodore Huff, *The Birth of a Nation Shot Analysis* (New York, 1961).

50. Gish, *Movies, Mr. Griffith, and Me*, 140.

51. Richard Slotkin, *The Crater* (New York, 1980); Agee, *Agee on Film*, 313.

52. Schickel, *Griffith*, 227.

53. The arms belong, on close inspection, to little sister, but they are easily mistaken for the mother's. Gilbert Seldes, for example, wrote, "From behind the door, as the soldier enters, comes the arm of his mother drawing in her son" (quoted in Richard Griffith et al., *The Movies*, rev. ed. [New York, 1981], 32). Shot lengths are in Huff, *Shot Analysis*.

54. Cf. Arlene Croce, quoted in Williams, *Griffith*, 74; and Jay Leyda, "The Art and Death of D. W. Griffith," in Geduld, *Focus on D. W. Griffith*, 161–67. Leyda offers, nonetheless, the best analysis I have seen of the differences between the two halves of the film.

55. Dixon, *Clansman*, 127, 149, 163–64, 333.

56. Dixon, *Leopard's Spots*, 468, 447.

57. Ibid., 418, 420.

58. Hart, *Man Who Invented Hollywood*, 26–28; Schickel, *Griffith*, 30–31; Wilson, *Reunion*, 60; Silva, *Focus on The Birth of a Nation*, 35; Dixon,

Clansman, 39. Klansmen liked to be called, and to convince blacks they were, the "ghosts of the Confederate dead." See Gladys-Marie Fry, *Night Riders in Black Folk History* (Knoxville, Tenn., 1975), 112, 136. Paul Thomas first showed me that the Klan sheets were shrouds.

59. D. W. Griffith, "My Early Life," *Photoplay* (1916), in Geduld, *Focus on D. W. Griffith*, 13–14, 39–40; Schickel, *Griffith*, 15, 555.

60. Dixon, *Leopard's Spots*, 9–13.

61. Geduld, *Focus on D. W. Griffith*, 13–14.

62. Williams, *Griffith*, 4; May, *Screening out the Past*, 68.

63. Schickel, *Griffith*, 15; Hart, *Man Who Invented Hollywood*, 73; Robert M. Henderson, *D. W. Griffith: His Life and Work* (Oxford, 1972), 54. In "Screen Memories," Freud wrote, "Our childhood memories show us our earliest memories not as they were but as they appeared at the later periods when the memories were revived. . . . And a number of motives, which had no concern with historical accuracy, had their part in thus forming them" (*Standard Edition* 3:322).

64. May, *Screening out the Past*, 80–86; Cripps, *Slow Fade to Black*, 56–62; Bogle, *Toms, Coons, Mulattoes*, 7; Francis Hackett, "Brotherly Love," *New Republic*, 20 March 1915, p. 185.

65. Stern, "*Birth of a Nation*, Part I," 170; Silva, *Focus on The Birth of a Nation*, 102; Schickel, *Griffith*, 277; Russell Merritt, "Dixon, Griffith, and the Southern Legend," *Cinema Journal* 3 (1972): 28.

66. Stern, "*Birth of a Nation*, Part I," 66, 123, 164.

67. Ibid., 66; "Films and Births and Censorships," *The Survey*, 3 April 1915, p. 4.

68. Friedman, *White Savage*, 57–68; Thomas Nelson Page, "The Lynching of Negroes—Its Cause and Prevention," *North American Review* 178 (1904): 36–39, 45; Hall, "Mind That Burns," 329; Stern, "*Birth of a Nation*, Part I," 123.

69. Stern, "*Birth of a Nation*, Part I," 123–24.

70. Griffith, in Geduld, *Focus on D. W. Griffith*, 15.

71. Dixon, in Silva, *Focus on The Birth of a Nation*, 79, 94–95; NAACP, Boston Branch, "Fighting a Vicious Film," in Geduld, *Focus on D. W. Griffith*, 94. Ann Banfield, in her interpretation of Artemesia Gentileschi's painting of Judith beheading Holofernes, first suggested to me the connection between castration and birth.

72. Dixon, *Leopard's Spots*, 336.

73. Hall, "Mind That Burns," 347n., 337.

74. Cf. Neil Hertz, "Medusa's Head: Male Hysteria Under Political Pressure," and Catherine Gallagher, "More About 'Medusa's Head,'" *Representations* 4 (Fall 1983): 27–57; Faulkner, *Light in August*, 437–40.

75. Dixon, *Clansman*, 20. *Light in August* is Faulkner's text for the castration, *Absalom, Absalom* for the brother-sister incest, and *Go Down Moses* for the displacement of mother-son by father-daughter incest.

76. This scene inverts Ahab's black mass on the *Pequod*. See Herman Melville, *Moby Dick* (New York, 1956), 140–41.

77. Friedman, *White Savage*, 155; Henry W. Bragdon, *Woodrow Wilson: The Academic Years* (Cambridge, Mass., 1967), 231.

78. René Girard, *Violence and the Sacred* (Baltimore, 1978), 4–22, 48–49, 56–64, 79–83, 203, 236, 307.

79. Stern, "*Birth of a Nation*, Part I," 3–4; Gish, *Movies, Mr. Griffith, and Me*, 139; Kevin Brownlow, *The Parade's Gone By* (New York, 1968), 54.

80. NAACP, Boston Branch, "Fighting a Vicious Film" 1 (Boston, 1915), 19.

81. Stern, "*Birth of a Nation*, Part I," 5, 14; Griffith, in Geduld, *Focus on D. W. Griffith*, 41.

82. Robert Toll, *Blacking up: The Minstrel Show in Nineteenth-Century America* (New York, 1974), 3–57, 202; Mackaye, "*The Birth of a Nation*," 45–46.

83. Mackaye, "*The Birth of a Nation*," 45–46.

84. D. W. Griffith, *The Rise and Fall of Free Speech in America* (Los Angeles, 1916), 1, 5.

85. Wagenknecht, *Movies in the Age of Innocence*, 78–79. The Sambo mask put on by blacks kept black feelings hidden from whites. Both black-face minstrelsy and Klan robes, as Gladys-Marie Fry pointed out, borrow the mask to use against its originators. See Fry, *Night Riders*, 6. For seeing the Klan as men in drag, I am indebted to Uli Knopfelmacher.

86. Dixon, *Leopard's Spots*, 152, 161, 244.

87. Hart, *Man Who Invented Hollywood*, 33.

88. Schickel, *Griffith*, 483; Bogle, *Toms, Coons, Mulattoes*, 26; May, *Screening out the Past*, 218. On dependence and autonomy see Hanna Fenichel Pitkin, *Fortune Is a Woman: Gender and Politics in the Thought of Niccolo Machiavelli* (Berkeley and Los Angeles, 1984).

89. Williams, *Griffith*, 62; May, *Screening out the Past*, 61.

90. D. W. Griffith, "Five-Dollar 'Movies' Prophesied," *The Editor*, 24 April 1915, in Geduld, *Focus on D. W. Griffith*, 25.

91. Brownlow, *Parade's Gone*, 50–53; Schickel, *Griffith*, 294; Lindsay, *Art of the Moving Picture*, 74.

92. Schickel, *Griffith*, 294; *New York Sun*, 4 March 1915, in Geduld, *Focus on D. W. Griffith*, 86. Cf. Catherine Gallagher, "The Politics of Culture and the Debate over Representation," *Representations* 5 (Winter 1984): 115–47.

93. May, *Screening out the Past*, 60.

94. Schickel, *Griffith*, 290; Stern, "*Birth of a Nation*, Part I," 103–18.

95. *New York American*, 28 February 1915, in Geduld, *Focus on D. W. Griffith*, 28–29.

96. D. W. Griffith, "The Future of the Two-Dollar Movie," in Silva, *Focus on The Birth of a Nation*, 100; Schickel, *Griffith*, 301; Brownlow, *Parade's Gone*, 628–29; May, *Screening out the Past*, 73.

97. Brown, *Adventures with Griffith*, 177–78.

98. Cf. above, pp. 96–97, and Michael O'Malley, "With a Thousand Eyes: Movies and the American Public, 1908–1918" (Unpublished seminar paper, Berkeley, Cal., 1985), 20. O'Malley quote is from George Creel, *How We Advertised America* (New York, 1920), xv, 5.

99. Davenport, "Dixon's Mythology," 341; Cook, *Fire from the Flint*, 184–85; May, *Screening out the Past*, 60; Merritt, "Griffith Directs the Great War," 47–57.

100. Schickel, *Griffith*, 353; May, *Screening out the Past*, 92.

101. Schickel, *Griffith*, 353–54; Merritt, "Griffith Directs the Great War," 51, 58–59.

102. Schickel, *Griffith*, 354–55; Henry C. Carr, "Griffith, Maker of Battle Scenes, Sees Real War," *Photoplay* 13 (March 1918): 23; "War, Shorn of Romance, Is Sounding Its Own Knell," *Current Opinion* 64 (April 1918): 258. (I am indebted to Michael O'Malley for this reference.)

103. Merritt, "Griffith Directs the Great War," 57.

104. G. Charles Niemeyer, "David Wark Griffith: In Retrospect, 1965," in Geduld, *Focus on D. W. Griffith*, 129; Stern, "*Birth of a Nation*, Part I," 67, 79–80; Link, *Wilson*, 246–47; Schickel, *Griffith*, 400–403.

105. Bloomfield, *The Leopard's Spots*, 395–96; Cook, *Fire from the Flint*, 196, 216–23.

106. May, *Screening out the Past*, 60–61.

107. Schickel, *Griffith*, 416–19, 560–64.

108. Silva, *Focus on The Birth of a Nation*, 9.

109. Henderson, *Griffith*, 280–84.

110. Ezra Goodman, *The Fifty-Year Decline and Fall of Hollywood* (New York, 1961), 4–5.

CHAPTER VIII. *KISS ME DEADLY*: COMMUNISM, MOTHERHOOD, AND COLD WAR MOVIES

1. Cf. chapters 2 and 7, above.

2. Cf. above, pp. 63–80.

3. Robert Justin Goldstein, *Political Repression in Modern America* (Cambridge, Mass., 1978), 100, 158.

4. Ibid., 328–29.

5. Cf. above, pp. 70–74.

6. On domestic ideology, cf. Barbara Welter, "The Cult of True Womanhood: 1820–1860," *American Quarterly* 18 (Summer 1966): 151–74; Ann Douglas, *The Feminization of American Culture* (New York, 1977); Jay Fliegelman, *Prodigals and Pilgrims: The American Revolution Against Patriarchal Authority* (New York, 1982); Kathryn Kish Sklar, *Catharine Beecher: A Study in American Domesticity* (New Haven, 1973); Michael Paul Rogin, *Fathers and Children: Andrew Jackson and the Subjugation of the American Indian* (New York, 1975), 63–72, and *Subversive Genealogy: The Politics and Art of Herman Melville* (New York, 1983), 27–30, 162–65, 187–92; and Catherine Gallagher, *The Industrial Reformation of English Fiction, 1832–1867: Social Discourse and Narrative Form* (Chicago, 1985), 113–86. Catherine Gallagher has deeply influenced my understanding of domestic ideology and its relation to cold war movies, here and throughout the essay.

7. On the relationship between female power in male-dominated societies and images of female pollution, see Mary Douglas, *Purity and Danger* (New York, 1966), 140–53.

8. On 1950s domestic ideology, see Betty Friedan, *The Feminine Mystique* (New York, 1963), and Sara Evans, *Personal Politics* (New York, 1979), 3–23.

See also Molly Haskell, *From Reverence to Rape: The Treatment of Women in the Movies* (New York, 1974).

9. Philip Wylie, *Generation of Vipers*, 2d ed. (New York, 1955), xii, 51–53, 191–216.

10. Philip Wylie, *Finnley Wren* (New York, 1934); Truman Frederick Keefer, *Philip Wylie* (Boston, 1977), 72, 85.

11. Wylie, *Generation of Vipers*, 194n; Keefer, *Philip Wylie*, 73, 78–79, 122, 127.

12. Keefer, *Philip Wylie*, 55, 77–78, 85, 95, 108–9; Wylie, *Generation of Vipers*, 196n, 216–17n, 318–20n. I am grateful to Todd Gitlin for calling my attention to Wylie's anti-Communism.

13. Keefer, *Philip Wylie*, 109, 125.

14. Ibid., 62–63, 125; Philip Wylie, *Tomorrow* (New York, 1954).

15. Richard J. Barnet, *Roots of War* (New York, 1972), 17; American Heritage, *History of Flight* (New York, 1952), 191–92, cited in Julie H. Wosk, "The Airplane in Anti-War Poetry and Art" (Unpublished paper, 1983).

16. Wylie, *Tomorrow*, 30, 50–59, 141, 161–64, 268–69, 296–97, 329–30, 359–60.

17. Ibid., 230–35, 350–53, 369, 372. In *Triumph* (New York, 1963) Wylie pursued the fantasy of a utopia constructed from atomic disaster.

18. Keefer, *Philip Wylie*, 85.

19. Ibid., 121–22; Philip Wylie, *The Disappearance* (New York, 1951).

20. Keefer, *Philip Wylie*, 125.

21. Victor S. Navasky, *Naming Names* (New York, 1980), 167–68; Nora Sayre, *Running Time: Films of the Cold War* (New York, 1982), 57–62. Both books have been indispensable for this project.

22. Goldstein, *Political Repression*, 344, 347; Navasky, *Naming Names*, 12.

23. Navasky, *Naming Names*, 12; Sayre, *Running Time*, 86–91.

24. Navasky, *Naming Names*, 225–26; University Art Museum, *Calendar*, October 1982, p. 8; Garry Wills, "Introduction," in Lillian Hellman, *Scoundrel Time* (New York, 1976), 4–6.

25. University Art Museum, *Calendar*, October 1982, p. 5.

26. Sayre, *Running Time*, 91.

27. Ralph de Toledano, *J. Edgar Hoover* (New Rochelle, N.Y., 1973), 260. In *Retreat Hell!* (1951) an overprotective mom tries to stop her son from fighting Communism in Korea. In *Strategic Air Command* (1955) the contest is between a wife at home and the all-male military hierarchy (with its eroticized B-47s and "the family of nuclear weapons they carry"). On these films, see Peter Biskind, *Seeing Is Believing* (New York, 1983), 313, 64–69. Biskind's brilliant political interpretation of 1950s film as a whole stresses ideological differences more than I do, but his book complements at numerous places the analysis of cold war cinema offered here.

28. Wylie, *Generation of Vipers*, 201.

29. Cf. above, pp. 3–4.

30. That is my surmise, based on Navasky, *Naming Names*, 100–101, 129–130, 151, 280.

31. Ibid., 232–38.

32. Cf. Murray Kempton, "Dishonorably Discharged," *The New York Review of Books*, 27 October 1983, p. 42.

33. Robert Warshow, *The Immediate Experience* (New York, 1975), 163–71; Gallagher, *Industrial Reformation*, chapters 5–7.

34. Michel Foucault, *The History of Sexuality* (New York, 1980); Christopher Lasch, *Haven in a Heartless World* (New York, 1977); Jacques Donzelot, *The Policing of Families* (New York, 1979).

35. Cf. Melanie Klein, *Contributions to Psychoanalysis* (London, 1948); Dorothy Dinnerstein, *The Mermaid and the Minotaur* (New York, 1977).

36. Sayre, *Running Time*, 91; University Art Museum, *Calendar*, November 1982, p. 8.

37. Navasky, *Naming Names*, 16, 210, 280; Sayre, *Running Time*, 151–66.

38. Cf. above, chapter 1.

39. Navasky, *Naming Names*, 79.

40. Ibid., 15; Sayre, *Running Time*, 99–149; Daniel Bell, ed., *The New American Right* (New York, 1954); Michael Paul Rogin, *The Intellectuals and McCarthy: The Radical Specter* (Cambridge, Mass., 1967), 1–7, 216–60; and see above, chapter 1.

41. Goldstein, *Political Repression*, 362, 377; University Art Museum, *Calendar*, October 1982, p. 9.

42. On the contrast between the classic monster movie and the 1950s creature feature, see Andrew Griffin, "Sympathy for the Werewolf," in Charles Muscatine and Marlene Griffith, eds., *The Borzoi College Reader*, 4th ed. (New York, 1980), 508–12.
A complementary transition is visible in the contrast between the two 3-D monster movies of the 1950s, *Creature from the Black Lagoon* (1954) and *It Came from Outer Space* (1953). *Creature* is in the classic tradition; the monster is supposed to be threatening; like the bad explorer who tracks him, he attacks the female lead. Until he is provoked by that explorer, however, the monster wants only to be left alone, and he is finally allowed by the good explorer to return to the sea to die. *It Came from Outer Space*, by contrast, intends to create sympathy for the aliens; they only need time to repair their spaceship and leave an earth that is not yet ready for them. But since the aliens take over human bodies (foreshadowing *Body Snatchers*) and since their symbol is an enormous (surveilling) eye, the audience rightly shares the townspeople's terror. The creature from the lagoon emerges from primitive and fecund nature; that presocial past is more sympathetic in American 1950s iconography, whatever the filmmakers thought they were doing, than the blankness of the desert in the other film and the outer space future to which it points. On the films' intentions, see Biskind, *Seeing is Believing* 107–8, 147–51.

43. University Art Museum, *Calendar*, November 1982, p. 9; Ron Rosen, "The House that Levitt Built," *Esquire*, December 1983, p. 380. For interpretation of *Body Snatchers* as a right-wing film, see Biskind, *Seeing is Believing*, 137–44.

44. Quoted in Lasch, *Haven*, 13.

45. Sayre, *Running Time*, 201.
46. Warshow, *The Immediate Experience*, 33–48, 127–203; Manny Farber, *Negative Space* (New York, 1971), 32–87; Pauline Kael, *I Lost It at the Movies* (New York, 1965), 3–94.
47. Walter Benjamin, "The Work of Art in the Age of Mechanical Reproduction," in *Illuminations*, Hannah Arendt, ed. (New York, 1968), 242.
48. Farber, *Negative Space*, 129.

CHAPTER IX. AMERICAN POLITICAL
DEMONOLOGY: A RETROSPECTIVE

1. The realist approach characterized progressive historiography. Cf. Charles Beard, *An Economic Interpretation of the Constitution of the United States* (New York, 1913); Arthur Schlesinger, *The Colonial Merchants and the American Revolution, 1763–1776* (New York, 1918); Merrill Jensen, *The Articles of Confederation* (Madison, Wis., 1940); Leo Huberman, *The Labor Spy Racket* (New York, 1937). More recent examples include Alan Wolfe, *The Seamy Side of Democracy* (New York, 1978); Robert Justin Goldstein, *Political Repression in Modern America* (Cambridge, Mass., 1978); David Wise, *The American Police State* (New York, 1976); Frank J. Donner, *The Age of Surveillance* (New York, 1980).

For the symbolist approach, cf. Richard Hofstadter, *The Paranoid Style in American Politics* (New York, 1965); David Brion Davis, ed., *The Fear of Conspiracy* (Ithaca, N.Y., 1971); Seymour Martin Lipset and Earl Raab, *The Politics of Unreason: Right-Wing Extremism in America, 1790–1970* (New York, 1971). Lipset and Raab attribute extremism to the dispossessed on pp. 29–30, 34–35, 43, 62–64, 100. For symbolist analyses of particular historical movements, see on McCarthyism, Daniel Bell, ed., *The New American Right* (New York, 1955), and Edward Shils, *The Torment of Secrecy* (Glencoe, Ill., 1956); on Populism, Richard Hofstadter, *The Age of Reform* (New York, 1955); on the abolitionists, Stanley Elkins, *Slavery* (Chicago, 1959), and David Donald, *Lincoln Reconsidered* (New York, 1961), 19–36; on the American Revolution, Bernard Bailyn, *The Ideological Origins of the American Revolution* (New York, 1967); on antebellum nativism, David Brion Davis, "Some Themes of Countersubversion: An Analysis of Anti-Masonic, Anti-Catholic, and Anti-Mormon Literature," *Mississippi Valley Historical Review* 47 (September 1960): 205–24, and "Some Ideological Functions of Prejudice in Ante-Bellum America," *American Quarterly* 15 (Summer 1963): 115–25.

The symbolists have also been called pluralists, a label that identifies the social vision of these scholars; symbolism calls attention to their concern with the disjunction between certain belief systems and the everyday world. It should be noted, however, that although pluralism is a name some of these writers have used about themselves, symbolism is not. In using that term, moreover, I do not mean to identify this group with earlier symbolist movements in the arts; there are certain similarities, but the uses of symbolism and the value placed upon it are very different. On the pluralists, see Michael Paul Rogin, *The Intellectuals and McCarthy* (Cambridge, Mass., 1967).

2. Cf. Peter Odegard, *Pressure Politics* (New York, 1928), and Joseph Gusfield, *Symbolic Crusade* (Urbana, Ill., 1963).

3. Rogin, *Intellectuals and McCarthy.*

4. American exceptionalism is acknowledged as a source of consensus theory in Seymour Martin Lipset, *Political Man* (New York, 1960), xxv–xxvi, 346, and Daniel Bell, *The Winding Passage* (Cambridge, Mass., 1980), 245–71. Consensus interpretations include, in addition to the above, Louis Hartz, *The Liberal Tradition in America* (New York, 1955); David M. Potter, *People of Plenty* (Chicago, 1954); Daniel Boorstin, *The Genius of American Politics* (Chicago, 1953); Richard Hofstadter, *The American Political Tradition* (New York, 1948).

5. On the status-class distinction, cf. Seymour Martin Lipset, "The Sources of the Radical Right," and Richard Hofstadter, "The Pseudo-Conservative Revolt," in Bell, *New American Right*, 168, 43–45.

6. Cf. Daniel Bell, "The Background and Development of Marxian Socialism in the United States," in Daniel Drew Egbert and Stow Persons, eds., *Socialism in American Life*, 2 vols. (Princeton, 1952), 1:213–405; Hofstadter, *American Political Tradition*, "Pseudo-Conservative Revolt," "Pseudo-Conservatism Revisited, A Postscript (1962)" in Daniel Bell, ed., *The Radical Right* (Garden City, N.Y., 1963), *Age of Reform*, and *Anti-Intellectualism in American Life* (New York, 1963). Comparison of the chapters on Roosevelt and the New Deal in *The American Political Tradition* and *The Age of Reform* is particularly instructive. Cf. also the discussion in Rogin, *Intellectuals and McCarthy*, 9–31.

7. Sacvan Bercovitch, *The Puritan Origins of the American Self* (New Haven, 1975); Mitchell Breitwieser, *Cotton Mather and Benjamin Franklin* (New York, 1984).

8. A disproportionate number of those who wrote in or influenced the paranoid style of discourse were the children of Jewish immigrants, had been Socialists, Communists, or Trotskyists in their youth, and had in the 1950s chosen America against Russia in the cold war—for example, Daniel Bell, Seymour Martin Lipset, Richard Hofstadter, Leslie Fiedler, Irving Kristol, Philip Selznick, Daniel Boorstin, Louis Hartz, and Sidney Hook. Bernard Bailyn, Stanley Elkins, and Edward Shils are also Jewish, but they did not, so far as I know, have radical pasts. Relevant work of these figures not previously cited includes Leslie Fiedler, "McCarthy," *Encounter* 3 (August 1954): 10–21, and *An End to Innocence* (Boston, 1955); Philip Selznick, *The Organizational Weapon* (1952; republished, Glencoe, Ill., 1960); Sidney Hook, *Heresy, Yes—Conspiracy, No!* (New York, 1953). As the son of a Jewish, Socialist trade unionist, I come from the next generation.

9. Cf. Immanuel Wallerstein, *The Modern World System* (New York, 1974); Francis Jennings, *The Invasion of America* (Chapel Hill, N.C., 1975); Stephen J. Greenblatt, "Learning to Curse" and the other essays, in Fredi Chiappelli, ed., *First Images of America*, 2 vols. (Berkeley and Los Angeles, 1976).

Also compare Hartz, *Liberal Tradition*, with Louis Hartz, *The Founding of New Societies* (New York, 1964), which moves beyond *Liberal Tradition* both in its comparisons among European "fragment" settler societies and in its treatment of race. Hartz, it should be said, is in a class by himself among consensus historians; whatever his blindnesses, he offers the most brilliant and enduring perspective on American politics to come out of the 1950s.

10. Cf. Lipset and Raab, *The Politics of Unreason*, 62–65, 83–87, 93–99, 116–31, 209–47. The authors do deal with the Red scare of 1919–20 (pp. 132–34), in the context of antiforeign but not anti-working-class agitation. And they finally recognize racial conflict, in their extensive analysis of support for George Wallace. But by treating the Wallace "backlash" as a response to the civil rights movement, they sever it from its roots in the racialist history of the United States. (Lipset and Raab not only elide racial oppression from American history; they also make workers into mainstays rather than victims of countersubversive movements.) Lipset, it should be noted, is perhaps the most eminent living American political sociologist and a past president of the American Political Science Association.

11. Compare David Brion Davis, "Some Themes of Countersubversion" and *The Slave Power Conspiracy and the Paranoid Style* (Baton Rouge, La., 1970) to *The Problem of Slavery in Western Culture* (Ithaca, N.Y., 1966) and *The Problem of Slavery in the Age of Revolution* (Ithaca, N.Y., 1975).

12. The evolution I have in mind can be followed in *Commentary* magazine from the 1950s to the 1980s and in the legacy of Hubert Humphrey in contemporary American politics, as it is carried out by former U.N. Ambassador Jeane Kirkpatrick and by arms negotiator Max Kampleman. There is a more troubled relationship between the New Right and such neoconservatives as Seymour Martin Lipset and Nathan Glazer. Cf. Peter Steinfels, *The Neoconservatives* (New York, 1979); Michael Rogin, "On the Jewish Question," *democracy*, Spring 1983, pp. 101–14; Alan Wolfe, "Why the Neocons are Losing Out," *Nation*, 3 September 1985, pp. 265, 281–82.

13. Cf. Lipset, *Political Man*, 439–56; Daniel Bell, *The End of Ideology* (Glencoe, Ill., 1960); Clifford Geertz, *The Interpretation of Culture* (New York, 1973); Grant Webster, *The Republic of Letters* (Baltimore, 1979); James E. Breslin, *From Modern to Contemporary: American Poetry, 1945–1965* (Chicago, 1984), 23–52.

14. A useful recent review essay is Gordon Wood, "Hellfire Politics," *New York Review of Books*, 28 February 1985, pp. 29–32. On republicanism, in addition to Bailyn, *Ideological Origins*, the most influential book is J. G. A. Pocock, *The Machiavellian Moment* (Princeton, 1975). On therapeutic politics, cf. Christopher Lasch, *The New Radicalism in America, 1889–1963* (New York, 1965), *Haven in a Heartless World* (New York, 1977), and *The Culture of Narcissism* (New York, 1979). Garry Wills has also sought an alternative to Lockean liberalism within America, first in local community in *Nixon Agonistes* (Boston, Mass., 1970), then in Scottish commonsense philosophy in *Inventing America* (Garden City, N.Y., 1978) and *Explaining America* (Garden City, N.Y., 1981). For a critique of these efforts to escape liberalism in America, see John P. Diggins, *The Lost Soul of American Politics* (New York, 1984).

15. Cf. the sources cited in n. 13 above; James Clifford, "On Ethnographic Authority," *Representations* 2 (Spring 1983): 118–46; Paul Rabinow, "Representations Are Social Facts: Modernity and Postmodernity in Anthropology," in James Clifford and George Marcus, eds., *Writing Culture* (Berkeley and Los

Angeles, 1986); Richard Slotkin, *The Fatal Environment* (New York, 1985), 15–32; Fredric Jameson, *The Political Unconscious* (Ithaca, N.Y., 1981).

16. Karl Marx, "On the Jewish Question," in Loyd D. Easton and Kurt H. Guddat, eds., *Writings of the Young Marx on Philosophy and Society* (Garden City, N.Y., 1967), 216–48, and "The Eighteenth Brumaire of Louis Bonaparte," in David Fernbach, ed., *Surveys from Exile* (New York, 1974). Cf. also Michael Paul Rogin, *Subversive Genealogy: The Politics and Art of Herman Melville* (New York, 1983), 16–21, and chapter 6, above; Paul Thomas, *Marx and the Anarchists* (London, 1980).

17. Cf. Sacvan Bercovitch, *The American Jeremiad* (Madison, Wis., 1978), xii–xiv, 18–22, 152–55. The quote is on p. 164. See also Bercovitch, *Puritan Origins*; Quentin Anderson, *The Imperial Self* (New York, 1971); Perry Miller, *Nature's Nation* (Cambridge, Mass., 1967). The president embodies the imperial self. Examples of presidential hagiography in normal political science are discussed in Joseph Cronin, *The State of the Presidency*, 2d ed. (Boston, 1980), 95–118. As Walter Dean Burnham has cited cross-national survey data to show, the more modernized a country, the less importance do respondents give to religion as a force in their lives. The single striking exception to this strong correlation is the United States, which is at once the most modernized and most religious among industrial nations. See Walter Dean Burnham, "The American Earthquake," in Thomas Ferguson and Joel Rogers, eds., *The Hidden Election* (New York, 1981), 132–39.

18. Theodore Draper, "On Nuclear War: An Exchange with the Secretary of Defense," *New York Review of Books*, 18 August 1983, pp. 27–33; Robert Scheer, *With Enough Shovels: Reagan, Bush, and Nuclear War* (New York, 1982), 19, 30–32, 60, 174–75; *San Francisco Chronicle*, 9 May 1985, p. 25.

19. On Marxist and Freudian theories of ideology, see Clifford Geertz, "Ideology as a Cultural System," in David Apter, ed., *Ideology and Discontent* (New York, 1964), 47–76. For examples of the replacement of ideology by psychology in 1950s social science, see Milton Rokeach, *The Open and Closed Mind* (New York, 1960); Philip Converse, "The Nature of Belief Systems in Mass Publics," in Apter, *Ideology and Discontent*, 206–61; and Herbert McClosky, "Conservatism and Personality," *American Political Science Review* 52 (March 1958): 27–45.

20. See Catherine Gallagher and Thomas Laqueur, eds., *Sexuality and the Social Body* (Berkeley and Los Angeles, 1987).

21. Cf. Lasch, *New Radicalism*; Jane Addams, "A Modern Lear," in Ray Ginger, ed., *American Social Thought* (New York, 1961), 189–203, and *Twenty Years at Hull House* (New York, 1910); Herbert Croly, *The Promise of American Life* (New York, 1909); Samuel Haber, *Efficiency and Uplift* (Chicago, 1964).

22. Cf. Philip Rieff, *Freud: The Mind of the Moralist* (New York, 1959) and *The Triumph of the Therapeutic* (New York, 1966); Russell Jacoby, *Social Amnesia* (Boston, 1975); Herbert Marcuse, *Eros and Civilization* (New York, 1962); Michel Foucault, *A History of Sexuality* (New York, 1978) and *Discipline and Punish* (New York, 1977); Carl Schorske, "Politics and Parricide in Freud's Interpretation of Dreams," in *Fin-de-Siècle Vienna, Politics and Culture* (New York, 1980), 181–207.

23. Eric Hobsbawm, *The Age of Capital, 1845–1875* (New York, 1975), 239–40.

24. Cf. C. B. MacPherson, *The Political Theory of Possessive Individualism* (London, 1964).

25. Carole Pateman, "Women and Democratic Citizenship" (Jeffersonian Memorial Lecture, University of California, Berkeley, 19 February 1985). On the American significance of the Lockean family, cf. Edgar G. Burrows and Michael Wallace, "The American Revolution: The Ideology and Psychology of National Liberation," *Perspectives in American History* 6 (1972), 167–206; Jay Fliegelman, *Prodigals and Pilgrims: The American Revolution Against Patriarchal Authority* (New York, 1982). On domestic ideology, cf. Catherine Gallagher, *The Industrial Reformation of English Fiction, 1832–1867: Social Discourse and Narrative Form* (Chicago, 1985), 113–84, and, for America, Barbara Welter, "The Cult of True Womanhood: 1820–1860," *American Quarterly* 18 (Summer 1966); Nancy Cott, *The Bonds of Womanhood* (New Haven, 1977); Michael Paul Rogin, *Fathers and Children: Andrew Jackson and the Subjugation of the American Indian* (New York, 1975), 63–72.

26. Cf. Melanie Klein, *Contributions to Psychoanalysis* (London, 1948), *New Directions in Psychoanalysis* (London, 1955), and *The Psychoanalysis of Children* (London, 1932); Norman O. Brown, *Life Against Death* (Middletown, Conn., 1959) and *Love's Body* (New York, 1966); Dorothy Dinnerstein, *The Mermaid and the Minotaur* (New York, 1976). (One need not accept Klein's periodization of the first two years of life to be influenced by her formulations as a whole.)

27. Nancy Chodorow, *The Reproduction of Mothering* (Berkeley and Los Angeles, 1978), 104–7.

28. In addition to the sources cited in the two previous notes, cf. Harry Guntrip, *Psychoanalytic Theory, Therapy, and the Self* (New York, 1971); Gayle Rubin, "The Traffic in Women: Notes on the Political Economy of Sex," in Rayna Reitter, ed., *Toward an Anthropology of Women* (New York, 1975), 157–210; and Christopher Lasch, *The Minimal Self* (New York, 1984) 163–96. I want also to acknowledge applications of feminist psychoanalytic theory to culture and politics that have influenced my own understanding: Lillian Rubin, *Intimate Strangers* (New York, 1983); Hanna Fenichel Pitkin, *Fortune is a Woman: Gender and Politics in the Thought of Niccolo Machiavelli* (Berkeley and Los Angeles, 1984); Kim Chernin, *The Hungry Self* (New York, 1985); Coppélia Kahn, *Man's Estate: Masculine Identity in Shakespeare* (Berkeley and Los Angeles, 1981); and Elizabeth Abel, *Virginia Woolf and the Fictions of Psychoanalysis* (forthcoming).

29. Cf. Mark Poster, *Critical Theory of the Family* (New York, 1978), and Eli Zaretsky, *Capitalism, the Family, and Personal Life* (New York, 1976).

30. Some writers, for example, have connected the terror of maternal invasion to social changes originating outside the home, changes that have both influenced the character of the family and had a direct impact on the psyche. This position links the breakdown of paternally based public authorities and the rise of pseudo-personal invasive institutions to the shift from neurotic symptoms (isolated within the character structure) to undifferentiated, pre-oedipal

character disorders that take over the whole personality. The changes these writers see, from production to consumption and from character to personality, bear on the rise of surveillance and the spectacle in late twentieth-century demonology. These developments, discussed in chapters 1 and 8, will be returned to at the end of this discussion. Cf. Leo Lowenthal, "Biography in Popular Magazines," in Paul Lazarsfeld and Frank N. Stanton, eds., *Radio Research, 1942–43* (New York, 1944); Alexander Mitscherlich, *Society Without the Father* (London, 1969); Lasch, *Haven* and *Narcissism*; Warren Susman, *Culture as History* (New York, 1984), xix–xxx, 271–86.

31. "Liberal Society and the Indian Question," first published in 1971, sought to restore to American history-writing not only the familial language of Indian removal but the fact of Indian dispossession as well. As recently as a decade ago, an interpretive review of Jacksonian historiography failed to mention westward expansion and Indian removal as important—much less defining—events of that period. See Ronald P. Formisiano, "Toward a Reorientation of Jacksonian Politics: A Review of the Literature, 1959–1975," *Journal of American History* 53 (June 1976): 42–65. Arthur Schlesinger's *The Age of Jackson* (Boston, 1945) was realist, New Deal history; Marvin Meyers's *The Jacksonian Persuasion* (New York, 1960) was symbolist history; both ignored Indians. The study that currently defines the Age of Jackson, Robert Remini's two-volume biography, *Andrew Jackson and the Course of American Empire* (New York, 1977) and *Andrew Jackson and the Course of American Freedom* (New York, 1981), embraces and celebrates Jacksonian expansion. My own book-length account of this subject, written as a biography of Jackson, is *Fathers and Children*.

32. Pitkin, *Fortune is a Woman*, 281.

33. Sigmund Freud, *Group Psychology and the Analysis of the Ego*, in James Strachey, ed., *The Standard Edition of the Complete Psychological Works of Freud*, 24 vols. (London, 1953–66), 18:67–144.

34. Cf. Sigmund Freud, *Moses and Monotheism*, in *Standard Edition*, 23:3–140; Michael Rogin, "On the Jewish Question"; Abel, *Virginia Woolf*.

35. R. D. Laing, *The Divided Self* (London, 1961).

36. Pierre Bourdieu, "The Social Space and the Genesis of Groups," *Social Science Information* 24 (1985): 215–17. Cf. Hanna Fenichel Pitkin, *The Concept of Representation* (Berkeley and Los Angeles, 1967).

37. Anthony Giddens, *The Nation-State and Violence* (Berkeley and Los Angeles, 1985), 193–94.

38. I take this point from ibid., 2–5, 179–97. State control of industrialized violence is, as Giddens says, the distinctive feature of relations among other states and foreign subjects.

39. Cf. the discussions in chapters 1, 7, and 8, above, and the analysis of the gaze in Jean-Paul Sartre, *Being and Nothingness*, Hazel E. Barnes, trans. (New York, 1966), 340–400, and Jacques Lacan, *The Four Fundamental Concepts of Psychoanalysis*, Jacques-Alain Miller, ed. (New York, 1977), 82–90. I am indebted to Ann Banfield for these references. For film the classic statement is Laura Mulvey, "Visual Pleasure and Narrative Cinema," in Karen Kay and Gerald Peary, eds., *Women and the Cinema* (New York, 1977), 412–28.

40. Jacques Lacan, "The Mirror Stage as Formative of the Function of the I as Revealed in Psychoanalytic Experience," in *Ecrits* (New York, 1977), 1–7; Otto Kernberg, *Borderline Conditions and Pathological Narcissism* (New York, 1975); Lasch, *Narcissism*, 31–51.

41. Cf. Erik Erikson, *Childhood and Society*, 2d ed. (Middlesex, Eng., 1965); D. W. Winnicott, "Mirror-Role of Mother and Family in Childhood Development," in *Playing and Reality* (London, 1971); Abel, *Virginia Woolf*; Hannah Arendt, *The Human Condition* (Chicago, 1958); Jessica Benjamin, "The End of Internalization: Adorno's Social Psychology," *Telos* 32 (Summer 1977): 42–64, and "Authority and the Family Revisited; or, A World Without Fathers," *New German Critique*, no. 13 (Winter 1978): 39–57.

42. I rely on the recent analysis by Christopher Pye, "The Sovereign, the Theater, and the Kingdome of Darknesse: Hobbes and the Spectacle of Power," *Representations* 8 (Fall 1984): 85–106. Cf. also Stephen J. Greenblatt, *Renaissance Self-Fashioning* (Chicago, 1980); Norman Jacobson, *Pride and Solace* (Berkeley and Los Angeles, 1978), 51–92; Hanna Fenichel Pitkin, "Hobbes's Concept of Representation," *American Political Science Review* 68 (June and December 1964): 328–40, 902–18; George Shulman, "The Lamb and the Dragon: Gerard Winstanley and Thomas Hobbes in the English Revolution" (Ph.D. diss., University of California, Berkeley, 1982).

43. Thomas Hobbes, *Leviathan* (New York, 1962), 125.

44. Ibid., 152.

45. Pye, "The Sovereign," 101–3.

Index

Compositor: Wilsted & Taylor
Text: 10/13 Sabon
Display: Sabon
Printer: Maple-Vail Book Mfg. Group
Binder: Maple-Vail Book Mfg. Group